W9-AVW-109

Putting It
Together

BASIC COLLEGE READING IN CONTEXT

186
192   Brown Box
193   Top Box
145 - Many early behaviors

Putting It Together

BASIC COLLEGE READING IN CONTEXT

Robert DiYanni

The College Board

BEDFORD/ST. MARTIN'S   Boston ◆ New York

For Bedford/St. Martin's

Developmental Editor: Aron Keesbury
Production Editor: Arthur Johnson
Senior Production Supervisor: Maria Gonzalez
Marketing Manager: Brian Wheel
Editorial Assistants: Joshua Levy and Jeffrey Voccola
Copyeditor: Barbara G. Flanagan
Text Design: Claire Seng-Niemoeller
Cover Design: Laura Shaw and Claire Jarvis
Cover Art: Bruce Baughman, *Autumn,* reverse acrylic painting on Lucite. By courtesy of the
    Bruce Baughman Studio and Gallery.
Composition: Stratford Publishing Services, Inc.
Printing and Binding: R.R. Donnelley & Sons Company

President: Charles H. Christensen
Editorial Director: Joan E. Feinberg
Editor in Chief: Karen S. Henry
Director of Marketing: Karen Melton
Director of Editing, Design, and Production: Marcia Cohen
Managing Editor: Elizabeth M. Schaaf

Library of Congress Control Number: 2001095135

Copyright © 2002 by Bedford/St. Martin's

All rights reserved. No part of this book may be reproduced, stored in a retrieval system, or transmitted in any form or by any means, electronic, mechanical, photocopying, recording, or otherwise, except as may be expressly permitted by the applicable copyright statutes or in writing by the Publisher.

Manufactured in the United States of America.

7   6   5   4   3   2
f   e   d   c   b

For information, write: Bedford/St. Martin's, 75 Arlington Street, Boston, MA 02116
(617-399-4000)

ISBN: 0–312–13689–7 (Student Edition)
       0–312–24790–7 (Instructor's Annotated Edition)

Acknowledgments

    Eric Berne, "Can People Be Judged by Their Appearance?" from *The Mind in Action* by Eric Berne. Copyright © 1947 by Eric Berne. Reprinted by permission of the author.
    Cecelie Berry, "It's Time We Rejected the Racial Litmus Test," *Newsweek,* February 7, 2000. All rights reserved. Reprinted by permission.

Acknowledgments and copyrights are continued at the back of the book on pages 510–12, which constitute an extension of the copyright page. It is a violation of the law to reproduce these selections by any means whatsoever without the written permission of the copyright holder.

Preface for Instructors

■ A New Book for the Reading Classroom

There has long been a need for a book that blends the best of traditional developmental reading pedagogy with new approaches. *Putting It Together* has been carefully designed to fill this need by providing a useful tool to help students become confident readers through a realistic application of the fundamental skills of college reading. Setting out to create such a book, I collaborated with the talented editors at Bedford/St. Martin's. From the beginning, our goal was to address concerns of the developmental reading classroom that other books have addressed only partially or not at all. Throughout the process, we were fortunate to receive substantial feedback, through interviews and extensive review programs, from a dedicated cache of developmental reading teachers around the country. Though their comments were broad and comprehensive, the concerns of those teaching developmental reading consistently highlighted three major areas of need, generally unfulfilled by other books. *Putting It Together* is built to address those needs.

First, instructors of developmental reading tell us that, while other books successfully help students isolate and learn the individual skills of college reading, in doing so they often oversimplify the complex process of reading. Although other books present the various components of reading and provide strategies for helping students learn to read, they do so without putting the skills back together into an integrated or holistic experience. Too often, the result is that students learn how to read fragmented or isolated passages and to take standardized tests based on a loose collection of skills—often at the expense of learning to read realistically.

Second, instructors tell us that, while developmental reading books include whole essays or textbook passages, they typically offer little in the way of a process, or program, to help students make the transition from reading isolated paragraphs to reading whole essays or extended passages. Having practiced their skills on very short excerpts, students often become intimidated when confronted with a complete and often complex reading selection. Discouraged, they often simply put the book down.

Finally, instructors overwhelmingly report that one of the most difficult obstacles they face teaching developmental reading is student motivation. Other books have tried with varying degrees of success to attack the problem head-on by offering students encouragement or metacognitive frameworks for understanding their motivational barriers. And while instructors relate that these measures sometimes persuade students of the importance of reading, it is nonetheless difficult to find readings that sufficiently engage students in the follow-through.

To address these concerns, *Putting It Together* blends a traditional learning model with a new, three-pronged approach. First, it enables students to put the distinct but interrelated skills of college reading back together into an integrated reading experience. Second, it provides them with an innovative program of readings and activities that guides them step-by-step through the often challenging process of applying those skills to whole readings. And third, the reading program in *Putting It Together* uses high-interest, topical essays and thematically linked textbook passages that will engage students' native interest, motivate them to practice reading, and—perhaps most important—show them the relevance of reading.

■ The Fundamental Skills of College Reading

In creating a new approach, *Putting It Together* has not abandoned the ideas and methodologies that have for many years proved successful in developmental reading classrooms all over the country. Rather, as the table of contents shows, it has built on the best of what has come before, developing its innovations around the familiar skills-based model.

- **Comprehensive coverage of the fundamental reading skills.** From vocabulary in context to main ideas and to understanding an author's purpose, the twelve skills-based chapters in *Putting It Together* teach step-by-step the developmental skills and strategies that prepare students for successful reading in college and in life.

- **Numerous and varied exercises that offer constant reinforcement.** Throughout the skills instruction are practice activities that isolate particular skills and give students a chance to succeed at smaller tasks before moving on to larger ones. These exercises, on perforated pages, can be used for self-study and practice, or they can be turned in to instructors as homework.

- **Critical thinking activities that keep students involved.** Every chapter begins and ends with a unique critical thinking apparatus especially designed to get students thinking about their own learning—both in and out of the classroom. At the beginning of every chapter, an introduction and Focusing Questions ask students to reflect on how the chapter is relevant to them. Everyday Reading boxes follow, inviting students to tie their in-class experience to their out-of-class lives. At the end of every chapter, Recall/Remember exercise questions and a chapter summary actively reinforce their learning.

- **Standardized test practice in the context of real readings.** Within the unique end-of-chapter Reading the Parts essay, fifteen questions—designed to resemble the kinds of questions asked on standardized tests—allow students to practice for statewide or schoolwide exams while they engage with real, high-interest readings.

■ An Innovative Approach

To help students integrate the various skills of reading together into a realistic reading experience, *Putting it Together* concludes each chapter with a specific step-by-step program of readings. This *Putting It Together* approach has three major components.

- **Reading the Parts** sections present engaging readings, divided into manageable two-to-three-paragraph parts. Each part is followed by five practice questions referring specifically back to those paragraphs. By "reading the parts," students are able to work their way successfully through a whole essay part by part, practicing their skills and receiving constant reinforcement.

- **Reading the Whole** sections reassemble the Reading the Parts essays and reprint them in their entirety. Having read an essay in its parts, students then reread with a higher level of confidence and a greater degree of success in both comprehension and critical thinking. Integrated Skills questions follow, encouraging students to put their newly learned skills together into an integrated and realistic approach to reading.

- **Reading Textbooks** sections guide students into academic texts. Thematically linked textbook passages that follow the Reading the

Whole readings in every chapter provide students with an opportunity to apply what they've learned to the kinds of readings they will encounter in their college courses. From disciplines as diverse as psychology, sociology, biology, economics, and marketing, for example, these textbook passages offer a broad range of interesting topics to help students negotiate their reading of college textbooks in every discipline.

■ Readings to Engage and Motivate Students

Students' motivation to read opens the door to practice and is ultimately at the heart of their success. To motivate students by engaging their native interest, *Putting It Together* provides interesting readings in innovative ways to give them reasons to read.

- **Exciting, topical, high-interest essays actually engage students in reading.** All the Reading the Parts and Reading the Whole essays are drawn from exciting contemporary sources such as newspaper editorial pages, student publications, and current magazines such as *Time* and *Newsweek*. On today's most interesting topics — sports, immigration, alcohol, and gun violence, for example — these essays are selected to channel student interest into the practice of reading.

- **Thematic links to textbook readings motivate students to read.** The textbook passage in each chapter is carefully selected for its direct topical connection to the other readings in the chapter. Explicit Thematic Connections at the beginning of each passage ask students to consider the relevance of the reading to the topics that interest them, drawing them into the reading, showing them how college reading can apply to their lives, and motivating them. A personal essay by Eva Hoffman about the experience of immigration, for example, is paired with a history passage that puts the author's experience into its fascinating historical context.

■ Supplements

A comprehensive ancillary package complements and supplements the pedagogy and practice extensively provided in *Putting It Together*. Bedford/St. Martin's has made available an impressive package with today's modern students and teachers in mind.

- **Instructor's Annotated Edition.** Available for teachers, this easy-to-use edition provides answers to all the book's exercises, printed in a different color and font.

- **Interactive Online Quizzing.** With hundreds of questions, this online quiz bank produces practice tests specifically keyed to the parts of the book. Students receive immediate feedback, and their results are collated automatically. Instructors can easily follow students' progress online. And because tests are generated randomly, no two students' tests will have the questions in the same order.

- **Overhead Transparency Masters** of the Reading the Parts readings and activities give instructors the option of going over these specially "chunked" readings and practice tests in class.

- **Companion Web site.** The Web site www.bedfordstmartins.com/ puttingittogether includes resources for students as well as for instructors, including links to the electronic online quizzing and access to Bedford/St. Martin's extensive resources for students.

■ Acknowledgments

From the beginning, *Putting It Together* has been a collaborative project. I have had the good fortune to profit from the wise counsel of many reviewers, who read each draft with scrupulous care. Thanks to the following for their assistance: Janice Beran, LearnCom Associates; James Bernarducci, Middlesex County College; Tamara Brawner, Thomas College; Elaine Fitzpatrick, Massasoit Community College; Lynna Geis, Rose State College; Karen Haas, Manatee Community College; Barbara A. Henry, West Virginia State College; Nancy Kreml, Midlands Technical Community College; Shuli Lamden, Santa Fe Community College; Patricia McDermott, Northern Essex Community College; Janice McIntyre, Kansas City Kansas Community College; Judith Y. McNeill, Portland Community College; Donna Yergovitch Nuzum, Fairmont State College; Ilene Rutan, Brookdale Community College; Jane Thielemann, University of Houston–Downtown; Anne Willekens, Antelope Valley College; and Robert Zweig, Borough of Manhattan Community College.

My work on the book as author has benefited tremendously from the support provided by Bedford/St. Martin's. Among the many who deserve my appreciation and thanks are Barbara Heinssen, who convinced me to begin work on the book more than five years ago, and Karen Allanson, the acquisitions editor who signed me to write the book. The then-president of St. Martin's College Division, Ed Stanford, also lent the project his authoritative support. I would like to thank Barbara, Karen, and Ed for their confidence in my ability to turn a good idea into an excellent book. Thanks also to Meg Spilleth, the book's first developmental editor, for her outstanding assistance.

I would also like to thank the publisher of Bedford/St. Martin's, Chuck Christensen, and the Editorial Director, Joan Feinberg, who were willing to renew the company's confidence in the book midway through its development at a point where I had hit a roadblock. They generously sent the manuscript out for a new set of reviews and then provided me with the support I needed to complete the book. I am grateful to both of these outstanding professionals for the chance to complete *Putting It Together* under their direction. Among the reasons for my thanks to Chuck and Joan is their decision to assign Aron Keesbury to the book as project editor. Aron's contribution to the development and the final form of *Putting It Together* has been critical, extending beyond offering ideas, suggesting readings, and helping the book to evolve. He contributed to the writing and textual editing in too many ways to count. Without Aron's work, *Putting It Together* would not exist as the book you now hold in your hands. I also had the good fortune of having two freelance editors help me further advance the project. My warm thanks and deep appreciation go to Marilyn Weissman and Maggie Barbieri for the outstanding editing they did to make *Putting It Together* the book it has now become.

In addition, Bedford/St. Martin's provided an outstanding staff of professionals who offered the first-rate assistance they are known for. Thanks are due to the production editor, Arthur Johnson, for his careful and painstaking work in bringing *Putting It Together* through the production process. His good-natured demeanor and professionalism made that process as pleasant as it was effective. Thanks to Joshua Levy and Jeff Voccola, the editorial assistants, who took on and handled myriad tasks with great aplomb. Thanks as well to Chris Stripinis for his work in clearing permissions and to Barbara Flanagan, the most meticulous of copyeditors. It was a privilege to work with this outstanding group of professionals.

Finally, I would like to thank my wife, companion, and best friend—Mary Hammond DiYanni. Mary has been with me on this project and on many others for more than thirty years, every one of them memorable and beautiful. I treasure her steadfastness and love, and I thank her with all my heart for helping me, throughout our married life, to put it all together.

Contents

PREFACE FOR INSTRUCTORS   v

INTRODUCTION: USING *PUTTING IT TOGETHER*   xxiii

1. Practicing Active Reading   1

Getting Ready   Chapter Overview   1

                           Focusing Questions   2

                           Everyday Reading   2

Learning the Skills   Thinking about Reading   3
                               Exercise 1-1   3

                           Basic Reading Strategies   5
                               ■ BOX: Strategies for Improving Concentration   5
                               Concentrating   6
                               Asking Questions   7

                           Reading Actively   10

Applying the Skills   Reading the Parts
                           Karen Epstein, *I'm a Barbie Girl*   13

                           Reading the Whole
                           Karen Epstein, *I'm a Barbie Girl*   19
                               Integrated Skills   21

                           Reading Textbooks
                           From Stephen J. Wayne, G. Calvin Mackenzie,
                           David M. O'Brien, and Richard L. Cole, *The Politics of
                           American Government*   22
                               Thinking about the Textbook Selection   23

Reviewing   Recall/Remember   24

                           Chapter Summary   24

2. Learning Vocabulary from Context Clues   25

Getting Ready

Chapter Overview   25

Focusing Questions   25

Everyday Reading   26

Learning the Skills

Restatement Context Clues   26
    Exercise 2-1   28

Example Context Clues   30
    Exercise 2-2   31

Contrast Context Clues   33
    Exercise 2-3   35

General Context Clues   37

Applying the Skills

Reading the Parts
Eva Hoffman, *Lost in Translation*   39

Reading the Whole
Eva Hoffman, *Lost in Translation*   45
    Integrated Skills   47

Reading Textbooks
From James A. Henretta, David Brody, and Lynn Dumenil,
America: A Concise History   48
    Thinking about the Textbook Selection   49

Reviewing

Recall/Remember   50

Chapter Summary   50

3. Learning Vocabulary by Analyzing Words   51

Getting Ready

Chapter Overview   51

Focusing Questions   51

Everyday Reading   52

Learning the Skills

Word Roots   52
   The Word Root port   52
   The Word Roots vid, vis, and spec   53
    Exercise 3-1   53
   Important Word Roots   54
    Exercise 3-2   56

Prefixes 57
  Prefixes Indicating Number   57
    Exercise 3-3   59
  Prefixes with Negative Meanings   61
    Exercise 3-4   62
  Prefixes Indicating Time, Space, and Position   63
    Exercise 3-5   65

Suffixes   66
  Exercise 3-6   68

Applying the Skills

Reading the Parts
Steve Rhodes and Kendall Hamilton, *Will Athletic Records Ever Stop Tumbling?*   69

Reading the Whole
Steve Rhodes and Kendall Hamilton, *Will Athletic Records Ever Stop Tumbling?*   73
  Integrated Skills   74

Reading Textbooks
From Ian Robertson, *Sociology*   76
  Thinking about the Textbook Selection   78

Reviewing

Recall/Remember   79

Chapter Summary   79

4. Recognizing Topics and Main Ideas in Paragraphs 81

Getting Ready

Chapter Overview   81

Focusing Questions   81

Everyday Reading   82

Learning the Skills

Finding Topics of Paragraphs   82
  Exercise 4-1   83
  Exercise 4-2   85

Finding Main Ideas in Paragraphs   87
  Identifying Topic Sentences   88
  Locating Topic Sentences   89
    Exercise 4-3   91
    Exercise 4-4   93

Applying the Skills

Reading the Parts
Cecelie Berry, *It's Time We Rejected the Racial Litmus Test*   97

Reading the Whole
Cecelie Berry, *It's Time We Rejected the Racial Litmus Test*   104
    Integrated Skills   106

Reading Textbooks
From Michael Cole and Sheila R. Cole, *The Development of Children*   107
    Thinking about the Textbook Selection   110

Reviewing   Recall/Remember   110

Chapter Summary   111

5. Understanding Major and Minor Supporting Details   113

Getting Ready   Chapter Overview   113

Focusing Questions   113

Everyday Reading   114

Learning the Skills   Identifying Supporting Details   114
    Exercise 5-1   115
    Exercise 5-2   116

Identifying Major Supporting Details   118
    Exercise 5-3   120

Identifying Minor Supporting Details   121
    Exercise 5-4   123

Using Supporting Details to Understand Unstated Main Ideas   125
    Exercise 5-5   126

Applying the Skills   Reading the Parts
Ben Krull, *The Lost Art of Nicknaming*   129

Reading the Whole
Ben Krull, *The Lost Art of Nicknaming*   134
    Integrated Skills   135

Reading Textbooks
From William G. Nickels and Marian Burk Wood, *Marketing: Relationships, Quality, Value*   136
    Thinking about the Textbook Selection   138

Reviewing   Recall/Remember   139

Chapter Summary   139

6. Identifying Main Ideas in Longer Selections — 141

Getting Ready   Chapter Overview   141

                             Focusing Questions   141

                             Everyday Reading   142

Learning the Skills   Identifying Thesis Statements   142
                                Exercise 6-1   144
                                Exercise 6-2   148

                             Thinking about Titles   151

                             Identifying Supporting Paragraphs   151

                             Looking at Introductions and Conclusions   154
                                Introductions   154
                                Conclusions   156

                             Identifying Unstated Main Ideas in Longer Selections   158
                                Exercise 6-3   159

Applying the Skills   Reading the Parts
                             Susan Brink, *Your Brain on Alcohol*   163

                             Reading the Whole
                             Susan Brink, *Your Brain on Alcohol*   169
                                Integrated Skills   171

                             Reading Textbooks
                             From Sylvia S. Mader, *Inquiry into Life*   172
                                Thinking about the Textbook Selection   173

Reviewing   Recall/Remember   174

                             Chapter Summary   174

7. Recognizing Patterns of Organization — 175

Getting Ready   Chapter Overview   175

                             Focusing Questions   176

                             Everyday Reading   176

Learning the Skills   Recognizing Patterns of Organization   177

                             Narration   178

                             Description   179
                                Exercise 7-1   180

Definitions   181
   Exercise 7-2   183

Examples   185
   Exercise 7-3   187

Lists and Sequences   188
   Exercise 7-4   189

Comparison, Contrast, and Analogy   191
   Comparison and Contrast   191
   Analogy   194
      Exercise 7-5   196
      Exercise 7-6   197

Classification   198
   Exercise 7-7   201

Cause and Effect   202
   Exercise 7-8   204

Mixing the Patterns   205
   Exercise 7-9   207

Applying the Skills

Reading the Parts
Jim Bobryk, *Navigating My Eerie Landscape Alone*   209

Reading the Whole
Jim Bobryk, *Navigating My Eerie Landscape Alone*   215
   Integrated Skills   217

Reading Textbooks
From Don H. Hockenbury and Sandra E. Hockenbury,
Discovering Psychology   218
   Thinking about the Textbook Selection   221

Reviewing

Recall/Remember   221

Chapter Summary   221

8. Making Observations and Connections   223

Getting Ready

Chapter Overview   223

Focusing Questions   224

Everyday Reading   224

Learning the Skills

Making Observations   224
   Observing Organization and Structure   225
      Exercise 8-1   226

Observing Examples   228
   Exercise 8-2   230
Observing Details   232
Observing Repetition   232

Using Writing to Develop Your Observation Skills   233
Annotating   234
   Exercise 8-3   236
Listing   237
   Exercise 8-4   237

Making Connections   237
Identifying Relationships   238
   Exercise 8-5   240
Practicing Making Connections   241

Applying the Skills

Reading the Parts
Cathy Young, *Trigger Guards Are Not Answer, but Moral Fiber Is*   243

Reading the Whole
Cathy Young, *Trigger Guards Are Not Answer, but Moral Fiber Is*   249
   Integrated Skills   251

Reading Textbooks
From David V. Edwards and Allessandra Lippucci, *Practicing American Politics*   252
   Thinking about the Textbook Selection   253

Reviewing

Recall/Remember   253

Chapter Summary   254

9. Making Inferences and Drawing Conclusions   255

Getting Ready

Chapter Overview   255

Focusing Questions   256

Everyday Reading   256

Learning the Skills

Developing Inferences   256
   Exercise 9-1   257
   Exercise 9-2   258

Reading Inferentially   259

Practicing Making Inferences   260
   Exercise 9-3   263

Drawing Conclusions   265
Exercise 9-4   269

Writing to Aid Reading Comprehension   273
■ BOX: Guidelines for Writing a Summary   274
Exercise 9-5   275

Applying the Skills

Reading the Parts
David Gergen, *Keeping the Flame Alive*   277

Reading the Whole
David Gergen, *Keeping the Flame Alive*   284
Integrated Skills   286

Reading Textbooks
From Lanny B. Fields, Russell J. Barber, and Cheryl A. Riggs, *The Global Past*   287
Thinking about the Textbook Selection   292

Reviewing

Recall/Remember   292
Chapter Summary   292

10. Becoming a Critical Reader   295

Getting Ready

Chapter Overview   295
Focusing Questions   296
Everyday Reading   296

Learning the Skills

Identifying an Author's Purpose   296
Exercise 10-1   300

Determining an Author's Point of View   302
Exercise 10-2   304

Distinguishing between Facts and Opinions   305
Exercise 10-3   307

Recognizing and Making Judgments   308
Exercise 10-4   309
Exercise 10-5   311
■ BOX: Guidelines for Critical Reading   313

Applying the Skills

Reading the Parts
Abbie Gibbs, *Witnessing Execution*   315

Reading the Whole
Abbie Gibbs, *Witnessing Execution*   321
Integrated Skills   322

Reading Textbooks
From David G. Myers, *Psychology*   324
    Thinking about the Textbook Selection   326

Reviewing   Recall/Remember   327
                         Chapter Summary   327

11. Skimming, Scanning, and Understanding the Parts of a Book   329

Getting Ready   Chapter Overview   329
                         Focusing Questions   329
                         Everyday Reading   330

Learning the Skills   Skimming a Reading Selection   330
                             ■ BOX: Guidelines for Skimming   331
                             Exercise 11-1   331
                             Exercise 11-2   334
                             Exercise 11-3   337

                         Scanning a Reading Selection   341
                             ■ BOX: Guidelines for Scanning   341
                             Exercise 11-4   343
                             Exercise 11-5   347

                         Understanding the Parts of a Textbook   350
                             The Table of Contents   *350*
                                 Exercise 11-6   350
                             The Index   *351*
                                 Exercise 11-7   351
                             Other Parts of a Book   *352*
                                 Exercise 11-8   353
                                 Exercise 11-9   354

Applying the Skills   Reading the Parts
                         Mark Trahant, *Every Symbol Tells a Story*   355

                         Reading the Whole
                         Mark Trahant, *Every Symbol Tells a Story*   362
                             Integrated Skills   365

                         Reading Textbooks
                         From James L. Roark, Michael P. Johnson, Patricia Cline
                         Cohen, Sarah Stage, Alan Lawson, and Susan M. Hartmann,
                         The American Promise   366
                             Thinking about the Textbook Selection   368

Reviewing   Recall/Remember   369

                                  Chapter Summary   369

12. Developing Visual Literacy   371

Getting Ready   Chapter Overview   371

                                  Focusing Questions   372

                                  Everyday Reading   372

Learning the Skills   Types of Graphics   372
                                  ■ BOX: Guidelines for Reading Graphics   373
                                  Photographs   374
                                      Exercise 12-1   375
                                      Exercise 12-2   376
                                  Maps   376
                                      Exercise 12-3   377
                                      Exercise 12-4   378
                                  Diagrams   378
                                      Exercise 12-5   379
                                      Exercise 12-6   380
                                  Charts   381
                                      Exercise 12-7   382
                                      Exercise 12-8   382
                                      Exercise 12-9   385
                                  Graphs   385
                                      Exercise 12-10   385
                                      Exercise 12-11   387
                                      Exercise 12-12   389
                                      Exercise 12-13   389
                                  Tables   390
                                      Exercise 12-14   391
                                      Exercise 12-15   393

                                  Understanding Text and Graphics Together   393
                                  ■ BOX: Guidelines for Linking Graphics and
                                      Written Text   394
                                  Exercise 12-16   394
                                  Exercise 12-17   395
                                  Exercise 12-18   395

Applying the Skills   **Reading the Parts**
                                  Robert Kunzig, *Erectus Afloat*   397

                                  Reading the Whole
                                  Robert Kunzig, *Erectus Afloat*   404
                                      Integrated Skills   406

Reading Textbooks
From Sylvia S. Mader, *Inquiry into Life*   408
Thinking about the Textbook Selection   409

Reviewing   Recall/Remember   410

Chapter Summary   410

13. Reading a Textbook Chapter   **413**

Getting Ready   Chapter Overview   413

Focusing Questions   414

Everyday Reading   414

Learning the Skills   Preparing to Read a Textbook   415

Textbook Elements   415
Preliminary Elements   415
Body Elements   416
Concluding Elements   418
Exercise 13-1   418

Reading/Writing Connection   421

Skimming the Sample Chapter   421

Finding the Main Idea and Comprehending the
Chapter   423

Applying the Skills   **Reading Textbooks**
From Dan O'Hair, Gustav W. Friedrich, John M. Wiemann,
and Mary Wiemann, *Competent Communication*   425
Thinking about the Textbook Selection   461

Reviewing   Recall/Remember   461

Chapter Summary   461

APPENDIX A: AN ANTHOLOGY OF READINGS   463

Bill Cosby, *How To Read Faster*   463

Amy Dickinson, *When Mommy or Daddy Dates*   469

Robert H. Frank, *The Downside of Hearing Whoopi at the Mall*   471

Ellen Goodman, *The Suspected Shopper*   474

Dana Hawkins, *Lawsuits Spur Rise in Employee Monitoring*   477

Douglas McCollam, *The Bull Shark*   480

Susannah Meadows, *The Water of the Moment*   485

Miki Meek, *You Can't Hide Those Lying Eyes in Tampa*   488

A. M. Rosenthal, *The Way She Died*   491

Michael Utley, *My Personal Bolt of Lightning*   494

APPENDIX B: USING A COLLEGE DICTIONARY   497

INDEX OF USEFUL TERMS   *Inside back cover*

Introduction: Using
Putting It Together

■ The Need for Reading

The single most important skill necessary for success in college is reading with understanding. Reading is necessary not only in school but also on the job and in the world at large. If you want to make your way in the world, you will need to read with competence and confidence. And if you want to succeed in your college courses, you will need not only to read with understanding but also to become a good critical reader. *Putting It Together* can help you succeed in becoming that kind of reader.

■ What Is Critical Reading?

But just what is critical reading? And how do you go about doing it— reading critically? It is important to know that critical reading is not simply being "critical" of everything you read. Critical reading does not mean always disagreeing, always finding something to criticize. Instead, critical reading is a process of reflective, thoughtful reading. It is a kind of reading in which you think carefully about what a writer is saying. You give the writer's ideas a chance—you consider them. You evaluate a writer's ideas in terms of your own experience. You think about how those ideas relate to what you have learned in school and in everyday life.

Critical reading involves asking questions about what a writer is saying. It involves extending a writer's ideas by adding ideas and examples of your own in support. Critical reading is active, engaged reading. Critical reading is the kind of reading you do when you care, when what is being said matters to you.

When you read critically, you do a number of things at the same time. First, you make observations. You notice what the author is saying and how he or she is saying it. Second, you make connections between different details of the author's writing, and you make further connections with what you already know about the subject. Third, you make educated guesses, also called *inferences*, based on your observations and connections. That is, you "fill in" and "read between the lines." This is one of the most exciting and challenging aspects of reading. And fourth, you figure out exactly what the author is saying, and then you form your own opinion about it—you develop a point of view about what you read.

Putting It Together helps you become this kind of critical reader, active and engaged by what you read. First, you will be introduced to all the different skills that make up the process of becoming a critical reader. And second, you will be given a chance to practice those skills separately and then—most important—all together.

■ Learning the Skills of College Reading

Every chapter in *Putting It Together* is designed to help you focus on a particular skill of college reading. For example, in one chapter you will focus on increasing your vocabulary by figuring out the meanings of words based on the words surrounding them, called their *contexts*. In another chapter, you will learn to figure out the meanings of words by breaking them down into parts, or analyzing them. In another chapter, you will focus on learning to identify a writer's main point and how, exactly, a writer makes that point.

Every chapter begins with three elements that will help you prepare to learn the skill that chapter presents. First, a Chapter Overview will let you know what skill, or skills, the chapter will cover. Next, a set of Focusing Questions will show you why that skill is important for reading. Third, an exercise called Everyday Reading will get you looking for the kinds of reading you do outside of college.

After these three introductory elements, the chapters in *Putting It Together* each explain the different skills involved in college reading. Clear explanations of each skill are followed by brief examples of readings for you to practice on. After the instruction and the examples, you will find useful, clear exercises especially designed to help you learn that skill through more extended practice.

■ The Skills of College Reading in Context

At the end of every chapter is a special set of essays and textbook passages. This set of readings is carefully designed to help you practice the different skills of critical reading. What's special about these readings is that they will also help you learn to put the different skills of college reading back together to read whole essays realistically.

READING THE PARTS

The first reading in the series of readings, called Reading the Parts, is usually an article from a newspaper or magazine on an interesting topic, such as sports records or gun violence. The Reading the Parts essay is divided into small sections with questions following each section. After reading each section, you will answer the questions about that section and then move on to the next section, practicing throughout.

READING THE WHOLE

The next reading in the series is called Reading the Whole. It is the same essay or article that you read in Reading the Parts, but this time it is not divided, so that you can read the whole article without being interrupted. Rereading the essay or article will give you a better, fuller sense of what the author is saying. More important, it will give you a chance to succeed at putting your new skills together into a real reading experience. At the end of the selection are questions that will help you integrate the skills you just learned and applied.

READING TEXTBOOKS

The third and final reading in the series is called Reading Textbooks. As you can probably tell from its title, the Reading Textbooks selection is a passage taken from a college-level textbook. Since the purpose of your college reading class and *Putting It Together* is to help you hone and practice the skills of college reading, every chapter ends by giving you a chance to practice your reading skills on one of the many kinds of readings you will encounter in college.

■ Practicing on Interesting Readings

The articles and textbook passages in *Putting It Together* are special in another way—they are interesting and relevant to your world today. The Reading the Parts and Reading the Whole essays were first published in popular books, student newspapers from around the country, and magazines like *Time, Newsweek, Discover,* and *U.S. News and World Report.* Since critical reading involves actively thinking about what you are reading, it's best to begin by reading selections that are interesting. The Reading the Parts and Reading the Whole essays are not only the kinds of readings you will do on your own, outside of class, but they are also well written and will give you a lot to think about—so active critical reading should come more easily.

The Reading Textbook readings are interesting, too, but in a different way. Every Reading Textbooks reading is connected directly to the other readings in the chapter. With Thematic Connections before them, the Reading Textbooks readings will actually teach you something useful—or will answer important questions—about the Reading the Parts and Reading the Whole essays. An essay about what it is like to be blind, for example, is followed by a passage from a psychology textbook that talks about how the eye works. An essay about what it was like for one woman to come to America is followed by a passage from a history textbook about immigration. The textbook passages *inform* the chapter's other essays. And rather than simply practicing your reading skills on college textbooks, you will also learn something useful about the world—and you'll find that reading is not only relevant and useful, but can also sometimes even be fun.

■ Three Essential Elements of Learning College Reading

Along with the editors at Bedford/St. Martin's, I've worked hard to make this book as good as it can be—and as useful to you as possible. But no book by itself can make you into a better, more competent, and confident reader. This book is one of three critical elements in that process. A second essential element is your instructor. Your reading instructor will guide you and coach you and coax you along the way. With his or her assistance, you will make progress.

The third and most important element of all, however, is you. You must *want* to succeed in improving your reading skills. This desire is fundamental and critical to your success. If you want to improve, and you are willing to do the work to succeed, your instructor and *Putting It Together* can help you achieve your goal.

If you are ready to tackle the job of learning to read well and to become a critical reader, here are a few preliminary suggestions to help you get started on realizing your dream.

1. Make reading a habit—in school and out. Read a little every day.

2. Read different types of things, like newspapers, magazines, and books.

3. Read about things that interest you—sports, music, food, love and sex, people and places, animals, cars, clothes. Read about anything you care about.

4. Find a consistent time or place to read a little each day—before bedtime, riding the subway, at breakfast or lunch, or whatever works for you.

5. Talk about what you read with friends, classmates, and family.

6. Keep a log of your reading—a simple list of what you read each day and week and month. You'll be surprised at how it adds up and how much you learn.

7. Purchase and use a dictionary to look up and learn the new words you encounter in your reading.

8. Make a reading plan—something like an exercise plan—for yourself.

By using *Putting It Together* faithfully and thoughtfully, by working with your reading instructor, and by being faithful to your reading plan, you can succeed in improving your reading ability. Your competence as a reader will increase dramatically. From this improvement in your reading competence will come confidence in your reading ability. You can do it—if you really want to and if you are willing to do the work necessary to achieve your goals. And in the end, you will be happy you did.

Chapter 1

Getting Ready	1
Learning the Skills	3
Applying the Skills	
• Reading the Parts	13
• Reading the Whole	19
• Reading Textbooks	22
Reviewing	24

Practicing Active Reading

Getting Ready

This chapter invites you to think about your reading habits and reading experiences both in and out of school. The aim of the chapter is to help you become a more active reader. **Active reading** requires an attentive mind for thinking and a busy hand for writing about your reading. This opening chapter also will get you thinking about the different kinds of reading you do in your everyday life and will offer an approach to help you read more effectively.

The chapter provides an opportunity to think about why and how you read (or why you don't). It invites you to participate by **asking questions,** working with others in small-group discussions, writing, and sharing your thoughts. Some strategies are provided for **concentrating,** staying focused, and building confidence in your reading ability. These strategies will help you read more confidently and successfully.

You may wish to make becoming an active reader a major goal of your current academic semester. Setting such a goal along with a time frame in which to accomplish it can provide the motivation you need to succeed. This chapter provides strategies through which you can achieve that success. But you will make real and sustained progress only when you decide that becoming an active and confident reader is truly important to you.

Chapter Overview

Focusing Questions

Describe your reading habits. Where and when do you read? Do you read quickly or slowly?

Why do you read, or why do you avoid reading?

How do your feelings and reactions affect your reading?

What was the best reading experience you can remember having? What did you read? Why was it a "good read"?

How does talking about what you read increase your understanding of reading selections?

What are your goals when reading newspapers and magazines?

What are your goals when you read textbooks?

Why do you think active reading might be important? How do you think active reading can help you read better?

What are some ways you can be active when you read?

Everyday Reading

"Everyday reading" refers to the kinds of reading you do in your everyday life outside of school. You use reading in your daily life more than you realize. Throughout this book, you will find invitations to think about and practice the many kinds of everyday reading you do as a normal part of your day. Like the reading you do in school, your everyday reading helps you participate in life more fully. The Everyday Reading boxes in this book provide activities that link your everyday life with the work of reading.

For this first Everyday Reading exercise, make a list of five different things you read outside of school. Try to think of things that you read for different purposes. For each kind of reading you put on your list, add the specific purpose or reason you do that kind of reading. Think about reading you do at work, reading you do in your free time, reading you do as you travel to and from work and school, reading you do to accomplish specific tasks, such as acquiring a driver's license, and so on.

Meet with a small group of classmates to discuss the kinds of everyday reading on one another's lists. Add types of reading and reasons for reading from others' lists to your own.

Learning the Skills

■ Thinking about Reading

Like nearly everything else we do, our reading is affected by our habits. In fact, we might say that just as each of us has particular eating, exercising, conversational, and sleeping habits, we also have reading habits. People's reading habits are not all the same. Their reading habits differ just as their other habits do.

Take a few minutes and jot answers to the questions about your reading habits in the following exercise.

Exercise 1-1
. . . .

Write brief responses to the following questions.

1. How often and how much do you read? Daily? Weekly? As little or as much as you can? Why?

   _____

   _____

   _____

2. What do you read most often? Magazines? Newspapers? Paperback books? Textbooks? Why?

   _____

   _____

   _____

3. Where do you read? Do you have a special place to read? Do you require special conditions—quiet, for example, or a comfortable chair?

   _____

   _____

   _____

   _____

4. What is your favorite kind of reading? What is your least favorite? Why?

_____

_____

_____

_____

5. Have all your reading experiences been similar, or have some differed from others? Explain.

_____

_____

_____

_____

_____

· ·

All learning begins with making observations, with noticing things — all kinds of things. Whether you are learning to swim or to play soccer, to work with a computer software program or to play a musical instrument, you learn in part through observation. The same is true of reading. To become a successful reader you need to make observations about the selections that you read.

The various things you learn to observe when you read are explained in detail in Chapter 8, but they begin with noticing the kinds of words writers use and the kinds of details and examples they include. You can begin that kind of observation in this chapter with the reading passage provided for practice.

Along with making careful observations while you read, you need to learn to make connections among the words, details, and examples you notice the writer using. These connections will form the basis for questions you can ask yourself about reading selections. Thinking about the questions and connections will lead you to a deeper understanding of what you read.

■ Basic Reading Strategies

When you read for your college courses, you need to make sense of what the authors of the reading selections say. Comprehension, or understanding, is most often the main goal.

But what should you do if you are bored by a reading selection or if you find yourself annoyed, angry, or frustrated by what you are reading? There is nothing wrong with finding some selections tedious, frustrating, or boring. Some reading selections *are* boring. Be honest with yourself and acknowledge what you are feeling. But don't stop there. You will also need to find a way to get past that feeling. To achieve academic success, you will need to concentrate on reading and on understanding what you read, even when an assignment does not interest you. You may even find that learning what is in the reading eventually excites you.

Strategies for Improving Concentration

1. **Focus on a small part.** Focus first on reading and understanding the first page of the assignment, for example, or the first paragraph. Then go on to the next small part.

2. **Set goals for yourself.** If a reading assignment appears overwhelming, break it into sections. Tackle one section during one reading session and other sections in later ones. Smaller successes quickly add up to bigger ones.

3. **Work for limited but intense periods of time.** Prepare yourself to read an assignment for forty to fifty minutes. Break that chunk of time into two or three smaller chunks of approximately fifteen minutes each, and take short breaks between the smaller periods of time.

4. **Take a longer break every hour.** Instead of reading straight for a full hour, take a ten-minute break a few minutes before the end of the hour. If you need to read for a second hour, build in a second ten-minute break.

5. **Reward yourself during your break.** Perhaps you will want to have a snack. For longer reading and study sessions, you can allow yourself other kinds of rewards, such as viewing a favorite TV program or going out with friends.

CONCENTRATING

Doing anything well requires concentration. To be an effective pitcher on the baseball diamond, an effective shooter on the basketball court, an effective student government representative—to be effective at anything—you have to concentrate on what you are doing. Effective reading requires similar kinds of concentration and a similar degree of effort.

Learning to concentrate is one of the essential keys to academic success. It is much easier to concentrate on something that interests you. What do you do when you find it hard to concentrate on reading? Look at the boxed list on page 5 for a few suggestions.

Apply the concentration strategies described in the list to the following passage—the first six paragraphs of Annie Dillard's essay "The Chase." Since the passage is relatively short, you can emphasize the first three strategies for concentrating. You will be reading the entire essay in parts throughout this chapter.

On one weekday morning after Christmas, six inches of new snow had just fallen. We were standing up to our boot tops in snow on a front yard on trafficked Reynolds Street, waiting for cars. The cars traveled Reynolds Street slowly and evenly; they were targets all but wrapped in red ribbons, cream puffs. We couldn't miss.

I was seven; the boys were eight, nine, and ten. The oldest two Fahey boys were there—Mikey and Peter—polite blond boys who lived near me on Lloyd Street, and who already had four brothers and sisters. My parents approved of Mikey and Peter Fahey. Chickie McBride was there, a tough kid, and Billy Paul and Mackie Kean too, from across Reynolds, where the boys grew up dark and furious, grew up skinny, knowing, and skilled. We had all drifted from our houses that morning looking for action, and had found it here on Reynolds Street.

It was cloudy but cold. The cars' tires laid behind them on the snowy street a complex trail of beige chunks like crenellated castle walls. I had stepped on some earlier; they squeaked. We could have wished for more traffic. When a car came, we all popped it one. In the intervals between cars we reverted to the natural solitude of children.

I started making an iceball—a perfect iceball, from perfectly white snow, perfectly spherical, and squeezed perfectly translucent so no snow remained all the way through. (The Fahey boys and I considered it unfair actually to throw an iceball at somebody, but it had been known to happen.)

I had just embarked on the iceball project when we heard tire chains come clanking from afar. A black Buick was moving toward us down the street. We all spread out, banged together some regular snowballs, took aim, and, when the Buick drew nigh, fired.

A soft snowball hit the driver's windshield right before the driver's face. It made a smashed star with a hump in the middle.

Think about your experience reading the passage. What did you discover when you tried to concentrate on reading this selection? Did it hold your interest, or did your mind wander? If your mind wandered, what did you do? Did you read the passage in one take or break it down into smaller parts? Did you read it more than once? Why or why not?

ASKING QUESTIONS

As you may have already noticed, concentrating on the beginning of a reading assignment is usually not enough. You need to keep focused, to sustain your concentration throughout the whole piece. One way to accomplish this is to ask yourself questions before, during, and after your reading session. Asking questions about your reading will help you remain actively engaged with the material. The questions can also help you assess how much you are learning.

Before you begin reading, for example, have a general question in mind to guide you during your reading session. This question can be a motivating question such as "What do I hope to accomplish in doing this reading?" or "How can this reading help me toward success in the course?" You can also ask questions about the topic of the reading selection, such as "What do I already know about the topic of this selection?" or "What do I expect to find out?"

During your reading session, continue to ask yourself questions about the reading to keep yourself focused on it. You can ask questions such as "Why is this fact or detail included?" or "How does this example support the writer's point?" or "How is this information or idea related to what I read or learned earlier—on the previous page, or in the previous chapter, or in class?"

After your reading session, jot down a couple of questions that the reading left unanswered. You can ask yourself two kinds of questions: (1) questions that focus on the key facts, details, or ideas of the reading selection—these will be questions you can answer; (2) questions you would like to ask in class because you are uncertain or confused about some element of the reading assignment—these are questions you cannot yet answer.

Asking questions before, during, and after reading a selection not only helps you keep focused on it but also provides you with study aids when it comes time to review for a test. Bringing your questions to the teacher in the classroom helps you contribute to class discussion, which may help your overall grade. Finally, asking questions allows you to see what you understand (the questions you can answer) and what you do not (the questions you need answered by the instructor).

The following passage is a continuation of the Annie Dillard essay that you began on page 6. Before you read, jot down two "before reading" questions for the selection in your notebook. As you read, keep these questions in mind, and continue to ask yourself "during reading" questions, such as "What have I learned so far?"—or, for a particular passage, "How does this relate to what I've already read?" or "What does this mean?"

Often, of course, we hit our target, but this time, the only time in all of life, the car pulled over and stopped. Its wide black door opened; a man got out of it, running. He didn't even close the car door.

He ran after us, and we ran away from him, up the snowy Reynolds sidewalk. At the corner, I looked back; incredibly, he was still after us. He was in city clothes: a suit and tie, street shoes. Any normal adult would have quit, having sprung us into flight and made his point. This man was gaining on us. He was a thin man, all action. All of a sudden, we were running for our lives.

Wordless, we split up. We were on our turf; we could lose ourselves in the neighborhood backyards, everyone for himself. I paused and considered. Everyone had vanished except Mike Fahey, who was just rounding the corner of a yellow brick house. Poor Mikey, I trailed him. The driver of the Buick sensibly picked the two of us to follow. The man apparently had all day.

He chased Mikey and me around the yellow house and up a backyard path we knew by heart: under a low tree, up a bank, through a hedge, down some snowy steps, and across the grocery store's delivery driveway. We smashed through a gap in another hedge, entered a scruffy backyard and ran around its back porch and tight between houses to Edgerton Avenue; we ran across Edgerton to an alley and up our own sliding woodpile to the Halls' front yard; he kept coming. We ran up Lloyd Street and wound through mazy backyards toward the steep hilltop at Willard and Lang.

He chased us silently, block after block. He chased us silently over picket fences, through thorny hedges, between houses, around garbage cans, and across streets. Every time I glanced back, choking for breath, I expected he would have quit. He must have been as breathless as we were. His jacket strained over his body. It was an immense discovery, pounding into my hot head with every sliding, joyous step, that this ordinary adult evidently knew what I thought only children who trained at football knew: that you have to fling yourself at what you're doing, you have to point yourself, forget yourself, aim, dive.

Now that you have read the passage, think about how you would answer your "before reading" questions. You knew something about the second passage from having read the earlier one. But you may also know something about the general topic or situation described in the passage from your observation or experience.

Now look at the questions you asked yourself during your reading of the second passage. Did you ask yourself about the meaning of any words? Which ones? Did you ask about why a particular detail or example was included? Which ones? Did you ask about how the second passage related to the first?

If you did not ask those kinds of questions, return to the second passage and read it again, this time asking those questions. Begin to formulate answers in your mind. If you did ask those kinds of questions, now ask further questions—the kind you might raise in class or in conversation with other students. Finally, return to the second passage and read it once again. Jot down whatever "after reading" questions you have—for example, "What was the writer's point?" or "Do I understand what the writer was getting at?"

■ Reading Actively

Active reading refers to the process of actually doing something while you read. You have already begun the process of active reading by asking and answering questions about "The Chase." Another dimension of active reading involves establishing personal goals for reading. In reading actively you read for a purpose. Part of your purpose, of course, is to understand what the passage says or means. But you might have other purposes as well—to challenge yourself, to concentrate and remain focused, to develop questions to ask in class, and more.

Establish your own personal goals when you read. Consider what you want to achieve in doing the reading. And think about how doing the reading can help you. It might help prepare you for class discussion or for a test. It might give you information you can use in your everyday life. It might provide you with something to talk about with a friend or a new acquaintance.

It will help you to read actively if you read with a pen or pencil in hand. You can jot notes while you read. You can underline passages, circle key words and phrases, underline new vocabulary words, and write out some questions. You can draw arrows and use other symbols, such as a question mark (?) to indicate something that confuses you or an exclamation point (!) to indicate something you agree with.

Here is an example of active reading applied to a continuation of the Annie Dillard story you have been reading in pieces throughout this chapter. As you read, note what this active reader did, and think of what notes you might make. Also pay particular attention to the continuation of the story. You will have a chance to practice active reading on the story's final section.

high? excited?—
dismayed: upset?

He catches the
kids

> Mikey and I had nowhere to go, in our own neighborhood or out of it, but away from this man who was chasing us. He <u>impelled</u> us forward; we <u>compelled</u> him to follow our route. The air was cold; every breath tore my throat. We kept running, block after block; we kept improvising, backyard after backyard, running a <u>frantic</u> course and choosing it simultaneously, failing always to find small places or hard places to slow him down, and discovering always, (exhilarated,) (dismayed,) that only bare speed could save us—for he would never give up, this man—and we were losing speed.
>
> He chased us through the backyard labyrinths of ten blocks before he <u>caught us</u> by our jackets. He <u>caught us</u> and we all stopped.

We three stood staggering, half blinded, coughing, in an obscure hilltop backyard: a man in his twenties, a boy, a girl. He had released our jackets, our (pursuer,) our (captor,) our (hero:) he knew we weren't going anywhere. We all played by the rules. Mikey and I unzipped our jackets. I pulled off my sopping mittens. Our tracks multiplied in the backyard's new snow. We had been breaking new snow all morning. We didn't look at each other. I was cherishing my excitement. The man's lower pants legs were wet; his cuffs were full of snow, and there was a prow of snow beneath them on his shoes and socks. Some trees bordered the little flat backyard, some messy winter trees. There was no one around: a clearing in a grove, and we the only players.

Why does he chase the kids?

Why don't they try to get away?

Why the details about snow on his pants and shoes?

The man is all 3 — pursuer, captor, hero — why hero?

— he's wet

Notice how some words are underlined and other words and phrases are circled. Notice too the marginal questions and notations. And finally, look at the questions the reader made about the passage. These marks and questions reveal a mind at work—a mind reading actively and attentively. This is the kind of active reading you should strive for.

Use active reading as you read the conclusion of the story in the passage that follows. Read with a pen in hand to underline, circle, write symbols, and jot questions and comments.

It was a long time before he could speak. I had some difficulty at first recalling why we were there. My lips felt swollen; I couldn't see out of the sides of my eyes; I kept coughing.

"You stupid kids," he began perfunctorily.

We listened perfunctorily indeed, if we listened at all, for the chewing out was redundant, a mere formality, and beside the point. The point was that he had chased us passionately without giving up, and so he had caught us. Now he came down to earth. I wanted the glory to last forever.

But how could the glory have lasted forever? We could have run through every backyard in North America until we got to Panama.

continued

But when he trapped us at the lip of the Panama Canal, what precisely could he have done to prolong the drama of the chase and cap its glory? I brooded about this for the next few years. He could only have fried Mikey Fahey and me in boiling oil, say, or dismembered us piecemeal, or staked us to anthills. None of which I really wanted, and none of which any adult was likely to do, even in the spirit of fun. He could only chew us out there in the Panamanian jungle, after months or years of exalting pursuit. He could only begin, "You stupid kids," and continue in his ordinary Pittsburgh accent with his normal righteous anger and the usual common sense.

If in that snowy backyard the driver of the black Buick had cut off our heads, Mikey's and mine, I would have died happy, for nothing has required so much of me since as being chased all over Pittsburgh in the middle of winter — running terrified, exhausted — by this sainted, skinny, furious red-headed man who wished to have a word with us. I don't know how he found his way back to his car.

Applying the Skills

Reading the Parts

This essay, written by Karen Epstein for her college newspaper, *The Tufts Daily,* discusses her experience with Barbie dolls. Epstein wrote the essay when she was a senior at Tufts University in 1997; the trigger was the announcement by the Mattel toy company that Barbie's figure was being made more realistic. As you read the essay, use the strategies for active reading you learned in this chapter, including asking questions and taking notes. After reading each section of the essay, answer the questions and move on to the next section. You will have a chance to read the whole essay when you finish.

KAREN EPSTEIN
I'm a Barbie Girl

It wasn't her curvaceous hips. Or her Scarlett O'Hara–esque waist. Or even her unnaturally voluptuous bustline. The only things that bothered me were her feet. Those tiny little plastic feet were bent up in this permanent high-heel position that was extremely aggravating because I could never get those itsy-bitsy high-heel pumps to stay on. Ah, but the handsome Ken: he had these big, wide, "manly" feet that were perfectly flat. Those sensible shoes never fell off. Poor Barbie, on the other hand, never got to wear shoes in my house.

To my dismay, the Mattel toy company has not yet announced whether they will bring in their podiatry experts to examine thirty-eight-year-old Barbie's feet before her upcoming surgery. Earlier this week, the company told the world that the shapely Barbie is scheduled for some extensive nips and tucks—a wider waist, slimmer hips, and a smaller bustline. She's even getting a new face, minus the toothy grin.

Many who felt that the pop icon Barbie doll upheld an unrealistic standard of beauty are hailing Mattel's decision to make her look more like a real woman. And her highly unrealistic 38-18-34 figure (according to some estimates) gives girls a negative body ideal from a young age. "I actually think it's healthy because we are surrounded by cultural icons that create unrealistic expectations in

> adult women. . . . Barbie's change is a wholesome step in the right direction," retired plastic surgeon Sharon Webb told the *Boston Globe*.

1. According to Epstein, why might Barbie need a "podiatry expert"?

   a. to give her plastic surgery

   b. to fix the problems with her feet

   c. to study her heart

   d. to work on her teeth

2. Why do many people, according to Epstein, have a problem with the way the Barbie doll looks?

   a. Many feel that the doll upholds an unrealistic standard of beauty.

   b. Many feel that not all ethnicities are represented by the Barbie doll line.

   c. Many feel that there should be more of a waistline on the Barbie doll.

   d. Many feel that Barbie's feet should be flat, not arched.

3. What effect does the construction of the Barbie doll have on girls, according to Epstein in paragraph 3?

   a. It makes them feel good, like they have something positive to work toward.

   b. It makes them feel like they, too, should be cultural icons.

   c. It may cause them to have a negative body image from a young age.

   d. It may cause them to play with Ken more.

4. According to Epstein, how is Mattel reacting to the negative publicity regarding Barbie's body type?

   a. They aren't going to do anything to change it.

   b. They are going to hold focus groups with young girls to see if there is a problem.

   c. They are going to launch a new line of dolls called "Maxie."

   d. They are going to remodel Barbie so that her body and face are more realistic.

5. What was the overall reaction to Mattel's decision, as reported by Epstein in paragraph 3?

    a. People didn't care.

    b. Many were happy with the decision.

    c. Many felt that Mattel didn't go far enough with its plan.

    d. Many hoped that Mattel would take Barbie off toy shelves.

I don't know about you, but for me, Barbie was always, well, a doll. When Barbie's skinny plastic legs popped out of their sockets, I knew she wasn't real. When my friend Lauren's bratty, semicannibalistic six-year-old neighbor chewed off Barbie's foot, and Barbie kept up that same cheery grin, I knew she wasn't real. I never deluded myself into thinking we little girls were supposed to grow up to have 38-18-34 figures. My mom didn't look like that. My teenage sisters didn't look like that. NO women I knew looked like Barbie. She was fun. She was a fantasy. And she sure did have some nice clothes.

4

I've always been a big fan of Barbie. I'm not alone. According to M. G. Lord, the author of *Forever Barbie*, the average American girl owns eight Barbie dolls—eight gals, that is, to "one pathetic, overextended Ken," she says. That was the case with me, although I think the number far exceeded eight. I don't remember all of their official names anymore, but I remember many in the lineup: there was punk-rocker Barbie, bride Barbie, "day-to-night" Barbie (her outfit converted from a work suit to evening wear, tres yuppie 1980s), the Barbie that came with an assortment of "fashion wigs," the Barbie with the funky hair-curler, birthday Barbie, ballerina Barbie, and, my favorite, permanently puckered kissing Barbie, who, at the push of a button on her back, would give Ken a big smooch. I was very upset when Barbie's kissing button stopped working. Looking back on it, I realize perhaps she just didn't like Ken anymore.

5

My Ken was a busy fella. He was forced to play the boyfriend, brother, father, husband, "insert male role here" role in every one of my Barbies' adventures. What a nice guy. And, oh, those adventures. I could dress her in fancy clothes and send her on a romantic date with Ken, give her a bath in my Barbie bubble bath, put her to bed in the Barbie dream house (I didn't actually have one, but I could pretend). It was a fantasy. "I mean, they say Barbie is unrealistic. But she's got a Ferrari, a Malibu dream house, and big plastic boobs. Here in LA, you can't get more realistic than that," said late-night TV host Jay Leno earlier this week.

6

6. What was the author's attitude toward Barbie when she was young?

   a. She thought Barbie offered an unrealistic body type and refused to play with the doll.

   b. She never played with dolls.

   c. She liked Ken better.

   (d.) She was a big fan of Barbie.

7. According to the author in paragraph 5, why do you think the "average American girl owns eight Barbie dolls"?

   a. Girls like to have more than one doll.

   (b.) Every Barbie doll is different and represents a different "type" of woman.

   c. Ken had too many roles to play.

   d. Girls have multiple Ken dolls and think that they need one Barbie for every Ken.

8. The author states in paragraphs 4–6 that she never viewed Barbie as anything but a doll. Which of the following sentences or phrases is *not* one of the reasons the author gives in the selection for her realistic view of the doll?

   a. Barbie's legs popped out of the sockets.

   b. Her friend's neighbor chewed off Barbie's feet.

   c. Her mother and sisters did not look like Barbie.

   (d.) The doll was made of plastic and therefore not real to the author.

9. "My Ken was a busy fella." What role did the Ken doll play in the author's fantasy, as described in paragraph 6?

   a. He always played the role of policeman.

   (b.) He played any number of male roles in the author's play with Barbie.

   c. He was always Barbie's husband.

   d. He played any number of male or female roles in the author's play with Barbie.

10. The author quotes Jay Leno in one of his opening monologues on *The Tonight Show*: ". . . she's got a Ferrari, a Malibu dream

house, and big plastic boobs. Here in LA, you can't get more realistic than that." Why does Epstein include this quote?

a. to show that there are many "dream houses" like Barbie's in Los Angeles

b. to show that many people own Ferraris in Los Angeles

(c.) to show that there is a stereotype of young women in Los Angeles looking like Barbie

d. to show that Jay Leno talks about Barbie

Don't get me wrong. I do understand the concern many have with Barbie's current look. And, although her incredibly unrealistic body image did not affect me consciously as a child, there is a good chance it did affect me unconsciously. There is no one cause of the obsession with body image in this country and the rampant eating disorders young girls and women develop. While I place more of the blame on unattainable images of sickly thin women in advertising, movies, and television for the perpetuation of unrealistic standards of beauty, I must say that, despite my love for the Barbie I grew up with, Mattel is making the right move. If it helps one girl to not internalize the ridiculous ideal of big-busted thinness as perfection, it's worth it. But I'll never forget my Barbie. 7

Even Christina Hoff Sommers, the author of a book entitled *Who Stole Feminism?*, told the *Boston Globe,* "The new Barbie is more attractive, and she did need a makeover. But I didn't mind the fact the older one reflected earlier ideals of feminine beauty. I liked Barbie as a child. She was glamorous. And part of being a child is fantasy and play, not an exercise in self-esteem." 8

In the end, she's a doll. A fantasy. An unanatomically correct piece of plastic with a ridiculously extensive wardrobe. And funny feet. 9

11. How does Epstein feel about Mattel's decision to change Barbie's form, as stated in paragraph 7?

a. She disagrees with the decision.

(b.) She agrees with the decision.

c. She thinks that Barbie should be taken off toy shelves permanently.

d. She thinks that more Barbies should look like middle-aged women.

12. The author writes, "I do understand the concern many have with Barbie's current look." What is the concern?
    a. Barbie's possible effect on young girls' body image
    b. Barbie's facial features
    c. Barbie's feet
    d. Barbie's relationship with Ken

13. "If it helps one girl to not *internalize* the ridiculous ideal of big-busted thinness as perfection, it's worth it." Considering this sentence in paragraph 7, what do you think the word *internalize* means?
    a. referring to internal organs
    b. to juxtapose
    c. to mix up
    d. to personalize

14. As stated in paragraph 8 of Epstein's essay, what is Christina Hoff Sommers' view of Barbie?
    a. She likes the new Barbie and the old Barbie.
    b. She likes the new Barbie better and thinks the old Barbie should be made extinct.
    c. She likes the old Barbie better and thinks that many have blown the issue of Barbie's form out of proportion.
    d. She thinks that the people who oppose the old Barbie should "get a life."

15. Besides the word *doll,* Karen Epstein uses one word repeatedly throughout the selection to describe Barbie. What is it?
    a. dummy
    b. blonde
    c. fantasy
    d. bombshell

Reading the Whole

Now that you've had a chance to read Karen Epstein's "I'm a Barbie Girl" in its parts and to practice active reading, you will be better prepared to reread it. As you read the whole essay reprinted here, continue to use your active reading strategies, this time asking different questions of the text as they occur to you. Continue to take whatever new notes will help you put the parts together, and take a look at Epstein's essay, this time from a broader perspective.

KAREN EPSTEIN

I'm a Barbie Girl

It wasn't her curvaceous hips. Or her Scarlett O'Hara–esque waist. Or even her unnaturally voluptuous bustline. The only things that bothered me were her feet. Those tiny little plastic feet were bent up in this permanent high-heel position that was extremely aggravating because I could never get those itsy-bitsy high-heel pumps to stay on. Ah, but the handsome Ken: he had these big, wide, "manly" feet that were perfectly flat. Those sensible shoes never fell off. Poor Barbie, on the other hand, never got to wear shoes in my house.

To my dismay, the Mattel toy company has not yet announced whether they will bring in their podiatry experts to examine thirty-eight-year-old Barbie's feet before her upcoming surgery. Earlier this week, the company told the world that the shapely Barbie is scheduled for some extensive nips and tucks—a wider waist, slimmer hips, and a smaller bustline. She's even getting a new face, minus the toothy grin.

Many who felt that the pop icon Barbie doll upheld an unrealistic standard of beauty are hailing Mattel's decision to make her look more like a real woman. And her highly unrealistic 38-18-34 figure (according to some estimates) gives girls a negative body ideal from a young age. "I actually think it's healthy because we are surrounded by cultural icons that create unrealistic expectations in adult women. . . . Barbie's change is a wholesome step in the right direction," retired plastic surgeon Sharon Webb told the *Boston Globe*.

I don't know about you, but for me, Barbie was always, well, a doll. When Barbie's skinny plastic legs popped out of their sockets, I knew she wasn't real. When my friend Lauren's bratty,

1

2

3

4

semicannibalistic six-year-old neighbor chewed off Barbie's foot, and Barbie kept up that same cheery grin, I knew she wasn't real. I never deluded myself into thinking we little girls were supposed to grow up to have 38-18-34 figures. My mom didn't look like that. My teenage sisters didn't look like that. NO women I knew looked like Barbie. She was fun. She was a fantasy. And she sure did have some nice clothes.

I've always been a big fan of Barbie. I'm not alone. According to M. G. Lord, the author of *Forever Barbie,* the average American girl owns eight Barbie dolls—eight gals, that is, to "one pathetic, overextended Ken," she says. That was the case with me, although I think the number far exceeded eight. I don't remember all of their official names anymore, but I remember many in the lineup: there was punk-rocker Barbie, bride Barbie, "day-to-night" Barbie (her outfit converted from a work suit to evening wear, tres yuppie 1980s), the Barbie that came with an assortment of "fashion wigs," the Barbie with the funky hair-curler, birthday Barbie, ballerina Barbie, and, my favorite, permanently puckered kissing Barbie, who, at the push of a button on her back, would give Ken a big smooch. I was very upset when Barbie's kissing button stopped working. Looking back on it, I realize perhaps she just didn't like Ken anymore.

My Ken was a busy fella. He was forced to play the boyfriend, brother, father, husband, "insert male role here" role in every one of my Barbies' adventures. What a nice guy. And, oh, those adventures. I could dress her in fancy clothes and send her on a romantic date with Ken, give her a bath in my Barbie bubble bath, put her to bed in the Barbie dream house (I didn't actually have one, but I could pretend). It was a fantasy. "I mean, they say Barbie is unrealistic. But she's got a Ferrari, a Malibu dream house, and big plastic boobs. Here in LA, you can't get more realistic than that," said late-night TV host Jay Leno earlier this week.

Don't get me wrong. I do understand the concern many have with Barbie's current look. And, although her incredibly unrealistic body image did not affect me consciously as a child, there is a good chance it did affect me unconsciously. There is no one cause of the obsession with body image in this country and the rampant eating disorders young girls and women develop. While I place more of the blame on unattainable images of sickly thin women in advertising, movies, and television for the perpetuation of unrealistic standards of beauty, I must say that, despite my love for the Barbie I grew up with, Mattel is making the right move. If it helps one girl to not internalize the ridiculous ideal of big-busted thinness as perfection, it's worth it. But I'll never forget my Barbie.

Even Christina Hoff Sommers, the author of a book entitled *Who Stole Feminism?*, told the *Boston Globe*, "The new Barbie is more attractive, and she did need a makeover. But I didn't mind the fact the older one reflected earlier ideals of feminine beauty. I liked Barbie as a child. She was glamorous. And part of being a child is fantasy and play, not an exercise in self-esteem." 8

In the end, she's a doll. A fantasy. An unanatomically correct piece of plastic with a ridiculously extensive wardrobe. And funny feet. 9

Integrated Skills

1. What do you think of Barbie—either before or after her figure makeover?

2. Do you think that Barbie's unrealistic figure has influenced the eating behavior and self-image of girls? Why or why not?

3. What other qualities does Barbie possess, according to the author or to Christina Hoff Sommers, whom she quotes?

4. What role does Ken play in Barbie's doll life? Why isn't there more of a fuss made about him?

Reading Textbooks

Thematic Connections. The following selection comes from a political science textbook, *The Politics of American Government* by Stephen J. Wayne, G. Calvin Mackenzie, David M. O'Brien, and Richard L. Cole. The passage is a special feature that highlights people who influenced political action or political ideas. The passage focuses on Gloria Steinem, a political activist, who founded the feminist magazine *Ms.* As you will learn from reading the selection, Steinem has worked as a Playboy bunny and has written books on issues important to women.

As you read the passage, pay particular attention to the issues that Steinem sees as important for women—women's issues, basically. Look also for what she says in the words the author quotes from her. And finally, ask yourself how this passage helps you understand the historical and social context of Karen Epstein's "I'm a Barbie Girl."

Vocabulary Preview

political activist (para. 1): one who takes action to achieve a political goal (n.)

exposé (para. 1): an article that exposes something (n.)

trenchant (para. 2): very effective (adj.)

assertive (para. 4): willing to state things clearly and boldly (adj.)

People in Politics

Gloria Steinem: Thoroughly Modern Feminist

Political activist and writer Gloria Steinem first came to notice as a voice for the newly emerging women's movement in 1963 with the publication of her exposé article "I Was a Playboy Bunny." From that beginning Steinem rose to national prominence as a political feminist. In 1971, along with Betty Friedan, Bella Abzug, and Shirley Chisholm, Steinem founded the National Women's Political Caucus (NWPC), an organization dedicated to encouraging women to run for public office. 1

In 1972, Steinem became the founding editor of *Ms.* magazine. Within a year, *Ms.* had attained a circulation of 500,000. Many of today's most significant women's issues—equal pay, reproductive freedom, maternity leave, date rape, sexual harassment—were first identified and discussed in the pages of that publication. In a very 2 real sense, *Ms.* raised the consciousness of an entire generation of women. But because advertisers were reluctant to appear in a "radical" magazine, Steinem spent most of her time on the road, speaking on campuses and in towns and cities around the country to raise money. She still found time to write trenchant articles and books, most notably a collection of essays called *Outrageous Acts and Everyday Rebellions,* first published in 1983.

Steinem remains an editorial consultant to *Ms.* She is also very **3** active as a lecturer, organizer, and spokesperson for the feminist movement and issues of equality. Over the years, she has helped to found the *Ms.* Foundation for Women, Voters for Choice, the Women's Action Alliance, and the Coalition of Labor Union Women.

Recently Steinem has come to take a wider view of feminism, **4** tying it to larger questions of self-esteem and self-knowledge for both women and men. "Progress for women," she says, "lies in becoming more assertive, more ambitious, more able to deal with conflict. Progress for men will lie in becoming more empathetic, more compassionate, more comfortable working inside the home." Her 1992 book *Revolution from Within: A Book of Self-Esteem* explores these issues.

Although she has now slowed the pace of her public appear- **5** ances, Steinem has hardly given up on organized feminism. She frequently points out that the issues first raised by feminists in the early 1970s are still in the news today—but as national, not feminist, issues. We will know progress has been made, says Steinem, "when young men on campuses get up and ask as much as young women do, 'How can I combine a career and family?'"

Thinking about the Textbook Selection

1. What does the author convey about Gloria Steinem as a political activist?

2. What can you learn about Gloria Steinem's interests and approach from the titles of her books—*Outrageous Acts and Everyday Rebellions* and *Revolution from Within: A Book of Self-Esteem*?

3. Do you agree with Steinem's idea that women can achieve progress through "becoming more assertive, more ambitious, more able to deal with conflict"? Why or why not?

4. Do you agree with her view that men will make progress by "becoming more empathetic, more compassionate, more comfortable working inside the home"? Why or why not?

Reviewing

Recall / Remember

1. What are the basic goals of reading? Why is it important to understand your own reading habits?

2. What is everyday reading, and how can you make it a more significant part of your reading life?

3. Why is it necessary to make observations and connections about what you read?

4. Identify some strategies for concentrating and maintaining your focus on what you read.

5. What is active reading, and how can you practice it?

Chapter Summary

This opening chapter introduces you to the goals of reading and offers preliminary advice about how to read more effectively. You have learned about the importance of concentrating and remaining focused on your reading. And you have been provided with some strategies to become an active reader.

In addition, it introduces you to the book's features, which you will find in the remaining chapters. These features include (1) a chapter overview with focusing questions and an Everyday Reading suggestion; (2) a reading selection broken into sections and accompanied by instruction and exercises; (3) a split-up reading with test questions between the parts; (4) the split-up reading selection put back together, or reconstituted; (5) an additional reading selection accompanied by a vocabulary preview and thinking questions; and (6) review questions followed by a chapter summary like this one.

Learning Vocabulary from Context Clues

Chapter 2

Getting Ready	25
Learning the Skills	26
Applying the Skills	
• Reading the Parts	39
• Reading the Whole	45
• Reading Textbooks	48
Reviewing	50

Getting Ready

Whenever people read, they usually have to figure out the meaning of words that are unfamiliar to them. They do this by using the words they *do* know to help them understand the words they *don't* know. They use the **context**—the surrounding words—to help them understand the unfamiliar words. They make **inferences**—reasoned, educated guesses—about the meaning of words that are new to them.

In this chapter, you will study four kinds of **context clues,** techniques authors use to help readers learn unfamiliar words. These four kinds of context clues are **restatement, example, contrast,** and **general context clues.**

Chapter Overview

When you encounter an unfamiliar word, **how** do you usually determine its meaning? To what extent do you try to figure it out from the words you *do* know?

What do you do when you learn new vocabulary?

How might you put newly learned words to use?

From **what** kinds of reading do you learn new words?

Focusing Questions

Everyday Reading

One kind of reading unrelated to your college work may be reading you do with children. If you are a parent, you may read to your child. If you have younger brothers or sisters, you may read to them.

When a child doesn't understand a word, how do you go about explaining its meaning? Do you have the child consult a dictionary? Do you examine the context—the passage in which the word appears?

The next time you read to a child, look for the context clues described in this chapter. You may wish to explain to the child how he or she can arrive at the meaning of an unfamiliar word through the context. Encourage the child to use the new words in speaking and in writing.

Learning the Skills

■ Restatement Context Clues

Writers want to be sure that their readers understand what they have written. Therefore, when they use an important term, phrase, or idea, they may restate it in words they think are familiar to their readers. The restatement may be a precise, formal definition as if from a dictionary, or it may be a general, informal definition. Either way, these definitions are called **restatement context clues.**

You will frequently find restatement context clues in college textbooks. The specialized vocabulary of a particular field of study is often explained through straightforward definitions. Here is an example from the math textbook *For All Practical Purposes* by the Consortium for Mathematics and Its Applications:

> A *bar code* is a series of dark bars and light spaces that represent characters.

The definition is formal and precise, and the purpose of the whole sentence is to present that definition.

The definition that follows, from the textbook *Exploring the World of Business* by Kenneth Blanchard, Charles Schewe, Robert Nelson, and Alexander Hiam, appears almost as an aside. The purpose of the sentence is not to define the term *revenues*. However, the author does want to be sure that readers understand what he means when he uses the term.

> Revenues—the money the business takes in—must be greater than expenses over the long run for the business to maintain itself and profit its owners.

The words immediately after *revenues* explain what *revenues* are. Notice that the restatement—the definition—is set off by dashes. Restatements may also be set off by commas or parentheses.

> For every *aphorism*, a statement of wisdom or a saying, you can usually find another one that presents the opposite point of view.
> In ancient Greek mathematics, the atoms of the earth were supposed to have the shape of *hexahedrons* (cubes).

Restatements may begin with words like *that is* or *or*.

> The children were asked to resolve a major *dilemma*, or difficult choice, between two alternatives.

Restatements may be included in a new sentence.

> Athletes who play many sports usually work on their *aerobic conditioning*. Improving the efficiency of the heart and lungs is important, no matter what the level of play.

The restatement clue to help readers understand *aerobic conditioning,* "improving the efficiency of the heart and lungs," appears at the beginning of the second sentence.

A restatement, or definition, may also appear *before* the term that is defined. Notice where the term *mantra* is defined in the following sentence about meditation, from the textbook *Discovering Psychology* by Don H. Hockenbury and Sandra E. Hockenbury.

> When a sound is used, it is typically a short word or a religious phrase, called a *mantra*, that is mentally repeated.

The definition of *mantra,* "a short word or a religious phrase," appears *before* the specialized term *mantra* is named.

Exercise 2-1

All the boldface words have restatement context clues. Underline each restatement. Then write a sentence of your own in which you use the boldface word(s).

Example:

Trees that shed their leaves during a specific season, called **deciduous** trees, create problems every fall for property owners.

SENTENCE: *Deciduous trees can be full of life in the summer but then bare and depressing in the winter.*

1. To **commend** means to express approval or to praise someone.

   SENTENCE: I will commend my friend on what I know.

2. A **draglift** is a kind of ski lift that pulls the skiers up the slopes.

   SENTENCE: I use a draglift last time I went sking.

3. The earliest **crustaceans,** animals whose bodies are encased in hard shells, were much smaller than the lobsters and crabs of today.

   SENTENCE: We have a crustaceans in my house.

4. I have an **equilibrist** in my family. My uncle performs all kinds of balancing acts, including tightrope walking.

   SENTENCE: I am an equilibrist when I am on my unicycle.

5. Whales and porpoises are **mammals,** warm-blooded animals with a covering of hair on their skin who nurse their young.

   SENTENCE: There are lots of mammals at the zoo.

6. The president's statement was **ambiguous;** it was unclear whether he favored sending in troops or was opposed to the idea.

   SENTENCE: My friend was ambiguous because he was very excited.

7. For lip-readers, one-on-one conversations are easiest if the **interlocutors** — that is, the talkers — are familiar with each other.

   SENTENCE: There are lots of interlocutors at parties

8. **Computer hackers** — experts at working with computer programs and codes — sometimes use their expertise to break into government databases.

   SENTENCE: Computer hackers can get into any computer from anywhere.

9. Some people born with malformed arms or legs wear **prostheses,** or artificial limbs, all their lives.

   SENTENCE: I saw someone with a prosthes. leg before.

10. **Small talk,** which might strike you as phony, is actually important in the beginning of a relationship. This light, impersonal conversation breaks the ice and opens the way for a more personal exchange.

    SENTENCE: Boddy started the small talk at the party.

■ Example Context Clues

Writers often provide examples to illustrate and clarify the meaning of an unfamiliar word. Such examples are known as **example context clues.** Like other context clues, examples may be set off in the sentence by commas, dashes, or parentheses.

> *Legumes*—green or snap beans, lima beans, green peas, chick-peas, navy beans, and so on—are a valuable, although incomplete, source of protein.

If you did not know the meaning of the word *legumes,* the examples given would help you realize that legumes are kinds of beans and peas.

Example context clues may appear in the same sentence as the unfamiliar word, as they do in the legume sentence, or they may be longer examples that take up a sentence or two.

> In the Old Testament, God is described as an *anthropomorphic* being. He walks in the Garden of Eden with Adam and Eve, talks with Moses in the desert, and becomes angry with the human race.

The second sentence gives examples of ways in which God is described in the Old Testament as being *anthropomorphic:* God walks, talks, and becomes angry. Those examples should help you figure out that *anthropomorphic* means "having human qualities."

Examples are sometimes introduced by words like *for example, for instance, such as,* and *including.*

> *Percussionists,* including those who play kettledrums, bass drums, cymbals, and triangles, usually have their own section in an orchestra.

The examples given should help you figure out that *percussionists* are musicians who play instruments that produce their sounds by being struck.

Exercise 2-2

. . . .

The boldface words all have example context clues. First underline
the example context clue. Next write the meaning of the boldface
word(s) on the line provided. Then write a sentence of your own
using the boldface word(s).

Example:

> **Homophones** present spelling problems that computer spell checkers
> cannot correct: *too* for *two*, for example, or *your* for *you're*.
>
> **Homophones** means _words that sound the same but have different_
> _meanings and spellings._
>
> SENTENCE: _Do you consider the words "Mary," "marry," and "merry"_
> _homophones, or do you pronounce each one differently?_

1. The way people use **cutlery** — knives, forks, and spoons — differs from
   culture to culture.

   Cutlery means _utensils used to eat with._

   SENTENCE: _we use alot of cutlery._

2. As hard as we try, we cannot always avoid **pathogens**, which include
   many kinds of bacteria, viruses, and parasites.

   Pathogens means _disease + germs._

   SENTENCE: _I get pathogens when I get sick._

3. The origin of an **idiom** — for instance, "to let one's hair down," "raining
   cats and dogs," and "talking through your hat" — is sometimes hard to
   understand and sometimes easy to figure out.

   Idiom means _something hard but easy to figure out._

   SENTENCE: _Someone I know says alot of idioms._

4. Marilyn took an **eclectic** approach to learning Spanish: She skimmed a grammar book, listened to a short conversational tape, and spent a little time with her Spanish-speaking relatives.

   Eclectic means _learning in many different ways_

   SENTENCE: _I like ectectic learning when it comes to music_

5. When visiting a foreign country, tourists should observe proper **etiquette**. In Iran, for example, visiting women should keep their arms and legs covered. In Japan and China, tourists should address new acquaintances by their full names. In many European countries, visitors should keep their fork in their left hand when eating.

   Etiquette means _culture manners_

   SENTENCE: _My friend bobby has no etiquette manners._

6. Some of baseball's famous long-ball hitters have hit a **"tape-measure job."** Josh Gibbons hit a home run 512 feet, Mickey Mantle slugged one more than 565 feet, and Mark McGwire hammered a ball about 545 feet.

   "Tape-measure job" means _How fall they have done_

   SENTENCE: _I had a tap-measure job in the summer_

7. The monastic orders founded in the Middle Ages were orders of **contemplative** monks and nuns. They spent their days in silence thinking about God. They thought about the state of their souls and other spiritual things.

   Contemplative means _thoughtful_

   SENTENCE: _The profreser was thoughtful_

8. He is the most **loquacious** person I have ever met. He spends hours talking on the telephone. He talks at length in meetings. He talks so much and so often that he rarely if ever listens to anyone else.

   Loquacious means _____

   SENTENCE: _____

   _____

9. Her argument seemed **incontrovertible.** She provided excellent reasons and a lot of evidence.

   Incontrovertible means _Not opend to quesdons_

   _____

   SENTENCE: _It was inconstrovertible_

   _____

10. Research has shown that some people can be cured of certain medical problems with **phototherapy.** This can mean sitting in front of bright lights for several hours a day—or getting outside the minute any sunshine peeks through the cloudy winter sky.

    Phototherapy means _to kill disease with Phototherapy_

    SENTENCE: _I kiy disease with Phototherapy_
    when I am sick.

· ·

■ Contrast Context Clues

Contrast is an important element in writing. Writers use contrast—that is, opposite meanings—to indicate differences. By knowing differences readers can better understand similarity. Consider how the contrast in the following sentence helps the reader understand the meaning of the italicized word.

> We expected him to be *compliant,* but instead we found him stubborn and uncooperative.

Even though you may not know the exact meaning of *compliant,* you can tell from the context that it means the opposite of "stubborn and uncooperative."

Notice too how the words *but* and *instead* indicate that an opposite meaning is coming. Without noticing *those* words, you would not realize that *stubborn* and *uncooperative* help you understand the meaning of *compliant.*

Here's another example:

> Although the senator is usually loquacious, he has been *taciturn* in recent weeks.

In this example, *taciturn* is contrasted with *loquacious.* You know from the previous exercise that *loquacious* means "talkative." You also know that *taciturn* is opposite in meaning to *loquacious.* Thus, *taciturn* means "saying little" or "keeping silent."

You can expect that an opposite is going to be presented because the sentence contains the word *although.* *Although* suggests that an exception or difference is about to follow. Here is a list of other words that indicate that a contrast clue is coming.

WORDS INDICATING CONTRAST

although	nevertheless
but	on the other hand
however	rather than
instead	unlike

Verbs like *differ(ed)*, *contrast(ed)*, *prefer(red)*, and so on also can indicate that a contrast clue is coming.

> His loquaciousness contrasted sharply with her taciturnity.

Also be alert for phrases like *in contrast to* or *opposed to.*

Exercise 2-3

Each boldface word has a contrast context clue. Use the contrast clue to figure out the meaning of the boldface word. Write the meaning on the line provided. Then write a sentence of your own using the boldface word.

Example:

Instead of being lazy and avoiding hard work, they were **diligent** about tackling the project.

Diligent means *not lazy, hardworking.*

SENTENCE: *I am diligent when it comes to keeping up with my assignments; that diligence always pays off.*

1. His **reticence** contrasted with her willingness to talk in any situation.

   Reticence means _____

   SENTENCE: _____

   _____

2. No matter what kinds of arguments they used, they could not **dissuade** him from attending the all-night party. He was determined to go, and no amount of pressure would convince him otherwise.

   Dissuade means ___To dissuade someone___

   SENTENCE: ___I will dissuade by him.___

   _____

3. It is hard to imagine a **benevolent** dictator because, historically, dictators like Hitler or Stalin have been brutal tyrants and oppressors.

   Benevolent means ___To do good___

   SENTENCE: ___Hittler was never a benevolent
   person___

4. Instead of being **amenable** to her request, they were resistant and stubborn.

   Amenable means _to be flexable_

   SENTENCE: _I am not an Amenable_
   when I go to school

5. Some educators want to **integrate** rather than separate academic courses. They fear that dividing courses into many different subjects has students learning bits and pieces without seeing the big picture.

   Integrate means _try to bring something together_

   SENTENCE: _When someone bImtegrate_
   to gettier.

6. His skin condition was **chronic.** Unfortunately, it would not disappear after a few more medical treatments.

   Chronic means _long term_

   SENTENCE: _I have chronic back pain._

7. Their behavior was anything but **altruistic.** They were determined to get as much as they could for themselves.

   Altruistic means _Not selfish_

   SENTENCE: _Mike is a Altruisttz person_

8. Unlike a simile, which uses the word *like* or *as* to create a comparison ("She danced like an angel"), a **metaphor** works its magic without any extra words ("He is a rock").

   Metaphor means _____

   SENTENCE: _She is a metaphor to heaven_

9. He **feigned** enthusiastic interest in the award-winning movie, but he really felt bored and irritated.

Feigned means _faken it,_

SENTENCE: _I Feigned it when I_
didn't want to go.

10. In contrast to her amusing light comedies, her latest play is dramatic and **somber.**

Somber means _glooming_

SENTENCE: _Its a somber day._

· ·

■ General Context Clues

Sometimes unfamiliar words will appear without restatement, example, or contrast context clues. Even though these three types of clues are not available to help you determine the meaning of the unfamiliar word, you may still be able to make an educated guess. You can do so based on your general knowledge of the context. In the sentence below, for example, the word *incongruous* is not defined. However, from your general knowledge, you can make an educated guess about what it means.

> It seemed incongruous to have the rusted, old-fashioned skeleton key open the door of a high-tech, top-secret laboratory.

By knowing that the skeleton key was "old-fashioned" and "rusted," you can guess that it doesn't really belong at a high-tech laboratory. Therefore, you might have guessed that *incongruous* means something out of place; something that doesn't make sense. By using your general knowledge, you were able to infer the meaning of the term *incongruous*.

From the following sentences, try to figure out the meaning of the word *palpitations*.

> George's doctor was concerned. When George got excited, he could feel his heart making irregular palpitations.

Using your general knowledge of what happens to your heart when you get excited, and knowing that doctors are concerned with medical problems, you can reasonably guess that palpitations are strong, fast heartbeats.

Anytime you determine a word's meaning from context, you may not understand every small facet of its meaning. From the previous example, you may have been able to guess only that palpitations have something to do with the heart. Using a word's context to understand its meaning is a useful tool for learning words, but in some cases it may help you only to continue your reading uninterrupted by giving you a general sense of the word's meaning. If you are not sure that you fully understand a word, use annotating techniques and underline the word so that you can look it up in a dictionary later.

Reading the Parts

This essay, written by Eva Hoffman, is taken from her 1989 book *Lost in Translation: A Life in a New Language.* Hoffman, who emigrated from Poland to Canada in 1959, is the author of two other books, *Shtetl: The Life and Death of a Small Town and the World of Polish Jews* (1997) and *Exit into History: A Journey through the New Eastern Europe* (1993). As you read, pay attention to words that are unfamiliar to you, noting especially the places where their meanings are given through restatement, example, contrast, and general context clues. After reading each section and answering the questions that follow, move on to the next section. You will have a chance to read the whole essay when you finish.

EVA HOFFMAN

Lost in Translation

It is April 1959, I'm standing at the railing of the *Batory*'s upper deck, and I feel that my life is ending. I'm looking out at the crowd that has gathered on the shore to see the ship's departure from Gdynia—a crowd that, all of a sudden, is irrevocably on the other side—and I want to break out, run back, run toward the familiar excitement, the waving hands, the exclamations. We can't be leaving all this behind—but we are. I am thirteen years old, and we are emigrating. It's a notion of such crushing, definitive finality that to me it might as well mean the end of the world. 1

My sister, four years younger than I, is clutching my hand wordlessly; she hardly understands where we are, or what is happening to us. My parents are highly agitated; they had just been put through a body search by the customs police, probably as the farewell gesture of anti-Jewish harassment. Still, the officials weren't clever enough, or suspicious enough, to check my sister and me—lucky for us, since we are both carrying some silverware we were not allowed to take out of Poland in large pockets sewn onto our skirts especially for this purpose, and hidden under capacious sweaters. 2

1. Judging from the context of this sentence in paragraph 1 — "I'm looking out at the crowd that has gathered on the shore to see the ship's departure from Gdynia — a crowd that, all of a sudden, is irrevocably on the other side — and I want to break out . . ."—the word *irrevocably* means

   a. irreversibly.　　　c. unhappily.

   b. contentedly.　　　d. dejectedly.

2. Based on the general context surrounding these sentences in paragraph 1 —"We can't be leaving all this behind — but we are. I am thirteen years old, and we are emigrating"—what is the meaning of the word *emigrating*?

   a. leaving one's country to live elsewhere

   b. eating with friends

   c. celebrating with relatives

   d. arriving in a new country

3. "My parents are highly agitated; they had just been put through a body search by the customs police." In the context of this sentence in paragraph 2, what is the meaning of the word *agitated*?

   a. happy　　　　　c. content

   b. nervous　　　　d. suspicious

4. As used in paragraph 2, where Hoffman refers to "anti-Jewish harassment," *harassment* means

   a. good-byes.　　　c. badgering.

   b. happiness.　　　d. send-offs.

5. Using what you know about context clues, consider the following: "lucky for us, since we are both carrying some silverware we were not allowed to take out of Poland in large pockets sewn onto our skirts especially for this purpose, and hidden under capacious sweaters." What is the meaning of *capacious* in paragraph 2?

   a. tight　　　　　c. snug

   b. roomy　　　　d. small

When the brass band on the shore strikes up the jaunty mazurka rhythms of the Polish anthem, I am pierced by a youthful sorrow so powerful that I suddenly stop crying and try to hold still against the pain. I desperately want time to stop, to hold the ship still with the force of my will. I am suffering my first, severe attack of nostalgia, or *tęsknota*—a word that adds to nostalgia the tonalities of sadness and longing. It is a feeling whose shades and degrees I'm destined to know intimately, but at this hovering moment, it comes upon me like a visitation from a whole new geography of emotions, an annunciation of how much an absence can hurt. Or a premonition of absence, because at this divide, I'm filled to the brim with what I'm about to lose—images of Cracow, which I loved as one loves a person, of the sun-baked villages where we had taken summer vacations, of the hours I spent poring over passages of music with my piano teacher, of conversations and escapades with friends. Looking ahead, I come across an enormous, cold blankness—a darkening, an erasure, of the imagination, as if a camera eye has snapped shut, or as if a heavy curtain has been pulled over the future. Of the place where we're going—Canada—I know nothing. There are vague outlines of half a continent, a sense of vast spaces and little habitation. When my parents were hiding in a branch-covered forest bunker during the war, my father had a book with him called *Canada Fragrant with Resin* which, in his horrible confinement, spoke to him of majestic wilderness, of animals roaming without being pursued, of freedom. That is partly why we are going there, rather than to Israel, where most of our Jewish friends have gone. But to me, the word "Canada" has ominous echoes of the "Sahara." No, my mind rejects the idea of being taken there, I don't want to be pried out of my childhood, my pleasures, my safety, my hopes for becoming a pianist. The *Batory* pulls away, the foghorn emits its lowing, shofar sounds, but my being is engaged in a stubborn refusal to move. My parents put their hands on my shoulders consolingly; for a moment, they allow themselves to acknowledge that there's pain in this departure, much as they wanted it.

3

Many years later, at a stylish party in New York, I met a woman who told me that she had had an enchanted childhood. Her father was a highly positioned diplomat in an Asian country, and she had lived surrounded by sumptuous elegance, the courtesy of servants, and the delicate advances of older men. No wonder, she said, that when this part of her life came to an end, at age thirteen, she felt she had been exiled from paradise, and had been searching for it ever since.

4

6. In paragraph 3, what is the meaning of the word *nostalgia*? The sentence in which the word appears—"I am suffering my first, severe attack of nostalgia, or *tęsknota*—a word that adds to nostalgia the tonalities of sadness and longing"—gives you a restatement context clue.

    a. longing for the past

    b. contentment with things as they are

    c. sadness

    d. frustration over what has happened

7. Using what you know about restatement context clues, what is the meaning of the Polish word *tęsknota* as used by Hoffman in paragraph 3?

    a. "vague outlines of half a continent"

    b. "a word that adds to nostalgia the tonalities of sadness and longing"

    c. "horrible confinement"

    d. "stubborn refusal to move"

8. Using what you know about example context clues, what does the word *erasure* mean in paragraph 3, where Hoffman writes, "Looking ahead, I come across an enormous, cold blankness—a darkening, an erasure, of the imagination"?

    a. addition   c. deleting

    b. imagination   d. without weight

9. In paragraph 3, Hoffman refers to the book *Canada Fragrant with Resin* as one of her father's possessions. From context, what do you think the word *majestic* means in the same sentence?

    a. soiled   c. barren

    b. fragrant   d. magnificent

10. In the first sentence of paragraph 4, Hoffman describes meeting a woman who had had an "enchanted childhood." In the next sentence she gives a context clue to the meaning of the word *enchanted:* "Her father was a highly positioned diplomat in an Asian country, and she had lived surrounded by sumptuous elegance, the courtesy of servants, and the delicate advances of older men." In this context, what do you think the word *enchanted* means?

a. sad

(c.) charmed

b. morose

d. mysterious

> No wonder. But the wonder is what you can make a paradise out   5
> of. I told her that I grew up in a lumpen apartment in Cracow,
> squeezed into three rudimentary rooms with four other people,
> surrounded by squabbles, dark political rumblings, memories of
> wartime suffering, and daily struggle for existence. And yet, when it
> came time to leave, I, too, felt I was being pushed out of the happy,
> safe enclosures of Eden.
>
> I am lying in bed, watching the slowly moving shadows on the   6
> ceiling made by the gently blowing curtains, and the lights of an
> occasional car moving by. I'm trying hard not to fall asleep. Being
> awake is so sweet that I want to delay the loss of consciousness. I'm
> snuggled under an enormous goose-feather quilt covered in hand-
> embroidered silk. Across the room from me is my sister's crib. From
> the next room, "the first room," I hear my parents' breathing. The
> maid—one of a succession of country girls who come to work for
> us—is sleeping in the kitchen. It is Cracow, 1949, I'm four years
> old, and I don't know that this happiness is taking place in a coun-
> try recently destroyed by war, a place where my father has to hustle
> to get us a bit more than our meager ration of meat and sugar. I
> only know that I'm in my room, which to me is an everywhere, and
> that the patterns on the ceiling are enough to fill me with a feeling
> of sufficiency because . . . well, just because I'm conscious, because
> the world exists and it flows so gently into my head. Occasionally, a
> few blocks away, I hear the hum of the tramway, and I'm filled by a
> sense of utter contentment. I love riding the tramway, with its brac-
> ing but not overly fast swaying, and I love knowing, from my bed,
> the street over which it is moving; I repeat to myself that I'm in
> Cracow, Cracow, which to me is both home and the universe.

11. Considering the general description of the apartment—
    "squeezed into three rudimentary rooms with four other people,
    surrounded by squabbles, dark political rumblings, memories
    of wartime suffering, and daily struggle for existence"—in
    paragraph 5, what do you think the word *lumpen* means?

    a. high class

    (c.) lower class

    b. middle class

    d. sophisticated

12. In paragraph 6, Hoffman describes "the maid—one of a succession of country girls who come to work for us." What does *succession* mean?

    a. lack

    (b) series

    c. houseful

    d. intermission

13. In paragraph 6, Hoffman writes, "I only know that I'm in my room, which to me is an everywhere, and that the patterns on the ceiling are enough to fill me with a feeling of sufficiency." What does the word *sufficiency* mean?

    a. sadness

    b. joy

    c. mourning

    (d.) adequacy

14. From Hoffman's description in paragraph 6 of "the tramway, with its bracing but not overly fast swaying, and . . . the street over which it is moving," what is a *tramway*?

    a. a highway overpass

    b. an automobile

    (c.) a streetcar line

    d. a street sweeper

15. Using the general context surrounding the word *contentment* in paragraph 6, what is its meaning?

    (a.) happiness

    b. anxiety

    c. fear

    d. excitement

Reading the Whole

Now that you have read the excerpt from Eva Hoffman's *Lost in Translation* in its several parts and practiced learning unfamiliar words by context clues, you will be able to reread the essay in its entirety, absorbing more fully the author's meaning and relating, perhaps, to the author's experience.

EVA HOFFMAN
Lost in Translation

It is April 1959, I'm standing at the railing of the *Batory*'s upper deck, and I feel that my life is ending. I'm looking out at the crowd that has gathered on the shore to see the ship's departure from Gdynia—a crowd that, all of a sudden, is irrevocably on the other side—and I want to break out, run back, run toward the familiar excitement, the waving hands, the exclamations. We can't be leaving all this behind—but we are. I am thirteen years old, and we are emigrating. It's a notion of such crushing, definitive finality that to me it might as well mean the end of the world. 1

My sister, four years younger than I, is clutching my hand wordlessly; she hardly understands where we are, or what is happening to us. My parents are highly agitated; they had just been put through a body search by the customs police, probably as the farewell gesture of anti-Jewish harassment. Still, the officials weren't clever enough, or suspicious enough, to check my sister and me—lucky for us, since we are both carrying some silverware we were not allowed to take out of Poland in large pockets sewn onto our skirts especially for this purpose, and hidden under capacious sweaters. 2

When the brass band on the shore strikes up the jaunty mazurka rhythms of the Polish anthem, I am pierced by a youthful sorrow so powerful that I suddenly stop crying and try to hold still against the pain. I desperately want time to stop, to hold the ship still with the force of my will. I am suffering my first, severe attack of nostalgia, or *tęsknota*—a word that adds to nostalgia the tonalities of sadness and longing. It is a feeling whose shades and degrees I'm destined to know intimately, but at this hovering moment, it comes upon me like a visitation from a whole new geography of emotions, an annunciation of how much an absence can hurt. Or a premonition of absence, because at this divide, I'm filled to the brim with what 3

I'm about to lose—images of Cracow, which I loved as one loves a person, of the sun-baked villages where we had taken summer vacations, of the hours I spent poring over passages of music with my piano teacher, of conversations and escapades with friends. Looking ahead, I come across an enormous, cold blankness—a darkening, an erasure, of the imagination, as if a camera eye has snapped shut, or as if a heavy curtain has been pulled over the future. Of the place where we're going—Canada—I know nothing. There are vague outlines of half a continent, a sense of vast spaces and little habitation. When my parents were hiding in a branch-covered forest bunker during the war, my father had a book with him called *Canada Fragrant with Resin* which, in his horrible confinement, spoke to him of majestic wilderness, of animals roaming without being pursued, of freedom. That is partly why we are going there, rather than to Israel, where most of our Jewish friends have gone. But to me, the word "Canada" has ominous echoes of the "Sahara." No, my mind rejects the idea of being taken there, I don't want to be pried out of my childhood, my pleasures, my safety, my hopes for becoming a pianist. The *Batory* pulls away, the foghorn emits its lowing, shofar sounds, but my being is engaged in a stubborn refusal to move. My parents put their hands on my shoulders consolingly; for a moment, they allow themselves to acknowledge that there's pain in this departure, much as they wanted it.

Many years later, at a stylish party in New York, I met a woman who told me that she had had an enchanted childhood. Her father was a highly positioned diplomat in an Asian country, and she had lived surrounded by sumptuous elegance, the courtesy of servants, and the delicate advances of older men. No wonder, she said, that when this part of her life came to an end, at age thirteen, she felt she had been exiled from paradise, and had been searching for it ever since.   4

No wonder. But the wonder is what you can make a paradise out of. I told her that I grew up in a lumpen apartment in Cracow, squeezed into three rudimentary rooms with four other people, surrounded by squabbles, dark political rumblings, memories of wartime suffering, and daily struggle for existence. And yet, when it came time to leave, I, too, felt I was being pushed out of the happy, safe enclosures of Eden.   5

I am lying in bed, watching the slowly moving shadows on the ceiling made by the gently blowing curtains, and the lights of an   6 occasional car moving by. I'm trying hard not to fall asleep. Being awake is so sweet that I want to delay the loss of consciousness. I'm snuggled under an enormous goose-feather quilt covered in hand-embroidered silk. Across the room from me is my sister's crib. From the next room, "the first room," I hear my parents' breathing. The maid—one of a succession of country girls who come to work for us—is sleeping in the kitchen. It is Cracow, 1949, I'm four years old, and I don't know that this happiness is taking place in a country recently destroyed by war, a place where my father has to hustle to get us a bit more than our meager ration of meat and sugar. I only know that I'm in my room, which to me is an everywhere, and that the patterns on the ceiling are enough to fill me with a feeling of sufficiency because . . . well, just because I'm conscious, because the world exists and it flows so gently into my head. Occasionally, a few blocks away, I hear the hum of the tramway, and I'm filled by a sense of utter contentment. I love riding the tramway, with its bracing but not overly fast swaying, and I love knowing, from my bed, the street over which it is moving; I repeat to myself that I'm in Cracow, Cracow, which to me is both home and the universe.

Integrated Skills

1. Why does Eva Hoffman say that in leaving her homeland, Poland, she feels that her life is ending? What do you think she means?

2. Why do Hoffman and her sister have silverware in large pockets sewn onto their skirts as they leave Poland?

3. What does Hoffman remember about her life in Poland as she is leaving it? And what does she imagine her new life in Canada will be like?

4. How do you think you would feel if you had to leave your home country for another? If you have already done this, explain how you felt when you left.

Reading Textbooks

Thematic Connections. You've just read about the experience of Eva Hoffman as she prepared to leave her native Poland to begin a new life in Canada. In her essay, she hints at the political situation in Poland that led her parents to decide to move. While the following reading discusses the political and social situation in the United States at around the same time, it will help you understand the similar circumstances that Hoffman and her family experienced when they arrived in North America. Taken from the textbook *America: A Concise History* by James A. Henretta, David Brody, and Lynn Dumenil, this reading will contain a number of unfamiliar words. Use what you have learned in this chapter to try to figure out their meanings from context.

Vocabulary Preview

influx (para. 1): mass immigration (n.)
complexion (para. 1): makeup (n.)
intermingling (para. 2): interacting (v.)
gravitated (para. 2): moved towards (v.)

congested (para. 2): crowded (adj.)
capitalizing (para. 3): taking advantage (v.)
patronized (para. 3): went to (v.)
composed (para. 3): made up (v.)

Newcomers

At the turn of the century upwards of 30 percent of the residents of New York, Chicago, Boston, Cleveland, Minneapolis, and San Francisco were foreign-born. The biggest ethnic group in Boston was Irish; in Minneapolis, Swedish; in most other northern cities, German. But by 1910 the influx from southern and Eastern Europe had changed the ethnic complexion of many of these cities. In Chicago Poles took the lead; in New York, Eastern European Jews; in San Francisco, Italians.

As the older "walking cities" disappeared, so did the opportunities for intermingling with the older populations. The later arrivals from southern and eastern Europe had little choice about where they lived; they needed to find cheap housing near their jobs. Some gravitated to the outlying factory districts; others settled in the congested downtown ghettos. The immigrants tended to settle by ethnic group. In New York Italians crowded into the Irish neighborhoods west of Broadway, and Russian and Polish Jews pushed the Germans out of the Lower East Side. A colony of Hungarians lived around Houston Street, and Bohemians occupied the Upper East Side between Fiftieth and Seventy-sixth Streets.

Capitalizing on fellow-feeling within ethnic groups, institutions of many kinds sprang up to meet the immigrants' needs. Wherever substantial numbers lived, newspapers appeared. In 1911 the 20,000 Poles in Buffalo, New York, supported two Polish-language daily papers. Immigrants throughout the country avidly read *Il Progresso Italo-Americano* and the Yiddish-language *Jewish Daily Forward,* both published in New York City. Companionship could always be found on street corners, in barbershops and club rooms, and in saloons. Italians marched in saint's day parades, Bohemians gathered in singing societies, and New York Jews patronized a lively Yiddish theater. To provide help in times of sickness and death the immigrants organized mutual-aid societies. The Italians of Chicago had sixty-six of these organizations in 1903, each mostly composed of people from a particular province or district. Immigrants built a rich and functional institutional life in urban America to an extent unimagined in their native villages.

3

Thinking about the Textbook Selection

1. What connections do you see between Eva Hoffman's experience as she describes it in her essay taken from *Lost in Translation* and this reading selection from a history textbook? How are the two passages related?

2. Where did the immigrants come from? What did they bring with them to their new country?

3. How did the immigrants maintain their customs and experiences from their native countries?

4. Where did the immigrants live? Why? How did their living arrangements help them survive in their new country?

5. What kinds of things did the immigrants do to stick together?

Reviewing

Recall / Remember

1. Explain what context clues are and how they can help you when you read.

2. Identify the four types of context clues and explain each type.

3. List four key words that suggest that a contrast is being made in a sentence. Explain how these contrast words help you understand what you read.

Chapter Summary

In this chapter you have been introduced to some strategies for developing a college-level vocabulary. These include using different types of context clues—restatement, example, contrast, and general—to determine a word's meaning. You have also had the opportunity to read a selection closely and carefully one section at a time to practice your vocabulary building. And you have had a chance to experience the value of rereading a selection in its entirety to think about the author's experience and ideas.

Getting Ready	51
Learning the Skills	52
Applying the Skills	
• Reading the Parts	69
• Reading the Whole	73
• Reading Textbooks	76
Reviewing	79

Learning Vocabulary by Analyzing Words

Getting Ready

You learned in Chapter 2 that one way to figure out the meaning of unfamiliar words is to use context clues as you read. A second way, of course, is to look up new words in a dictionary. (See Appendix B, Using a College Dictionary, at the back of this book for guidance.) In this chapter, you will learn yet another way. You can determine the meaning of unfamiliar words by using **word analysis**—that is, by breaking down words and thinking about their smaller parts. Understanding the meanings of the parts of a word can help you understand the meaning of the entire word.

In this chapter, you will study the word parts known as **roots, prefixes,** and **suffixes.** A knowledge of common roots, prefixes, and suffixes is extremely helpful for figuring out unfamiliar words, especially long ones.

Chapter Overview

Have you ever tried to break down a long word into smaller parts? Why is a *supermarket* called what it is? How about a *submarine*?

Do you know what a word root is? A prefix? A suffix?

How can you learn the meaning of many words at once—whole families of words?

How can a larger vocabulary help you be more successful?

Focusing Questions

Everyday Reading

In the next few days, write down a dozen long words you come across, even if you already know the words. You might find the words on forms you have to fill out at work or at school. You might find them in a newspaper or a magazine, in an article or an advertisement. You might get some of them from posters and billboards, even from graffiti. The important thing is to become more word-conscious—to notice the words around you.

As you study this chapter, begin analyzing the words you have chosen. Break them into parts: prefixes, roots, suffixes. Try to figure out the meaning of each word by using word analysis.

Learning the Skills

■ Word Roots

Many, but not all, words are formed from a **word root,** a word part that often comes from an ancient language like Latin or Greek. This root carries the main meaning of the word. Other word parts, called **affixes,** may be attached to either the beginning or the ending of the root, but it is the root that provides the central meaning of the word. A word may contain more than one root, and many contain more than one affix. This section of the chapter will discuss some important word roots, what they mean, and how to use your understanding of them to analyze unfamiliar words.

THE WORD ROOT *port*

The word root *port,* for example, comes from the Latin word *portare,* which means "to carry." You can probably see immediately that the English word *portable* means "able to be carried." Therefore, a *portable* stereo system is a stereo system that can be easily carried. Many words that you know have the root *port.* The word *transportation,* for example, includes the root *port* and therefore involves "carrying." *Transportation* roughly means "something that carries people or goods." Let's also consider the word *import.* As a noun (a thing), an *import* is something that is carried *into* a country from another place. As a verb (an action), *to import* is to carry (bring) something in from a foreign country.

Notice from these examples that a root—in this case, *port*—can appear at the beginning of a word (*portable*), in the middle of a word (*transportation*), or at the end of a word (*import*). You might also have noticed the affixes, the word parts that are attached to the root *port*. The affix *able* makes *portable* mean "able to be carried." The affix *trans* in *transportation* means "across," and the affix *tion* means "the act of." Therefore, the more accurate meaning of *transportation* is "the act of carrying across."

THE WORD ROOTS *vid, vis,* AND *spec*

Different roots can have nearly the same meaning. The word root *vid* comes from the Latin word *vidēre,* which means "to see." The root *vis* comes from another form of the same Latin word. These words are found in many English words: *video,* for example, which means "image that we see," and *visible,* which means "able to be seen."

The root *spec,* which comes from the Latin word *specere,* also means "to look at," "to see," or "to watch." Thus, we have words like *spectator,* "someone who watches," and *inspect,* "to look at carefully."

Exercise 3-1

On your own or in a small group with other students, identify three more words that have the root *port,* four that have the root *vid* or *vis,* and three that have the root *spec.* Give the meaning of each new word.

Example:

   port   NEW WORD: *porter*

   MEANING: *someone who carries baggage*

1. *port*   NEW WORD: _____

   MEANING: _____

2. *port*   NEW WORD: _____

   MEANING: _____

3. *port*   NEW WORD: _____

   MEANING: _____

4. *vid* or *vis*   NEW WORD: _____

   MEANING: _____

5. *vid* or *vis*   NEW WORD: _____

   MEANING: _____

6. *vid* or *vis*   NEW WORD: _____

   MEANING: _____

7. *vid* or *vis*   NEW WORD: _____

   MEANING: _____

8. *spec*   NEW WORD: _____

   MEANING: _____

9. *spec*   NEW WORD: _____

   MEANING: _____

10. *spec*   NEW WORD: _____

   MEANING: _____

. . . .

IMPORTANT WORD ROOTS

Here is a list of common word roots and their meanings. Each root has an example of a word containing it, along with a definition of the example. Be sure to consider the meaning of the example in connection with the meaning of the root. Try to memorize these roots. They can help you increase your vocabulary enormously.

Root	Meaning	Example
bio	life	**biology:** the science of life
chron, chrono	time	**chronological:** arranged in time order
corp	body	**corpse:** a dead body
cred	to believe	**incredulous:** unbelieving
dic, dict	to say	**diction:** choice of words in speaking and writing
duc, duct	to bring forth	**product:** something brought forth by someone's or something's effort

Root	Meaning	Example
equ	equal	**equivalent:** equal in value or force or meaning
fac, fact	to make, do	**facsimile:** an exact copy (something made the same)
geo	earth	**geography:** the study of the earth and its features
graph	to write	**holograph:** something written in the handwriting of the person whose signature it bears
logue, loq	to talk	**loquacious:** very talkative
mis, mit	to send	**remittance:** money that is sent
mor, mort	death	**immortal:** never dying
path	emotion	**empathy:** the act of identifying with someone else's feelings
phono	sound	**stereophonic:** using two or more channels for producing sound
photo	light	**photosynthesis:** the process whereby green plants break down water and carbon dioxide using light as the energy source
port	to carry	**transport:** to carry from one place to another
pos	to place	**position:** a place or location
scop, scope	to see	**periscope:** an instrument that allows one to see from a position not in the direct line of sight
scrib, scrip	to write	**scribble:** write carelessly
sen, sent	to feel	**sensation:** a feeling in the body
spec, spic	to look, see	**introspective:** examining one's own thoughts and feelings (looking inward)
tang	to touch	**tangent:** a line that touches but does not intersect another line
ten, tain	to hold	**detain:** delay (hold from going forward)
tend, tens, tent	to stretch	**extend:** to stretch out
terr, terre	land, earth	**territory:** an area of land

Root	Meaning	Example
theo	god	**theology:** the study of the nature of god
vid, vis	to see	**vision:** eyesight

Exercise 3-2

Choose ten of the roots listed on pages 54–56. Find another example of a word that uses each root. Then use each new word in a sentence.

Example:

ROOT: *scrib*　　　NEW WORD: *inscribe*

SENTENCE: *The ring was inscribed with the words "From Jim to Kay."*

1. ROOT: _____ NEW WORD: _____

    SENTENCE: _____

2. ROOT: _____ NEW WORD: _____

    SENTENCE: _____

3. ROOT: _____ NEW WORD: _____

    SENTENCE: _____

4. ROOT: _____ NEW WORD: _____

    SENTENCE: _____

5. ROOT: _____ NEW WORD: _____

    SENTENCE: _____

6. ROOT: _____ NEW WORD: _____

    SENTENCE: _____

7. ROOT: _____ NEW WORD: _____

    SENTENCE: _____

8. ROOT: _____ NEW WORD: _____

    SENTENCE: _____

9. ROOT: _____ NEW WORD: _____

SENTENCE: _____

10. ROOT: _____ NEW WORD: _____

SENTENCE: _____

· ·

■ Prefixes

Many, but not all, words have prefixes. A **prefix** is an affix, or word part, that is added to the *beginning* of a word. A word may have more than one prefix. Just as learning the meaning of important roots will increase your word power, learning the meaning of important prefixes can open up new avenues for understanding unfamiliar words.

Consider the prefix *trans*. When we looked at the root *port* in the word *transportation*, you learned that the affix *trans* means "across." You now know that *trans* is a prefix because it is attached to the beginning of the word. Knowing that *trans* means "across" allows you to see that the word *translation*, for example, involves moving something "across" languages. Taking a *transcontinental* flight puts you, at least for a little while, "across" a continent. This section of the chapter will discuss several important prefixes and how to use your knowledge of them to understand unfamiliar words.

PREFIXES INDICATING NUMBER

Many prefixes indicate number. The prefixes *uni* (from Latin) and *mono* (from Greek) both mean "one." Thus, the word *uniform* indicates that something is of one type only, such as a *uniform style* or a *uniform look*. The word *monologue* consists of the prefix *mono* and the Greek root *logue*, which means "to talk." Thus a *monologue* is talking that involves only one person.

Counting from one to ten through prefixes is easy enough. The prefixes *bi* and *di* both mean "two." Thus, we have the words *bicycle* ("a vehicle with two wheels") and *dialogue* ("a conversation between two people"). The prefix *tri* means "three." Thus, a semester divided into three parts is called a *trimester*. The prefix *quadr* means "four." You can see this prefix in words like *quadrilateral*, which means "four-sided figure," and *quadruplets*, "four offspring born in a single birth."

The following list gives prefixes from both Latin and Greek that indicate numbers from one to ten. Be sure to connect the meaning of the example with the meaning of each prefix. Review these number prefixes carefully; try to memorize them.

NUMBER PREFIXES

Root	Meaning	Example
uni, mono	one	**unison:** the state of being together as one **monochrome:** being in a single color
bi, di, du, dy	two	**bipartisan:** supported by members of two parties **dilemma:** difficult choice between two options
tri	three	**tripod:** a three-legged object
quadr, tetr	four	**quadriceps:** the four-part muscle at the front of the thigh **tetrapod:** an animal with four legs
quint, penta	five	**quintuplet:** one of five offspring born in a single birth **pentagon:** a five-sided figure
sex, hexa	six	**sexagenarian:** a person in his or her sixties **hexagonal:** having six sides
sept, hepta	seven	**septennial:** occurring every seven years **heptagon:** a seven-sided figure
oct, octo, octa	eight	**octogenarian:** a person in his or her eighties
non, nov	nine	**nonagenarian:** a person in his or her nineties
deca, deci	ten	**decathlon:** an athletic contest with ten events

Other prefixes also indicate numbers or ideas related to numbers. The prefix *cent,* for example, means "one hundred." Thus, we have the word *centigram,* a unit equivalent to one-hundredth of a gram. The prefix *mill* means "thousand," and we have the word *millennium,* which means "a thousand years."

Other prefixes relate to numbers without specifying a particular number. The prefixes *semi* (Latin) and *hemi* (Greek) both mean "half." You might, for example, get paid *semimonthly,* "at half-month intervals," and perhaps you can guess that a *hemicycle* is a half circle.

The prefixes *multi* (Latin) and *poly* (Greek) both mean "many." Thus, we have words like *multipurpose,* meaning "used for many purposes" and *polygamy,* meaning "marriage at the same time to many spouses." (*Bigamy* means being married to two spouses.)

The following list shows these number and number-related prefixes. It will be worth your effort to learn these.

MORE NUMBER PREFIXES

Root	Meaning	Example
cent	hundred	**centennial:** related to a period of a hundred years
mill	thousand	**millisecond:** one-thousandth of a second
semi, hemi	half	**semiannual:** happening every half year **hemisphere:** half of a sphere
multi, poly	many	**multilingual:** expressed in many languages **polytechnic:** related to instruction in many arts and sciences

Exercise 3-3

On your own or in a small group with other students, choose ten number prefixes from the two charts in this section. Think of an additional example that uses each prefix. Then write a sentence using that prefix.

Example:

PREFIX: *cent*   NEW EXAMPLE: *centipede*

SENTENCE: *If I have two left feet now, how would I function as a*

centipede?

1. PREFIX: _____ NEW EXAMPLE: _____

SENTENCE: _____

2. PREFIX: _____ NEW EXAMPLE: _____

   SENTENCE: _____

   _____

3. PREFIX: _____ NEW EXAMPLE: _____

   SENTENCE: _____

   _____

4. PREFIX: _____ NEW EXAMPLE: _____

   SENTENCE: _____

   _____

5. PREFIX: _____ NEW EXAMPLE: _____

   SENTENCE: _____

   _____

6. PREFIX: _____ NEW EXAMPLE: _____

   SENTENCE: _____

   _____

7. PREFIX: _____ NEW EXAMPLE: _____

   SENTENCE: _____

   _____

8. PREFIX: _____ NEW EXAMPLE: _____

   SENTENCE: _____

   _____

9. PREFIX: _____ NEW EXAMPLE: _____

   SENTENCE: _____

   _____

10. PREFIX: _____ NEW EXAMPLE: _____

   SENTENCE: _____

   _____

PREFIXES WITH NEGATIVE MEANINGS

A prefix can change the meaning of a word. The prefix *in*, for example, can mean "not" or "without." Thus, when *in* is added to the beginning of a word, it may change the meaning of the word from positive to negative. Take the words *visible* ("able to be seen"), *exact* ("precise"), and *gratitude* ("thankfulness"). When *in* is added to the beginning of these words, the meanings become just the opposite. *Invisible* means "not able to be seen," *inexact* means "not precise," and *ingratitude* means "without thankfulness."

The spelling of the prefix *in* can change depending on the spelling of the word to which it is added. In front of the letter *l*, the prefix *in* becomes *il*, as in *illegal* ("not legal") or *illogical* ("not logical"). In front of the letters *b, m,* and *p*, the prefix *in* becomes *im*, as in *imbalance* ("not in a balanced state"), *immovable* ("not able to be moved"), and *imperfect* ("not perfect"). In front of the letter *r*, the prefix *in* becomes *ir*, as in *irregular* ("not regular") or *irreversible* ("not able to be reversed").

Other prefixes also mean "not" and "without." Still other prefixes have slightly different negative meanings, like "badly," "wrongly," or "against" (in the sense of "opposed to"). The following list gives common prefixes with negative meanings. Connect the meaning of the prefix with the meaning of the example word. Try to memorize the prefixes.

PREFIXES WITH NEGATIVE MEANINGS

Root	Meaning	Example
a	not; without	**amoral:** without regard for right or wrong
anti	against	**antipoverty:** against poverty
contra	against	**contradict:** to express the opposite
dis	not	**disobedient:** not obedient
in (il, im, ir)	not	**incomprehensible:** not able to be understood **illegible:** not able to be read **immeasurable:** not able to be measured **irresponsible:** not responsible
mal	badly	**malfunction:** to function badly
mis	wrongly	**misinform:** to inform wrongly
non	not	**nonrecoverable:** not able to be recovered
un	not	**unfortunate:** not lucky

Exercise 3-4

Change each of the following words into its opposite by adding the prefix *il, im, in, ir, un,* or *non.* Check your answers in the dictionary if you are unsure. Then write a sentence using the negative form of the word.

Example:

    smoker   NEGATIVE FORM: *nonsmoker* _____

    SENTENCE: *Most nonsmokers do not understand how hard it is to stop*

    smoking. _____

1. *equal*   NEGATIVE FORM: _____

    SENTENCE: _____

    _____

2. *credible*   NEGATIVE FORM: _____

    SENTENCE: _____

    _____

3. *legible*   NEGATIVE FORM: _____

    SENTENCE: _____

    _____

4. *lucky*   NEGATIVE FORM: _____

    SENTENCE: _____

    _____

5. *familiar*   NEGATIVE FORM: _____

    SENTENCE: _____

    _____

6. *mobile*   NEGATIVE FORM: _____

    SENTENCE: _____

    _____

7. *sense*   NEGATIVE FORM: _____

    SENTENCE: _____

    _____

8. *decisive*   NEGATIVE FORM: _____

SENTENCE: _____

_____

9. *replaceable*   NEGATIVE FORM: _____

SENTENCE: _____

_____

10. *negotiable*   NEGATIVE FORM: _____

SENTENCE: _____

_____

. . . .

PREFIXES INDICATING
TIME, SPACE, AND POSITION

Many prefixes indicate time in the sense of "before" or "after." The prefix *pre,* for example, means "before" or "beforehand." You will find the prefix *pre* in many words: *pregame* means "before the game"; *precooked* means "cooked beforehand"; *predict* means "to say beforehand." Some bookstores even advertise *preread books,* supposedly a more positive way of saying "used books."

The prefix *post,* which means "after," is also very common, as in *postgame* ("after the game"), *postwar* ("after the war"), and *postscript* ("after the writing"), which we abbreviate P.S. at the end of a letter. Other prefixes indicating time are shown in the list on page 64.

The prefix *in,* which you already know can mean "not," can also mean "into" or "within." Thus, we have words like *inbound* (often meaning "into a city"), *incision* ("a cut into something"), and *infield* (in baseball "the area enclosed by home plate and the three bases").

Study the following lists of prefixes indicating time and those indicating space and position. Note that the spelling of *co,* meaning "with," changes depending on the spelling of the word to which it is added. In front of the letter *l,* the prefix *co* becomes *col,* as in *collaborate* ("to work together with"). In front of the letter *m,* the prefix *co* becomes *com,* as in *commiserate* ("to sympathize"). In front of the letter *n,* the prefix *co* becomes *con,* as in *connect* ("to join with").

Be sure to connect the meaning of each prefix in the list with the meaning of the example given. The more of these prefixes you can memorize, the more words you will be able to understand.

PREFIXES INDICATING TIME

Root	Meaning	Example
ante	before	**antecedent:** something that comes before
fore	before	**foretell:** to predict (tell beforehand)
pre	before	**pretrial:** a proceeding held before a trial
post	after	**postoperative:** happening after surgery
re	again	**rebuild:** to build again

PREFIXES INDICATING SPACE AND POSITION

Root	Meaning	Example
ab	away from	**abduct:** to kidnap (lead away from)
ad	to, for	**adhere:** to stick to
circum	around	**circumnavigate:** to go completely around
co (col, com, con)	with	**coexist:** to exist together with
de	away from	**deport:** to expel (carry away from)
e, ex	outside, out of, away from	**eject:** to throw out forcefully
in	into, within	**instill:** to introduce (put into) by gradual efforts
inter	between, among	**interact:** to act with (between) another
intra	within	**intramural:** carried on within a group
mid	middle	**midmorning:** the middle of the morning
pro	earlier, before, standing for	**pronoun:** a word that stands for a noun
retro	back	**retrograde:** moving backward
sub	under	**submarine:** a ship that operates underwater
super	above, over, superior	**superscript:** a letter set above (for example, the 2 in x^2)
trans	across	**transition:** the passage (across) from one form to another

Exercise 3-5

. . . .

Identify the prefix in the following words and write it on the line provided. Then write the meaning of the prefix on the line provided, followed by the definition of the whole word.

Example:

  circumscribe   PREFIX: *circum*＿＿＿＿＿   MEANING: *around*＿＿＿＿＿

  WORD DEFINITION: *to make a circle*＿＿＿＿＿＿＿＿＿＿＿＿＿＿＿＿＿＿＿＿＿

1. *retroactive*   PREFIX: ＿＿＿＿＿＿＿＿＿   MEANING: ＿＿＿＿＿＿＿＿＿

   WORD DEFINITION: ＿＿＿＿＿＿＿＿＿＿＿＿＿＿＿＿＿＿＿＿＿＿＿＿＿＿＿＿

2. *intravenous*   PREFIX: ＿＿＿＿＿＿＿＿＿   MEANING: ＿＿＿＿＿＿＿＿＿

   WORD DEFINITION: ＿＿＿＿＿＿＿＿＿＿＿＿＿＿＿＿＿＿＿＿＿＿＿＿＿＿＿＿

3. *subterranean*   PREFIX: ＿＿＿＿＿＿＿＿＿   MEANING: ＿＿＿＿＿＿＿＿＿

   WORD DEFINITION: ＿＿＿＿＿＿＿＿＿＿＿＿＿＿＿＿＿＿＿＿＿＿＿＿＿＿＿＿

4. *forefathers*   PREFIX: ＿＿＿＿＿＿＿＿＿   MEANING: ＿＿＿＿＿＿＿＿＿

   WORD DEFINITION: ＿＿＿＿＿＿＿＿＿＿＿＿＿＿＿＿＿＿＿＿＿＿＿＿＿＿＿＿

5. *interposed*   PREFIX: ＿＿＿＿＿＿＿＿＿   MEANING: ＿＿＿＿＿＿＿＿＿

   WORD DEFINITION: ＿＿＿＿＿＿＿＿＿＿＿＿＿＿＿＿＿＿＿＿＿＿＿＿＿＿＿＿

6. *prescribe*   PREFIX: ＿＿＿＿＿＿＿＿＿   MEANING: ＿＿＿＿＿＿＿＿＿

   WORD DEFINITION: ＿＿＿＿＿＿＿＿＿＿＿＿＿＿＿＿＿＿＿＿＿＿＿＿＿＿＿＿

7. *inspect*   PREFIX: ＿＿＿＿＿＿＿＿＿   MEANING: ＿＿＿＿＿＿＿＿＿

   WORD DEFINITION: ＿＿＿＿＿＿＿＿＿＿＿＿＿＿＿＿＿＿＿＿＿＿＿＿＿＿＿＿

8. *postcolonial*   PREFIX: ＿＿＿＿＿＿＿＿＿   MEANING: ＿＿＿＿＿＿＿＿＿

   WORD DEFINITION: ＿＿＿＿＿＿＿＿＿＿＿＿＿＿＿＿＿＿＿＿＿＿＿＿＿＿＿＿

9. *transmittal*   PREFIX: ＿＿＿＿＿＿＿＿＿   MEANING: ＿＿＿＿＿＿＿＿＿

   WORD DEFINITION: ＿＿＿＿＿＿＿＿＿＿＿＿＿＿＿＿＿＿＿＿＿＿＿＿＿＿＿＿

10. *supervise*   PREFIX: _____   MEANING: _____

WORD DEFINITION: _____

. . . .

■ Suffixes

Many, but not all, words have suffixes. A **suffix** is an affix, or word part, that is added to the *end* of a word. Examples of suffixes are *ful,* as in *hopeful; ess,* as in *happiness;* and *ion,* as in *demonstration.* A word may have more than one suffix, like the word *beautifully,* which has the suffix *ful* as well as the suffix *ly.*

Suffixes can help you recognize the part of speech of a word. Take the suffix *ful,* for example. It means "full of" and is found in words like *hopeful* ("full of hope"), *joyful* ("full of joy"), and *beautiful* ("full of beauty"). The suffix *ful* usually indicates that the word is an adjective — that is, a word describing a noun or a pronoun. Examples are a *hopeful student* and *We* are *joyful.*

Many suffixes indicate the existence of a condition or a quality. The suffix *hood,* for example, usually indicates that a particular condition or quality exists — for example, *motherhood* ("the condition of being a mother") or *falsehood* ("the quality of being false"). Words with the suffix *hood* are almost always nouns.

The suffix *ness* also indicates a quality or state or condition: *happiness, brightness, weakness* — that is, "the state of being happy," "the state of being bright," "the state of being weak." The suffix *ion* (sometimes spelled *tion*) can also indicate a quality or state or condition — for example, *frustration* ("the state of being frustrated"). The suffix *ion* can also mean an action or process, like *completion* ("the act of completing") or *expression* ("the act of expressing").

Suffixes like *er, or,* and *ist* often indicate a person — for example, *teacher* ("a person who teaches"), *adviser* ("one who advises"), *instructor* ("one who instructs"), or *physicist* ("one who is an expert in physics").

The following are three lists of important suffixes.

SUFFIXES INDICATING AN ACTION, PROCESS, STATE, CONDITION, OR QUALITY

Suffix	Example
ance, ence	admittance, preference
hood	childhood
ice	justice
ion, tion, ation	percussion, combination, approximation
ism	heroism
ity, ty	inferiority, royalty
ment	containment
ness	rudeness
ship	kinship

SUFFIXES INDICATING A PERSON

Suffix	Example
ee	referee
eer	engineer
er, or	employer, editor
ist	journalist

SUFFIXES INDICATING ADJECTIVES

Suffix	Example
able, ible	enjoyable
al	seasonal
ent	independent
ful	wonderful
ic	toxic
ish	childish
ive	aggressive
less	clueless
ly	lovely
ous	humorous
y	dizzy

Exercise 3-6

....

Add at least one appropriate suffix to each of the following words.

Example:

consume   SUFFIX ADDED: *consumer* _____

1. *friend*   SUFFIX ADDED: _____

2. *meaning*   SUFFIX ADDED: _____

3. *corrupt*   SUFFIX ADDED: _____

4. *adapt*   SUFFIX ADDED: _____

5. *sleep*   SUFFIX ADDED: _____

6. *appoint*   SUFFIX ADDED: _____

7. *hero*   SUFFIX ADDED: _____

8. *art*   SUFFIX ADDED: _____

9. *suggest*   SUFFIX ADDED: _____

10. *invent*   SUFFIX ADDED: _____

....

Applying the Skills

Reading the Parts

This essay, originally published in *Newsweek* magazine in October 1997, was written by *Newsweek* reporters Steve Rhodes and Kendall Hamilton. As you read, be particularly aware of words with prefixes and suffixes—even if you already know the words. After reading each section and answering the questions that follow, move on to the next section. You will have a chance to read the whole essay when you finish.

STEVE RHODES AND KENDALL HAMILTON

Will Athletic Records Ever Stop Tumbling?

In 1919, after baseball deity Babe Ruth set a single-season record by slamming his 29th home run, his manager, Edward Barrow, declared the mark "far and away out of reach of any other player the game is likely to develop." By the mid-1920s, top big-league batters were routinely besting that total. The record Ruth set in 1927, when he belted 60 homers, did stand up for 34 years—but then Roger Maris hit 61 in '61. This season [1997], two players, Seattle's Ken Griffey Jr. and Mark McGwire of St. Louis, have made a run at Maris's milestone. Neither may succeed this year, but rest assured that someday someone will.

The Guinness Book of World Records doesn't put out a new edition every year for nothing. "The notion that records are invulnerable is foolish," says Bill James, a Kansas author widely considered the father of statistical baseball analysis. Still, some feats are more easily bettered than others. Watching Michael Jordan dominate a basketball game, it's tough to imagine what a better player might look like. To see sprinter Donovan Bailey cover 100 meters in 9.84 seconds, as he did at last year's Olympic Games in Atlanta, is to wonder just how much faster a human being could possibly run. As we head into the 21st century, it may seem that we're reaching the outer limits of human athletic potential. Can sports records really continue to fall indefinitely?

1. Considering that *vulnerable* means "unprotected," what does *invulnerable* mean in paragraph 2?

    a. impossible to attack

    b. impossible to lower

    c. never to be recorded

    d. susceptible to attack

2. Which of the following words from paragraphs 1 and 2 does *not* have a suffix?

    a. foolish   c. invulnerable

    b. statistical   d. season

3. In paragraph 2 of the selection, Rhodes and Hamilton write, "Can sports records really continue to fall *indefinitely*?" Using what you know about prefixes with negative meanings, what do you think *indefinite* means?

    a. having distinct limits

    b. without limits

    c. defined

    d. determined

4. Which of the following words from the first two paragraphs of the selection has a suffix indicating a person?

    a. athletic   c. sprinter

    b. foolish   d. potential

5. In paragraph 2, Bill James is described as "the father of statistical baseball analysis." What do you think *statistical* means?

    a. concerning the collection of numbers and data

    b. algebra

    c. geometric tables

    d. pioneering ideas

> Records based on longevity certainly can. For example, baseball great Lou Gehrig's streak, playing in 2,130 consecutive games, "was one record we assumed would never be broken," says Lyle Spatz, records-committee chair of the Statistical Association of

Baseball Research. Pampered modern-day players were thought to lack the grit of earlier competitors—until Baltimore's Cal Ripken played his 2,131st straight game two years ago. He's since added more than 300 games to the streak. "Whenever Cal gets that one done, it'll be a herculean task to break it," says Steve Stone, a former big-league pitcher who now broadcasts for the Chicago Cubs.

Records in team sports also tend to be subject to adjustments in the game. Football running back Eric Dickerson broke O.J. Simpson's season rushing record in 1984, but he had the benefit of two extra games in which to do it. Maris had eight more games in which to hit his 61 homers than Ruth did to hit his 60. Rules changes favorable to batters—notably the smaller strike zone—have placed just about every hitting record in jeopardy. Perhaps the only baseball landmark considered unassailable is pitcher Cy Young's 511 career victories. Pitchers today simply don't play enough games over the course of a career.

4

In track-and-field events, the playing field remains more constant. A marathon will always be 26.2 miles long and humans will never have more than two feet. Harder tracks, better shoes, and more efficient training have led to great gains in athletic performance over the past century. But the margins by which records are broken is decreasing. Scientists generally agree that there's a ceiling to human athletic performance, but just where it lies is unknown. "We're out in the ozone when we're dealing with sports performance," says Dr. David Martin, chairman of sports science for USA Track & Field. "The athletes are in uncharted territory." For instance, the current marathon record—2:06:50, set by Belayneh Densimo in 1988—isn't likely to be beaten by much, but it is likely to be beaten. "I've long since learned that you just don't tell these people they can't do something," says Martin. In other words, where there's a will, there's a way.

5

6. As used in paragraph 3 of Rhodes and Hamilton's selection, what do you think the word *longevity* means?

   a.   state of short life

   (b.) state of long life

   c.   sudden death

   d.   records that are tied

7. "For example, baseball great Lou Gehrig's streak, playing in 2,130 *consecutive* games, 'was one record we assumed would never be broken.'" Considering what you know about word roots and suffixes indicating adjectives, what do you think the word *consecutive* means?

   a. out of sequence

   b. on every other Monday

   c. continuous

   d. deliberate

8. If *assail* means "to attack," what do you think *unassailable*, as used in paragraph 4, means in the sentence "Perhaps the only baseball landmark considered *unassailable* is pitcher Cy Young's 511 career victories"?

   a. able to be beaten

   b. not able to be beaten

   c. subject to change

   d. broken

9. How would you change the suffix of the word *competitors*, as used in paragraph 3, to an adjective?

   a. add *ively* to make the word *competitively*

   b. add *ion* to make the word *competition*

   c. add *ent* to make the word *competent*

   d. add *ive* to make the word *competitive*

10. Using what you know about prefixes with negative meanings, and knowing that the word *chart* means "map or outline," what do you think *uncharted* means in paragraph 5: "'The athletes are in *uncharted* territory'"?

    a. definite   c. unknown

    b. known   d. drawn

Reading the Whole

Now that you have read "Will Athletic Records Ever Stop Tumbling?" in its parts and paid close attention to the prefixes, suffixes, and root words, you will better be able to put the parts together. As you reread the whole essay, notice how your understanding of vocabulary helps you to appreciate the larger points that Rhodes and Hamilton are making.

STEVE RHODES AND KENDALL HAMILTON

Will Athletic Records Ever Stop Tumbling?

In 1919, after baseball deity Babe Ruth set a single-season record by slamming his 29th home run, his manager, Edward Barrow, declared the mark "far and away out of reach of any other player the game is likely to develop." By the mid-1920s, top big-league batters were routinely besting that total. The record Ruth set in 1927, when he belted 60 homers, did stand up for 34 years—but then Roger Maris hit 61 in '61. This season [1997], two players, Seattle's Ken Griffey Jr. and Mark McGwire of St. Louis, have made a run at Maris's milestone. Neither may succeed this year, but rest assured that someday someone will.

The Guinness Book of World Records doesn't put out a new edition every year for nothing. "The notion that records are invulnerable is foolish," says Bill James, a Kansas author widely considered the father of statistical baseball analysis. Still, some feats are more easily bettered than others. Watching Michael Jordan dominate a basketball game, it's tough to imagine what a better player might look like. To see sprinter Donovan Bailey cover 100 meters in 9.84 seconds, as he did at last year's Olympic Games in Atlanta, is to wonder just how much faster a human being could possibly run. As we head into the 21st century, it may seem that we're reaching the outer limits of human athletic potential. Can sports records really continue to fall indefinitely?

Records based on longevity certainly can. For example, baseball great Lou Gehrig's streak, playing in 2,130 consecutive games, "was one record we assumed would never be broken," says Lyle Spatz, records-committee chair of the Statistical Association of Baseball Research. Pampered modern-day players were thought to lack the grit of earlier competitors—until Baltimore's Cal Ripken played his 2,131st straight game two years ago. He's since added more than 300 games to the streak. "Whenever Cal gets that one done, it'll be a herculean task to break it," says Steve Stone, a former big-league pitcher who now broadcasts for the Chicago Cubs.

Records in team sports also tend to be subject to adjustments in the game. Football running back Eric Dickerson broke O.J. Simpson's season rushing record in 1984, but he had the benefit of two extra games in which to do it. Maris had eight more games in which to hit his 61 homers than Ruth did to hit his 60. Rules changes favorable to batters—notably the smaller strike zone—have placed just about every hitting record in jeopardy. Perhaps the only baseball landmark considered unassailable is pitcher Cy Young's 511 career victories. Pitchers today simply don't play enough games over the course of a career.

4

In track-and-field events, the playing field remains more constant. A marathon will always be 26.2 miles long and humans will never have more than two feet. Harder tracks, better shoes, and more efficient training have led to great gains in athletic performance over the past century. But the margins by which records are broken is decreasing. Scientists generally agree that there's a ceiling to human athletic performance, but just where it lies is unknown. "We're out in the ozone when we're dealing with sports performance," says Dr. David Martin, chairman of sports science for USA Track & Field. "The athletes are in uncharted territory." For instance, the current marathon record—2:06:50, set by Belayneh Densimo in 1988—isn't likely to be beaten by much, but it is likely to be beaten. "I've long since learned that you just don't tell these people they can't do something," says Martin. In other words, where there's a will, there's a way.

5

Integrated Skills

1. What is the authors' point—that is, what do they want their readers to think about?

2. Why do you think the authors use examples from baseball, football, and track—as opposed to other sports?

3. Why do think no women's sports records are mentioned?

4. What does the last sentence of the article mean: "Where there's a will, there's a way"? What opinion about sports performance is conveyed by it?

5. What sports records have been broken in the past few years?

6. What sports records do you think might be broken soon? Which ones do you think might never be broken? Why?

Reading Textbooks

Thematic Connections. You've read Steve Rhodes and Kendall Hamilton's essay about sports records made and broken by professional athletes. In the essay, the authors discuss the importance of records to professional sports and the various changes that professional sports have undergone throughout the years. The reading that follows is taken from the textbook *Sociology* by Ian Robertson. In it, the author discusses the overall place that sports hold in society in general, both professionally and recreationally. As you read, think about how the textbook reading helps to place the earlier reading by Rhodes and Hamilton in a larger context. Pay attention as well to unfamiliar words and how you can understand them by understanding their roots, prefixes, and suffixes.

Vocabulary Preview

vigorous (para. 2): strong (adj.)
emulation (para. 2): imitation (n.)
participants (para. 2): those taking part (n.)
parallel (para. 3): match or are similar to (v.)
predominantly (para. 3): mostly (adv.)

spurred (para. 3): stimulated (v.)
facilitated (para. 3): made easier (v.)
proliferated (para. 3): increased; multiplied (v.)
revenues (para. 4): monies (n.)

Sport in American Society

In American society, sport is an important institution directly affecting the lives of the majority of the population who are either participants in, or spectators of, various sports. Three out of four Americans report that they discuss sports frequently, and an event like the Superbowl may attract well over 100 million viewers. The sports section of newspapers is by far the most popular part of the paper; in fact, it is the only section that millions of Americans ever read. Clearly, sport is not a trivial aspect of American life. Indeed, in recent years it has been the subject of extensive sociological study. 1

Like any other institution, sport serves various functions for the social system as a whole. Among the functions that have been identified are the following: 2

1. *Leisure activities.* Sport provides organized leisure activities for the population—a useful function in a society where people have a good deal of free time.

2. *Physical exercise.* Sport encourages people to engage in vigorous physical activity, which is important in a society where people get little exercise.

3. *Role models.* Sport provides, through famous athletes, role models whose skills and determination are held up for public emulation.

4. *Outlet for energies.* Sport may act as a "safety valve" for spectators and participants, allowing them to express aggressive or competitive energies in a generally harmless way.

5. *Reinforcement of values.* Sport serves to reinforce many of the basic values of society, such as teamwork, competition, discipline, and obedience to rules.

Changes in sport, like those in any other institution, parallel changes in the wider society. Until about a hundred years ago, Americans' favorite sports were such activities as foot racing, boat racing, cockfighting, hunting, and fishing; the large-scale spectator sports of football, baseball, hockey, and basketball were virtually unknown, and became popular only as the nation was transformed from a predominantly rural, agricultural society into an urban, industrial one. The development of these mass sports were spurred by several social factors: economic development, which led to a shorter work week and more leisure time; the growth of cities, which provided the concentrated populations necessary to support huge stadiums; the spread of radio and television, which brought spectator sport into homes across the nation; and innovations in land and air transport, which facilitated competition among regions and even among nations. Other changes in sport have likewise reflected trends in the wider society. As workers in general have become more and more specialized, a new role has emerged, that of the full-time professional athlete who specializes not only in a single sport but also in a single status, such as pitcher or quarterback. Similarly, as large organizations have proliferated in society, control of sport has passed from small, primary groups of players to large, secondary groups like unions, associations, and even corporations.

The American economic institution emphasizes free enterprise and the pursuit of profit, and its capitalist spirit inevitably affects sport. The teams of the major professional sports are corporate organizations, similar in most respects to other businesses; they even buy, sell, and trade players, as though athletes were economic commodities. Sport, in fact, is a big business that generates huge revenues, running into billions of dollars each year. But who benefits from the immense wealth generated by the industry? Conflict theorists argue that here, as elsewhere in the society, the wealth is unequally shared, with most of it going to high-status people such as sports "stars" and the owners of the various businesses that directly or indirectly profit from sport. Few people who participate in sport get rich, a fact that is perhaps obscured by the enormous earnings of the tiny minority of athletes who do. The full-time players in the four major team sports are, in fact, well paid, but their total number is less than 2,500; and only a handful of athletes in other sports are able to make a good living from the profession. Nevertheless, millions of Little Leaguers and other juvenile athletes are encouraged to aspire to become professionals in their sport, a status more than 99 percent of them will fail to achieve. The idea that sport is an avenue to social and economic success is part of the general "rags to riches" dream that pervades American life. It is widely believed in America that if you work hard, you will grow rich—even though, in fact, most people do not get especially rich, no matter how hard they work (about 95 percent of American taxpayers earn less than $50,000 a year).

Thinking about the Textbook Selection

1. Identify the five basic functions of sport in society, as described in the selection. Which ones do you think are the most important? Why?

2. Of the sports the author mentions, which are team sports and which are sports for individuals rather than teams? What are some of the differences in those two different kinds of sports? Which type of sports do you prefer? Why?

3. Do you agree with the author's explanations for the value of the five functions? Do you think, for example, that professional sports provide—or should provide—"role models" for people, especially for children? Why or why not?

4. What do you think of what the author says about sports and riches? Do you think sports are a good avenue to wealth?

Reviewing

1. Explain how to do word analysis. Identify the three parts of words that can help you analyze their meanings.
2. Provide three examples of word analysis. Explain why each word means what it does.
3. Explain how the learning strategies of observing, connecting, and inferring can be used to determine the meanings of words.

**Chapter
Summary**

In this chapter you have been introduced to some strategies for developing a college-level vocabulary. One strategy is to use word analysis of prefixes, suffixes, and roots to understand the meanings of words by breaking them down into parts. Another strategy is to build your vocabulary by linking words in groups or families of related words.

You have gained additional practice in using the basic technique of learning that this book applies—observing, connecting, and inferring—to comprehend what you read. Finally, you have had the opportunity to apply your word acquisition skills to a variety of reading selections.

Chapter 4

Getting Ready	81
Learning the Skills	82

Applying the Skills
• Reading the Parts	97
• Reading the Whole	104
• Reading Textbooks	107

| Reviewing | 110 |

Recognizing Topics and Main Ideas in Paragraphs

Getting Ready

An author's topic is what he or she is writing about. An author's **main idea** is his or her key point. In a paragraph, the main idea is usually expressed in a single sentence called the **topic sentence**. This chapter explains how to identify the topic, or subject, of a paragraph and how to identify the topic sentence, which states what the writer wants to say about the topic. We will look at many different paragraphs, some from textbooks and others from magazines and general-reading books. The aim will always be to understand what point the author wants to make.

Chapter Overview

What is the difference between a paragraph's topic and its main idea?

What is the difference between a paragraph's topic and the topic sentence?

What strategies do you use to find the main idea in a paragraph?

How do you know when you have found the writer's main idea?

Focusing Questions

Everyday Reading

As you study this chapter, look for main ideas in writing you encounter outside of your textbooks. Look, for example, for the main idea of newspaper articles and editorials, advertisements, and posters. You can also look for main ideas in letters, notes, and e-mail you receive from family or friends.

Learning the Skills

■ Finding Topics of Paragraphs

The **topic** of a paragraph is its subject—what the paragraph is about. The topic is the broad, general subject under discussion. The topic is often referred to over and over. The same word may be repeated, words that have the same or a similar meaning may be substituted, or pronouns may be substituted. It is usually clear, however, what the topic of a paragraph is—what broad subject is being discussed. Look, for example, at the following paragraph, taken from the textbook *Economics* by Timothy Tregarthen and Libby Rittenberg.

> **Economics** is the study of how people choose among the alternatives available to them. It's the study of little choices ("Should I take the chocolate or the strawberry?") and big choices ("Should we require a reduction in energy consumption in order to protect the environment?"). It's the study of individual choices, choices by firms, and choices by governments. Life presents each of us with a wide range of alternative uses of our time and other resources; economists examine how we choose among those alternatives.

The topic of this paragraph is *economics*. We know that because the first sentence introduces and defines the term. (Boldface type is often a clue to a topic about to be discussed.) The second sentence begins with *It's*. What does the *It* refer to? Economics. The third sentence also starts with *It's*. Again the *It* refers to economics. In the fourth sentence, *economists* are mentioned, another reference to economics. In a four-sentence paragraph, therefore, the subject of economics has been referred to four times. *Economics* is the topic—the broad subject—of the paragraph.

Sometimes, as in the preceding example paragraph, the topic of a paragraph can be stated in one word. At other times, a phrase (a group of words) is needed to state the topic. Consider the following paragraph, adapted from the book *Source Imagery* by Sandra G. Shuman.

The opening up of a person's creativity has a healthy impact on his or her life in a number of unexpected ways. Sometimes as a result of discovering creative abilities, a person identifies a new career path or establishes more satisfying personal relationships. Often it can foster a new level of self-awareness and confidence, helping a person become more effective in his or her current career. If someone is already an artist, it can provide him or her with new inspiration and material to work with.

At first glance the topic of this paragraph may seem to be *creativity*. But that is too broad a topic. The paragraph is really about *opening up creativity*, not just *creativity* itself. The idea of opening up creativity is referred to over and over again. For example, the phrase *discovering creative abilities* in the second sentence restates the idea of opening up creativity. The word *it* in the third sentence refers to opening up creativity, not just to creativity itself. Similarly, the word *it* in the fourth sentence refers back to the same concept.

When you look for the topic of a paragraph, try to find the very core of what is under discussion. For example, while *creativity* is too broad a topic for this example paragraph, identifying the topic as *creativity and new career paths* is too narrow. *New career paths* is a specific example of how opening up creativity can improve someone's life. *Career paths* is not a repeated idea in the paragraph. Only the topic *opening up creativity* covers all the material in the paragraph.

Exercise 4-1

Identify the topic of each paragraph by checking the appropriate letter below it.

Example:

Contrary to popular myth, entrepreneurs do not enjoy taking risks. Granted, a certain amount of risk is unavoidable in business, but the thrill of the start-up doesn't come from defying the odds. It comes from creating a viable company, and you improve your chances of doing that if you keep the level of risk as low as possible. (Norm Brodsky, "The Road Not Taken," *Inc.*, March 2000)

a. __✓__ risks   c. _____ business

b. _____ entrepreneurs   d. _____ myths

1. A democracy is a form of government in which citizens have a right to control their own destiny. Democracy works on the principle of popular consent. The term itself comes from the Greek words *demos,* meaning "people," and *kratos,* meaning "authority." The people have authority; they have the right to make or influence decisions that affect their everyday lives. (Stephen J. Wayne, G. Calvin Mackenzie, David M. O'Brien, and Richard L. Cole, *The Politics of American Government*)

a. _____ the Greeks   c. _____ types of government

b. _____ democracy   d. _____ Greek word roots

2. A ripe guava is yellow, although some varieties have a pink tinge. The skin is thick, firm, and sweet. Its heart is bright pink and almost solid with seeds. The most delicious part of the guava surrounds the tiny seeds. If you don't know how to eat a guava, the seeds end up in the crevices between your teeth. (Esmeralda Santiago, *When I Was Puerto Rican*)

a. _____ how to eat a guava

b. _____ guavas

c. _____ delicious fruits

d. _____ guava seeds

3. Wild salmon waken, at birth, to the pebbles and clear flow of a high mountain stream. The tiny fish bond not to a parent fish, but to the stones and flow of their birth stream. For a full year or longer, these young fish cling to the parent stream, taking in its unique chemistry, memorizing all they can about it. Then at the unpromising size of five inches, they obey their blood and the parent stream's downward urging and set out on a journey that makes *The Odyssey* look tame. (David James Duncan, "Salmon's Second Coming," *Sierra,* March/April 2000)

a. _____ birth streams   c. _____ wild salmon

b. _____ baby fish   d. _____ impossible journeys

4. Today the word "politics" is often used ⟨disparagingly⟩ Political candidates who accuse their opponents of "playing politics" mean to imply that the other candidate has been somehow unethical, or at least underhanded. In the 1992 presidential campaign, independent candidate H. Ross Perot appealed to many Americans precisely because of his contempt for "traditional politics." Bill Clinton's equivocation in answering questions about his past and his changing positions on some key issues made him vulnerable to the charge that he was a "typical" politician. (Stephen J. Wayne et al., *The Politics of American Government*)

    a. _____ politicians   c. _____ "traditional politics"

    b. _____ "playing politics"   d. _____ the word *politics*

5. When there are no relatives living within easy visiting distance (less than an hour away), we speak of an isolated nuclear family. This family form usually results from a geographic move to another part of the country in response to a job offer. Less frequently it results from an intermarriage or the need to escape extended-family conflicts. The isolated nuclear family is completely independent, economically and emotionally, from the extended family. Family members borrow from banks rather than from relatives. If they are in trouble, they seek advice from outsiders — friends, professionals, or other experts. Relatives exert no influence on nuclear family decisions. The isolated nuclear family visits with relatives infrequently, usually during holidays and ceremonial occasions (weddings and funerals). (Betty Yorburg, *Family Relationships*)

    a. _____ isolated nuclear families

    b. _____ having no one to turn to

    c. _____ family members

    d. _____ missing one's relatives

Exercise 4-2

. . . .

Write the topic of the paragraph on the line below each of the following paragraphs.

Example:

The first time I heard Zora Neale Hurston's name, I was auditing a black-literature class taught by the great poet Margaret Walker, at Jackson State

College in Jackson, Mississippi. The reason this fact slipped my mind was that Zora's name and accomplishments came and went so fast. The class was studying the usual "giants" of black literature: Chesnutt, Toomer, Hughes, Wright, Ellison, and Baldwin, with the hope of reaching LeRoi Jones very soon. Women writers like Zora Neale Hurston were names appended, like verbal footnotes, to the illustrious all-male list that paralleled them. (Alice Walker, *In Search of Our Mothers' Gardens*)

TOPIC: *Zora Neale Hurston*

1. The social environment is all the people who affect the performance of a business or are affected by it. It includes a business's customers as well as its employees, the communities and countries in which it operates, and all the beliefs, customs, and laws of those people and their societies. (Kenneth Blanchard, Charles Schewe, Robert Nelson, and Alexander Hiam, *Exploring the World of Business*)

TOPIC: the social environment

2. Water spews from the Earth as geysers. It circles the globe as clouds and falls from the sky as the gentle rain or in thundering torrents. Frozen, it covers parts of Antarctica to a depth of 3,000 meters (10,000 feet) or more. Vast oceans of it submerge much of the planet. Water is one of the key ingredients that makes life on Earth possible. It makes up as much as 95 percent of the weight of some living things. (William K. Purves, Gordon H. Orians, H. Craig Heller, and David Sadava, *Life: The Science of Biology*)

TOPIC: Water

3. Why is autobiography the most popular form of fiction for modern readers? Why are so many people moved to write their life stories today? And what is it about the genre that makes it appeal to readers not just in the Western world, but also in non-Western cultures, like those of Japan and India or the many cultures of Africa? (Jill Ker Conway, *When Memory Speaks*)

TOPIC: autobiography

4. It was a long time before we began to understand the content of our crab Buster's character. He required more patient observation than we were in the habit of giving to a small, cold-blooded life. As months went by, we would periodically notice with great disappointment that Buster seemed to be dead. Or not entirely dead but ill, or maybe suffering the crab equivalent of blues. He would burrow into a gravelly corner, shrink deep into his shell, and not move, for days and days. We'd take him out to play or dunk him in water—nothing. He wanted to be still. (Barbara Kingsolver, *High Tide in Tucson*)

   TOPIC: _Crab Buster's character._

5. The frequency with which Americans are exposed to the mass media invites the assumption that the media play a significant role as socializing agents. The evidence, however, is mixed. The media play an important role in setting the boundaries of political debate and in identifying important issues. Most studies have shown that they are an important source of political information, that citizens' familiarity with issues comes primarily from the communications media. The spread of AIDS, overworked air traffic control systems, the demise of communism in eastern Europe—people learn about issues like these principally from the print and broadcast media. But there is little evidence to suggest that the media have much independent effect on political attitudes. In other words, most people's opinions and political behavior are not altered significantly by their exposure to the mass media. (Stephen J. Wayne et al., *The Politics of American Government*)

   TOPIC: _Mass media_

· ·

■ Finding Main Ideas in Paragraphs

The main idea of a paragraph expresses the writer's opinion or point of view about a topic. The topic of a paragraph might be, for example, *recent trends in rap music*, or it might be *U.S. presidential campaigns*. To find the main idea—the writer's opinion about the topic—you need to ask yourself what the paragraph is actually saying about the topic, what opinion or point of view is expressed. You would need to ask yourself, for example, "What point does the writer make about recent trends in rap music?" or "What is the writer suggesting about U.S. presidential campaigns?" When you can answer questions like these, you have understood the paragraph.

IDENTIFYING TOPIC SENTENCES

The main idea is often stated directly in a paragraph. The sentence in which the main idea appears is called the **topic sentence.** Read the following paragraph, taken from the textbook *The Politics of American Government* by Stephen J. Wayne, G. Calvin Mackenzie, David M. O'Brien, and Richard L. Cole.

> Power is exerted by and within all institutions of government. Presidents exercise power when they persuade reluctant legislators to support their policy positions, as President Clinton did in 1993, when he convinced a majority of the members of Congress to support his deficit reduction plan despite their many misgivings. Congress exercises power when it initiates policy and obtains reluctant presidential support, as the Democratic majority did in 1990 when it persuaded then-President George Bush to generate new deficit-reducing revenues through taxes despite his campaign promise not to raise taxes. Interest groups exercise power when they convince political leaders to reverse their positions on policy matters, as senior citizens' groups did in 1989 when they virtually forced Congress to withdraw a tax to finance the catastrophic health-care plan enacted in the previous year, and as they continued to do in 1993 and 1994, when they participated in the debate over the content of President Clinton's health-care proposals.

The topic of the preceding paragraph is *power. Power* is the broad subject that is constantly referred to. The main idea is expressed in the first sentence: "Power is exerted by and within all institutions of government." That is the point the writer wants to make about the subject of power. Although there are many kinds of power and many ways of looking at power, this writer wants to tell us that power is exercised by and in all government institutions. In this paragraph, the first sentence is the topic sentence. It directly states the writer's main idea.

One way to identify the main idea in a paragraph is to look for the most general opinion or point of view expressed. The most general opinion is the broadest one, the viewpoint that covers or includes all the narrower or more specific ideas. In the preceding example paragraph, the general statement (the main idea) is that all government institutions exert power. The author then goes on to give specific examples: Presidents exert power, Congress exerts power, interest groups exert power. Each of these is a specific example of a government institution that exerts power. The main idea, however, covers all of them. The topic sentence expresses, in general terms, that all government institutions exert power.

LOCATING TOPIC SENTENCES

The topic sentence (the sentence that states the writer's main idea) is very often the first sentence in the paragraph. Here is another example of the topic sentence as first sentence. The paragraph is taken from the article "Bad Choices" by Mary Ann Chapman, which appeared in the October 1999 issue of *Psychology Today*.

> Our day-to-day bad choices have alarming results. For example, one-third of Americans are overweight, costing the U.S. government $100 billion each year in treatment of related illnesses. We're also steeped in debt: The Consumer Federation of America calculates that 60 million households carry an average credit card balance of $7,000, for a total national credit card debt topping $455 billion. Our failure to make sacrifices now for rewards later is particularly devastating when it comes to following prescribed medical regimes. Studies have found that only half of us take antidepressants, antihypertensives, asthma medications and tuberculosis drugs as prescribed. Such lack of compliance is the major cause of hospital admissions in people who have previously had heart failure, and it's entirely preventable.

The topic of this paragraph is *bad choices*. What does the writer want to say about bad choices? She wants to say that day-to-day bad choices have alarming results. She expresses that thought in the first sentence, which we can now identify as the topic sentence. She then goes on to give specific examples of bad choices with alarming results: medical treatments related to being overweight; credit card debts related to spending habits; hospitalizations related to failure in following medical treatment plans. The topic sentence is the "umbrella" sentence: the statement that covers all the specific examples.

Sometimes authors will put the topic sentence somewhere other than the beginning of the paragraph. One writing technique is to build up to the main idea by giving the examples first and the topic sentence at the end of paragraph. This can be a very effective and dramatic way of making a point. Look, for example, at this paragraph by Jon Krakauer from his book *Into Thin Air.*

> Straddling the top of the world, one foot in China and the other in Nepal, I cleared the ice from my oxygen mask, hunched a shoulder against the wind, and stared absently down at the vastness of Tibet. I understood on some detached level that the sweep of earth beneath my feet was a spectacular sight. I'd been fantasizing about this moment, and the release of the emotion that would accompany it, for many months. But now that I was finally here, actually standing on the summit of Mount Everest, I just couldn't summon the energy to care.

The topic of the paragraph is *reaching the summit of Mount Everest.* In this paragraph, Krakauer has put the topic sentence (the statement of the main idea—what he wants to *say* about reaching the summit of Mount Everest) at the end of the paragraph. And what he wants to say (the main idea) is that when he finally reached the top of the world's highest mountain, he didn't have the energy to care.

The sentences that lead up to the last sentence, the topic sentence, give the specific examples that illustrate Krakauer's lack of energy and emotion. Only after the first three sentences does he state the main idea: that once he reached his goal, he was too tired to care. That lack of energy and emotion has already been shown in specific examples: He stared absently; he understood on a detached level; he was not feeling what he had fantasized beforehand that he would feel.

The topic sentence (the stated main idea of the paragraph) can also appear in the middle of the paragraph. Look at the following paragraph from the astronomy textbook *Universe* by William J. Kaufmann III and Roger A. Freedman.

> A rock tossed into a lake sinks to the bottom, while an air bubble produced at the bottom of a lake (for example, by the air tanks of a scuba diver) rises to the top. These are examples of a general principle: An object sinks in a fluid if its average density is greater than that of the fluid but rises if its average density is less than that of the fluid. The average density of water is 1000 kg/m^3, which is why a typical rock (with an average density of about 3000 kg/m^3) sinks while an average air bubble (average density of about 1.2 kg/m^3) rises.

The topic of this paragraph is *the sinking and rising of objects in water.* The topic sentence—what the authors want to say about the sinking and rising of objects in water—appears in the middle of the paragraph: "An object sinks in a fluid if its average density is greater than that of the fluid but rises if its average density is less than that of the fluid."

Notice that the authors begin the paragraph with specific examples: A rock sinks; an air bubble rises. They then present the topic sentence, the umbrella statement that covers the specific examples. After the topic sentence, they return to the examples, now explaining more specifically (by giving the weights of rocks and air bubbles) why these objects sink and rise, respectively.

Often the statement of the main idea is part of a longer sentence. The introductory words, like "These are examples of a general principle" (as in the astronomy example) or "What I am going to speak about today," or ending words, like "We can certainly arrive at this conclusion," will help you recognize that a general topic sentence is included. At other times, you may find that the full main idea is contained in two sentences, so that the topic sentence is really a combination of two sentences.

Exercise 4-3

You have already determined the topics of the following paragraphs. Now look for what the author is saying *about* each topic. Identify the topic sentence in each paragraph by underlining it.

Example:

> Economics is the study of how people choose among the alternatives available to them. It's the study of little choices ("Should I take the chocolate or the strawberry?") and big choices ("Should we require a

reduction in energy consumption in order to protect the environment?"). It's the study of individual choices, choices by firms, and choices by governments. Life presents each of us with a wide range of alternative uses of our time and other resources; economists examine how we choose among those alternatives. (Timothy Tregarthen and Libby Rittenberg, *Economics*)

1. A democracy is a form of government in which citizens have a right to control their own destiny. Democracy works on the principle of popular consent. The term itself comes from the Greek words *demos,* meaning "people," and *kratos,* meaning "authority." The people have authority; they have the right to make or influence decisions that affect their everyday lives. (Stephen J. Wayne et al., *The Politics of American Government*)

2. When there are no relatives living within easy visiting distance (less than an hour away), we speak of an isolated nuclear family. This family form usually results from a geographic move to another part of the country in response to a job offer. Less frequently it results from an intermarriage or the need to escape extended-family conflicts. The isolated nuclear family is completely independent, economically and emotionally, from the extended family. Family members borrow from banks rather than from relatives. If they are in trouble, they seek advice from outsiders— friends, professionals, or other experts. Relatives exert no influence on nuclear family decisions. The isolated nuclear family visits with relatives infrequently, usually during holidays and ceremonial occasions (weddings and funerals). (Betty Yorburg, *Family Relationships*)

3. The opening up of a person's creativity has a healthy impact on his or her life in a number of unexpected ways. Sometimes as a result of discovering creative abilities, a person identifies a new career path or establishes more satisfying personal relationships. Often it can foster a new level of self-awareness and confidence, helping a person become more effective in his or her current career. If someone is already an artist, it can provide him or her with new inspiration and material to work with. (Sandra G. Shuman, *Source Imagery*)

4. Today the word "politics" is often used disparagingly. Political candidates who accuse their opponents of "playing politics" mean to imply that the other candidate has been somehow unethical, or at least underhanded. In the 1992 presidential campaign, independent candidate H. Ross Perot appealed to many Americans precisely because of his contempt for "traditional politics." Bill Clinton's equivocation in answering questions about his past and his changing positions on some key issues made him vulnerable to the charge that he was a "typical" politician. (Stephen J. Wayne et al., *The Politics of American Government*)

5. The frequency with which Americans are exposed to the mass media invites the assumption that the media play a significant role as socializing agents. The evidence, however, is mixed. The media play an important role in setting the boundaries of political debate and in identifying important issues. Most studies have shown that they are an important source of political information, that citizens' familiarity with issues comes primarily from the communications media. The spread of AIDS, overworked air traffic control systems, the demise of communism in eastern Europe — people learn about issues like these principally from the print and broadcast media. But there is little evidence to suggest that the media have much independent effect on political attitudes. In other words, most people's opinions and political behavior are not altered significantly by their exposure to the mass media. (Stephen J. Wayne et al., *The Politics of American Government*)

Exercise 4-4

. . . .

For each of the following paragraphs, identify the topic and the topic sentence by writing them on the lines provided.

Example:

A transfer is a lateral, or sideways, move from one job to another with a similar level of authority and compensation. Some transfers are required by the organization. Ford Motor Company and many other firms now require managers and other employees to increase their flexibility by serving stints in various parts of the organization, where they can gain a larger view of the company and learn a variety of jobs and processes. Organizations also sometimes transfer troublesome employees, reassigning them to a different manager or work team where they may fit in better or be more productive. (Kenneth Blanchard et al., *Exploring the World of Business*)

TOPIC: <u>*transfers*</u>

TOPIC SENTENCE: <u>*A transfer is a lateral, or sideways, move from one job*</u> *to another with a similar level of authority and compensation.*

1. Women's boxing, which has struggled in the shadow of the men's sport, is coming into its own. The estimated 300 professional female boxers in the United States are being joined by rapidly increasing numbers internationally. The Internet swarms with Web sites devoted to the sport, and its commercial value is also building. Cable television ratings for women's boxing are consistently high, and its cinematic possibilities have surfaced in films like *Girlfight,* which won a Grand Jury Prize at the Sundance festival, and the documentary *Shadow Boxers,* which earned rave reviews on the festival circuit. (Katherine Dunn, "Rijker's Island," *New York Times Magazine,* February 27, 2000)

TOPIC: <u>Women Boxing</u>

TOPIC SENTENCE: <u>Women boxing which has struggled in the shadow</u>

2. Most forms of psychotherapy, including most group therapies, tend to see a person's problems — and the solutions to those problems — as primarily originating within the individual. Family therapy operates on a different premise, focusing on the whole family rather than on an individual. The major goal of family therapy is to alter and improve the ongoing interactions among family members. Typically, family therapy involves every member of the family, even young children, and may also include important members of the extended family, such as grandparents or in-laws. (Adapted from Don H. Hockenbury and Sandra E. Hockenbury, *Discovering Psychology*)

TOPIC: _Family therapy_

TOPIC SENTENCE: _Family therapy operates on a different premise, focusing on the whole family_

3. Floppies are fine for moving a particular document from one machine to another, but they aren't reliable for long-term storage. They aren't hermetically sealed, so they can go bad — victims of humidity or dust or an overturned cup of coffee. Usually, you won't realize the disk is bad until you insert it into the computer and see the words "Disk error" or "Disk cannot be read" or a similar message that can ruin an otherwise ideal day. Many people routinely use one particular floppy to back up a spreadsheet or a daily reminder and learn a lesson in betrayal when it goes sour on them. (Robert Stephens, *The Geek Squad Guide to Solving Any Computer Glitch*)

TOPIC: _Floppies_

TOPIC SENTENCE: _Floppies are fine for moving a particular document from one machine to another, but they aren't reliable for long-term storage_

4. Suppose your best friend has invited you for a spaghetti dinner. As you walk in the front door, you're almost overwhelmed by the odor of onions and garlic cooking on the stove. However, after just a few moments, you no longer notice the smell. This example demonstrates one of the characteristics of our senses. After being exposed to a steady stimulus for a time, we become less aware of it. Why? Because our sensory receptor cells become less responsive to a constant stimulus. This gradual decline in sensitivity to a constant stimulus is called sensory adaptation. (Adapted from Don H. Hockenbury and Sandra E. Hockenbury, *Discovering Psychology*)

TOPIC: _Sensory adaptation_

TOPIC SENTENCE: _This gradual decline in sensitivity to a constant stimulus is called sensory adaptation._

5. Like many other children, I read to be scared witless, to be less lonely, to believe in other possibilities. But we all become different readers in how we respond to books, why we need them, what we take from them. We become different in the questions that arise as we read, in the answers that we find, in the degree of satisfaction or unease we feel with those answers. We differ in what we begin to consider about the real world and the imaginary one. We differ in what we think we can know—or would want to know—and in how we continue to pursue that knowledge. (Amy Tan, *The Best American Short Stories 1999*)

TOPIC: different kinds of readers

TOPIC SENTENCE: But we all become different readers in how we respond to books, why we need them, what we take from them.

Applying the Skills

Reading the Parts

The following essay was written by Cecelie Berry, a writer living in Montclair, New Jersey, and a contributor to Salon.com's "Mothers Who Think." The essay was originally published in *Newsweek*, February 7, 2000. As you read, pay special attention to the topic and main idea of each paragraph. After reading each section and answering the questions that follow, move on to the next section. You will have a chance to read the entire essay when you finish.

CECELIE BERRY

It's Time We Rejected the Racial Litmus Test

I recognize the sassy swivel of the head, the rhythmic teeth sucking and finger snapping. My son Spenser has come home from kindergarten talking like he's black. Never mind that he *is* black; somehow his skin color is no longer adequate to express his racial identity. Sometimes, in diverse schools like the one he attends, black children feel pressure to "act" black. My 8-year-old son Sam asks me to tell Spenser not to use "that phony accent" around his friends. "I'll talk to him," I say with a sigh. 1

"Be yourself" seems insufficient at times like this. I know from my experience with integration that it takes a long time to own your identity. In an all-black elementary school in Cleveland, I carried around a dogeared copy of *A Little Princess* and listened to Bach on my transistor radio. Nobody paid attention. When my family moved to Shaker Heights, an affluent suburb known for its successfully integrated schools, I encountered the war over who was authentically black. I had hoped that when I raised my own children there wouldn't be any more litmus tests, that a healthy black identity could come in many styles. But the impulse to pigeonhole each other endures. 2

1. Which statement best expresses the topic of paragraph 1 of Berry's essay?

    a. integrated schools

    b. racial identity

    c. the author's family

    d. kindergarten

2. Identify the topic sentence of paragraph 1—that is, the sentence that best expresses the main idea of that paragraph.

    a. My son Spenser had come home from kindergarten talking like he's black.

    b. Never mind that he *is* black; somehow his skin color is no longer adequate to express his racial identity.

    c. Sometimes, in diverse schools like the one he attends, black children feel pressure to "act" black.

    d. My 8-year-old son Sam asks me to tell Spenser not to use "that phony accent" around his friends.

3. The topic of paragraph 2 is

    a. a healthy black identity.

    b. stereotypes.

    c. Shaker Heights.

    d. litmus tests.

4. What is the topic sentence of the second paragraph?

    a. "Be yourself" seems insufficient at times like this.

    b. I know from my experience with integration that it takes a long time to own your identity.

    c. I had hoped that when I raised my own children there wouldn't be any more litmus tests, that a healthy black identity could come in many styles.

    d. But the impulse to pigeonhole each other endures.

5. The main idea of the two paragraphs taken together is that

    a. finding one's identity is a complex process.

    b. parents' wisdom should be passed on to their children.

    c. parents need to talk to their children about race.

    d. communities should be better integrated.

As I considered what to say to Spenser, I recalled my own struggles over my accent. In seventh grade, I was rehearsing a play after school when a group of black girls passed by. "You talk like a honky," their leader said. "You must think you're white." In the corner of my eye, I could see her bright yellow radio, shaped like a tennis ball, swinging like a mace. A phrase I'd found intriguing flashed through my mind: "The best defense is a good offense." I stepped forward and slapped her hard.

3

I was suspended for that fight, but I felt I deserved a medal. My true reward came later, when I heard two girls talking about me in the hallway. "I heard she's an oreo," one said. "Don't let her hear you say that," the other replied, "'cause she'll kick your butt!"

4

I hesitate to tell Spenser to be himself because I know it's not that simple. From integration, I learned that you have to fight for the right to be yourself, and often, your opponents have the same color skin as you. My sons will discover, as I did, that you can feign a black accent, but your loyalty will continue to be tested as long as you allow it.

5

6. Which word or phrase best expresses the topic of paragraph 3?

   a. children's tendency to bully

   b. female classmates

   c. the author's conflicts with black schoolmates

   d. fighting

7. Which sentence expresses the main idea of paragraph 3?

   a. As I considered what to say to Spenser, I recalled my own struggles over my accent.

   b. In seventh grade, I was rehearsing a play after school when a group of black girls passed by.

   c. A phrase I'd found intriguing flashed through my mind: "The best defense is a good offense."

   d. I stepped forward and slapped her hard.

8. The topic sentence in paragraph 4 that best expresses the paragraph's main idea is

   a. I was suspended for that fight but I felt I deserved a medal.

   b. My true reward came later, when I heard two girls talking about me in the hallway.

   c. "I heard she's an oreo," one said.

   d. "Don't let her hear you say that," the other one replied, "'cause she'll kick your butt!"

9. What word or phrase best expresses the topic of paragraph 5?

   a. skin color   c. dealing with bullies

   b. being yourself   d. responding to challenges

10. The topic sentence of paragraph 5 is:

   a. I hesitate to tell Spenser to be himself because I know it's not that simple.

   b. From integration, I learned that you have to fight for the right to be yourself, and often, your opponents have the same color skin as you.

   c. My sons will discover, as I did, that you can feign a black accent, but your loyalty will continue to be tested as long as you allow it.

   d. None of the above.

> In high school, I enhanced my reputation as an "oreo" by participating in activities that most black students didn't: advanced-placement classes, the school newspaper and the debate team. Mostly, I enjoyed being different. It put me in a unique position to challenge the casually racist assumptions of my liberal classmates. I remember a question posed by my social-studies teacher, "How many of you grew up addressing your black housekeepers by their first names?" Many students raised their hands. "And how many of you addressed white adults that way?" The hands went down. One girl moaned: "That's not racist. Everybody does that."   6
>
> "We never addressed our housekeeper that way," I said. In the silence that followed, I could feel myself being reassessed. I'd challenged my classmate on the fairness of a privilege she had, like many whites, taken completely for granted. I had defied the unspoken understanding of how blacks in white settings are supposed to be: transparent and accommodating.   7
>
> If black students inflicted upon each other a rigid code of "blackness," liberal whites assumed that the blacks in their midst would not dispute their right-mindedness. Being myself, I found, could be lonely. In high school, I grew weary of walking the tightrope between black and white.   8

11. The topic of paragraph 6 of Berry's essay is

    a. black housekeepers.   c. racist assumptions.

    b. "oreos."   d. white students.

12. The topic sentence of paragraph 6 is

    a. In high school, I enhanced my reputation as an "oreo" by participating in activities that most black students didn't.

    b. Mostly, I enjoyed being different.

    c. It put me in a unique position to challenge the casually racist assumptions of my liberal classmates.

    d. I remember a question posed by my social-studies teacher, "How many of you grew up addressing your black house-keepers by their first names?"

13. What is the topic of paragraph 7?

    a. the assessment of the author by her white classmates

    b. challenging stereotypes of blacks in white settings

    c. privileges

    d. accommodation

14. Which sentence expresses the main point of paragraph 7?

    a. "We never addressed our housekeeper that way," I said.

    b. In the silence that followed, I could feel myself being reassessed.

    c. I'd challenged my classmate on the fairness of a privilege she had, like many whites, taken completely for granted.

    d. I had defied the unspoken understanding of how blacks in white settings are supposed to be: transparent and accom-modating.

15. What word or phrase best expresses the topic of paragraph 8?

    a. the tightrope between black and white

    b. white right-mindedness

    c. "blackness"

    d. rigid codes

By college, I was eating regularly at the controversial "black tables" of Harvard's Freshman Union. I talked black, walked black and dated black men. My boyfriend, an Andover graduate, commented on my transformation by saying that I had never been an oreo; I was really a "closet militant." I laughed at the phrase; it had an element of truth. I had learned that people—black or white—tend to demonize what they don't understand and can't control. So I sometimes hid the anger, ambition and self-confidence that provoked their fear. Integration taught me to have two faces: one that can get along with anybody and one that distrusts everybody.

9

I've seen both sides, now. I've "hung" white and I've "hung" black, and been stereotyped by both groups. I choose integration for my children, not out of idealism, but a pragmatic assessment of what it takes to grow up. When it comes to being yourself—and finding out who that person is—you're on your own. Experimentation is a prerequisite, trying on various accents and dress styles, mandatory. Diversity is the best laboratory for building individuality.

10

I am about to explain this to Spenser, when I see him change, like quicksilver, into someone else. Playfully, he stretches his arm out toward my face, turns his gap-toothed smile in the opposite direction and, in a tone as maddening as it is endearing, he says, "Mom, talk to the hand."

11

16. The topic of paragraph 9 of Berry's essay is

   a. the controversial "black tables" at Harvard.

   b. "closet militants."

   c. the author's "black identity" in college.

   d. getting along with anyone and distrusting everyone.

17. The topic sentence of paragraph 9 is

   a. I talked black, walked black and dated black men.

   b. I was really a "closet militant."

   c. I had learned that people—black or white—tend to demonize what they don't understand and can't control.

   d. So I sometimes hid the anger, ambition, and self-confidence that provoked their fear.

18. What is the topic of paragraph 10?

    a. building individuality

    b. stereotypes

    c. experimentation

    d. diversity

19. Which sentence best states the main idea of paragraph 10?

    a. I've seen both sides, now.

    b. I've "hung" white and I've "hung" black, and been stereo-typed by both groups.

    c. When it comes to being yourself—and finding out who that person is—you're on your own.

    d. Diversity is the best laboratory for building individuality.

20. The phrase that best expresses the topic of paragraph 11 is

    a. Spenser's individuality.

    b. Spenser's playfulness.

    c. Spenser's lack of respect for his mother.

    d. Berry's feelings about Spenser.

Reading the Whole

Now that you've read Cecelie Berry's essay "It's Time We Rejected the Racial Litmus Test" in its parts and carefully studied each paragraph's topic and topic sentence, you will be better able to reread the selection in its entirety. As you read, your understanding of the paragraph topics and topic sentences should help you better appreciate Berry's whole experience and perhaps to understand the subtleties of her point of view.

CECELIE BERRY

It's Time We Rejected the Racial Litmus Test

I recognize the sassy swivel of the head, the rhythmic teeth sucking and finger snapping. My son Spenser has come home from kindergarten talking like he's black. Never mind that he *is* black; somehow his skin color is no longer adequate to express his racial identity. Sometimes, in diverse schools like the one he attends, black children feel pressure to "act" black. My 8-year-old son Sam asks me to tell Spenser not to use "that phony accent" around his friends. "I'll talk to him," I say with a sigh.

"Be yourself" seems insufficient at times like this. I know from my experience with integration that it takes a long time to own your identity. In an all-black elementary school in Cleveland, I carried around a dogeared copy of *A Little Princess* and listened to Bach on my transistor radio. Nobody paid attention. When my family moved to Shaker Heights, an affluent suburb known for its successfully integrated schools, I encountered the war over who was authentically black. I had hoped that when I raised my own children there wouldn't be any more litmus tests, that a healthy black identity could come in many styles. But the impulse to pigeonhole each other endures.

As I considered what to say to Spenser, I recalled my own struggles over my accent. In seventh grade, I was rehearsing a play after school when a group of black girls passed by. "You talk like a honky," their leader said. "You must think you're white." In the corner of my eye, I could see her bright yellow radio, shaped like a tennis ball, swinging like a mace. A phrase I'd found intriguing

1

2

3

flashed through my mind: "The best defense is a good offense." I stepped forward and slapped her hard.

I was suspended for that fight, but I felt I deserved a medal. My true reward came later, when I heard two girls talking about me in the hallway. "I heard she's an oreo," one said. "Don't let her hear you say that," the other replied, "'cause she'll kick your butt!"

I hesitate to tell Spenser to be himself because I know it's not that simple. From integration, I learned that you have to fight for the right to be yourself, and often, your opponents have the same color skin as you. My sons will discover, as I did, that you can feign a black accent, but your loyalty will continue to be tested as long as you allow it.

In high school, I enhanced my reputation as an "oreo" by participating in activities that most black students didn't: advanced-placement classes, the school newspaper and the debate team. Mostly, I enjoyed being different. It put me in a unique position to challenge the casually racist assumptions of my liberal classmates. I remember a question posed by my social-studies teacher, "How many of you grew up addressing your black housekeepers by their first names?" Many students raised their hands. "And how many of you addressed white adults that way?" The hands went down. One girl moaned: "That's not racist. Everybody does that."

"We never addressed our housekeeper that way," I said. In the silence that followed, I could feel myself being reassessed. I'd challenged my classmate on the fairness of a privilege she had, like many whites, taken completely for granted. I had defied the unspoken understanding of how blacks in white settings are supposed to be: transparent and accommodating.

If black students inflicted upon each other a rigid code of "blackness," liberal whites assumed that the blacks in their midst would not dispute their right-mindedness. Being myself, I found, could be lonely. In high school, I grew weary of walking the tightrope between black and white.

By college, I was eating regularly at the controversial "black tables" of Harvard's Freshman Union. I talked black, walked black and dated black men. My boyfriend, an Andover graduate, commented on my transformation by saying that I had never been an oreo; I was really a "closet militant." I laughed at the phrase; it had an element of truth. I had learned that people—black or white—tend to demonize what they don't understand and can't control. So I sometimes hid the anger, ambition and self-confidence that provoked their fear. Integration taught me to have two faces: one that can get along with anybody and one that distrusts everybody.

I've seen both sides, now. I've "hung" white and I've "hung" black, and been stereotyped by both groups. I choose integration for my children, not out of idealism, but a pragmatic assessment of what it takes to grow up. When it comes to being yourself—and finding out who that person is—you're on your own. Experimentation is a prerequisite, trying on various accents and dress styles, mandatory. Diversity is the best laboratory for building individuality.

I am about to explain this to Spenser, when I see him change, like quicksilver, into someone else. Playfully, he stretches his arm out toward my face, turns his gap-toothed smile in the opposite direction and, in a tone as maddening as it is endearing, he says, "Mom, talk to the hand."

Integrated Skills

1. How does your understanding of the topic and topic sentence of each paragraph help you understand Cecelie Berry's overall topic? What is her overall topic?

2. What main ideas in Berry's paragraphs carry through the entire reading selection? What is her main idea in the whole piece?

3. What examples of being or acting black does Berry include? Why do you think she uses them?

4. What does the author mean when she describes her reputation as an "oreo"?

5. What do you think Berry means when she writes that she "grew weary of walking the tightrope between black and white"?

Reading Textbooks

Thematic Connections. Cecelie Berry's essay "It's Time We Rejected the Racial Litmus Test" discusses how cultural attitudes have affected the development of her own and her children's racial identity. The following passage from the child psychology textbook *The Development of Children* by Michael Cole and Sheila R. Cole is taken from the chapter "Schooling and Development in Middle Childhood." It explores some of the ways that broader cultural ideas and attitudes—particularly those of teachers—affect children's academic development. The passage hints at larger implications that might help you to place Berry's experience and that of her children into context. As you read, carefully note the topic and main idea of each paragraph, and consider how the textbook reading as a whole helps you understand Berry's essay.

Vocabulary Preview

controversial (para. 2): arguable; disputed (adj.)

initiated (para. 2): begun; started (v.)

colleagues (para. 2): coworkers (n.)

groundless (para. 2): without foundation; unsubstantiated (adj.)

spurt (para. 3): quick increase or growth (n.)

candidates (para. 4): those chosen or selected (n.)

provocative (para. 5): stimulating; thought-provoking (adj.)

regarding (para. 5): with respect to; about (prep.)

factor (para. 6): element; part (n.)

recipients (para. 6): receivers; subjects (n.)

inattentiveness (para. 7): lack of attention (n.)

Focus on Research
Expectations and Performance

Most of you have spent more than a dozen years in classrooms and know from personal experience that teachers' attitudes toward students vary. Teachers expect some students to do better than others in mastering academic material. Research has shown that these attitudes and expectations influence students' performance in a variety of ways. 1

Perhaps the most famous, and certainly the most controversial, research on the effect of teachers' expectations was initiated in the 2

1960s by Robert Rosenthal and his colleagues. These researchers found that a teacher's expectations about a child's academic ability may become a self-fulfilling prophecy, even when the expectations are groundless. That is, the teacher's expectations in themselves may lead to behavior that causes the expectations to be realized.

To demonstrate the power of teachers' expectations, Rosenthal and Lenore Jacobsen gave children in all six grades of an elementary school a test that, they told the teachers, would identify children who were likely to "bloom" intellectually during the coming year. After the testing, the researchers gave the teachers the names of those children who would supposedly show a spurt in intellectual development during the school year. In fact, the names of the predicted "bloomers" were chosen at random (with a few exceptions, to be described in due course).

At the end of the school year, the children were tested again. This time the researchers found that at the first- and second-grade levels there was in fact a difference between the "bloomers" and "non-bloomers"; the children who had been randomly identified as likely candidates for rapid intellectual growth actually gained an average of 15 points on their IQ scores, while their classmates' IQ scores remained unchanged. In this study, the IQs of children in grades 3 through 6 did not change, but in a follow-up study Rosenthal and his colleagues found that older schoolchildren's performance on IQ tests could also be influenced by the teachers' expectations. Since the children identified as those likely to bloom intellectually were chosen at random, Rosenthal and his colleagues concluded that teachers' expectations influence their own behavior and thus their students', making their teaching more effective with children they believe to be academically able.

A particularly provocative finding in Rosenthal and Jacobsen's study concerned race, ethnic, and class differences in academic performance. Teachers often have lower expectations regarding the academic performance of minority-group and poor children than they do regarding that of their white, middle-class counterparts. To test the possibility that these lowered expectations actually lower minority and poor children's academic performance, Rosenthal and Jacobsen included a group of poor Mexican-American children among those they identified as likely to bloom during the coming year. These children made particularly large gains in IQ test performance. In fact, the children whom the teachers identified as most

"Mexican-looking" made the largest gains, perhaps because the teachers, recognizing that these students were the ones from whom they would ordinarily have expected the least, paid them all the more attention.

Such results immediately attracted the attention of researchers and the public at large. Hundreds of studies have since been conducted on the role of teachers' expectations in students' academic performance. Many school districts even have special training programs to ensure that their teachers are sensitive to the ways in which their expectations may negatively affect some children. However, despite general acceptance of the idea that teachers' expectations are a significant factor in children's academic performance, some psychologists and educators remain skeptical. One basis for doubt is that many studies fail to find any such effects. Why? When researchers attempted to find out by observing teachers and children in interaction in classrooms, they found that teachers differ in their approach to the children they expect little of. Some teachers ignore those children and focus on the ones they consider more capable, but other teachers seem to give extra help and encouragement to those children. This research also makes it clear that children are not passive recipients of teachers' expectations. Children influence those expectations by their own classroom behavior.

Research by Carol Dweck and her colleagues . . . has shown one way in which the interplay between teachers' expectations and children's behavior may shape academic development. Dweck studied teachers' differing expectations for boys and girls. In general, girls are better behaved than boys during the elementary school years. Consequently, teachers expect boys to challenge classroom decorum and girls to support it. Dweck and her colleagues found that these differences in children's behavior and teachers' expectations led teachers to respond differently to boys and girls. Overall, teachers criticize boys more than girls. Often this criticism focuses on boys' lack of decorum, their failure to do their work neatly, or their inattentiveness. Their criticism of girls, by contrast, is likely to focus on ability and intellectual performance. At the same time, when teachers offer praise, its focus is likely to be girls' cooperative social behavior and boys' intellectual accomplishments.

These differences in teachers' expectations for boys and girls and in the kind of feedback they provide have been found to be related to the kinds of expectations that children form about their own behavior. When girls are told that they have failed, they usually believe that the teacher has correctly assessed their intellectual capacity, so they tend to stop trying. Boys interpret such criticism differently: they blame their poor performance on someone else, on their situation, or on bad luck and retain faith in their own ability to do better next time.

Thinking about the Textbook Selection

1. What is the main connection between Berry's magazine piece and the textbook reading selection? How are the two pieces related?

2. Identify the topic, topic sentence, and main idea of two different paragraphs in the textbook selection. Explain why you chose those paragraphs.

3. What do the textbook authors mean by the following terms: "self-fulfilling prophecy," "bloomers," and "nonbloomers"?

4. What do the textbook authors suggest about the effect that teachers' expectations have for their students?

5. What do the authors suggest about the relationship between teachers' low expectations of some groups of students and the academic performance of those students?

Reviewing

**Recall /
Remember**

1. What is a "main idea"? How is a paragraph's main idea different from its topic?

2. Explain the difference between the topic of a paragraph and a paragraph's topic sentence.

3. Explain why finding a paragraph's main idea is important for reading.

4. Identify two strategies for finding the main idea in a paragraph.

In this chapter you learned how to recognize a writer's main idea and to distinguish between the main idea and the topic of a paragraph. You also learned to distinguish between a paragraph's topic and its topic sentence. In addition, you practiced using specific strategies to find the main idea in a paragraph. And finally, you had a chance to practice finding the main ideas, topics, and topic sentences for paragraphs in longer reading selections, one from a magazine and another from a textbook.

Chapter Summary

Understanding Major and Minor Supporting Details

Chapter 5

Getting Ready	113
Learning the Skills	114
Applying the Skills	
• Reading the Parts	129
• Reading the Whole	134
• Reading Textbooks	136
Reviewing	139

Getting Ready

Writers often use specific details to explain or clarify a main idea. That is, they try to convince readers that the main idea is true by giving specific examples, illustrations, and instances that support their opinion or point of view. In this chapter we will look at different kinds of **supporting details**. We will also distinguish between **major supporting details** and **minor supporting details**. Finally, we will look at how supporting details can communicate the main idea when a paragraph does not contain a topic sentence—that is, when the main idea is not expressed directly.

Chapter Overview

What else do you want to know after you have identified a writer's main idea? What else do you look for?

Are all the specific details that a writer gives you equally important? Why or why not?

How can you identify a writer's main idea if the idea is not directly stated in the writing?

Focusing Questions

Everyday Reading

As you study this chapter, begin to look at magazine advertisements for their main ideas. What specific details does each advertisement use? If the main idea is stated, do the details—including details in pictures as well as in writing—support the stated idea? You may find that the details support another idea entirely. If the main idea is unstated, do the details lead you to the main idea that the advertiser seems to be promoting—or do the details lead you to something entirely different?

Make a list of five advertisements, writing out their main ideas and then listing all the details beneath them. In your lists, underline those details that support the main idea and circle those that do not.

Learning the Skills

■ Identifying Supporting Details

Topic sentences are supported by examples, illustrations, statistics, explanations—any specific details that will convince readers of the truth of the writer's main idea. Consider, for example, this topic sentence from a paragraph in the textbook *Health in the New Millennium* by Jeffrey S. Nevid, Spencer A. Rathus, and Hannah R. Rubenstein: "There are three types of blood vessels." What kind of support would you expect to follow that statement? You would probably expect each of the three types of blood vessels to be named and explained. And they are: The paragraph goes on to name and explain arteries, capillaries, and veins.

Here is another example from the same textbook: "Skin cancer is the most common and most rapidly increasing type of cancer in the United States." What type of support would you expect to back up that statement? For the explanation of "most common," you might expect statistics of the frequency of skin cancer in comparison with other cancers. For the explanation of "most rapidly increasing type of cancer," you might expect statistics that show the growth in the number of cases of skin cancer in comparison with other cancers. You might possibly also expect an explanation of what factors in the modern world might be causing such growth.

Even when the topic sentence is not as factual as the two topic sentences just mentioned, the idea of support is the same. Supporting details explain or develop or prove the topic sentence. Here is a more personal topic sentence, from Annie Dillard's book *For the Time Being:* "All my life I have loved this sight: a standing wave in the boat's wake, shaped like a thorn." What kind of support would you expect from a statement like that? Why Dillard loves that particular kind of wave? A description of the beauty or action of the wave? Instances when she saw such a wave? Any of those would support Dillard's topic sentence.

Exercise 5-1

After reading the following topic sentences, which are all taken from college textbooks, decide what kinds of details could support the statements. Include at least one example of possible support for each topic sentence. (Even if you are not familiar with the particular subject matter, you should be able to figure out what kind of support the topic sentence needs.)

Example:

TOPIC SENTENCE: U.S. elections are in need of serious changes.

POSSIBLE SUPPORT: *Reasons why elections are in need of change — for example, that there are too many different ways to cast votes*

1. TOPIC SENTENCE: As a group, birds eat almost all types of animal and plant material. (William K. Purves, Gordon H. Orians, H. Craig Heller, and David Sadava, *Life: The Science of Biology*)

   POSSIBLE SUPPORT: The birds can eat warms,

2. TOPIC SENTENCE: Countries cannot depend solely on the goods and services produced within their own boundaries for three reasons. (Kenneth Blanchard, Charles Schewe, Robert Nelson, and Alexander Hiam, *Exploring the World of Business*)

   POSSIBLE SUPPORT: depends on Nactinal recarces, ~~eve~~

3. TOPIC SENTENCE: Although politics sometimes leads to excesses and abuses, in itself it is neither bad nor dangerous. (Stephen J. Wayne, G. Calvin Mackenzie, David M. O'Brien, and Richard L. Cole, *The Politics of American Government*)

   POSSIBLE SUPPORT: people can protest

4. TOPIC SENTENCE: The use of coded messages today has advanced far beyond detective stories and puzzles. (Harold R. Jacobs, *Mathematics: A Human Endeavor*)

   POSSIBLE SUPPORT: _____

   _____

5. TOPIC SENTENCE: Each different chemical element is made of a specific type of atom. (William J. Kaufmann III and Roger Freedman, *Universe*)

   POSSIBLE SUPPORT: _____

   _____

Exercise 5-2

Each topic sentence is followed by four statements. Cross out the statement that does *not* provide support for the topic sentence.

Example:

You don't have to go to the Louvre to see art in Paris.

a. ~~The Louvre is the world's largest palace as well as the world's largest museum.~~

b. At the Musée d'Orsay, a museum that once was a Paris train station, you can see magnificent Impressionist art.

c. In the section of Paris known as Montmartre, you can see outdoor exhibits as well as watch artists painting on street corners.

d. Paris is filled with smaller museums, including some devoted to a particular artist, like Picasso or the sculptor Rodin.

1. Here are some ways to recover from DOMS, delayed onset muscle soreness — the pain, tenderness, and stiffness that occur in muscles a day or two after exercise.

   a. Light massage gets your blood moving and breaks up scar tissue, which speeds proper healing.

   b. You usually don't feel sore on the same day you do the heavy exercise.

   c. Ice or cold water reduces inflammation, which may be a cause of DOMS.

    d.   In the next few days you should do some light aerobic cross-training, which helps clean out the waste built up by extended effort.

(Adapted from Ed Eyestone, "Your Road to Recovery," *Runner's World,* April 2000)

2.   For centuries, explorers have risked their lives venturing into the unknown for reasons that were usually economic and nationalistic.

    a.   Christopher Columbus went west to look for better trade routes to the Orient and to promote the greater glory of Spain.

    b.   Lewis and Clark journeyed into the American wilderness to find out what the United States had acquired in the Louisiana purchase.

    c.   The Apollo astronauts rocketed to the moon in a dramatic flexing of technological muscle during the cold war.

    d.   In the twenty-first century, science may take a leading role along with economics and nationalism.

(Adapted from Glenn Zorpette, "Why Go to Mars?" *Scientific American,* March 2000)

3.   It is impossible to get away from music these days.

    a.   The music is turning our minds to mush.

    b.   A merciless stream of 1960s golden oldies drenches our suburban shopping malls.

    c.   In the back of the taxi all the way to the airport, the radio thumps out disco revivals.

    d.   Tinny Muzak bleats from storefronts as we walk along the sidewalk.

(Adapted from J. Bottum, "The Soundtracking of America," *Atlantic Monthly,* March 2000)

4.   Few people realize how precisely their private lives can be tracked online.

    a.   Little tags called "cookies" are often placed on your computer by the Web sites you visit.

    b.   Cookies can implant a unique ID number, which tells a site exactly who you are when you return.

c. Your Internet service provider can help you get rid of cookies.

d. When you buy a new computer and transfer your data from your old one, the cookies come along.

(Adapted from Jane Bryant Quinn, "Fighting the Cookie Monster," *Newsweek*, February 28, 2000)

5. The quality, intensity, and distribution of light determine which plants to grow and where to plant them.

a. Plants that require four to six hours of sun a day should be planted in parts of the garden that are on an east–west axis.

b. As the sun shifts in the sky and as the clouds come and go, patterns of light and shade vary endlessly.

c. Plants that require six to eight hours of full sun a day are best situated in west- or south-facing exposures.

d. Plants that need gentle morning sun should go in the farthest east regions of the garden; plants that need some strong sunlight should go in the farthest west regions.

(Adapted from Lucy Hardiman, "The Many Shades of Sunlight," *Horticulture*, March 2000)

■ Identifying Major Supporting Details

All the supporting details that we have discussed so far are **major supporting details.** Major supporting details support the topic sentence *directly.* They are essential for supporting an author's main idea. They give basic information, reasons, or evidence to convince readers of the truth or validity of the author's opinion or viewpoint. You can often identify major supporting details because the sentences that contain them refer directly to the topic sentence. These sentences will often repeat key words from the topic sentence or use synonyms—words with the same meaning—for those key words. Usually the sentences that contain major supporting details will expand on the concepts presented in the topic sentence, providing more information about them.

Look at the following paragraph adapted from the textbook *Discovering Psychology* by Don H. Hockenbury and Sandra E. Hockenbury.

> Factors such as body weight, gender, food consumption, and the rate of alcohol consumption affect blood alcohol levels. A slender person who quickly consumes three drinks on an empty stomach will become more than twice as intoxicated as a heavier person who consumes three drinks with food. If a man and a woman of equal weight consume the same number of drinks, the woman will become more intoxicated.

The topic sentence in this passage is the first sentence. It states the main idea of the paragraph. The major supporting details give specific evidence that illustrates the more general topic sentence. The fact that body weight and food consumption affect blood alcohol levels (stated in the topic sentence) is explained in the second sentence (a major supporting detail): specifically, that a slim person who has three drinks on an empty stomach will become more than twice as intoxicated as a heavier person who has three drinks with food. The fact that body weight and gender affect blood alcohol levels (stated in the topic sentence) is explained in the third sentence (a major supporting detail): specifically, that a woman will become more intoxicated than a man although she weighs the same amount and drinks the same amount.

For another example of major supporting details, let's look again at the paragraph on power from *The Politics of American Government.*

> Power is exerted by and within all institutions of government. Presidents exercise power when they persuade reluctant legislators to support their policy positions, as President Clinton did in 1993, when he convinced a majority of the members of Congress to support his deficit reduction plan despite their many misgivings. Congress exercises power when it initiates policy and obtains reluctant presidential support, as the Democratic majority did in 1990 when it persuaded then-President George Bush to generate new deficit-reducing revenues through taxes despite his campaign promise not to raise taxes. Interest groups exercise power when they convince political leaders to reverse their positions on policy matters, as senior citizens' groups did in 1989 when they virtually forced Congress to withdraw a tax to finance the catastrophic health-care plan enacted in the previous year, and as they continued to do in 1993 and 1994, when they participated in the debate over the content of President Clinton's health-care proposals.

We have already identified the topic of this paragraph (*power*) and the main idea as expressed in the topic sentence ("Power is exerted by and within all institutions of government"). The three major supporting details in this paragraph are (1) "Presidents exercise power when they persuade reluctant legislators to support their policy positions"; (2) "Congress exercises power when it initiates policy and obtains reluctant presidential support"; and (3) "Interest groups exercise power when they convince political leaders to reverse their positions on policy matters." By pointing out the three different government institutions (presidents, Congress, and interest groups) and showing how each exerts power, the authors provide support for their statement that power is exerted by and within all institutions of government.

Highlighting major supporting details as you read can be very useful for reviewing material later or studying for tests. Certainly it will help you to gain a fuller understanding of the author's main idea. On exams, you may be asked for evidence (major supporting details) that illustrates or explains or clarifies a writer's main ideas.

——Exercise 5-3

Double underline the topic sentence and then underline the major supporting details in the following paragraphs, adapted from *Exploring the World of Business* by Kenneth Blanchard, Charles Schewe, Robert Nelson, and Alexander Hiam.

Example:

Businesses use natural resources. Iron ore is made into the steel chassis of cars. Trees are made into the paper that books are printed on. Energy is used to power equipment. A grocery store, for example, depends on the energy of the waterfall, uranium, or coal used to generate the electricity that runs its coolers, freezers, lights, air conditioning, and cash registers. And, of course, rain, sun, and soil are needed to grow the vegetables and fruit with which the grocery store's coolers are stocked.

1. Businesses also use the natural environment in less obvious ways. They use up space in landfills when customers throw away the packaging of their products. They use up the capacity of air, soil, and water to absorb waste products when their wastes enter the environment. They affect the natural environment when they build new factories or offices, sometimes unknowingly destroying the habitats of plants and animals.

2. Businesses have traditionally treated the preservation of the natural environment passively, as a secondary concern. They simply complied with environmental regulations. They avoided any major catastrophes that would make bad headlines.

3. Today, however, businesses are taking an active approach to helping to preserve the natural environment. One example is the waste exchanges that businesses have formed in many parts of the United States and Canada. For instance, the paper that one company throws away can often be recycled to make packing materials by another company.

4. Groups like the Canadian Waste Materials Exchange, the Hawaii Waste Exchange, and the Indiana Waste Exchange now recycle six million tons of refuse for businesses yearly. Business is beginning to take responsibility for its impact on the natural environment, but it is only a first step. So far, waste exchanges handle less than 10 percent of the total waste generated in the United States.

5. Ford Motor Company does a lot of recycling. It grinds up about fifty million plastic soda bottles each year to make luggage racks, door padding, and grille opening reinforcements for cars. It makes brake pedal pads from recycled tires, taillight housings from old plastic bumpers, and splash shields from auto battery casings. Think about that the next time you turn in your empties.

. . . .

■ Identifying Minor Supporting Details

All the details in a paragraph are not equally important. **Minor supporting details** add extra information to major supporting details. The minor supporting details may add interest to the writing, but they are not essential for understanding the author's main idea. They are less important than the major supporting details.

Minor supporting details explain, clarify, give examples, and support major supporting details. You can often identify minor supporting details because the sentences that contain them refer to the sentences containing major supporting details. Minor supporting details are often introduced with phrases like "for example" or "that is" that tell you an example or a clarification is coming up. If we look once again at the paragraph about political power on page 119, we see that each minor supporting detail gives a specific example to support the major supporting detail.

MAJOR SUPPORTING DETAIL:

Presidents exercise power when they persuade reluctant legislators to support their policy positions,

▶ MINOR SUPPORTING DETAIL:

as President Clinton did in 1993, when he convinced a majority of the members of Congress to support his deficit reduction plan despite their many misgivings.

The minor supporting detail gives a specific example of when and how a president exerted power. We see the same pattern in the next sentence.

MAJOR SUPPORTING DETAIL:

Congress exercises power when it initiates policy and obtains reluctant presidential support,

▶ MINOR SUPPORTING DETAIL:

as the Democratic majority did in 1990 when it persuaded then-President George Bush to generate new deficit-reducing revenues through taxes despite his campaign promise not to raise taxes.

The minor supporting detail gives a specific example of when and how Congress exerted power. We see the same pattern once again in the final sentence.

MAJOR SUPPORTING DETAIL:

Interest groups exercise power when they convince political leaders to reverse their positions on policy matters,

▶ MINOR SUPPORTING DETAIL:

as senior citizens' groups did in 1989 when they virtually forced Congress to withdraw a tax to finance the catastrophic health-care plan enacted in the previous year, and as they continued to do in 1993 and 1994, when they participated in the debate over the content of President Clinton's health-care proposals.

The minor supporting details give specific examples of when a special interest group (in this case, senior citizens) exerted power.

Let's take a look at another paragraph adapted from *Health in the New Millennium.*

> Because no two people agree on everything, conflict is inevitable in relationships — even in healthy relationships. Conflicts can arise over money. Partners may have different ideas about how much should be spent for food, for example, or whether or not to leave the lights on when no one is home. Conflicts can arise from communication difficulties. Some couples, for example, do not discuss problems until an explosion occurs. Conflicts can arise over children. Partners may disagree over how many children to have, when to have them, and how to raise them.

The first sentence in this paragraph is the topic sentence, the general statement that conflict is inevitable in relationships. The major supporting details are the large categories that support the topic sentence: (1) "Conflicts can arise over money"; (2) "Conflicts can arise from communication difficulties"; (3) "Conflicts can arise over children." The minor supporting details are the specific examples that illustrate the three major supporting details: (1) Food and lights are examples of money disagreements; (2) explosions are an example of communication difficulties; (3) the number, spacing, and raising of children are examples of conflicts over children.

Exercise 5-4

In the following paragraphs, each sentence is numbered. On the lines below each paragraph, write the number of each sentence that is a minor supporting detail. (The number of blank lines indicate the number of minor supporting details.)

Example:

(1) Two moons move around Mars in orbits close to the planet's surface. (2) Phobos is the inner and larger of the Martian moons. (3) It circles Mars in only seven hours and thirty-nine minutes. (4) Deimos is farther from Mars and somewhat smaller than Phobos. (5) As seen from the Martian surface, Deimos rises in the east and takes about three full

days to creep slowly from one horizon to the other. (Adapted from William J. Kaufmann III and Roger A. Freedman, *Universe*)

SENTENCES THAT PROVIDE MINOR SUPPORTING DETAILS: <u>3</u> , <u>5</u>

1. (1) Our capacity for remembering disconnected items is severely limited. (2) We rarely can remember more than four to seven separate items. (3) These include unconnected words, numbers, and letters. (Adapted from E. D. Hirsch Jr., *Cultural Literacy*)

   SENTENCE THAT PROVIDES MINOR SUPPORTING DETAILS: <u>3</u>

2. (1) Euphemisms (the substitution of more acceptable words for less acceptable ones) can be divided into two general types—positive and negative. (2) The positive ones inflate and magnify, making the euphemized terms seem altogether grander and more important than they really are. (3) Examples are words like *emporiums, parlors, salons,* and *shoppes* to describe small business establishments. (4) The negative ones deflate and diminish, deleting from the language everything that people prefer not to deal with directly. (5) Examples are phrases like *fallen asleep, gone to meet their Maker, passed over the river,* and so on, to describe dying. (Adapted from Hugh Rawson, *A Dictionary of Euphemisms and Other Doubletalk*)

   SENTENCES THAT PROVIDE MINOR SUPPORTING DETAILS: <u>3</u> , <u>5</u>

3. (1) Plants can get sick. (2) Our environment is filled with agents that cause diseases in plants. (3) For example, we know of more than one hundred diseases that can kill a tomato plant. (4) Viruses, fungi, and bacteria can attack tomato leaves. (5) A tiny roundworm can attack the tomato root. (6) Some fungi attack the tomato stem. (7) One bacterium can attack any part of the tomato plant, producing a tumor that gives rise to further tumors. (William K. Purves et al., *Life: The Science of Biology*)

   SENTENCES THAT PROVIDE MINOR SUPPORTING DETAILS: <u>4</u> , <u>5</u> , <u>6</u> , <u>7</u>

4. (1) Over the course of any year, about a third of the adult population is troubled by a bout of insomnia. (2) Such sleeping difficulties can often be traced to stressful life events. (3) Most common among these events are job or school difficulties, troubled relationships, the death of a loved

one, or financial problems. (4) Concerns about sleeping itself can add to whatever waking anxieties the person may already be experiencing. (Adapted from Don H. Hockenbury and Sandra E. Hockenbury, *Discovering Psychology*)

SENTENCE THAT PROVIDES MINOR SUPPORTING DETAILS: ___3___

5. (1) One purpose served by contemporary realistic fiction is to help children learn to cope with their own problems. (2) For example, many children worry about being accepted by their peers, and reading or hearing stories about characters who share this concern may help children deal with it better. (3) In *Will You Be My Friend?* Allison is a typical preschool child, wistfully hoping for a playmate. (4) In *The Hundred Dresses*, a poor Polish girl attempts to win acceptance by talking about the many clothes she has. (5) In *The Popular Girls Club*, the heroine deals with the problem of being excluded from an exclusive club. (Adapted from John Stewig, *Children and Literature*)

SENTENCES THAT PROVIDE MINOR SUPPORTING DETAILS: ___3___ , ___4___ ,
___5___

· ·

■ Using Supporting Details to Understand Unstated Main Ideas

In much of your reading, the main idea will be expressed directly. Paragraphs often have a topic sentence that states the main idea. On many occasions, however, the main idea will be unstated. It will be implied — expressed indirectly. The way a main idea is expressed indirectly is through a group of details that suggest an idea without actually stating it.

Here is an example, adapted from *For All Practical Purposes* by the Consortium for Mathematics and Its Applications.

> Economists, financial advisers, and policy makers in government and business study the latest data on unemployment and inflation. Physicians must understand the origin and trustworthiness of the data that appear in medical journals. Business decisions are based on market research data that reveal consumer tastes. Engineers gather data on the quality and reliability of manufactured products.

In this paragraph, the main idea is not stated directly in a topic sentence. However, we can draw conclusions about that main idea. The unstated main idea is "Data are important in the work of many different professions."

How do we arrive at that statement as the expression of the unstated main idea? First, we identify the topic of the paragraph. We know that the topic is the subject that the paragraph refers to again and again. That subject is *data,* which is mentioned in every sentence. What does the author want to say about the topic of *data*? At first we don't know, but as the author gives one example after another of professionals who use data in their work, we begin to see the connection among the details. By seeing what these supporting details have in common, we can arrive at the conclusion that the main idea is that data are important in the work of many different professions.

Here is another example, adapted from *Life: The Science of Biology.*

Humans generally eat several meals a day. A lion may eat once in several days. A boa constrictor may eat once a month. Hibernating animals may go five to six months without eating.

What is the topic of the paragraph—the subject that is referred to again and again? If you said *eating,* you are correct. What does the author want to say about the topic of *eating*? At first we don't know, but as the author gives specific details about how often different animals eat, we begin to see the connections among the examples. By noticing what the details have in common, we can figure out the general statement that they illustrate. If you said something like "Different animals can go without eating for different lengths of time," you have correctly inferred the unstated main idea.

Exercise 5-5

Identify the unstated main idea for each of the following paragraphs adapted from *Health in the New Millennium.*

Example:

Offering food to guests can be considered a symbol of hospitality, and refusing food can be perceived as refusing hospitality. Food can become a symbol of parental love, and parents may feel hurt if a child doesn't eat all the food on his or her plate. We celebrate achievements, family reunions, and holidays with food. In addition, we often turn to food when our emotional needs are not met.

a. _____ Food is needed for physical survival.

b. __✔__ Food has many symbolic meanings.

1. Weight watchers often try to save calories by skipping breakfast, but that strategy deprives your body of the nutrition it needs to get started on the day. It may also lead to overeating later in the day as your body seeks to make up for the missed meal. Skipping breakfast can lead to eating unplanned snacks or overeating at other meals.

   a. __✓__ Skipping breakfast is not healthy.

   b. _____ Watching your weight is difficult.

2. What does it matter if your frozen waffles have no fat if you pour on gobs of butter and syrup? A cup of fresh unsweetened peaches contains about 72 calories. Yet when it is packed in heavy syrup, it has 190 calories. And if you eat your fruit in cream, you are truly pouring on the fat and calories. A baked potato with skin contains about 220 calories and a trace of fat. One tablespoon of butter adds 11 grams of fat and 100 calories. Covering a meat dish with a cup of canned beef gravy adds some 125 calories. Chicken gravy adds 190 calories; mushroom gravy 120 calories.

   a. __✓__ Food add-ons—butter, syrups, gravies, and so on— are major sources of calories.

   b. _____ A cup of any kind of gravy adds more calories to a dish than a tablespoon of butter does.

3. Choose fat-free popcorn (the air-popped variety) over potato chips. Choose fat-free pretzels (read the labels). Switch from high-fat ice cream to low-fat or fat-free ice cream. Substitute fruits and vegetables for high-calorie snack foods. Fresh fruits make delicious, low-calorie snacks. Most fruits and vegetables are also rich sources of vitamins and fiber.

   a. __✓__ Low-fat snacks are healthier than high-fat ones.

   b. _____ Fruits and vegetables are healthful.

4. A binge is the consumption of a huge amount of food in a short period of time. Have you ever dreaded an approaching test and downed a carton of ice cream to quell your anxiety? We may attempt to drown emotions like anxiety, fear, and depression in chocolate cake. Stuffing ourselves can be the equivalent of stuffing down our anger.

   a. _____ Frequent binge eating can lead to guilt.

   b. __✓__ Negative emotions can lead to bingeing.

5. Some people are so obsessed with their weight that they desire to achieve an exaggerated image of thinness. They may engage in a cycle of binge eating and vomiting to control their weight. They can be subject to many diseases and conditions as a result of malnutrition. They sometimes literally starve themselves to death.

   a. __✓__ Being obsessed with weight can be a great danger to one's health.

   b. _____ People have different ideas about thinness.

Reading the Parts

This essay by Ben Krull appeared on the *New York Times* opinion page on May 10, 2001. A lawyer and avid sports fan, Krull uses many examples throughout the essay to illustrate his point. As you read, pay close attention to the major and minor supporting details and how, exactly, they support each paragraph's main idea. After reading each section and answering the questions that follow, move on to the next section. You will have a chance to read the entire essay when you finish.

BEN KRULL

The Lost Art of Nicknaming

Nicknames aren't what they used to be. Compare A-Rod, the nickname for Alex Rodriguez, baseball's highest-paid player, with the Human Vacuum Cleaner, Brooks Robinson's alias while playing third base for the championship Baltimore Orioles a generation ago. 1

While the nicknames Hammerin' Hank and the Sultan of Swat helped fans of yesteryear envision the home runs hit by Hank Aaron and Babe Ruth, Big Mac makes me think more about hamburgers than the record-breaking home runs slugged by Mark McGwire. The Splendid Splinter effectively depicted the lean frame of Ted Williams. But Junior fails to offer a visual account of Ken Griffey Jr. (To be fair, there are some current baseball nicknames that match up with those given to the old timers. Rocket fits Roger Clemens's rising fastball. Of course, he acquired "Rocket" as a rookie about 17 years ago. If Clemens were starting out today he would probably be called Clem.) 2

1. All of the following are nicknames described in the two paragraphs except

   a. the Human Vacuum Cleaner.

   b. Hammerin' Hank.

   c. Piazza Delivery.

   d. Sultan of Swat.

2. What do the nicknames "Hammerin' Hank" and "Sultan of Swat" help fans envision, according to Ben Krull?

   a. the home runs hit by Ken Griffey Jr. and Ty Cobb

   b. the home runs hit by Hank Aaron and Babe Ruth

   c. the many singles hit by Hank Aaron and Babe Ruth

   d. the record-breaking home runs hit by Sammy Sosa and Mark McGwire

3. Which of the following sentences from the first two paragraphs of Ben Krull's essay best supports the topic sentence "Nicknames aren't what they used to be"?

   a. To be fair, there are some current baseball nicknames that match up with those given to old timers.

   b. Of course, he acquired "Rocket" as a rookie about 17 years ago.

   c. If Clemens were starting out today he would probably be called Clem.

   d. Compare A-Rod, the nickname for Alex Rodriguez, baseball's highest-paid player, with the Human Vacuum Cleaner, Brooks Robinson's alias while playing third base for the championship Baltimore Orioles a generation ago.

4. Why is the nickname "Junior" for Ken Griffey Jr. not effective, according to Krull?

   a. He is not the namesake of a famous baseball player.

   b. It fails to offer a visual account of Ken Griffey Jr.

   c. Someone else on Griffey's team is called "Junior" by his teammates.

   d. It makes Griffey sound like a child.

5. What is the most important element of a good nickname, as implied by Krull?

   a. The nickname must help fans envision the physical and athletic characteristics of the player.

   b. It must be something the fans can remember easily.

   c. It must be something that has never been used before.

   d. It must rhyme with the player's name.

Indeed, outside of wrestling and boxing, sports has become a haven for dumbed-down nicknames. Consider basketball. Whereas the last-second heroics of Jerry West inspired Los Angeles Laker fans of the 1960's to call him Mr. Clutch, the best that today's Angelenos can do for the intimidating Shaquille O'Neal is Shaq. And New York Knick fans, who once chanted "Clyde" in recognition of Walt Frazier's stylish dress, have been reduced to shouting "Spree" when Latrell Sprewell scores a basket. In college basketball, nicknames for winning coaches have devolved from names like the Wizard of Westwood for U.C.L.A.'s John Wooden to pronunciation helpers like Coach K for Mike Krzyzewski of Duke.

3

The diminishing nickname has spread beyond sports. Witness the journey from Old Blue Eyes for Frank Sinatra to J-Lo for Jennifer Lopez. And what about the fall-off from Silent Cal for President Calvin Coolidge to Hill and Bill; from Little Flower for New York City's Depression-era mayor Fiorello La Guardia to today's Rudy?

4

6. Ben Krull states that "sports has become a haven for dumbed-down nicknames," with the exception of two sports. What are they?

   a. basketball and hockey

   b. hockey and tennis

   c. wrestling and boxing

   d. boxing and hockey

7. Why did Los Angeles Laker fans call Jerry West "Mr. Clutch," according to Krull?

   a. Jerry West drove a pickup truck with a broken clutch.

   b. Jerry West carried a clutch bag with his equipment in it.

   c. Jerry West performed well in the last seconds of games, making "clutch" plays and baskets.

   d. Jerry West's middle name is "Clutch," a name he shared with his father, Jerrold Clutch West.

8. Which of the following sentences from paragraphs 3 and 4 best supports the topic sentence "sports has become a haven for dumbed-down nicknames"?

    a.   Consider basketball.

    b.   The diminishing nickname has spread beyond sports.

    c.   Witness the journey from Old Blue Eyes for Frank Sinatra to J-Lo for Jennifer Lopez.

    d.   In college basketball, nicknames for winning coaches have devolved from names like Wizard of Westwood for U.C.L.A.'s John Wooden to pronunciation helpers like Coach K for Mike Krzyzewski of Duke.

9. While New York fans once chanted "Clyde" in recognition of Walt Frazier's stylish dress, they now chant another player's nickname instead, evidence of the lack of good sports nicknames, according to Krull. What is the nickname and who is the player?

    a.   Shaq for Shaquille O'Neal

    b.   The Rocket for Maurice Richard

    c.   The Messiah for Mark Messier

    d.   Spree for Latrell Sprewell

10. What examples does Krull give to support the sentence "The diminishing nickname has spread beyond sports"?

    a.   Frank Sinatra and Jennifer Lopez

    b.   The Rock and Rowdy Roddy Piper

    c.   Slick Willy and "Sullen" Mike Dukakis

    d.   Jesse "the Body" Ventura and Al "the Bore" Gore

> Nicknames once had an important function. Joe DiMaggio's moniker, the Yankee Clipper, helped those who couldn't make it to the ballpark envision the great outfielder chasing fly balls with the grace of a clipper ship gliding on water. Television and other media have increased the visibility of sports figures, politicians, and celebrities, allowing images to supplant words as the primary way people relate to them. As a result, nicknames have been reduced from descriptive tools to a type of shorthand, much like the abbreviated words and uncapitalized letters used in e-mail. 5
>
> Perhaps, though, inspiration for a nickname revival will come from President Bush, who, despite being tagged with the lackluster W, has a penchant for dispensing creative monikers like The Adding Machine, Big Country, and Ostrich Legs. 6

11. In paragraph 5, what example does Krull give to support the topic sentence "Nicknames once had an important function"?

    a.   Mike Piazza as the Pizza Man

    b.   Brooks Robinson as the Human Vacuum Cleaner

    c.   Joe DiMaggio as the Yankee Clipper

    d.   Todd "the Tank" Pratt

12. From whom does Krull think a nickname revival will originate, as stated in paragraph 6?

    a.   Al Gore

    b.   Will Ferrell

    c.   Lorne Michaels

    d.   George W. Bush

13. Who and/or what does Ben Krull credit with increasing "the visibility of sports figures, politicians, and celebrities"?

    a.   television and other media

    b.   Amazon.com and other dot-com companies

    c.   the Internet and the Web

    d.   Ahmad Rashad and the cast of *Survivor*

14. To what, according to Krull in paragraph 5, have nicknames been reduced?

    a.   a type of shorthand

    b.   stupid, catchall phrases

    c.   insipid descriptors

    d.   baby talk

15. Which of the following is not one of the nicknames the author credits George W. Bush with dispensing?

    a.   The Adding Machine

    b.   The Teflon President

    c.   Big Country

    d.   Ostrich Legs

Reading the Whole

Now that you have had a chance to read Ben Krull's essay in its parts and to practice looking for major and minor supporting details, you are better prepared to read the essay in its entirety. As you read, remain aware of how the major and minor supporting details contribute to your understanding of each paragraph. However, also pay attention to the whole flow of the essay. You may find that Krull's humor appeals to you or that you can particularly relate to his opinions. In any case, pay particular attention to the points he makes, and ask yourself whether you think they are valid and why.

BEN KRULL
The Lost Art of Nicknaming

Nicknames aren't what they used to be. Compare A-Rod, the nickname for Alex Rodriguez, baseball's highest-paid player, with the Human Vacuum Cleaner, Brooks Robinson's alias while playing third base for the championship Baltimore Orioles a generation ago. 1

While the nicknames Hammerin' Hank and the Sultan of Swat helped fans of yesteryear envision the home runs hit by Hank Aaron and Babe Ruth, Big Mac makes me think more about hamburgers than the record-breaking home runs slugged by Mark McGwire. The Splendid Splinter effectively depicted the lean frame of Ted Williams. But Junior fails to offer a visual account of Ken Griffey Jr. (To be fair, there are some current baseball nicknames that match up with those given to the old timers. Rocket fits Roger Clemens's rising fastball. Of course, he acquired "Rocket" as a rookie about 17 years ago. If Clemens were starting out today he would probably be called Clem.) 2

Indeed, outside of wrestling and boxing, sports has become a haven for dumbed-down nicknames. Consider basketball. Whereas the last-second heroics of Jerry West inspired Los Angeles Laker fans of the 1960's to call him Mr. Clutch, the best that today's Angelenos can do for the intimidating Shaquille O'Neal is Shaq. And New York Knick fans, who once chanted "Clyde" in recognition of Walt Frazier's stylish dress, have been reduced to shouting "Spree" when Latrell Sprewell scores a basket. In college basketball, nicknames for winning coaches have devolved from names like 3 the Wizard of Westwood for U.C.L.A.'s John Wooden to pronunciation helpers like Coach K for Mike Krzyzewski of Duke.

The diminishing nickname has spread beyond sports. Witness the journey from Old Blue Eyes for Frank Sinatra to J-Lo for Jennifer Lopez. And what about the fall-off from Silent Cal for President Calvin Coolidge to Hill and Bill; from Little Flower for New York City's Depression-era mayor Fiorello La Guardia to today's Rudy?   4

Nicknames once had an important function. Joe DiMaggio's moniker, the Yankee Clipper, helped those who couldn't make it to the ballpark envision the great outfielder chasing fly balls with the grace of a clipper ship gliding on water. Television and other media have increased the visibility of sports figures, politicians, and celebrities, allowing images to supplant words as the primary way people relate to them. As a result, nicknames have been reduced from descriptive tools to a type of shorthand, much like the abbreviated words and uncapitalized letters used in e-mail.   5

Perhaps, though, inspiration for a nickname revival will come from President Bush, who, despite being tagged with the lackluster W, has a penchant for dispensing creative monikers like The Adding Machine, Big Country, and Ostrich Legs.   6

Integrated Skills

1. What is Ben Krull's main idea about the topic of nicknames?

2. What major supporting details does Krull provide to support his idea?

3. What minor details can you identify in Krull's piece about nicknames?

4. What is your own experience with nicknames? How do your nicknames or the nicknames of your friends compare with the kinds of nicknames described by Krull?

Reading Textbooks

Thematic Connections. You've just read sports fan Ben Krull's opinion about nicknames in sports. At first glance, it may seem quite separate from the following passage from the textbook *Marketing: Relationships, Quality, Value* by William G. Nickels and Marian Burk Wood. However, as you read the selection you will see some similarities. The following reading touches on some of the same issues that Krull discusses. Though the *Marketing* passage is about products and Krull writes about sports personalities, ask yourself as you read how the two selections are similar.

Vocabulary Preview

differentiates (para. 1): distinguishes; shows differences (v.)

shorthand (para. 2): abbreviation (n.)

channel partners (para. 3): "middlemen" in business (n.)

convention (para. 4): practice; way of doing things (n.)

pharmaceutical (para. 7): drug; pharmacy (n.)

provocative (para. 9): stimulating; inciting (adj.)

exclusivity (para. 10): specialness; lack of sharing (n.)

Branding Reinforces Marketing Relationships

As a marketer, how can you reinforce marketing relationships by identifying your value package as separate and distinct from competing products? The answer is to use a **brand,** a name, phrase, design, symbol, or a combination that identifies your products and differentiates them from rival products. [1]

To customers, brands are a kind of shorthand representing the unique combination of feature and benefits offered by each branded product. Customers nowadays make so many purchases on the Internet and through telephone and mail orders that branding is essential as a way of distinguishing a marketer's products. Both products and companies can be branded for identification and differentiation. [2]

BRAND TYPES

Both manufacturers and channel partners can use brands to distinguish their value packages from those of competitors and to strengthen customer relationships. A **manufacturer brand,** which is owned by the product's maker, is also known as a *national brand* [3] because it is frequently advertised throughout the country. For example, Hewlett-Packard puts the HP LaserJet brand on certain laser printers, and ConAgra puts the Healthy Choice brand on certain frozen and prepared foods.

When two or more marketers collaborate on a product, they may apply *cobranding,* using more than one manufacturer's brand to identify a jointly developed product. This convention alerts customers to the added value they're getting from a product with two trusted brand names. For example, United Airlines and Visa offer a cobranded credit card that rewards loyalty by giving users one frequent-flier mile for every dollar charged. These mileage awards allow customers to accumulate points that will enable them to travel free.

A **private brand** is one that is owned by a wholesaler or retailer. Also called a *private-label* or *store brand,* this type of identification is used to strengthen relationships with customers. From the customer's perspective, private brands are a lower-priced alternative to manufacturer brands, which accounts for their popularity. Private-brand products are usually made by companies other than the retailer or wholesaler.

Supermarkets, for example, pay manufacturers to make private-brand food and household products. A&P, which introduced private-brand groceries to the industry, offers products under a basic private brand, America's Choice, as well as a premium private brand, Master's Choice. Private-brand groceries account for $30 billion in annual sales in the United States, challenging sales of manufacturer brands.

A **generic brand** carries no brand name. It is identified by the product category alone. Generic brands usually receive no promotional support from marketers or retailers, so they are cheaper than other brands. Drugs marketed in this way, for example, are available as lower-priced substitutes for many pharmaceutical products. For obvious reasons, the practice of generic branding appeals to price-conscious shoppers.

EFFECTIVE BRANDING

To help customers keep a product in mind and tell it apart from others, a brand should be simple, memorable, and distinctive. Brand names such as Ivory and Xerox are easy to say and easy to remember. An effective brand name should also remind customers of the product's key features and benefits. For example, think of Ruffles, the brand name for Frito-Lay's potato chips that have ridges to hold snack dip, or Diet Coke, the brand name for Coca-Cola's low-calorie soft drink. If a brand will be available in other areas or cultures, be sure it is appropriate and translates well. Check also for any legal or regulatory restrictions that might prevent the brand from being used.

Julie Lobdell, cofounder of a California chain of cinnamon roll shops, tells how she and her partner planned the brand name. "We knew 'Bodacious Buns' would be well received in Southern California, but we wanted to make sure it would not be too provocative or misunderstood in other parts of the country," she says. The partners hired a lawyer to review use of the brand in other states. They also legally registered the trademark.

9

What many marketers fear is having their brand names become generic. A *generic name* identifies an entire product category. Did you know that *aspirin, linoleum, nylon, escalator,* and *zipper* were once brand names? When the brands became identified with all versions of the products, they lost their distinctiveness and became generic. The trademark owners could no longer enforce their exclusivity. The manufacturers then had to come up with new brand names. The original Aspirin, for example, became Bayer aspirin. It's easy to see why Rollerblade's lawyers want people to say "in-line skating" rather than using the brand name as the generic term for this activity.

10

Thinking about the Textbook Selection

1. What connections can you identify between Ben Krull's essay on nicknames in sports and this textbook selection on brand names?

2. Why are brands important? What does a brand include, besides its special brand name?

3. Explain the differences among the following: manufacturer's brand, private brand, store brand, and generic brand.

4. What are some qualities of effective branding?

Reviewing

1. Explain what supporting details are and why it is important to recognize them in reading selections.
2. What is the relationship between the supporting details of a paragraph and that paragraph's main idea?
3. Explain the difference between major and minor supporting details.
4. Explain how you can understand the main idea of a paragraph or a passage when it is implied or not stated directly.

In this chapter you learned how to identify supporting details—the specific examples, illustrations, instances, and reasons that support a writer's idea or point of view. You learned to distinguish between major and minor supporting details and had opportunities to practice identifying them in different reading selections. And you also learned how to identify a writer's main idea when it is implied or not stated directly. In addition, you had the chance to practice each of these skills on longer reading selections from a magazine and a textbook.

Chapter 6

Identifying Main Ideas in Longer Selections

Getting Ready   141

Learning the Skills   142

Applying the Skills
• Reading the Parts   163
• Reading the Whole   169
• Reading Textbooks   172

Reviewing   174

Getting Ready

Like paragraphs, longer selections—including whole essays—have a main idea that an author wants to get across to readers. In this chapter, you will look for main ideas in longer selections. Main ideas in longer readings are often called **controlling ideas** because they control the content of an entire piece of writing. The controlling idea of a reading is often stated directly in what is called a thesis statement. This chapter focuses on **thesis statements** and shows how they are supported by **titles**, major and minor **supporting paragraphs**, and **introductions and conclusions.** You will also learn to identify **unstated, or implied, main ideas.**

Chapter Overview

What strategies do you currently use to find the main idea in a longer selection?

What role do major and minor supporting paragraphs and major and minor supporting details play in a longer selection?

Can you **recognize** introductory and concluding paragraphs? Are you aware of the function they serve?

Focusing Questions

Everyday Reading

You have already looked for main ideas of paragraphs in newspaper articles and editorials, advertisements, and other writings outside of college textbooks. For one week, focus on the opinion/editorial page of your favorite newspaper, collecting editorials and reader letters on a single, recurring subject. Make a list of the headlines of each selection and under the headline restate the selection's main point. As you read, carefully note how the authors support their main ideas with major and minor supporting details, introductions, and conclusions. Begin to notice what works well in a piece of writing and what doesn't. Notice, too, how many main ideas can come from the same subject.

Learning the Skills

■ Identifying Thesis Statements

A thesis statement is to a longer reading what a topic sentence is to a paragraph. Both are direct statements of an author's main idea. In a longer reading, you will very often find the thesis statement in the first paragraph. In fact, the thesis statement is sometimes the first sentence of the first paragraph, as it is in the following passage, titled "Bad Luck Superstitions about Umbrellas," adapted from *Panati's Extraordinary Origins of Everyday Things* by Charles Panati.

> Bad luck superstitions about umbrellas began with the Egyptians, who gave religious significance to their intricately designed umbrellas of papyrus and peacock feathers. These early umbrellas were never intended to protect against rain (which was rare and a blessing in arid Egypt), but served as sunshades in the blistering heat of day.
>
> The Egyptians believed that the canopy of the sky was formed by the body of the goddess Nut. With only her toes and fingertips touching the earth, her body spanned the planet like a vast umbrella. Human-made umbrellas were regarded as early embodiments of Nut. Umbrellas, therefore, were suitable only to be held above the heads of nobility. The shade cast by an umbrella outdoors was considered sacred. For a commoner to even accidentally step into that shade was seen as a sin that would lead to bad luck.

Just as we did with paragraphs, we can find the topic—the subject that is repeated again and again—of a longer selection. Also as with paragraphs, determining the topic can be the first step in finding a longer selection's main idea. What is the topic of this writing, the term that is repeated again and again? It is, of course, *umbrellas*. Then we need to ask, "What does the writer want to say about the topic, in this case umbrellas?"

The writer's main idea, the point, the controlling idea, of the two paragraphs is that "bad luck superstitions about umbrellas began with the Egyptians, who gave religious significance to their intricately designed umbrellas." That idea is stated in the first sentence of the first paragraph; that first sentence is the thesis statement of the entire passage. The remainder of the passage describes a bad luck superstition, with religious significance, that the Egyptians held about umbrellas.

Here is the beginning of another selection, called "Benefits of Bone-Strengthening Exercise," adapted from the textbook *Health in the New Millennium* by Jeffrey S. Nevid, Spencer A. Rathus, and Hannah R. Rubenstein.

> Bones are living tissues. They grow in length until age twenty-one, but they continue to change in density, or thickness, throughout life. Unless bones are worked, they become thinner and more brittle. Density gives bones their strength. Stronger bones are less vulnerable to fractures or breaks. When bones are not stressed through repeated use, they begin to lose density as the result of loss of calcium.
>
> Resistance training helps maintain bone density. Resistance training involves working against a weight or force, such as in lifting weights. On average, the bone density of those who exercise regularly is six to eight percent greater than it is in those who don't exercise.

Once more, we ask, "What is the topic of this passage?" What is the subject that is repeated again and again? The answer is *bones*. What do the authors want to say about bones? What is the main idea, the controlling idea, that the authors want to get across to readers? It is that "unless bones are worked, they become thinner and more brittle." The thesis statement of this reading—the sentence that contains the controlling idea—is the third sentence in the first paragraph. All the other sentences describe bones, bone density, and maintaining bone density.

Sometimes the thesis statement may appear at the end of the first paragraph rather than at the beginning, or it may appear in the second paragraph. Sometimes you may even have to put two sentences together to get a complete thesis statement. However, in any long piece of writing, the thesis statement almost always appears in the first few paragraphs. In addition, as we have seen with topic sentences in paragraphs, the main idea may not be stated directly. You may have to infer the main idea—make an educated guess—based on supporting paragraphs and supporting details. We will discuss finding unstated main ideas in longer selections in more detail later in this chapter.

Exercise 6-1

Identify the thesis statement in each of the following selections.

Example:

Your Life and the Internet

I am living proof of the following statement. Health information on the Internet can help save your life. A few years ago, over a period of months my doctor treated me for a variety of medical symptoms. It seemed as if as soon as one symptom was under control, another developed. Finally, based on my symptoms, my medical history, and recent tests, my doctor suggested a diagnosis that might explain everything. I had an ignorant, lay-person's view of the illness he mentioned and rejected his diagnosis.

I continued getting more and more sick—and more and more scared. In desperation, I turned to the Internet. Within minutes, I found a National Institutes of Health site that offered several documents about the illness my doctor had mentioned. I had to read only the first two pages to realize that my doctor's diagnosis was correct. I immediately returned to him and started treatment—a treatment that I'm fully convinced saved my life. Today, with ongoing treatment I'm largely able to control my illness and lead a normal life.

My case is an extreme example of the benefits available from Internet health information. Yet millions of people have similar—if less dramatic—stories to tell about how health information they found on the Internet has helped improve their lives. (Bruce Maxwell, *How to Find Health Information on the Internet*)

a. _____ I am living proof of the following statement.

b. _✓_ Health information on the Internet can help save your life.

1. **Automatic Behavior**

Have you ever said "excuse me" to a store mannequin or written a check in January with the previous year's date? When we're in the automatic behavior mode, we take in and use limited signals from the world around us without letting other signals penetrate as well.

Once, in a small department store, I gave a cashier a new credit card. Noticing that I hadn't signed it, she handed it back to me to sign. Then she took my card, passed it through her machine, handed me the receipt, and asked me to sign it. I did as I was told. The cashier then held the receipt next to the newly signed card to see if the signatures matched. (Ellen J. Langer, *Mindfulness*)

a. _____ When we're in the automatic behavior mode, we take in and use limited signals from the world around us without letting other signals penetrate as well.

b. _____ Have you ever said "excuse me" to a store mannequin or written a check in January with the previous year's date?

2. **Industrial versus Consumer Markets**

Industrial marketing involves exchanges among manufacturers. Industrial marketing involves exchanges that eventually get to consumers, but there are many differences between industrial markets and consumer markets. Here are some of these differences.

The demand for industrial goods is *derived from* the demand for consumer goods. For example, the demand for lumber depends on the demand for new houses, and much of the demand for steel is based on the demand for new cars.

The demand for industrial goods is *less price sensitive* than is the demand for consumer goods. For example, an industrywide price increase in tires will not stop automakers from putting tires on new cars — but it may stop some consumers from replacing old tires.

Industrial purchases often involve a *long negotiating period*. A consumer product may be purchased in a matter of seconds, but months or years may elapse before a final sale is made of some types of industrial products, such as large machines for manufacturing. (Adapted from Kenneth Blanchard, Charles Schewe, Robert Nelson, and Alexander Hiam, *Exploring the World of Business*)

a. _____ Industrial marketing involves exchanges among manufacturers.

b. _____ Industrial marketing involves exchanges that eventually get to consumers, but there are many differences between industrial markets and consumer markets.

3. **Personality Disorders**

The student of abnormal psychology faces two problems in learning about personality disorders. One problem is that not all experts agree that such disorders are legitimate psychological syndromes. The disagreement hinges on the question of whether or not such traits really exist as consistent ways of responding across life situations. For example, is an individual antisocial in all life situations?

The second problem is the unreliability of the diagnosis. Some of the individual personality disorders are considered too unreliable for practical usefulness. It is difficult to decide at which point a disorder really exists. The symptoms of personality disorders range from expressions commonly found in a normal population to severely pathological expressions. For example, dependency of a mild sort is found in the interpersonal relationships of otherwise happily well-adjusted individuals. (Timothy W. Costello and Joseph T. Costello, *Abnormal Psychology*)

a. _____ The symptoms of personality disorders range from expressions commonly found in a normal population to severely pathological expressions.

b. _____ The student of abnormal psychology faces two problems in learning about personality disorders.

4. **Sports Choices**

We all have different reasons for selecting and sticking with (or not) our sports of choice and the accompanying hard work. Most of the athletes we interviewed said that the main reason they got into their sport was "because it seemed like fun." All of the younger children we interviewed also said that they participate in sports for fun. While their parents may be signing them up for exercise, social, and even baby-sitting purposes, the kids clearly believe fun is the reason for joining a sport.

There are some exceptions, of course. For example, baseball player Croteau says she initially wanted a high school varsity letter. Some women athletes got into sports because an older brother said they couldn't. Some, like 6'5" basketball star Lisa Leslie, took up a sport because someone assigned it to them: "You should play basketball!"

For whatever the reasons we participate competitively or recreationally, whether for weight loss or rehabilitation or Olympic gold or just to get away from the kids (or parents), we've probably wondered at some point, "Why am I doing this? Why do I bother?" Whatever the reasons to start, and whatever the reasons to continue or to stop, they are sure to be of a personal nature. (Alexandra Powe-Allred and Michelle Powe, *The Quiet Storm: A Celebration of Women in Sport*)

a. _____ Most of the athletes we interviewed said that the main reason they got into their sport was "because it seemed like fun."

b. _____ We all have different reasons for selecting and sticking with (or not) our sports of choice and the accompanying hard work.

5. Farewell, My Lovely

I see by the new Sears Roebuck catalogue that it is still possible to buy an axle for a 1909 Model T Ford, but I am not deceived. The great days of the Model T have faded. The end is in sight. Only one page in the current catalogue is devoted to parts and accessories for the Model T; yet everyone remembers springtimes when the Ford gadget section was larger than men's clothing, almost as large as household furnishings. The last Model T was built in 1927, and the car is fading from what scholars call the American scene, which is an understatement. To a few million people who grew up with it, the old Ford practically *was* the American scene.

It was the miracle God had wrought. And it was the sort of thing that could only happen once. Mechanically uncanny, it was like nothing that had ever come to the world before. Flourishing industries rose and fell with it. As a vehicle, it was hard-working, commonplace, heroic; and it often seemed to transmit those qualities to the persons who rode in it. My own generation identifies it with Youth, with its gaudy irretrievable excitements. (Lee Strout White, "Farewell, My Lovely," in Cleanth Brooks, John Thibaut Purser, and Robert Penn Warren, *An Approach to Literature*)

a. _____ I see by the new Sears Roebuck catalogue that it is still possible to buy an axle for a 1909 Model T Ford, but I am not deceived.

b. _____ The great days of the Model T have faded. The end is in sight.

Exercise 6-2

Underline the thesis statement in each of the following selections, adapted from the college textbook *Life: The Science of Biology* by William K. Purves, Gordon H. Orians, H. Craig Heller, and David Sadava.

Example:

Red Maples

One of the most familiar native trees in the eastern United States is the red, or scarlet, maple. The red maple does not provide us with a great variety of useful products, but it enriches us by its beauty.

Not only is it abundant in forests, but we admire it in parks and as a street tree growing as high as ten to thirty meters tall. We use its wood as lumber, although the sugar maple is a more important commercial source of maple wood.

The red maple leaf—the symbol of Canada—consists of a single blade with three to five lobes and with veins that radiate from a single focal point. These leaves are among the brilliant contributors to the fall colors of eastern forests. The small, scarlet flowers have four sepals, four petals, eight stamens, and one pistil. The distinctive winged fruit of the maple family contains two seeds.

1. **Coconut Palms**

   In some cultures, the coconut palm is called the tree of life because every aboveground part of the plant has value to humans. People use the stem—the trunk—of this tropical coastal lowland tree for lumber. They dry the sap from its trunk to use as a sugar, or they ferment it to drink. They use the leaves to thatch their homes and to make hats and baskets. They eat the bud at the top of the trunk in salads.

   The coconut fruit also serves many purposes. The hard shell can be used as a container or burnt as fuel. The middle layer of the fruit wall can be made into mats and ropes. The seed of the coconut palm provides both coconut milk and coconut meat. Because the refreshing and delicious milk contains no bacteria or other pathogens, it is a particularly important drink wherever the water is not fit for drinking.

   Millions of people get most of their protein from coconut meat. In addition, coconut oil is the most widely used vegetable oil in the world; it is used in the manufacture of a range of products from hydraulic brake fluid to synthetic rubber and, although nutritionally poor, as food.

2. **Three Principal Plant Organs**

   The body of many plants is divided into three principal organs: the **leaves,** the **stem,** and the **roots.** Taken together, a stem, its leaves, and any flowers are called a shoot. The **shoot system** of a plant consists of all stems and leaves. The **root system** consists of all primary and secondary roots.

   Broadly speaking, the leaves are the chief organs of photosynthesis. The stem holds and displays the leaves to the sun, allowing the greatest possible amount of photosynthesis and providing the transporting connections between the roots and the leaves. Roots anchor the plant in place, and their extreme branching and fine form adapt them to absorb water and mineral nutrients from the soil.

3. **Root Systems**

   Water and minerals usually enter the plant through the root system, of which there are two principal types. Some plants have a **taproot system:** a single, large, deep-growing root accompanied by smaller secondary roots. The taproot itself often functions as a food storage organ, as in carrots and radishes.

By contrast, other plants have a **fibrous root system,** which is composed of numerous thin roots roughly equal in diameter. Fibrous root systems often have a tremendous surface area for the absorption of water and minerals. A fibrous root system holds soil very well, giving grasses that have such systems a protective role on steep hillsides where runoff from rain could cause erosion.

4. **Plant Support Systems**

Water holds up plants that grow in water, but plants that grow on land must either sprawl on the ground or somehow be supported against gravity. There are two principal types of support for land plants. One type of support comes from what is called the turgor pressure of the cells in the plant body. Turgor pressure is like the air pressure in a tire. A small plant can maintain an erect posture if its cells are turgid, but it collapses—wilts—if the turgor pressure falls too low.

Support by the turgor pressure is often strengthened by the second type of support, the presence of strengthening tissue. Some strengthening tissue is flexible while others provide rigid, stronger support.

The most important support for many plants is wood. Wood is such a strong yet lightweight material that we have used it in buildings, furniture, and other structures for millennia.

5. **Colonization and Extinction**

When Polynesian people settled in Hawaii about 2,000 years ago, they quickly exterminated, probably by hunting, thirty-nine species of native land birds, including seven species of geese, three species of owls, at least fifteen finches, and a small hawk.

No people lived in New Zealand until about 1,000 years ago, when the Polynesian ancestors of the Maori colonized the island. Hunting by the Maori caused the extinction of thirteen species of flightless birds called moas, some of which were larger than ostriches.

When humans arrived in North America over the Bering land bridge, about 20,000 years ago, they encountered a rich variety of large mammals. Most of those species were exterminated within a few thousand years. A similar extermination of large animals followed the human colonization of Australia, about 40,000 years ago. All the species in thirteen major categories of animals had become extinct by 18,000 years ago.

Do you see a pattern here? <u>Human-caused extinction of species has lessened the biological diversity of the Earth.</u>

. . . .

◼ Thinking about Titles

A title can be a shortcut to identifying the topic—the subject—of a longer piece of writing. If we ask the same question of the title of a longer reading as we do about the topic of a paragraph—"What does the author want to say about this?"—we may be able to zero in on the thesis statement in the same way that we were able to zero in on the topic sentence of a paragraph. Once you have looked at the title and have spent enough time with the selection to determine the general topic, the question "What point does the author want to make about this subject?" will lead you directly to the thesis sentence. When you find the sentence in the selection that best describes the author's point, that is the thesis statement.

Look again at some of the titles of the selections in this chapter's exercises—for example, "Bad Luck Superstitions about Umbrellas," "Your Life and the Internet," and "Red Maples." What does the author want to say about "bad luck superstitions about umbrellas"? He wants to make the point that bad luck superstitions about umbrellas began with the Egyptians, who gave religious significance to their umbrellas. What point does the author want to make about "your life and the Internet"? He wants to make the point that health information on the Internet can save your life. What point do the authors want to make about "red maples"? They want to make the point that the red maple doesn't give us many useful products but enriches us with its beauty.

◼ Identifying Supporting Paragraphs

Just as details can support a topic sentence in a single paragraph, whole paragraphs can support a thesis statement in a longer reading. Supporting paragraphs provide examples, statistics, facts, illustrations, information, and so on that prove, illustrate, clarify—in short, support— the thesis statement. With what you know about supporting details in paragraphs, you will see this easily in longer readings. Look at the support for the thesis statement in some of the passages you have already seen.

Bad Luck Superstitions about Umbrellas

Bad luck superstitions about umbrellas began with the Egyptians, who gave religious significance to their intricately designed umbrellas of papyrus and peacock feathers. These early umbrellas were never intended to protect against rain (which was rare and a blessing in arid Egypt), but served as sunshades in the blistering heat of day.

The Egyptians believed that the canopy of the sky was formed by the body of the goddess Nut. With only her toes and fingertips touching the earth, her body spanned the planet like a vast umbrella. Human-made umbrellas were regarded as early embodiments of Nut. Umbrellas, therefore, were suitable only to be held above the heads of nobility. The shade cast by an umbrella outdoors was considered sacred. For a commoner to even accidentally step into that shade was seen as a sin that would lead to bad luck.

We have already identified the thesis statement as the first sentence of the first paragraph: "Bad luck superstitions about umbrellas began with the Egyptians, who gave religious significance to their intricately designed umbrellas of papyrus and peacock feathers." The second paragraph is a supporting paragraph. Through the description of the goddess Nut and her connection with the umbrella, the paragraph gives an example of a bad luck superstition about umbrellas that is directly related to Egyptian religion.

Here is another passage you have seen before. You have already determined that the thesis statement is the second sentence in the first paragraph. How does the second paragraph support the thesis statement?

Automatic Behavior

Have you ever said "excuse me" to a store mannequin or written a check in January with the previous year's date? When we're in the automatic behavior mode, we take in and use limited signals from the world around us without letting other signals penetrate as well.

Once, in a small department store, I gave a cashier a new credit card. Noticing that I hadn't signed it, she handed it back to me to sign. Then she took my card, passed it through her machine, handed me the receipt, and asked me to sign it. I did as I was told. The cashier then held the receipt next to the newly signed card to see if the signatures matched.

You are correct if you said something like "The second paragraph is a specific example of someone in automatic behavior mode." Because the cashier *always* checked the signature on the receipt with the signature on the credit card, she did so in this case. But this case was different. Both signatures had just been written. Of course they would be the same! If the card had been stolen, there would be no way to know that by checking the signatures. The cashier hadn't let "other signals penetrate."

You can apply everything you have learned about major and minor supporting details to supporting paragraphs. The second paragraph in the preceding passage is a major supporting paragraph. It gives an example that directly supports the thesis statement.

Here is another passage you have seen before.

Plant Support Systems

Water holds up plants that grow in water, but plants that grow on land must either sprawl on the ground or somehow be supported against gravity. There are two principal types of support for land plants. One type of support comes from what is called the turgor pressure of the cells in the plant body. Turgor pressure is like the air pressure in a tire. A small plant can maintain an erect posture if its cells are turgid, but it collapses—wilts—if the turgor pressure falls too low.

Support by the turgor pressure is often strengthened by the second type of support, the presence of strengthening tissue. Some strengthening tissue is flexible while others provide rigid, stronger support.

The most important support for many plants is wood. Wood is such a strong yet lightweight material that we have used it in buildings, furniture, and other structures for millennia.

In this passage, the thesis statement is "There are two principal types of support for land plants." The two major supporting details, as you would expect, explain exactly what those two principal types of support are. The first major supporting detail is in the first paragraph: "One type of support comes from what is called the turgor pressure of the cells in the plant body." The second major supporting detail is in the second paragraph: "Support by the turgor pressure is often strengthened by the second type of support, the presence of strengthening tissue."

But now look at the third paragraph, which describes wood. The third paragraph is a minor supporting paragraph because it supports a major supporting paragraph, the second one. The third paragraph gives the most important example of the second major supporting detail, the second type of plant support.

■ Looking at Introductions and Conclusions

INTRODUCTIONS

Introductory sentences or introductory paragraphs sometimes lead the way into the thesis statement. These introductions often grab readers' attention so that they will want to read further to see what the author is getting at. Look again at the beginning of "Automatic Behavior."

> Have you ever said "excuse me" to a store mannequin or written a check in January with the previous year's date? When we're in the automatic behavior mode, we take in and use limited signals from the world around us without letting other signals penetrate as well.

The first sentence is an introductory sentence. It is a lighthearted, specific, interesting example that makes a person want to read on. It leads directly into the more general, more serious thesis statement.

The selection "Your Life and the Internet" begins similarly. An attention-catching statement is followed by the thesis statement.

> I am living proof of the following statement. Health information on the Internet can help save your life.

Sometimes authors will use an entire paragraph — or even more — to lead up to the thesis statement. Here is an example from an essay called "Elvis Presley's Purple Cadillac," in Harvey Rachlin's book *Jumbo's Hide, Elvis's Ride, and the Tooth of the Buddha.*

The car languished in a backyard shed for many years, then was left out in an open field, where, exposed to the elements, it began to crumble away. The 1956 convertible Cadillac Eldorado Baritz had been a precious possession of Elvis Presley's when he was a hot young rock 'n' roll star, but just as he faded from public view for a time in his later years only to reemerge in a new blaze of glory, so his car was forgotten until it was rescued at an auction and restored by a used car dealer and his wife, both Elvis fans.

Elvis Presley had a passion for cars. Once his new fame had accorded him sufficient income, he purchased a pink Cadillac in December 1954. Some months later this car caught on fire and was destroyed, and in the summer of 1955 Elvis acquired another Cadillac, a pink Fleetwood. The next year he bought a pink Cadillac limousine. When it became widely known that Elvis was driving pink Cadillacs, he was forced to give them up, as his car would be mobbed.

The thesis statement is the first sentence of the second paragraph: "Elvis Presley had a passion for cars." The whole first paragraph is an introduction. That introductory paragraph captures readers' attention by beginning with the story of a deserted Cadillac.

Instead of functioning only as "interest grabbers," introductory paragraphs often give background information. Look at this excerpt from the reference book *Twentieth-Century American Literature*.

Zora Neale Hurston

Zora Neale Hurston was probably born on January 7, 1901, in America's first all-black incorporated town, Eatonville, Florida. In her teens, five years after the death of her mother, Hurston left Eatonville to work as a maid for a traveling Gilbert and Sullivan troupe. She studied at Morgan College in Baltimore and at Howard University, where her first short story appeared in the college literary magazine. She later won a scholarship to Barnard College to study with the famous anthropologist Franz Boas. While living in New York, Hurston worked as a secretary to the popular novelist Fannie Hurst.

Hurston is considered a major force in the Harlem Renaissance of the 1920s and 1930s. She collaborated on several plays with other

continued

writers, including Langston Hughes. Boas arranged a fellowship for Hurston, which allowed her to travel throughout the South and collect folklore. The result of these travels was the publication of a collection of black folk tales, *Mules and Men* (1935). Hurston is thought to be the first black American to have collected and published Afro-American folklore. In later years, her interest in anthropology took her to several Latin American countries, including Jamaica, Haiti, and Honduras.

Hurston's first novel, *Jonah's Gourd Vine,* is loosely based on the lives of her parents in Eatonville. Her best-known work is the novel *Their Eyes Were Watching God.* She published two collections of black folklore, which are considered an excellent source for myths and legends about black culture. Her autobiography, *Seraph on the Suwanee,* appeared in 1948. Hurston's other honors included Guggenheim Fellowships in 1936 and 1938. She died on January 28, 1960, in Fort Pierce, Florida.

The first paragraph of the selection is an introductory paragraph that gives background information; it tells about the early life of author Zora Neale Hurston. The thesis statement is the first sentence of the second paragraph: "Hurston is considered a major force in the Harlem Renaissance of the 1920s and 1930s." Most of the second and third paragraphs support the thesis statement; that is, they explain the achievements that caused Hurston to be considered a major force in the black literary movement of the 1920s that flourished in the Harlem district of New York City.

CONCLUSIONS

A concluding sentence or a concluding paragraph "closes" a reading and makes it feel finished. The preceding selection on Zora Neale Hurston ends with a concluding sentence: "She died on January 28, 1960, in Fort Pierce, Florida." Unlike the other sentences in the third paragraph, this sentence does not support the thesis statement. It serves instead to bring the whole reading to a conclusion. Notice how it balances the first sentence of the reading. It brings us full circle, from Hurston's birth to her death.

A concluding paragraph sometimes restates the thesis statement that appears early in the piece. You may recall that the thesis statement in "Sports Choices" is the first sentence: "We all have different reasons for selecting and sticking with (or not) our sports of choice and the accompanying hard work." Here again is the last paragraph of that selection.

> For whatever the reasons we participate competitively or recreationally, whether for weight loss or rehabilitation or Olympic gold or just to get away from the kids (or parents), we've probably wondered at some point, "Why am I doing this? Why do I bother?" Whatever the reasons to start, and whatever the reasons to continue or to stop, they are sure to be of a personal nature.

The last sentence in this concluding paragraph is a restatement of the original thesis statement. Repeating the thesis statement, or restating it in different words, is another way of coming full circle in a piece of writing. It gives the reader a sense of closure; it feels like an ending.

Concluding sentences or concluding paragraphs can also make predictions about the future, tell readers where to get further information, or suggest further avenues of thought. Look at the following passage, from *For All Practical Purposes: Mathematical Literacy in Today's World* by a group of authors called the Consortium for Mathematics and Its Applications.

> ## The Mathematical Bernoullis
>
> Few families have made more contributions to mathematics than the Bernoullis of Basel, Switzerland. No fewer than seven Bernoullis, over three generations spanning the years between 1680 and 1800, were distinguished mathematicians. Four of them helped build the new mathematics of probability.
>
> Jakob (1654–1748) and Johann (1667–1748) were sons of a prosperous Swiss merchant, but they studied mathematics against the will of their practical father. Both were among the finest mathematicians of their times, but it was Jakob who concentrated on probability. He was the first to see clearly the idea of a long-run proportion as a way of measuring chance.
>
> Johann's son Daniel (1700–1782) and Jakob and Johann's nephew Nicholas (1687–1759) also studied probability. Nicholas saw that the pattern of births of male and female children could
>
> *continued*

be described by probability. Despite his own rebellion against his father's strictures, Johann tried to make his son Daniel a merchant or a doctor. Daniel, undeterred, became yet another Bernoulli mathematician. In the field of probability, he worked to fairly price games of chance and gave evidence for the effectiveness of inoculation against smallpox.

The Bernoulli family in mathematics, like their contemporaries the Bachs in music, is an unusual example of talent in one field appearing in successive generations. The Bernoullis' work helped probability to grow from its birthplace in the gambling hall to a respectable tool with worldwide applications.

The first paragraph of this selection contains the thesis statement, which consists of the second and third sentences. The next two paragraphs are major supporting paragraphs that describe the four Bernoullis who helped build the mathematics of probability.

The final paragraph, the concluding paragraph, makes a general statement about the Bernoullis, comparing them with the Bach family, and then goes on to bring the Bernoullis' work up to the present.

■ Identifying Unstated Main Ideas in Longer Selections

Just as the main idea in a paragraph may be stated or unstated, the main idea in a longer selection may also be stated or unstated. In longer selections, readers have more information to understand and it is more likely that the main idea will be stated directly in a thesis statement to help them. However, sometimes writers leave the main idea of a longer selection unstated, or implied.

In the same way that you find a paragraph's unstated main idea by examining its supporting details, you will use the introduction, supporting paragraphs, and conclusion of a longer selection to help you identify the selection's unstated main idea. To determine the main idea of a longer selection when it is unstated, try following these five steps:

1. Identify the topic of the selection.
2. Observe the major and minor supporting details and the major and minor supporting paragraphs.
3. Look for connections among the details.

4. Answer these two questions: What do the details reveal about the topic? What idea about the topic do the details imply?

5. State the implied main idea in one sentence, using your own words.

When you state the implied main idea of a reading selection in your own words, you are making **inferences** based on your **observations** about details the passage includes. From your observations and your inferences, you draw a conclusion about the main idea of the passage. You will learn more about this process in Chapters 8 ("Making Observations and Connections") and 9 ("Making Inferences and Drawing Conclusions"), but you already have a sense of what is involved from your reading of Chapter 1.

Exercise 6-3

Read the following passage, adapted from the textbook *Health in the New Millennium,* and answer the questions that follow. The questions will help you analyze this longer reading selection.

The Healthy Personality

Who are you? Are you optimistic or pessimistic? Are you independent or group-minded? Are you one of your favorite people, or do you get down on yourself? Are you hard-driving or easy-going? 1

No two of us are quite alike. Your personality is distinct, but is it healthy? Though professionals may argue about the particular group of traits that constitute a healthy personality, there is general agreement that both self-esteem and self-confidence enter the picture. 2

Self-esteem refers to our sense of self-worth. Psychologically healthy people have positive self-esteem. They value themselves and consider themselves worthy of success. They also recognize their deficits and limitations. Thus they have a positive but realistic view of themselves. 3

Self-esteem plays a critical role in the choices we make about our health. Those with high self-esteem are less likely to abuse their health by drinking to excess, ignoring guidelines for safer sex, or denying the signs of illness. 4

Our self-esteem rises when we are good to ourselves. Eliminating unhealthful habits enhances self-esteem. Virtually all former smokers feel better about themselves than they did when they were smoking. So do people who eat a balanced diet and exercise regularly. 5

Psychologically healthy people are also self-confident. They believe   6
in their ability to get things done, such as completing a college course or
doing a back flip off a diving board. They are more likely to face the
challenges of life rather than retreat from them. They are more likely to
grasp opportunities, such as starting a new career, taking up a new sport
or hobby, and making healthful changes in their behavior. They are also
more likely to stick to their efforts, even when they confront obstacles
in their path.

Self-confidence and success go hand in hand. People who have self-   7
confidence are more likely to succeed in accomplishing the tasks that
they undertake. Yet success also boosts self-confidence. This is one reason that "success experiences" are so important to children and adults
alike.

Self-confidence is a strong predictor of positive health outcomes. It   8
predicts who will recover most successfully from a heart attack and
who will be better able to cope with the pain of arthritis. During child-
birth, women with more self-confidence are more likely to waive pain-
killing medication. People with self-confidence are less likely to relapse
once they have quit smoking or lost weight.

People with healthy personalities do not see their health as a matter   9
of luck or chance. They see themselves as responsible for their fates.
What about you? Are you the master of your fate? Or do you see your
prospects as subject to the whim of others or to blind luck?

Example:

Which question will better help you to understand the main
idea of this selection?

a. ___✔___ What point do the authors want to make about the
healthy personality?

b. _____ Is self-esteem more important than self-confidence
for a healthy personality?

1. What is the function of paragraph 1?

a. _____ It provides major supporting details.

b. _____ It is an introductory paragraph.

2. Which is the thesis statement of this selection?

    a. _____ No two of us are quite alike. Your personality is distinct, but is it healthy?

    b. _____ Though professionals may argue about the particular group of traits that constitute a healthy personality, there is general agreement that both self-esteem and self-confidence enter the picture.

3. What is the function of paragraph 3?

    a. _____ It is a major supporting paragraph.

    b. _____ It is a minor supporting paragraph.

4. What is the function of paragraph 4?

    a. _____ It is a major supporting paragraph.

    b. _____ It is a minor supporting paragraph.

5. What is the function of paragraph 5?

    a. _____ It is a major supporting paragraph.

    b. _____ It is a minor supporting paragraph.

6. What is the function of the first sentence of paragraph 6?

    a. _____ It is a major supporting detail.

    b. _____ It is a minor supporting detail.

7. What is the function of the first sentence of paragraph 7?

    a. _____ It is a major supporting detail.

    b. _____ It is a minor supporting detail.

8. What is the function of paragraph 9?

    a. _____ It is a major supporting paragraph.

    b. _____ It is a concluding paragraph.

9. How does paragraph 9 work?

    a. _____ It repeats the thesis statement.

    b. _____ It balances the first paragraph by asking readers questions about themselves.

10. Which sentence better states the main idea of the selection?

    a. _____ Self-esteem is the same as self-confidence.

    b. _____ Self-esteem and self-confidence are both necessary.

Reading the Parts

This essay, from the May 7, 2001, issue of *U.S. News and World Report,* is written by Susan Brink, a senior writer who reports on science and technology issues. As you read, pay particular attention to how the title, the supporting paragraphs, the introduction, and the conclusion help you to identify the thesis statement. After reading each section and answering the questions that follow, move on to the next section. You will have a chance to read the entire essay when you finish.

SUSAN BRINK

Your Brain on Alcohol

Ask any alcoholic trying to take it just one day at a time, and he'll tell you that compulsive drinking is a disease—period. That's what the Big Book said, after all, the groundbreaking tome by Alcoholics Anonymous that came out way back in 1939. And that's what just about everyone has believed ever since.

But hold on. Technology, not for the first time, is forcing doctors and therapists to see things in a new light. With the aid of sophisticated new imaging techniques, scientists can look inside the brains of alcoholics at the very moment they're being tempted by thoughts of cold beers, crisp martinis, or fully ripened cabernet francs. The new science shows just how alcohol can rewire the circuitry of the brain, eroding its ability to feel pleasure and act wisely, and replacing it with a locus for intense craving and destructive behavior. "Alcoholism is a disease that interferes with home life, work, interpersonal relationships, and eventually with health," says James West, medical director emeritus of the Betty Ford Center in Rancho Mirage, Calif. "It's biological, but it's also psychosocial."

The picture is a scary one. But the good news is that it's changing the way doctors and specialists are thinking about the treatment of alcoholism. Until recently, largely believing they had nothing to offer, physicians have left such treatment to counselors, recovering drinkers, and clergy. The result has been a hodgepodge of therapies, some with good results, others merely good intentions.

1. Read paragraphs 1–3 and choose the phrase that best represents the topic of these three paragraphs.

   a. Alcoholics Anonymous and the treatment of alcoholics

   b. what doctors are learning about the effects of alcohol on the brain.

   c. biology and psychosocial behavior of alcoholics

   d. physicians who treat alcoholics

2. Considering paragraphs 1–3, what group does the author credit with the acknowledgment that compulsive drinking is a disease?

   a. the American Medical Association

   b. Mothers Against Drunk Driving

   c. Alcoholics Anonymous

   d. the American Bar Association

3. Reread paragraphs 1–3. Who is credited with saying that alcoholism is "biological, but it's also psychosocial"?

   a. Betty Ford   c. James West

   b. the Big Book   d. Gerald Ford

4. What or who is "forcing doctors and therapists to see things in a new light" regarding alcoholism, according to Susan Brink in paragraph 2?

   a. members of Alcoholics Anonymous

   b. patients at the Betty Ford clinic

   c. technology

   d. physicians studying alcoholism

5. In paragraph 3 Brink says, "The picture is a scary one." What is the good news about recent research developments concerning alcoholism?

   a. Physicians have discovered that alcoholism is totally biological and can be controlled.

   b. Doctors and specialists are changing the way they think about treatment of alcoholism.

   c. Doctors think that alcoholics can be cured.

   d. Doctors no longer should be treating alcoholics.

Now doctors are weighing in—big time. The most promising area of research is the new drugs that target specific areas of the brain to help ease the craving for liquor. One such drug—the first of its kind—has shown promise in quelling the terrible yen for a drink. Naltrexone has been approved by the Food and Drug Administration and is available by prescription. Two more drugs that also may ease craving are being tested in clinical trials.

4

But even proponents of pharmaceutical treatment say drugs aren't the whole answer. Most alcoholics will still need counseling or 12-step programs to help confront the harm they may have caused or the growing up they need to do. Yet just as Prozac got general practitioners interested in depression, anticraving drugs might get more physicians involved in alcoholism treatment. Says Keith Humphreys, a psychologist and addiction researcher at Stanford University: "Doctors want to be able to do something medically."

5

Brain Pain. The new brain-imaging technology will be the key to determining how much, and how effectively, doctors can help. Some 14 million people in the United States are alcoholics or abuse alcohol. They are skid-row bums and lace-curtain drunks, senseless rebels and charming rogues. They chill Louis Roederer Cristal champagne in silver buckets and swill Budweiser from plastic cups. They tell themselves they are not alcoholics because they never drink before 5 P.M., or because they make it to work every day, or because dinner is always on the table on time.

6

But their excuses can't overcome the damage they do. Inga fell down a flight of stairs with her infant in her arms. Mark had five wives, and five divorces. Betty polished off a pint of vodka, then carpooled fourth graders from soccer practice. Jeffrey committed strong-armed robbery. April, once shy, took off her clothes and danced for money. Martha threatened her husband with a carving knife. Paula slipped into the kitchen during dinner parties to swill down the last drops of wine left in dirty goblets. All are recovering alcoholics and they are ashamed of these recollections.

7

6. According to the information presented in paragraph 4, what is the most promising area of research regarding drugs for alcoholics?

   a.   those that target specific areas of the brain to help ease the craving for liquor

b. those that completely suppress the desire for alcohol

c. those that allow alcoholics to drink without feeling the negative effects of alcohol

d. those that treat the "whole patient" as opposed to just the symptoms

7. What drug, the first of its kind, has "shown promise in quelling the terrible yen for a drink," according to Susan Brink?

a. Zoloft

b. Anacin

c. Prozac

d. Naltrexone

8. Reread paragraph 6, under the heading "Brain Pain." How many people in the United States are alcoholics or abuse alcohol?

a. 1 million

b. 10 million

c. 14 million

d. 20 million

9. What is the main idea of paragraph 7?

a. funny alcoholics

b. the destructive things alcoholics can do when drunk

c. ashamed alcoholics and their families

d. drunk driving and alcoholics

10. Reread paragraphs 4 and 5. What is the main idea of this section of Susan Brink's essay?

a. new drugs for alcoholism and doctors' roles in treatment

b. Naltrexone and its effects

c. pharmaceutical companies and their opinions on new drugs

d. why alcoholics need 12-step programs

    For active alcoholics, drinking trumps reason. It distorts judgment. It severs the connection between behavior and consequence. It lays waste to marriages, friendships, and careers. It leaves children stranded. For alcoholics, love and logic can't hold a candle to liquor.   8

    And the damage is not limited to others. Over time, addiction becomes an enervating trial for the drinker. "I would always drink out of glasses that were opaque so my husband couldn't tell what I was drinking," says Jackie Clarke, sober for 16 years. "I would put   9 vodka in my wine because wine seemed more acceptable. I was always thinking about what I was going to drink, when I was going to drink, hiding bottles so my husband wouldn't know how much I drank. It was exhausting."

Just where alcohol abuse crosses the line into addiction remains blurry. John Schwarzlose, president of the Betty Ford Center, has his own simple criterion: An alcohol abuser might get stopped once while driving under the influence, and the experience will be mortifying—and sobering. For an alcoholic, however, the embarrassment is not enough. "Two or more DUIs—that is an alcoholic," says Schwarzlose. But it is often a meaningless distinction to family members, loved ones, and employers. They know that excessive drinking can ruin lives through betrayal, broken promises, lost jobs, car accidents, and a host of other personal tragedies.

10

11. Reread paragraph 8. Which sentence best describes how "active alcoholics" experience the situation of drinking as described by Susan Brink in this paragraph?

a. "Drinking trumps reason."

b. "They love to drink."

c. "They don't know when to stop."

d. "They can stop whenever they want."

12. According to John Schwarzlose in paragraph 10, what is one way to determine if someone is an alcoholic?

a. being stopped two or more times for driving under the influence

b. missing work because of alcohol

c. drinking in the morning

d. drinking all the time

13. In paragraph 9, what is one word that Jackie Clarke uses to describe her life as a drinker?

a. happy

b. exhausting

c. sad

d. depressing

14. According to the information Susan Brink presents in paragraph 10, which of the following is *not* one of the things specifically mentioned by the author that excessive drinking can bring about?

    a. betrayal

    b. car accidents

    c. divorce

    d. broken promises

15. Reread or scan the entire selection. What is the main idea of the entire selection by Susan Brink?

    a. how alcohol alters brain chemistry and affects lives, and how technology can help

    b. how doctors can help alcoholics

    c. new drugs to treat alcoholism

    d. people who are alcoholics and what they go through

Reading the Whole

Now that you have read Susan Brink's essay "Your Brain on Alcohol" in its parts and answered the questions about it, you may find it easier to understand its main point as you reread the essay in its entirety. Reading straight through, pay particular attention to how all the parts of the essay—the title, the introduction, the supporting paragraphs and details, and the conclusion—work together to create a single main point.

SUSAN BRINK

Your Brain on Alcohol

Ask any alcoholic trying to take it just one day at a time, and he'll tell you that compulsive drinking is a disease—period. That's what the Big Book said, after all, the groundbreaking tome by Alcoholics Anonymous that came out way back in 1939. And that's what just about everyone has believed ever since.

But hold on. Technology, not for the first time, is forcing doctors and therapists to see things in a new light. With the aid of sophisticated new imaging techniques, scientists can look inside the brains of alcoholics at the very moment they're being tempted by thoughts of cold beers, crisp martinis, or fully ripened cabernet francs. The new science shows just how alcohol can rewire the circuitry of the brain, eroding its ability to feel pleasure and act wisely, and replacing it with a locus for intense craving and destructive behavior. "Alcoholism is a disease that interferes with home life, work, interpersonal relationships, and eventually with health," says James West, medical director emeritus of the Betty Ford Center in Rancho Mirage, Calif. "It's biological, but it's also psychosocial."

The picture is a scary one. But the good news is that it's changing the way doctors and specialists are thinking about the treatment of alcoholism. Until recently, largely believing they had nothing to offer, physicians have left such treatment to counselors, recovering drinkers, and clergy. The result has been a hodgepodge of therapies, some with good results, others merely good intentions.

Now doctors are weighing in—big time. The most promising area of research is the new drugs that target specific areas of the brain to help ease the craving for liquor. One such drug—the first of its kind—has shown promise in quelling the terrible yen for a drink. Naltrexone has been approved by the Food and Drug Administration and is available by prescription. Two more drugs that also may ease craving are being tested in clinical trials.

But even proponents of pharmaceutical treatment say drugs aren't the whole answer. Most alcoholics will still need counseling or 12-step programs to help confront the harm they may have caused or the growing up they need to do. Yet just as Prozac got general practitioners interested in depression, anticraving drugs might get more physicians involved in alcoholism treatment. Says Keith Humphreys, a psychologist and addiction researcher at Stanford University: "Doctors want to be able to do something medically."

Brain Pain. The new brain-imaging technology will be the key to determining how much, and how effectively, doctors can help. Some 14 million people in the United States are alcoholics or abuse alcohol. They are skid-row bums and lace-curtain drunks, senseless rebels and charming rogues. They chill Louis Roederer Cristal champagne in silver buckets and swill Budweiser from plastic cups. They tell themselves they are not alcoholics because they never drink before 5 P.M., or because they make it to work every day, or because dinner is always on the table on time.

But their excuses can't overcome the damage they do. Inga fell down a flight of stairs with her infant in her arms. Mark had five wives, and five divorces. Betty polished off a pint of vodka, then carpooled fourth graders from soccer practice. Jeffrey committed strong-armed robbery. April, once shy, took off her clothes and danced for money. Martha threatened her husband with a carving knife. Paula slipped into the kitchen during dinner parties to swill down the last drops of wine left in dirty goblets. All are recovering alcoholics and they are ashamed of these recollections.

For active alcoholics, drinking trumps reason. It distorts judgment. It severs the connection between behavior and consequence. It lays waste to marriages, friendships, and careers. It leaves children stranded. For alcoholics, love and logic can't hold a candle to liquor.

And the damage is not limited to others. Over time, addiction becomes an enervating trial for the drinker. "I would always drink out of glasses that were opaque so my husband couldn't tell what I was drinking," says Jackie Clarke, sober for 16 years. "I would put vodka in my wine because wine seemed more acceptable. I was always thinking about what I was going to drink, when I was going

5

6

7

8

9

to drink, hiding bottles so my husband wouldn't know how much I drank. It was exhausting."

Just where alcohol abuse crosses the line into addiction remains   10 blurry. John Schwarzlose, president of the Betty Ford Center, has his own simple criterion: An alcohol abuser might get stopped once while driving under the influence, and the experience will be mortifying—and sobering. For an alcoholic, however, the embarrassment is not enough. "Two or more DUIs—that is an alcoholic," says Schwarzlose. But it is often a meaningless distinction to family members, loved ones, and employers. They know that excessive drinking can ruin lives through betrayal, broken promises, lost jobs, car accidents, and a host of other personal tragedies.

Integrated Skills

1. Why is alcoholism considered a disease—and not just a bad habit?

2. What are the consequences for the treatment of alcoholics when alcoholism is thought of as a disease?

3. Why does the author include the details about alcoholics' behavior in paragraph 7?

4. How does alcoholism affect people's lives?

5. What do you think can be done to help people who suffer from alcoholism?

Reading Textbooks

Thematic Connections. Susan Brink's essay "Your Brain on Alcohol" discusses some of the psychological and social repercussions of alcohol abuse. Brink also touches on technology that is helping doctors and scientists understand and treat alcoholism's physical effects. However, as you will see from the following reading, taken from the introductory biology textbook *Inquiry into Life* by Sylvia S. Mader, alcohol affects more than just one's brain, mind, and lifestyle. As you read this textbook selection, think about how knowing some of the other effects of alcohol helps you to understand alcohol in a larger context.

Vocabulary Preview

moderation (para. 1): the state in which something remains not large, great, or severe (n.)

ingestion (para. 1): the process of taking food or liquid into the body (n.)

biphasic (para. 2): having two stages or phases (adj.)

potentiates (para. 2): helps to make possible (v.)

inhibitory (para. 2): stopping or slowing a chemical reaction (adj.)

neurotransmitter (para. 2): a chemical that carries messages between nerves (n.)

engorged (para. 3): filled with blood (adj.)

overtaxed (para. 3): worked too hard (adj.)

inflammatory (para. 3): causing swelling, redness, heat, and pain (adj.)

impairment (para. 3): the state or condition of being damaged (n.)

deterioration (para. 4): breakdown in quality or strength (n.)

Alcohol: Most Abused Drug

The type of alcohol in beer, wine, and liquor is ethanol. While it is possible to drink alcohol in moderation, the drug is often abused. Alcohol use becomes "abuse," or an illness, when alcohol ingestion impairs an individual's social relationships, health, job performance, or ability to avoid legal difficulties. 1

HOW ALCOHOL WORKS

Alcohol effects on the brain are biphasic. After consuming several drinks, blood alcohol concentration rises rapidly and the drinker reports feeling "high" and happy (euphoric). Ninety minutes later — and lasting some 300–400 minutes after consumption — the drinker 2 feels depressed and unhappy (dysphoric). On the other hand, if the drinker continues to drink in order to maintain a high blood alcohol level, he or she will experience ever-increasing loss of control. Coma and death are even possible if a substantial amount of alcohol (1¼ pt of whiskey) is consumed within an hour. In the short run, research seems to indicate that alcohol potentiates GABA, an inhibitory neurotransmitter. Exactly how this leads to motor incoordination and poor judgment is not known. In the long run, alcohol causes the death of neurons, permanent brain damage, and cirrhosis of the liver.

CIRRHOSIS OF THE LIVER: FAT-FILLED AND SCARRED

3

The stomach and the liver contain the enzyme alcohol dehydrogenase, which begins the breakdown of alcohol to acetic acid. A new study reports that women have less of this enzyme in their stomach, and this may explain why they show a greater sensitivity to alcohol, including a greater chance of liver damage. Acetic acid can be used in the liver to produce energy, but the calories provided are termed "empty" because they contribute to energy needs and weight gain without supplying any other nutritional requirements. Worse still, the molecules (glucose and fatty acids) that the liver ordinarily uses as an energy source are converted to fats. Eventually, the liver cells become engorged with fat droplets. After a few years of being overtaxed, the liver cells begin to die, causing an inflammatory condition known as alcoholic hepatitis. Finally, scar tissue appears in the liver, and it is no longer able to perform its vital functions. This condition is called cirrhosis of the liver, a frequent cause of death among drinkers. Brain impairment and generalized deterioration of other vital organs also are seen in heavy drinkers.

4

It should be stressed that the early signs of deterioration can be reversed if the habit of drinking to excess is given up.

Thinking about the Textbook Selection

1. When does drinking alcohol become "alcohol abuse"?

2. What are the physical effects of drinking alcohol? Of drinking too much alcohol?

3. Why do women tend to have a greater sensitivity to alcohol than men do?

4. What is cirrhosis of the liver, and what causes it?

Reviewing

Recall / Remember

1. What is another term for "main idea"?
2. What is a thesis statement?
3. How is a thesis statement in a longer selection like a topic sentence in a paragraph?
4. What do introductory and concluding sentences in paragraphs do?
5. What do introductory and concluding paragraphs in longer passages do?

Chapter Summary

In this chapter you learned how to identify main ideas in longer reading selections. In longer selections, main ideas are also called controlling ideas because they control the content of the selection.

You also focused on the thesis statement, a sentence that states the main or controlling idea, usually near the beginning of a reading selection.

Finally, you practiced identifying major and minor supporting paragraphs, including introductions and conclusions, for a reading selection's main or controlling idea, and you learned to infer the main idea when it is not directly stated.

Recognizing
Patterns of
Organization

Chapter 7

Getting Ready	175
Learning the Skills	177
Applying the Skills	
• Reading the Parts	209
• Reading the Whole	215
• Reading Textbooks	218
Reviewing	221

Getting Ready

Very commonly, writers organize their ideas according to certain patterns in paragraphs and longer passages. This chapter explains these basic patterns and helps you identify them. Identifying the common patterns writers use to organize their ideas will help you better understand their main ideas, whether stated or implied. The following is a checklist of the different organizational patterns and brief definitions.

Chapter Overview

- **Narrations** tell stories.
- **Descriptions** highlight visual and other details of objects or scenes.
- **Definitions** provide the meanings of key terms or concepts.
- **Examples** give specific instances that illustrate or explain an idea.
- **Lists** are collections of details arranged one after another, in no particular order.
- **Sequences** are lists in which the order of the elements is important.
- **Comparison and contrast** investigate the similarities and differences of two or more separate things.
- **Analogies** are extended comparisons.
- **Classifications** put things into groups or classes.
- **Cause and effect analyses** show reasons why one thing leads to another.

Writers often use more than one pattern of organization in a paragraph or a section of an article, essay, or book chapter. **Mixing the patterns** provides more ways for readers to understand the subject. By carefully observing these organizational patterns—whether they are used separately or are mixed—you can make connections among the details the author includes to increase your comprehension of what you read.

Focusing Questions

How do you use lists in everyday life? How are they helpful?

When is the order of a list important in everyday life?

How can examples help you understand ideas when you read?

When do you compare two items or ideas—while shopping, while driving? What other personal decisions require comparison?

When is it important to you to understand the causes of things? Where do you encounter cause and effect analysis?

How might organizational patterns in general help you as a reader?

Everyday Reading

Find examples of different organizational patterns from among the many written messages you see around your campus or residence, such as an e-mail message from your instructor, an article in the campus newspaper, or something from your school course catalog. Look especially for things like lists, product comparisons, instructions, and advertisements. Select two of them and bring them to class.

Share the everyday reading materials with your classmates in a small group. Describe which of the patterns of organization—definitions, examples, lists, sequences, classification, comparison-contrast, cause and effect—they follow. Write at the top of each item which pattern you think was used and discuss your choice with your classmates. Remember—more than one pattern may have been used in a piece of writing.

Learning the Skills

■ Recognizing Patterns of Organization

As a reader, it is important to understand how the writer has organized the ideas you are reading. Recognizing the organizational patterns of paragraphs, passages, essays, articles, chapters, or longer sections of books will help you more readily understand a writer's main and supporting ideas. Recognizing patterns of organization can

- increase your comprehension of what you are reading
- make it easier to predict what will follow in a passage or selection and help you understand it better
- help you study and review your textbooks or class notes
- give you an opportunity to practice the patterns in your own thinking and writing

When you recognize the organizing pattern of a passage or part of a reading selection, you are able to follow it more easily. You know where you are while you are reading. You can also predict, to some degree, what might be coming next.

Think of your favorite half-hour television comedy. You know that the writers of the show have about twenty-two minutes (if you take out the commercials) to introduce the story, create a conflict or situation, and resolve it. So you as the viewer know that before the first commercial you will learn who the key players will be and what situation will occur. After the first commercial, you will learn the consequences of the conflict or situation and how the characters will resolve it. And how do you know this? Because you've watched the show or shows like it before, and you know how the action will be presented. The same can be said for reading. Once you learn the patterns of organization, you will become adept at predicting what will come next.

Writers tend to use the same few patterns of organization, to some degree, in all writing. They do so because readers tend to understand information better when it is presented in these patterns, which are the same patterns we use in our everyday lives to think with. For example, in deciding what kind of stereo equipment to buy, you compare and contrast one brand and one model with another. You may ask yourself, "This model has two speakers and the other has four. What do I want?"

Or "This brand is $200 more expensive than the other one I'm interested in. Why? What components does the more expensive one have, and do I need them?" In deciding which of two sections of a course to take, you consider their hours, their instructors, which of your friends might be taking one or the other, and so on. In selecting courses to take during an upcoming semester, you might categorize them by type — by their content, their level of difficulty, the degree of interest they hold for you, and so on. In considering whether to join a fraternity or sorority, to move off campus, or to change your major, you analyze the effects such an action would have.

These thinking patterns are just a few of the approaches to thinking you use every day. At the same time, they represent a few of the common patterns writers use to organize and develop their ideas. As a result, you will encounter these and other patterns of organization and thinking when you read. You can also use these patterns to organize your own thinking when you write. In fact, it's quite likely that your college writing course requires you to write paragraphs and essays specifically using these patterns of organization.

■ Narration

One of the most common patterns of organization that writers use is **narration.** To narrate is simply to tell a story. Narrations can be long, taking up a whole essay or passage, or can be short, taking up only a paragraph — or even a sentence. Writers use narration to engage readers, to illustrate concepts, or just to entertain readers by reporting what happened.

Usually narrations are in chronological order: They begin at the beginning and end at the end. Chronological narrations follow a story through time as it really progressed. Look at this example from the essay "Cornered" by John Monczunski, in which he recounts the story of how his quiet walk is interrupted.

> Then the spell breaks. Two blocks ahead a solitary figure emerges from a building. He wheels around and begins walking toward me. When I see him my stomach knots. I am not sure if he is even aware of me, but I know that I do not want to meet him. I decide on a tactical evasive maneuver and cross to the other side of the street. The man counters my move. Apparently he is intent on meet-

ing me and he reestablishes our collision course. We mirror each other's movements all the while slicing the gap between us. His long-distance telegraphed intentions add to my unease. Am I paranoid or prudent?

In this paragraph, Monczunski presents the story as it happened—in chronological order. First he notices the solitary figure. Then he crosses the street, followed by the figure. Finally the figure mirrors Monczunski's movements. By revealing the details of the story as it happened, Monczunski is able to build suspense. The passage leaves the reader with a feeling of anticipation similar to what he felt. This suspense makes the question he asks—"Am I paranoid or prudent?"—seem more important. (Later we learn that the figure was a man asking for donations for a worthy cause.)

Narration will not always be in chronological order. Sometimes, to build tension or suspense, writers will reveal later events before revealing earlier events. The following sentence begins with what happened last and then tells what happened first: "Before I got to class and put my books away, three people asked me if I had studied for the test." Narrations that present events out of order may be as short as this sentence or as long as whole essays or even books. Novels often tell stories out of order, "flashing back" to events earlier in a character's life.

To identify narration, whether the events in the story are presented in chronological order or not, simply look for accounts of events that pull together into a single story.

Description

When writers organize information around any of the five senses, they are using **description.** Descriptions highlight certain details from scenes or objects; they use words that appeal to the senses of sight, sound, touch, taste, and smell. Descriptions bring scenes or objects to life. An orange, for example, is orange and shiny. Its surface is dimpled. It tastes sweet and acidic. It feels heavy. Bus exhaust looks thick, dark, and smoky. You can hear the bus cough it out. It smells and tastes like gasoline.

Because writers cannot possibly describe every tiny aspect of a scene—to do so would take years and fill millions of pages—they pick out specific details to highlight. Look at how Marta K. Taylor describes a scene in the following excerpt from her essay "Desert Dance."

> Jon was sprawled out on his back, one arm up and one arm down, reminding me of Gumby or an outline chalked on the sidewalk in a murder mystery. His mouth was wide open and his regular breath rattled deeply in the back of his throat somewhere between his mouth and his nose. Besides the vibration of the wheels and the steady hum of the engine, no other sound disturbed the sacred silence of the desert night.

In this paragraph, Taylor uses descriptions of sight, sound, and touch to bring the scene to life. She describes how Jon *looked,* "sprawled out on his back, one arm up and one arm down," and how he *sounded,* "his regular breath rattled deeply." She also describes the feeling of the "vibration of the wheels."

You will be able to identify descriptions by the author's inclusion of sensory details. Very few descriptions will use all five senses, but many will use two or more. Look for words that help the reader see, hear, feel, smell, or taste particular details.

Exercise 7-1

Read each of the following passages and determine whether it is primarily description or narration. Write a **D** on the line for description, an **N** for narration. The first one is done for you.

Example:

"Then just before the revival ended, they held a special meeting for children, 'to bring the young lambs to the fold.' My aunt spoke of it for days ahead. That night I was escorted to the front row and placed on the mourners' bench with all the other young sinners, who had not yet been brought to Jesus." (Langston Hughes, "Salvation") __N__

1. "The brass instruments are the loudest of all the woodwinds because of the rather remarkable way their sound is produced. The player blows into a small cup-shaped mouthpiece of metal, and this actually makes the player's lips vibrate. The lip vibration activates vibration of the air in the brass tube." (Joseph Kerman and Gary Tomlinson, *Listen*) _____

2. "The first afternoon in the sandbox with Linda, he sat and watched with fascination as she conducted a tea party for her teddy bear and

bunny rabbit. After a while he placed several small containers in a row on the edge of the sandbox, filled a large container with sand, and then poured its contents into the smaller ones in perfect imitation of his cousin." (Michael Cole and Sheila R. Cole, *The Development of Children*) _____

3. "Like our Moon, Ganymede has two very different kinds of terrain. Dark, polygon-shaped regions are its oldest surface features, as judged by their numerous craters. Light-colored, heavily grooved terrain is found between the dark, angular islands." (Neil F. Comins and William J. Kaufmann III, *Discovering the Universe*) _____

4. "The Pacific turned ominously glossy during a Santa Ana period, and one woke in the night troubled not only by the peacocks screaming in the olive trees but by the eerie absence of surf. The heat was surreal. The sky had a yellow cast, the kind of light sometimes called 'earthquake weather.'" (Joan Didion, "Los Angeles Notebook") _____

5. "It is 7:25 on a Tuesday morning. I have showered, brushed my teeth, dressed, plucked, powdered, and curled my eyelashes. I grab my bag, shut my door, and head for the stairs, only to be stopped by my father, waiting always in dismay." (Cortney Keim, "Making the Bed") _____

. . . .

■ Definitions

Writers use **definitions** to provide the meanings of key terms or concepts. A definition may include examples, comparisons, and other kinds of explanation discussed later in this chapter. For example, look at the following paragraph from the textbook *Biology* by David Krogh. The last sentence in the excerpt gives the *scientific* definition of the word *theory*.

> It's unfortunate but true that *theory* means one thing in everyday speech and something almost completely different in scientific communication. In everyday speech, a theory can be little more than a hunch. It is an unproven idea that may or may not have any evidence to support it. In science, meanwhile, a theory is a general set of principles, supported by evidence, that explains some aspect of nature.

Sometimes writers provide a definition of a key term in a sentence. This kind of formal definition is much like what you might find in a dictionary.

Textbooks are often designed to make spotting definitions easy. The key term is often in **boldface** or *italics* and the entire definition might be as well. For example, look at the following passage from the business textbook *Exploring the World of Business* by Kenneth Blanchard, Charles Schewe, Robert Nelson, and Alexander Hiam.

> A **cooperative,** or customer-owned business, **is a business owned by a group of individuals working toward some common economic goal.** The goal may be to purchase products for the use of the members or to market the products produced by the cooperative.

In this case the key term, or word being defined, appears in boldface. The definition follows immediately and is also in bold. So a cooperative is a "business owned by a group of individuals working toward some common economic goal."

Another way to spot a definition is to look at word choice. The author's choice of a verb may indicate that a definition is contained in a sentence. For instance, if the key term is followed by *is, is defined as, refers to,* or *means,* you know that a definition will follow. Here is another example from the business textbook:

> **Acquisition** is the outright purchase of one corporation by another corporation, either in whole or in part.

The author begins the sentence with "Acquisition is." That is a clue that the following words will define the term *acquisition.*

One last way to spot a definition is to see if the author uses a dash or parentheses to define the terms. Here is an example of a definition contained within two dashes:

> In the 1980s mergers called *hostile takeovers*—the business equivalent of war—became popular.

As you can see, the key term, *hostile takeovers,* is in italics, and the definition, "the business equivalent of war," is contained inside the dashes. An example of a parenthetical definition (a definition contained inside parentheses) from the same textbook looks like this:

> A **precipitating event** (a change in the environment that spurs an individual to take action) takes various forms.

Often writers need to define concepts that are larger or more complicated than single words. Such definitions are usually longer than a sentence or even a paragraph. Many times definitions can span several paragraphs or even take up a whole essay. Defining the complicated feelings a parent has for a child, for example, may take many pages, since the definition cannot be summed up in a single word, phrase, or paragraph.

Since longer, or extended, definitions are spread over a larger area — sometimes over the whole essay — they may be harder to spot. Still, to identify them, you can apply variations of the same techniques discussed earlier for shorter definitions. For example, rather than stating the word to be defined just once in bold or italics, writers often repeat the word (or words) for what they are defining throughout a longer selection. Similarly, many longer definitions use examples to illustrate the concept being defined. Unlike shorter definitions, however, examples in longer definitions are often themselves quite long. Generally, to identify a longer definition, look for passages that explore in great detail all the things that are and are not included in whatever is being defined.

Exercise 7-2

Underline the definitions contained in each of the following paragraphs. The first one is done for you.

Example:

The third basic managerial function is leading. Some people consider leading to be both the most important and the most challenging of all managerial activities. Leading is the set of processes used to get people to work together to advance the interests of the organization. For example, Coca-Cola's chief executive officer constantly encourages the firm's managers to keep pushing for growth. (Kenneth Blanchard, Charles Schewe, Robert Nelson, and Alexander Hiam, *Exploring the World of Business*)

1. Today, we realize that the Milky Way is actually a disk tens of thousands of parsecs wide that contains several hundred billion stars, one of which is our own Sun, as well as vast quantities of gas and dust. It is one among myriads of galaxies, or systems of stars and interstellar matter. The disk of the Milky Way, along with a halo of stars that surrounds it, is called the Milky Way Galaxy. It is also called "the Galaxy" or "our Galaxy," with a capital G. (William J. Kaufmann III and Roger A. Freedman, *Universe*)

2. Economists argue that most choices are made "at the margin." The margin is the current level of an activity. Think of it as the edge from which a choice is to be made. (Timothy Tregarthen and Libby Rittenberg, *Macroeconomics*)

3. How can we choose a sample that is truly representative of the population? The easiest—but not the best—way to select a sample is to choose individuals close at hand. If we are interested in finding out how many people have jobs, for example, we might go to a shopping mall and ask people passing by if they are employed. A sample selected by taking the members of the population that are easiest to reach is called a convenience sample. Convenience samples often produce unrepresentative data. (Consortium for Mathematics and Its Applications, *For All Practical Purposes*)

4. Meditation refers to a group of techniques that induce an altered state of focused attention and heightened awareness. Meditation takes many forms and has been used for thousands of years as part of religious practices throughout the world. Virtually every major form of religion has a rich tradition of meditative practices—whether Hindu, Taoist, Buddhist, Jewish, Christian, or Muslim. (Don H. Hockenbury and Sandra E. Hockenbury, *Discovering Psychology*)

5. Psychologically healthy people have ego identity. Ego identity is a firm sense of who we are and what we stand for. Ego identity is based on understanding or creating our personal needs, values, and goals. Achievement of ego identity is a key developmental task of adolescence

and young adulthood. (Jeffrey S. Nevid, Spencer A. Rathus, and Hannah R. Rubenstein, *Health in the New Millennium*)

· ·

■ Examples

Writers often use **examples** to illustrate and explain an idea. Sometimes
they explain an idea by describing one example in detail. Look at this
paragraph from an introduction to film textbook, *Understanding Movies,*
by Louis D. Giannetti:

> Off-screen narration tends to give a movie a sense of objectivity
> and often an air of predestination. Many of the works of Billy
> Wilder are structured in flashbacks, with ironic monologues em-
> phasizing fatality: The main interest is not what happened, but how
> and why. In *Double Indemnity,* for example, the story is narrated
> by the fatally wounded hero, who admits his guilt at the opening of
> the film.

In this paragraph, it is easy to spot the example because the author uses
the words *for example.* He is describing the concept of predestination in
filmmaking and uses the film *Double Indemnity* to make his point.

Sometimes authors provide a series of examples but give each one a
brief treatment. Look at this passage from the health text *Health in the
New Millennium* by Jeffrey S. Nevid, Spencer A. Rathus, and Hannah R.
Rubenstein.

> In some cases, yesterday's prescription drug has become today's
> over-the-counter drug. Examples include the analgesics ibuprofen
> (Advil, Motrin, etc.) and naproxen sodium (Aleve), and medicines
> that are taken for allergies and asthma (such as Benadryl and
> Bronkaid Mist), skin irritations (Cortaid), heartburn and ulcers
> (Pepcid, Axid, Zantac, etc.), lice (Nix, etc.) and yeast infections
> (Monistat 7, Gyne-Lotrimin). Many sleeping pills and diet pills are
> also sold over the counter.

Here the authors have used parentheses to give instances of certain brands that fall into specific categories of drugs. Again, the authors use cue words—*such as, examples include*—to indicate that they are going to illustrate their point.

In the following passage from the political science textbook *Politics in a Changing World* by Marcus E. Ethridge and Howard Handelman, the authors explain how politics and government affect people's everyday lives. They illustrate their idea with a variety of different examples. Their way of stating their main idea is that "political decisions do have an extensive impact beyond purely 'governmental' matters." Their examples range over different areas of people's lives, including education, health, religion, art, the professions, war, and even death.

Many of the best things in life have little or nothing to do with politics. Personal relationships, the satisfaction of learning and working, artistic achievement and enjoyment, the challenges and deep fulfillment of raising a child—we can experience all these things without doing anything "political." Political institutions, issues, and movements are not necessarily involved in most aspects of our day-to-day lives. There is much more to life than politics.

— In the most basic sense, politics and government have to do with *public* policies and *public* decision making, concerns that most people think about only occasionally. Yet, however important the private sphere of life, political decisions do have an extensive impact beyond purely "governmental" matters. Parenting is often deeply involved with politics. In most countries, the government helps determine what children must learn in school and when they will learn it. Often it mandates what kinds of health-related precautions must be taken to protect students and what kinds of discipline and religious training they can be given. Art is restricted by government in most countries, both to limit expressions seen as improper and to restrict the dissemination of ideas that may produce dissent and disloyalty. Virtually everywhere, government regulates membership in selected professions (including not only law and medicine but also plumbing, architecture, and a wide range of others), limiting and often forcing career choices. Governments are the only institutions that may legally apply the death penalty to their citizens. And, of course, when nations decide to make war on one another, virtually all aspects of their citizens' personal lives may be drastically changed.

Exercise 7-3

Reread the preceding paragraph from *Politics in a Changing World* and answer the following questions. The first one is done for you.

Example:

What, "in the most basic sense," are politics and government concerned with?

Politics and government are concerned with public policies and

public decision making.

1. What is the main idea of paragraph 1?

2. Make a list of the examples included in paragraph 1.

3. What is the main idea of paragraph 2?

4. What five areas of life do the authors use as examples illustrating the main idea of paragraph 2?

5. List three examples included in paragraph 2 of governmental decisions that affect parenting.

■ Lists and Sequences

A **list** is a collection of details arranged one after another, often in no special order. The following is an example of a paragraph using lists, taken from the college composition textbook *The Bedford Reader* by X. J. Kennedy, Dorothy M. Kennedy, and Jane E. Aaron. In the paragraph, the authors use two short lists to show what it means to classify.

> To classify is to make sense of the world by arranging many units—trucks, chemical elements, wasps, students—into more manageable groups. To help us find books in a library, librarians classify books into categories: fiction, biography, history, psychology, and so forth. For the convenience of readers, newspapers run classified advertising, grouping many small ads into categories such as Help Wanted and Cars for Sale.

Sequences differ from lists because they follow a particular order of steps or stages. Sequence refers to the order in which things happen, as when a history book describes the series of events leading up to a war. Sequences are used to describe the development of the planet earth in geology, the emergence of evolutionary life forms in biology, and the influence of factors causing a disease, such as cancer, to occur.

Read the following example from the biology textbook *Life: The Science of Biology* by William K. Purves, Gordon H. Orians, H. Craig Heller, and David Sadava, and see if you can identify the signal words in the sequence.

> To determine the number of molecules in a sample of pure substance, we first determine the weight of the substance in grams, then we divide the grams by the relative weight of one molecule (the molecular weight defined earlier).

If you identified *first* and *then* as signal words, you are correct. These two words indicate that the authors were developing an idea that has steps or stages.

It is easy to identify a sequence when signal words are used. But how do you identify a sequence when such words are not used? Take a look at these paragraphs from the textbook *Exploring the World of Business*, and notice how the authors have incorporated a sequence.

Job applicants usually submit a résumé and cover letter to introduce themselves to a firm that has a job vacancy. A résumé is a brief summary of an applicant's relevant experience, ideally one or two pages in length. The cover letter highlights experience that particularly qualifies the applicant for the job and provides information on contacting him or her.

Individuals selected from the pool of applicants are usually called for an interview and tests, which in large firms are administered by the human resources department. There they are required to complete the company's own application form, which asks standard questions that enable the human resources employees to determine the candidate's experience level. The form also requests salary history, references, and other necessary information that will help in evaluating the candidate.

Employers almost always seek additional information through employment interviews, which are personal meetings with the candidate.

In addition to simply outlining all the materials a job applicant must prepare, these paragraphs also outline the steps — in order — the applicant must take to be considered for a job. Though no obvious signal words are included, it is still clear what those steps are: first submit a résumé and cover letter, then attend an interview and fill out an application form.

Exercise 7-4

Put the steps in each sequence in the proper order by numbering them on the lines provided. Rework the steps so they read as a sequence of events. The first one is done for you.

Example:

    3   Follow cleaning with a thorough washing with soap and warm water.

    1   Always clean a brush right after painting.

    2   Use the appropriate thinner or solvent for the paint with which the brush has been used.

1.   _2_   Cut fabric pieces are then carefully matched and sewn together using the latest sewing machine technology.

     _3_   Finally, our skilled upholsterers hand-pad and upholster the frame with layers of extra fiber for comfort.

     _1_   Our state-of-the-art fabric-cutting machine uses digitized pattern information to automatically cut pieces from bolts of fabric.

2.   _3_   Turn the washing machine to the "off" position after the cycle has been completed.

     _1_   Separate your clothes into whites and colors.

     _2_   Put the whites into the washing machine after you have put in your detergent and bleach.

3.   _3_   Increased blood levels of melatonin make you sleepy and reduce activity levels.

     _4_   Shortly before sunrise, the pineal gland all but stops producing melatonin, and you soon wake up.

     _2_   At night, blood levels of melatonin rise, peaking between 1:00 and 3:00 A.M.

     _1_   Exposure to sunlight and other bright light suppresses melatonin levels, and they remain very low throughout the day.

4.   _2_   Open the back of the camera and locate the film spool.

     _3_   Purchase one package of 400-speed color film.

     _4_   Wind the film around the spool inside the camera.

     _1_   Open the film package and expose the first inch of film so you can insert it into the camera.

5.   _5_   Pour the batter onto the waffle iron.

     _4_   Belgian waffles are a delicious but time-consuming treat.

     _3_   Then heat your waffle iron to the exact temperature indicated on the recipe, usually 250 degrees.

     _2_   First, buy the necessary ingredients; if the recipe calls for a specific brand, make sure to purchase that and not another type.

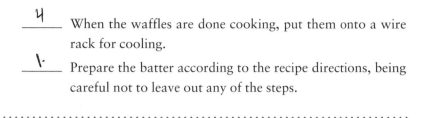

____4____ When the waffles are done cooking, put them onto a wire rack for cooling.

____1.____ Prepare the batter according to the recipe directions, being careful not to leave out any of the steps.

. . . .

■ Comparison, Contrast, and Analogy

COMPARISON AND CONTRAST

To illustrate or explain features of ideas or things, writers often compare them to, or contrast them with, other things. By setting one thing off against another, writers can provide a clearer picture of both. **Comparing** two things is looking at their similarities. **Contrasting** two things is noting the differences between similar aspects.

Comparing and contrasting are useful in writing and in real life. Imagine how you decide between two different television shows: one is funny and lasts only half an hour; one is serious and lasts a whole hour. Depending on how much time you want to watch television, and whether you want to laugh or think seriously, the results of your comparison and contrast will help you decide.

Writers use comparison and contrast similarly. For example, an essay may point out the differences between a Republican and a Democratic candidate for office; it may discuss the similarities between two different approaches to teaching; or it might highlight the similarities and differences between two ways of thinking about a social problem.

Certain signal or cue words help identify when a writer is comparing or contrasting two or more different topics or concepts. If you see the following types of words in a reading, they usually signal that the writer is comparing two or more things. Signal words used to indicate comparison include the following.

in comparison	parallels	similar
in the same way	resembles	similarly
like		

As you can see from the list, all of these words have one thing in common: They link things and indicate that an author will be looking at them to see how they are alike.

Similarly, certain words signal that a writer is contrasting rather than comparing things. The following are examples.

although	in contrast	on the other hand
but	instead	whereas
different	nevertheless	yet
however		

By definition, contrast indicates difference rather than similarity. So, unlike comparison, in which writers describe how things are alike, in contrast writers look at how things are different. Frequently, writers use both comparison (similarities) and contrast (differences) when writing about a topic.

Signal words are not necessary for making comparisons and contrasts in a passage. Sometimes the comparison and contrast organizational pattern omits signal words. In this case, it will be up to you to figure out if the writer is either comparing how two or more things are alike or contrasting two or more things to show how they are different.

Sometimes writers organize their comparison-contrast discussion in a "block" structure by discussing first one part fully and then the other. The following example of the block structure is taken from the essay "American Space, Chinese Place" by Yi-Fu Tuan.

> Americans have a sense of space, not of place. Go to an American home in exurbia, and almost the first thing you do is drift toward the picture window. How curious that the first compliment you pay your host inside his house is to say how lovely it is outside his house! He is pleased that you should admire his vistas. The distant horizon is not merely a line separating earth from sky, it is a symbol of the future. The American is not rooted in his place, however lovely: his eyes are drawn by the expanding space to a point on the horizon, which is his future. By contrast, consider the traditional Chinese home. Blank walls enclose it. Step behind the spirit wall and you are in a courtyard with perhaps a miniature garden around a corner. Once inside his private compound you are wrapped in an ambiance of calm beauty, an ordered world of buildings, pavement, rock, and decorative vegetation. But you have no distant view: nowhere does space open out before you. Raw nature in such a home is experienced only as weather, and the only open space is the sky above. The Chinese is rooted in his place. When he has to leave, it is not for the promised land on the terrestrial horizon, but for another world altogether along the vertical, religious axis of his imagination.

Writers may also use an alternating structure, in which they move back and forth between the things being compared by taking up one aspect at a time but for each of the compared items. The following is an example taken from the astronomy textbook *Universe* by William J. Kaufmann III and Roger A. Freedman.

> Although Saturn's rings are unique in the solar system, the planet itself has many similarities to its larger cousin Jupiter. Both planets exhibit differential rotation, taking less time to complete one rotation at the equator than near the poles. The chemical compositions of their atmospheres are also similar. Earth-based spectroscopic observations along with data from spacecraft confirm that, like Jupiter, Saturn has a hydrogen-rich atmosphere with trace amounts of methane, ammonia, and water vapor. These compounds are the simplest combinations of hydrogen with carbon, nitrogen, and oxygen. And like Jupiter, Saturn's atmosphere probably has three distinct cloud layers: an upper layer of frozen ammonia crystals, a middle layer of crystals of ammonium hydrosulfide, and a lower layer of water ice crystals.

The alternating structure is also illustrated in the following passage from John McPhee's essay "Oranges." In this paragraph, McPhee contrasts Florida oranges with oranges from California. Instead of discussing one type completely and then the other type, he moves back and forth between Florida and California oranges to describe differences in the amount of juice they contain, the kinds of skins they have, and how easy they are to eat.

> An orange grown in Florida usually has a thin and tightly fitting skin, and is also heavy with juice. Californians say that if you want to eat a Florida orange you have to get into a bathtub first. California oranges are light in weight and have thick skins that break easily and come off in hunks. The flesh inside is marvelously sweet, and the segments almost separate themselves. In Florida, it is said that you can run over a California orange with a ten-ton truck and not even wet the pavement. The differences from which these hyperboles arise will prevail in the two states even if the type of orange is
>
> *continued*

the same. In arid climates, like California's, oranges develop a thick albedo, which is the white part of the skin. Florida is one of the two or three most rained-upon states in the United States. California uses the Colorado River and similarly impressive sources to irrigate its oranges, but of course irrigation can only do so much. The annual difference in rainfall between the Florida and California orange-growing areas is one million one hundred and forty thousand gallons per acre. For years, California was the leading orange-growing state, but Florida surpassed California in 1942, and grows three times as many oranges now. California oranges, for their part, can safely be called three times as beautiful.

ANALOGY

Analogy is a special type of comparison, an extended comparison for the purpose of explanation. Writers use analogy to explain something unfamiliar to their readers by comparing it with something more familiar to them. For example, a science writer might explain how the heart functions by comparing it with a water pump. Or you might explain the game of football to someone who didn't understand it by making an analogy with war—the offense attacks the defense by attempting to invade its territory.

Appreciating how writers use analogy to clarify and explain their ideas can help you understand complex ideas. This example comes from the book *The Disuniting of America* by Arthur Schlesinger Jr.:

History is to the nation rather as memory is to the individual. As an individual deprived of memory becomes disoriented and lost, not knowing where he has been or where he is going, so a nation denied a conception of its past will be disabled in dealing with its present and its future.

In this analogy the author explains his idea about the need for a knowledge of history by comparing the loss of that knowledge to someone who has lost his way. Schlesinger uses his analogy to support his idea that historical memory is as important to the nation as individual memory is to each individual person.

The following selection, from the psychology textbook *Discovering Psychology* by Don H. Hockenbury and Sandra E. Hockenbury, presents an analogy between an experiment concerning rats in a maze and a person's ability to use a "cognitive map" to solve problems.

Many early behaviorists believed that complex, active behaviors were no more than a chain of stimulus-response connections that had been "stamped in" by their effects. But one early learning researcher, Edward C. Tolman (1898–1956), had a different view of learning. Tolman believed that, even in the lowly rat, cognitive processes were involved in the learning of complex behaviors. According to Tolman, although such cognitive processes could not be observed directly, they could still be experimentally verified and inferred by careful observation of outward behavior.

Much of Tolman's research involved rats in mazes. When Tolman began his research in the 1920s, many studies of rats in mazes had been done. In a typical experiment, a rat would be placed in the "start" box, and a food reward would be put in the "goal" box at the end of the maze. The rat would initially make many mistakes in running the maze. After several trials, it would eventually learn to run the maze quickly and with very few errors.

But what had the rats learned? According to traditional behaviorists, the rats had learned a *sequence of responses,* such as "first corner—turn left; second corner—turn left; third corner—turn right," and so on. Each response was associated with the "stimulus" of the rat's position in the maze. And the entire sequence of responses was "stamped in" by the food reward at the end of the maze.

Tolman disagreed with that view. He noted that several investigators had reported as incidental findings that their maze-running rats had occasionally taken their own shortcuts to the food box. In one case, an enterprising rat had knocked the cover off the maze, climbed over the maze wall and out of the maze, and scampered directly to the food box. To Tolman, such reports indicated that the rats had learned more than simply the sequence of responses required to get to the food. Instead, Tolman believed that the rat eventually builds up, through experience, a **cognitive map** of the maze—a mental representation of its layout.

As an analogy, think of the route that you typically take to get to your psychology classroom. If a hallway along the way were

continued

blocked off for repairs, you would use your "cognitive map" of the building to come up with an alternative route to class. Tolman showed experimentally that rats, like people, seem to form cognitive maps. And, like us, rats can use their cognitive maps to come up with an alternate route to a goal when the customary route is blocked.

Exercise 7-5

Identify the analogies in these passages by circling one thing being compared and underlining what it is compared to. The first one is done for you.

Example:

For example, Gay Balfour of Colorado recognized a problem—the need to remove prairie dogs from an area without killing them. When trying to come up with a way to get the prairie dogs out of their burrows, Balfour was struck by the analogy between a (vacuum cleaner) and the suction devices used to clean out septic tanks. Balfour devised a machine that sucks the critters out of the ground without harming them so they can be relocated. (Don H. Hockenbury and Sandra E. Hockenbury, *Discovering Psychology*)

1. At 5 feet 5 and 110 pounds, Amelia Greenberg was about as overweight as an earthworm. But last summer, as friends started dieting, she decided to lose five to ten pounds. Within a few months, Amelia, now 15, was on the death march called anorexia nervosa. (Claudia Kalb, "When Weight Loss Goes Awry," *Newsweek,* July 3, 2000)

2. Your brain is to your body as the hard drive is to your computer. Both act as storage units for information, but unlike your computer, your brain stores your thoughts, feelings, and memories as well.

3. The American Stock Exchange is smaller than the New York Stock Exchange, with fewer than 900 members. It is the Triple AAA Baseball League of stock exchanges because as companies grow, they often move up to the New York Stock Exchange when they become larger, not unlike a successful baseball player.

4. Soil, the uppermost layer of the earth's crust, is composed of rock fragments associated with organic material, both living and in various stages of decomposition. Think of it as your top layer of skin — exposed to the elements, often unprotected, and sometimes shed to reveal a new layer.

5. When spreading the top sheet across the mattress, leave extra sheet at the foot of the bed. Lift the mattress at the bottom, and tuck the sheet in there. This, ideally, keeps you in bed, helping to hold you still and secure. Pull the remaining sheet tight to the top of the bed, without untucking, and smooth out wrinkles with your palms from the bottom up and the center out. You'll be a kind of human iron, pressing out problems, regrouping each time for more steam. (Cortney Keim, "Making the Bed")

Exercise 7-6

Write a brief paragraph of two or three sentences using one of the analogies listed here. The first one is done for you.

Example:

Compare your favorite teacher to a season.

Dr. Kemp is easy, relaxing, and fun, like summer. I wait through my

other classes impatiently for his class like waiting through winter.

_____

1. Compare your apartment building to a beehive.

_____

_____

_____

2. Compare your family to the branches on a tree.

_____

_____

_____

3. Compare your commute to school or work to a video game.

_____

_____

_____

4. Compare preparing your favorite dinner to performing surgery.

_____

_____

_____

5. Compare your schoolwork to gardening.

_____

_____

_____

. . . .

■ Classification

To **classify** things is to categorize them—to put them into groups or classes. Classified ads in the newspaper organize goods for sale or services for hire. You can find listings for houses and apartments for rent or sale; cars both new and used for sale or lease; job opportunities; and merchandise or services. Each section of the classifieds is subdivided into smaller categories based on things such as location (for houses); size (for apartments); type of merchandise (domestic/imported for cars).

Textbooks use classification extensively. Often, the table of contents of a textbook includes ways of classifying the topics for the subject of the book. A psychology textbook, for example, might devote chapters to personality development, perception, consciousness, learning, memory, motivation, emotions, disorders, statistics, and other topics related to the study of human behavior. Textbooks use classification to organize information within chapters and parts of chapters as well. A discussion in a literature textbook may classify poems into the types narrative, lyric, and dramatic; or fiction into novels, novellas, and short stories. Biology textbooks often present the various classifications of animal and plant species. A music textbook may classify popular music as folk, country, rock, disco, reggae, blues, jazz, and other contemporary styles.

Sometimes it is helpful to look at a classification in an outline format to see what the author intended. For instance, classifying the different types of literature may look something like this:

I. Literature
    A. Poetry
        1. Narrative
        2. Lyric
        3. Dramatic
    B. Fiction
        1. Novels
        2. Novellas
        3. Short stories

This outline format helps you visualize the main topic (literature), the two subtopics (poetry and fiction), and the categories within each (narrative, lyric, dramatic; novels, novellas, short stories).

Writers use classification to organize information, to order data and information so readers can see connections between different concepts and different topics more readily. Classification enables writers to clarify their ideas; it enables readers to better understand the writers' points.

In the following passage from an essay titled "Can People Be Judged by Their Appearance?," the psychologist Eric Berne presents his theory that human beings can be classified into three basic types. He describes three types of physical build and relates these physical characteristics to differences in psychological disposition. Whether his theory is correct is disputable. Nonetheless, his classifications are clear.

Everyone knows that a human being, like a chicken, comes from an egg. At a very early stage, the human embryo forms a three-layered tube, the inside layer of which grows into the stomach and lungs, the middle layer into bones, muscle, joints, and blood vessels, and the outside layer into the skin and nervous system.

Usually these three grow about equally, so that the average human being is a fair mixture of brains, muscles, and inward organs. In some eggs, however, one layer grows more than the others, and when the angels have finished putting the child together, he may have more gut than brain, or more brain than muscle. When

continued

this happens, the individual's activities will often be mostly with the overgrown layer.

We can thus say that while the average human being is a mixture, some people are mainly "digestion-minded," some "muscle-minded," and some "brain-minded," correspondingly digestion-bodied, muscle-bodied, or brain-bodied. The digestion-bodied people look thick; the muscle-bodied people look wide; and the brain-bodied people look long. This does not mean the taller a man is the brainier he will be. It means that if a man, even a short man, looks long rather than wide or thick, he will often be more concerned about what goes on in his mind than about what he does or what he eats; but the key factor is slenderness and not height. On the other hand, a man who gives the impression of being thick rather than long or wide will usually be more interested in a good steak than a good idea or a good long walk.

Medical men use Greek words to describe these types of body-build. For the man whose body shape mostly depends on the inside layer of the egg, they use the word *endomorph*. If it depends mostly upon the middle layer, they call him a *mesomorph*. If it depends upon the outside layer they call him an *ectomorph*. We can see the same roots in our English words "enter," "medium," and "exit," which might just as easily have been spelled "ender," "mesium," and "ectit."

Since the inside skin of the human egg, or endoderm, forms the inner organs of the belly, the viscera, the endomorph is usually belly-minded; since the middle skin forms the body tissues, or soma, the mesomorph is usually muscle-minded; and since the outside skin forms the brain, or cerebrum, the ectomorph is usually brain-minded. Translating this into Greek, we have the viscerotonic endomorph, the somatotonic mesomorph, and the cerebrotonic ectomorph.

Words are beautiful things to a cerebrotonic, but a viscerotonic knows you cannot eat a menu no matter what language it is printed in, and a somatotonic knows you cannot increase your chest expansion by reading a dictionary. So it is advisable to leave these words and see what kinds of people they actually apply to, remembering again that most individuals are fairly equal mixtures and that what we have to say concerns only the extremes. Up to the present, these types have been thoroughly studied only in the male sex.

Exercise 7-7

In developing his classification of human males, Berne employs a number of techniques to make his meaning clear. Reread the selection and follow the directions in each question. The first question is done for you.

Example:

List four things that grow from the middle layer of the embryo's tube.

a. *bones*

b. *muscle*

c. *joints*

d. *blood vessels*

1. Identify the three layers of the embryo.

    a. _____

    b. _____

    c. _____

2. What three things develop from these three embryonic layers?

    a. _____

    b. _____

    c. _____

3. To what three categories of people does each of these three layers correspond?

    a. _____

    b. _____

    c. _____

4. What, according to Berne's groupings, are the three appearances of the human body?

    a. _____

    b. _____

    c. _____

5. What three inclinations correspond with Berne's groupings of the three appearances of the human body?

a. _____

b. _____

c. _____

· ·

■ Cause and Effect

One of the most common organizational patterns writers use is that of **cause and effect.** Sometimes referred to as *causal analysis,* the cause and effect organizational pattern explains why something happened or developed as it did. If you were to list, for example, your reasons for attending college, including why you chose the school and program you did, you would be thinking about causes. In listing the reasons for going to college — intellectual, social, financial — you complete a causal analysis of your decision to continue your education. In a historical account of the American Civil War or the French Revolution, the writer would explain both the causes of the war and the effects it had socially, politically, and economically.

Writers often use cause and effect as an organizing pattern when making an argument about why or how something happened and what might result from it. The causes of the event or situation are the reasons it occurred; the effects are its results or consequences. The following are typical words that signal causes: *because, cause, due to, for this reason, on account of,* and *since.* These words typically signal effects: *as a result, consequently, in effect, outcomes, result, therefore.*

In the following passage from the American history textbook *America's History* by James A. Henretta, David Brody, and Lynn Dumenil, the authors explain the causes of the revival of feminism in the 1960s.

Women's Changing Lives

Social movements do not just spring up when leaders announce a set of demands. Leaders arise only when there is a constituency ready to be mobilized. Preconditions for feminism lay in the changing social and demographic bases of women's lives, especially increased labor force participation, greater access to higher education, the declining birthrate, and changing patterns of marriage.

The most important factor was the dramatic rise in women's participation in the work force during the postwar years. In 1950 almost one-third of women were employed, and one-quarter of them were married. By 1970, 42.6 percent of women were working, and four out of ten working women were married. Especially significant was the growth in the number of working women with preschool children — up from 12 percent in 1950 to 30 percent in 1970. Working mothers had become both socially accepted and economically necessary.

Women also benefited from increased access to education. Immediately after World War II the percentage of women college students had declined: the GI Bill gave men a temporary advantage in access to higher education, and many college women dropped out of school to marry and raise families at the height of the baby boom. By 1960, however, the percentage of women students had climbed to 35 percent, and by 1970 to 41 percent.

The meaning of marriage was changing too. The baby boom only temporarily interrupted the century-long decline in the birthrate. The introduction of the birth control pill, first marketed in 1960, and the intrauterine device (IUD) helped women control their fertility, as did the legalization of abortion in the 1970s. Women had fewer children and, because of increased life expectancy (75 years in 1970, up from 54 years in 1920), spent fewer years of their lives involved primarily in childcare. At the same time, the divorce rate, which had risen slowly through the twentieth century, shot up. It doubled from 15 per thousand marriages in 1960 to 32 per thousand in 1975. Women could no longer assume that their marriages would last until "death do us part."

As a result of these changes, traditional gender expectations were dramatically undercut. To be female in America now usually included work and marriage, often childrearing and a career, and possibly bringing up children as a single parent after a divorce. These changing social realities created a major constituency for the revival of feminism in the 1960s.

Exercise 7-8

Refer to the selection "Women's Changing Lives" and answer the following questions. The first one is done for you.

Example:

In the last paragraph, what important signal words do the authors use to reinforce their cause and effect analysis?

a. _As a result_

b. _created_

1. List three signal words the authors use in this cause and effect selection.

a. _____

b. _____

c. _____

2. List three preconditions for feminism as outlined in the first paragraph.

a. _____

b. _____

c. _____

3. What was the "most important factor" the authors refer to in the second paragraph?

_____

_____

4. List five other factors the authors list in later paragraphs that contributed to the rise of feminism.

a. _____

b. _____

c. _____

d. _____

e. _____

5. List the three social changes the author identifies as the causes for the revival of feminism.

    a. _____

    b. _____

    c. _____

. . . .

■ Mixing the Patterns

Most often, writers employ more than one pattern of organization in a paragraph or a section of an article, essay, or chapter. You might find, for instance, that a paragraph or longer piece of writing classifies things while simultaneously analyzing their causes or effects. An essay may use examples to help define a word or concept. Similarly, an essay or paragraph may present all of the patterns that you have learned.

In the following paragraphs from the textbook *Economics* by Timothy Tregarthen and Libby Rittenberg, the authors use three different organizational patterns. See if you can identify them as you read.

The study of economics is generally divided into two broad branches. One focuses on individual components of economic activity; the other looks at the total of all economic activity. To understand this division, we must start with the goods and services that are produced and exchanged in the economy. A **good** is a tangible commodity, such as a chair or a watermelon, that people value. A **service** is an intangible commodity, such as the activity of a teacher or a waiter, that people value. A set of arrangements through which a particular good or service is produced and exchanged is called a **market**. An **economy** is a system of institutions that provides for the production and exchange of goods and services. An economy may include markets, but there may be other institutions, such as government agencies, that produce or distribute goods and services. The economy can have whatever geographical designation we care to give it. We may speak of the economy of a city, a nation, or a region.

Everyone who participates in the consumption or production of goods and services is part of the economy. Since all of us satisfy at

1

2

continued

least the first criterion, we are all part of the economy. Markets can take all sorts of forms. When economists speak of the market for food, for example, they are talking about an enormously complex mix of farmers, distributors, retail stores, government agencies, and consumers who interact to produce and exchange food. They may confine their analysis to the market for food in a small town or speak of the global market for food. Instead of focusing on food in general, an economist might speak of the market for veal, or for almonds, or for broccoli.

The two broad branches of economics are microeconomics and macroeconomics. Your economics course, for example, may be designated as a "micro" or as a "macro" course. **Microeconomics** is a branch of economics that focuses on the choices made by consumers and firms and the impacts those choices have on specific markets. **Macroeconomics** is a branch of economics that focuses on the impact of choices on the total level of economic activity. It deals particularly with the determination of total output, level of employment, and price level.

How does the weather in Argentina affect the producers and consumers of eggs in Oregon? Why do women end up doing most of the housework? Why do senior citizens get discounts on public transit systems? Why do we seem to make so little progress in the war on drugs? These questions are generally regarded as microeconomic because they focus on individual units or markets in the economy.

Is the total level of economic activity rising or falling? Is the rate of inflation increasing or decreasing? What's happening to the unemployment rate? These are questions that deal with aggregates, or totals, in the economy; they are problems of macroeconomics. The question about the level of economic activity, for example, refers to the total value of all production in the economy. Inflation is a measure of the rate of change in the average price level for the entire economy; it is a macroeconomic problem. The total levels of employment and unemployment in the economy represent the aggregate of all labor markets; unemployment is thus a topic of macroeconomics.

Both microeconomics and macroeconomics give attention to individual markets. But in microeconomics that attention is an end in itself; in macroeconomics it is aimed at explaining the movement of major economic aggregates—the level of total output, the level of employment, and the price level.

Exercise 7-9

Answer the following questions based on your reading of the preceding selection. The first one is done for you.

Example:

Identify the paragraph or paragraphs where the authors use
definition.

paragraphs 1, 2, 3, and 4 _____

1. What are two terms and their definitions that the authors pro-
    vide in the selection?

    a. _____

        _____

    b. _____

        _____

        _____

2. List three examples the authors use to support their main point.

    a. _____

        _____

    b. _____

        _____

    c. _____

        _____

3. Identify the places where the authors use lists or sequences.
    Make a list below of the items in either the lists or sequences.

    a. _____

        _____

        _____

        _____

    c. _____

        _____

4. Identify the paragraph or paragraphs where the authors use comparison and contrast.

   _____

5. Identify the paragraph or paragraphs where the authors use classification.

   _____

. . . .

As a collaborative exercise, work with two or three of your class-mates to find a piece of writing that exhibits a mixed pattern of organization. Once you have found such a piece, collaborate to identify the types of organizational patterns used. Label each pattern of organization in the margin next to where it is used in the reading selection.

Applying the Skills

Reading the Parts

Jim Bobryk, a California writer and executive, wrote this essay for the "My Turn" column in *Newsweek* magazine. The essay appeared in the March 8, 1999, issue. While Bobryk does not use every pattern of organization in his essay, many of his paragraphs provide excellent examples of the patterns in this chapter. As you read, pay close attention to how each paragraph is organized. After you read each section and answer the questions that follow, move on to the next section. You will have a chance to reread the whole essay when you finish.

JIM BOBRYK
Navigating My Eerie Landscape Alone

1   Now, as I stroll down the street, my right forefinger extends five feet in front of me, feeling the ground where my feet will walk.

2   Before, my right hand would have been on a steering wheel as I went down the street. I drove to work, found shortcuts in strange cities, picked up my two daughters after school. Those were the days when I ran my finger down a phone-book page and never dialed Information. When I read novels and couldn't sleep until I had finished the last page. Those were the nights when I could point out a shooting star before it finished scraping across the dark sky. And when I could go to the movies and it didn't matter if it was a foreign film or not.

3   But all this changed about seven years ago. I was driving home for lunch on what seemed to be an increasingly foggy day, although the perky radio deejay said it was clear and sunny. After I finished my lunch, I realized that I couldn't see across the room to my front door. I had battled glaucoma for 20 years. Suddenly, without warning, my eyes had hemorrhaged.

4   I will never regain any of my lost sight. I see things through a porthole covered in wax paper. I now have no vision in my left eye and only slight vision in my right. A minefield of blind spots make people and cars suddenly appear and vanish. I have no depth

209

perception. Objects are not closer and farther; they're larger and smaller. Steps, curbs, and floors all flow on the same flat plane. My world has shapes but no features. Friends are mannequins in the fog until I recognize their voices. Printed words look like ants writhing on the pages. Doorways are unlit mine shafts. This is not a place for the fainthearted.

My cane is my navigator in this eerie landscape. It is a hollow   5
fiber-glass stick with white reflector paint and a broad red band at the tip. It folds up tightly into four 15-inch sections, which can then be slipped into a black holster that attaches to my belt with Velcro.

1. In paragraph 2, which organizational pattern does Jim Bobryk use to describe his life before losing his sight?

   a. listing

   b. cause and effect analysis

   c. example

   d. classification

2. In paragraph 3, which pattern of organization does Bobryk use to explain how his life changed?

   a. narration   c. description

   b. example   d. analogy

3. In paragraph 4, Bobryk discusses the ways that his world has changed. The paragraph is primarily organized as which of the following?

   a. a sequence

   b. examples

   c. a cause and effect analysis

   d. comparison and contrast

4. Which of the following sentences from paragraph 4 is an example of an analogy?

   a. I will never regain any of my lost sight.

   b. I now have no vision in my left eye and only slight vision in my right.

c. Objects are not closer and farther; they're larger and smaller.

d. Printed words look like ants writhing on the pages.

5. Discussing his cane, Bobryk primarily organizes paragraph 5 by which of the following?

a. narration

b. cause and effect

c. description

d. comparison and contrast

Adults—unless they're preoccupied or in a hurry—will step aside without comment when they see me coming. Small children will either be scooped up apologetically or steered away by their parents. Only teenagers sometimes try to play chicken, threatening to collide with me and then veering out of the way at the last moment.   6

While I'm wielding my stick, strangers are often afraid to communicate with me. I don't take this personally—anymore. Certainly they can't be afraid that I'll lash at them with my rod. (Take *that,* you hapless sighted person! Whack!) No, they're probably more afraid *for* me. Don't startle the sword swallower. Don't tickle the baton twirler.   7

The trick for the sighted person is to balance courtesy with concern. Should he go out of his way or should he get out of the way? Will his friendliness be misconstrued by the disabled as pity? Will an offer of help sound patronizing? These anxieties are exaggerated by not knowing the etiquette in dealing with the disabled. A sighted person will do nothing rather than take the risk of offending the blind. Still, I refuse to take a dim view of all this.   8

When I peer over my cane and ask for help, no one ever cowers in fear. In fact, I think people are waiting for me to give them the green light to help. It makes us feel good to help.   9

6. Discussing some of the ways other people react to him on the street, Bobryk organizes paragraph 6 primarily around

a. description.   c. a list.

b. examples.   d. a sequence.

7. In the sentences "Don't startle the sword swallower. Don't tickle the baton twirler," Bobryk

    a. describes the causes and effects of using his cane.

    b. creates an analogy between his own behavior and that of performers.

    c. builds a sequence of possible reactions to him.

    d. narrates the experience of encountering others.

8. In paragraph 7, discussing the possible explanations for others' reactions to him, Bobryk contrasts which of the following?

    a. the theory that people are afraid *of* him with the theory that they are afraid *for* him

    b. sighted people with himself

    c. his violent reaction with other people's silence

    d. sword swallowing with baton twirling

9. The questions in paragraph 8 are

    a. a narration of how people might think.

    b. examples of how people might think.

    c. a description of sighted people.

    d. a cause and effect analysis.

10. Since Bobryk does not actually have the "green light" to which he refers in paragraph 9, that sentence is an example of

    a. a narration.   c. a description.

    b. an analogy.   d. None of the above

> When I ask for a small favor, I often get more assistance than I   10
> ever expect. Clerks will find my required forms and fill them out for
> me. A group of people will parade me across a dangerous intersec-
> tion. A salesclerk will read the price tag for me and then hunt for
> the item on sale. I'm no Don Juan, but strange (and possibly exotic)
> women will take my hand and walk me through dark rooms, mys-
> terious train stations, and foreign airports. Cabbies wait and make
> sure I make it safely into lobbies.
>
> It's not like it's inconvenient for friends to help me get around.   11
> Hey, have disabled parking placard—will travel. Christmas shop-

ping? Take me to the mall and I'll get us front-row parking. Late for the game? *No problema*. We'll be parking by the stadium entrance. And if some inconsiderate interloper does park in the blue zone without a permit, he'll either be running after a fleeing tow truck or paying a big fine.

Worried about those age lines showing? Not with me looking. 12 Put down that industrial-strength Oil of Olay. To me, your skin looks as clear and smooth as it was back in the days when you thought suntanning was a good idea.

So you see, I'm a good guy to know. I just carry a cane, that's all. 13

None of this is to make light of going blind. Being blind is dark 14 and depressing. When you see me walking with my cane, you may think I'm lost as I ricochet down the street. But you'll find more things in life if you don't travel in a straight line.

11. What is the primary organizational pattern of paragraph 10?

   a. narration   c. example

   b. description   d. cause and effect

12. What is the primary organizational pattern of paragraph 11?

   a. narration   c. example

   b. analogy   d. cause and effect

13. Which sentence from paragraphs 13 and 14 includes an analogy?

   a. So you see, I'm a good guy to know.

   b. I just carry a cane, that's all.

   c. None of this is to make light of going blind.

   d. When you see me walking with my cane, you may think I'm lost as I ricochet down the street.

14. What is the main point of paragraph 11?

   a. People help the writer cross intersections.

   b. Cabbies wait until he gets into his building.

   c. He receives more assistance than expected.

   d. Women guide him through dark rooms, airports, and train stations.

15. Which is the topic sentence of paragraph 14?

    a. None of this is to make light of going blind.

    b. Being blind is dark and depressing.

    c. When you see me walking with my cane, you may think I'm lost as I ricochet down the street.

    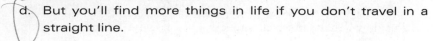 d. But you'll find more things in life if you don't travel in a straight line.

Reading the Whole

Now that you have had a chance to read Jim Bobryk's essay in its parts, identifying the patterns of organization within the essay, you will find that you have a deeper understanding of his main point when you reread the essay in its entirety. As you read, continue to pay attention to the patterns of organization. The ways Bobryk combines the patterns will shed new light on his experience.

JIM BOBRYK

Navigating My Eerie Landscape Alone

1   Now, as I stroll down the street, my right forefinger extends five feet in front of me, feeling the ground where my feet will walk.

2   Before, my right hand would have been on a steering wheel as I went down the street. I drove to work, found shortcuts in strange cities, picked up my two daughters after school. Those were the days when I ran my finger down a phone-book page and never dialed Information. When I read novels and couldn't sleep until I had finished the last page. Those were the nights when I could point out a shooting star before it finished scraping across the dark sky. And when I could go to the movies and it didn't matter if it was a foreign film or not.

3   But all this changed about seven years ago. I was driving home for lunch on what seemed to be an increasingly foggy day, although the perky radio deejay said it was clear and sunny. After I finished my lunch, I realized that I couldn't see across the room to my front door. I had battled glaucoma for 20 years. Suddenly, without warning, my eyes had hemorrhaged.

4   I will never regain any of my lost sight. I see things through a porthole covered in wax paper. I now have no vision in my left eye and only slight vision in my right. A minefield of blind spots make people and cars suddenly appear and vanish. I have no depth perception. Objects are not closer and farther; they're larger and smaller. Steps, curbs, and floors all flow on the same flat plane. My world has shapes but no features. Friends are mannequins in the fog until I recognize their voices. Printed words look like ants writhing on the pages. Doorways are unlit mine shafts. This is not a place for the fainthearted.

My cane is my navigator in this eerie landscape. It is a hollow fiber-glass stick with white reflector paint and a broad red band at the tip. It folds up tightly into four 15-inch sections, which can then be slipped into a black holster that attaches to my belt with Velcro. 5

Adults—unless they're preoccupied or in a hurry—will step aside without comment when they see me coming. Small children will either be scooped up apologetically or steered away by their parents. Only teenagers sometimes try to play chicken, threatening to collide with me and then veering out of the way at the last moment. 6

While I'm wielding my stick, strangers are often afraid to communicate with me. I don't take this personally—anymore. Certainly they can't be afraid that I'll lash at them with my rod. (Take *that,* you hapless sighted person! Whack!) No, they're probably more afraid *for* me. Don't startle the sword swallower. Don't tickle the baton twirler. 7

The trick for the sighted person is to balance courtesy with concern. Should he go out of his way or should he get out of the way? Will his friendliness be misconstrued by the disabled as pity? Will an offer of help sound patronizing? These anxieties are exaggerated by not knowing the etiquette in dealing with the disabled. A sighted person will do nothing rather than take the risk of offending the blind. Still, I refuse to take a dim view of all this. 8

When I peer over my cane and ask for help, no one ever cowers in fear. In fact, I think people are waiting for me to give them the green light to help. It makes us feel good to help. 9

When I ask for a small favor, I often get more assistance than I ever expect. Clerks will find my required forms and fill them out for me. A group of people will parade me across a dangerous intersection. A salesclerk will read the price tag for me and then hunt for the item on sale. I'm no Don Juan, but strange (and possibly exotic) women will take my hand and walk me through dark rooms, mysterious train stations, and foreign airports. Cabbies wait and make sure I make it safely into lobbies. 10

It's not like it's inconvenient for friends to help me get around. Hey, have disabled parking placard—will travel. Christmas shopping? Take me to the mall and I'll get us front-row parking. Late for the game? *No problema.* We'll be parking by the stadium entrance. And if some inconsiderate interloper does park in the blue zone without a permit, he'll either be running after a fleeing tow truck or paying a big fine. 11

Worried about those age lines showing? Not with me looking. Put down that industrial-strength Oil of Olay. To me, your skin looks as clear and smooth as it was back in the days when you thought suntanning was a good idea.   12

So you see, I'm a good guy to know. I just carry a cane, that's all.   13

None of this is to make light of going blind. Being blind is dark and depressing. When you see me walking with my cane, you may think I'm lost as I ricochet down the street. But you'll find more things in life if you don't travel in a straight line.   14

Integrated Skills

1. What is the author's attitude toward being blind? What is glaucoma?

2. What does the author mean when he writes, "My cane is my navigator in this eerie landscape"? And why does he describe his landscape as "eerie"?

3. What do you think sighted people should do when they encounter a blind person? What would you do? Why?

4. What benefits of being legally blind does the author describe?

Reading Textbooks

Thematic Connections. Jim Bobryk's essay "Navigating My Eerie Landscape Alone" recounts the experience of going blind from a personal perspective. His description of his blindness is limited to his own impressions. The reading that follows, which is taken from the textbook *Discovering Psychology* by Don H. Hockenbury and Sandra E. Hockenbury, describes the scientific process of seeing and will help you place Bobryk's experience in a broader perspective. As you read, pay attention to the patterns of organization the textbook authors use to make sense of how the human eye works.

Vocabulary Preview

receptor (para 1): something that receives (n.)

intricate (para. 2): complicated (adj.)

stimulus (para. 2): something that causes a reaction (n.)

minuscule (para. 4): tiny (adj.)

correspond (para. 4): match up (v.)

fibrous (para. 6): having many fibers (adj.)

transparent (para. 7): clear (adj.)

distinguish (para. 12): tell one from another (v.)

periphery (para. 13): outside edges (n.)

Vision

From Light to Sight

The eye contains receptor cells that are sensitive to the physical energy of light. What is the visible spectrum? What are the key structures of the eye? What are the functions of the rods and cones?   1

A lone caterpillar on the screen door, the pile of dirty laundry in the closet corner, a spectacular autumn sunset, the intricate play of color, light, and texture in a painting by Monet. The sense organ for seeing is the eye, which contains receptor cells that are sensitive to the physical energy of *light*. But before we can talk about how the eye functions to produce the sense of vision, we need to briefly discuss some characteristics of light as the visual stimulus.   2

WHAT WE SEE

The Nature of Light

Light is just one of many different kinds of electromagnetic energy that travel in the form of waves. Other forms of electro-   3 magnetic energy include X-rays, the microwaves you use to bake a potato, and the ultraviolet rays that give you a sunburn. The various types of electromagnetic energy differ in **wavelength,** which is the distance from one wave peak to another.

Humans are capable of visually detecting only a minuscule portion of the electromagnetic energy range. The visible portion of the electromagnetic energy spectrum can be further divided into different wavelengths. As we'll discuss in more detail later, the different wavelengths of visible light correspond to our psychological perception of different colors.

4

HOW WE SEE

The Human Visual System

Suppose you're watching your neighbor's yellow and white tabby cat sunning himself on the front steps. How do you "see" the cat? Simply seeing a yellow tabby cat involves a complex chain of events. We'll describe the process of vision from the object to the brain.

5

First, light waves reflected from the cat enter your eye, passing through the *cornea, pupil,* and *lens.* The **cornea,** a clear membrane that covers the front of the eye, helps gather and direct incoming light. The *sclera,* or white portion of the eye, is a tough, fibrous tissue that covers the eyeball except for the cornea. The **pupil** is the black opening in the middle of the eye. The pupil is surrounded by the **iris,** the colored structure that we refer to when we say that someone has brown or blue eyes. The iris is actually a ring of muscles that contract or expand to precisely control the size of the pupil and thus the amount of light entering the eye. In dim light, the iris widens the pupil to let light in; in bright light, the iris narrows the pupil.

6

Behind the pupil is the **lens,** another transparent structure. In a process called **accommodation,** the lens thins or thickens to bend or focus the incoming light so that the light falls on the retina. If the eyeball is abnormally shaped, the lens may not properly focus the incoming light on the retina. The result is a visual disorder, such as *nearsightedness, farsightedness,* or *astigmatism.*

7

THE RETINA

Rods and Cones

The **retina** is a thin, light-sensitive membrane that lies at the back of the eye, covering most of its inner surface. The retina contains

8

the two kinds of sensory receptors for light: **rods** and **cones.** When exposed to light, rods and cones undergo a chemical reaction that results in a neural signal.

Rods and cones differ in many ways. First, as their names imply, rods and cones are shaped differently. Rods are long and thin, with blunt ends. Cones are shorter and fatter, with one end that tapers to a point. The eye contains far more rods that cones. Each eye contains about 7 million cones, but more than 125 million rods!   9

Rods and cones are specialized for different visual functions. Although both are light receptors, rods are much more sensitive to light than cones. Once the rods are fully adapted to the dark, they are about a thousand times better than cones at detecting weak visual stimuli. Thus, we rely primarily on rods for vision in dim light and at night.   10

Rods and cones also react differently to *changes* in the amount of light. Rods adapt relatively slowly, reaching maximum sensitivity to light in about 30 minutes. In contrast, cones adapt quickly to bright light, reaching maximum sensitivity in about 5 minutes. That's why it takes several minutes for your eyes to adapt to the dim light of a darkened room, but only a few moments to adapt to the brightness when you switch on the lights.   11

You may have noticed that it is difficult or impossible to distinguish colors in very dim light. This difficulty occurs because only the cones are sensitive to the different wavelengths that produce the sensation of color, and cones require much more light than rods do to function effectively. Cones are also specialized for seeing fine details and for vision in bright light.   12

Most of the cones are concentrated in the **fovea,** which is a region in the very center of the retina. Cones are scattered throughout the rest of the retina, but they become progressively less common toward the periphery of the retina. There are no rods in the fovea. Images that do not fall on the fovea tend to be perceived as blurry or indistinct. For example, focus your eyes on the word *For* at the beginning of this sentence. In contrast to the sharpness of the letters in *For,* the words to the left and right are somewhat blurry. The image of the outlying words is striking the peripheral areas of the retina, where rods are more prevalent and cones are much less common.   13

Thinking about the Textbook Selection

1. Why does the author define *light*? How does the author define *light*?

2. Why does the author mention "your neighbor's yellow and white tabby cat"? What purpose does the tabby cat serve in the selection?

3. What are the cornea, pupil, and iris of the eye? What function does each of these parts of the eye perform?

4. What are rods and cones, and why are they important for seeing?

Reviewing

1. What are patterns of organization and why do writers use them?
2. Explain how recognizing patterns of organization can help you understand what you read.
3. Identify the common patterns of organization writers frequently use.
4. Why is it important to recognize mixed patterns of organization?
5. Which is your favorite pattern of organization? Why?

Recall / Remember

In this chapter you learned to identify the common patterns of organization writers use to develop their ideas. You can now recognize the following organizational patterns when you read: definitions, examples, lists and sequences, comparison and contrast, analogy, classification, and cause and effect. You have learned to use these patterns to understand reading selections. And you have seen how the patterns of organization can be combined.

In the chapters that follow, you will continue to practice your reading comprehension skills. Chapter 8 focuses on the process of reading through making careful observations about the details of a passage and making connections among those details as you begin to discover a pattern of meaning in the passage.

Chapter Summary

Making Observations and Connections

Getting Ready	223
Learning the Skills	224
Applying the Skills	
• Reading the Parts	243
• Reading the Whole	249
• Reading Textbooks	252
Reviewing	253

Getting Ready

The primary goal of reading is understanding. This chapter presents an approach and a series of strategies to help you understand what you read. In this chapter and throughout this book we use the term *comprehension* to describe the process of understanding involved in reading. This process entails four interrelated stages: making observations, making connections, drawing inferences, and formulating conclusions.

This chapter focuses on the first two of these steps: **making observations** and **making connections.** Observations are the things you notice when you read any kind of material, including key words and sentences, structure and organization, examples, and repetition.

This chapter also explains how to use your observations to make connections that lead to comprehension. You make connections among the details you observe. For example, you link your observations about repeated details. You make connections among your observations about the vocabulary of a reading selection, about its use of examples, and about its evidence and ideas.

Finally, this chapter provides you with a chance to practice these comprehension skills through exercises in reading and writing.

Chapter Overview

**Focusing
Questions**

In reading a chapter from one of your textbooks, **what** kinds of observations can you make about it?

In reading one of your textbook chapters, **what** connections can you make among your observations?

How can using a pen or pencil when you read help you to make observations and connections?

How can the beginning of a reading selection be connected to its middle and ending?

**Everyday
Reading**

All writing includes details, examples, structures, and key words and phrases that support the author's main ideas. Choose an article that interests you from a magazine that you enjoy. As you read it, pay attention to what stands out in your mind. When you have finished reading the article, make a list of five things you remember most strongly. You may find yourself listing examples, unusual ways that the article was structured, especially vivid details, or key words or phrases that jumped out at you. (If you have trouble coming up with five things, read the article again.) When you are finished your list, write a brief sentence after each, noting what was important about that item. When you've finished, write a brief summary of what all your items have in common.

Learning the Skills

■ Making Observations

Your first step toward comprehension is to observe things about what you are reading. In reading this paragraph, for example, you notice that it contains a heading — "Making Observations." You know that a heading in a textbook usually indicates the topic to follow. What does your observation about the heading "Making Observations" tell you? One thing it tells you is that this paragraph and those that follow will discuss the topic of making observations. What can you predict about this topic even before you continue reading? What might be some of the things this topic of making observations will focus on with regard to reading?

Many of the strategies described in the first seven chapters of this book require specific kinds of observation necessary for comprehending what you read. In Chapter 6, when you practiced the skill of identifying the main idea of a reading passage, for example, you made observations about a main idea and supporting details. Those observations helped you comprehend the meaning of what you read.

In reading your other textbooks, you observe that key terms are **boldface** or *italic* and that the chapters contain headings and subheadings. In reading newspaper and magazine advertisements, you observe headlines and pictures with captions. Comprehension of any material, written or visual, relies on observation. The observations you make while reading serve as the basis for your comprehension.

OBSERVING ORGANIZATION AND STRUCTURE

Organization refers to the way a writer presents information. In Chapter 7 you learned about some of the common organizing structures writers use, such as classification and comparison-contrast. Observing these kinds of organizing structures helps you comprehend an author's meaning. It helps you understand the relationship between main ideas and their supporting details and between one paragraph or section of a reading selection and another. And understanding these relationships helps you to follow an author's thinking.

Other ways that writers structure information are on a smaller scale than the organizational patterns you learned about in Chapter 7. They involve the order of sentences and paragraphs, for example, or the placement of headings, key words, key phrases, or illustrations, to name a few. These structures are not as easy to label as the common patterns of organization, but they are still important to understanding a writer's point. One strategy for noticing how authors structure their writing is to ask yourself the following questions as you read.

- How does this sentence relate to the ones immediately before and after it?
- How does this paragraph relate to the ones immediately before and after it?
- Where does the author state the main idea?
- Where does the author provide evidence to illustrate or support the main idea?

Read the following passage from the psychology textbook *Exploring Psychology* by David G. Myers and answer the questions in the list just given. We will then look at how the writer organized the passage. Understanding the structure of the passage will help you comprehend the author's meaning.

Perceptual Set

As everyone knows, to see is to believe. As many people also know, but do not fully appreciate, to believe is to see. Our experiences, assumptions, and expectations may give us a **perceptual set,** or mental predisposition, that greatly influences what we perceive. Is the image in the center picture of the following figure a man playing the saxophone or a woman's face? What we see in such a drawing can be influenced by first viewing either of the two unambiguous versions.

Which do you see in the center picture: the male saxophonist or the woman's face? Glancing first at one of the two unambiguous versions of the picture is likely to influence your interpretation.

Looking at the structure of this passage, you will observe that the paragraph begins with the heading "Perceptual Set." It includes a brief definition of *perceptual set* and then a series of pictures as an example. Notice that the passage begins first with a statement that you probably recognize — "to see is to believe" — but then turns that statement around as a way to explain what a perceptual set is. By noticing these details of structure, you no doubt were able to figure out that a perceptual set is an idea you already have that helps you understand new information.

Exercise 8-1

Look at the following textbook selections and identify the writers' organizing structure. Choose from the list on page 175.

Example:

As we say in the last chapter the eukaryotic cell, by virtue of its size and complexity, has a number of properties that made possible a great diversification of the unicellular eukaryotes in both structure and mode of life. These properties include the capacity to carry a great deal of genetic information and to transmit it reliably from generation to generation; the compartmentalization and specialization of different parts of the cell for different functions, leading to greater efficiency; the ability to acquire more food; and greater adaptability to life-threatening environmental changes. (Helena Curtis and N. Sue Barnes, *Invitation to Biology*)

list

1. Countries frequently are classified into two main economic categories based on GDP [Gross Domestic Product] per capita (that is, per person), or GDP divided by the number of people in the country. Developed countries are those in which per capita GDP is relatively high, over $10,000 per year. Developing countries are those in which per capita GDP is relatively low, less than $10,000 per year and typically below $5,000. Living standards in developing countries are often low, population growth high, and advanced technology unavailable to the vast majority of citizens. (Kenneth Blanchard, Charles Schewe, Robert Nelson, and Alexander Hiam, *Exploring the World of Business*)

2. Like any science, psychology is based on empirical evidence, or evidence that is the result of observation, measurement, and experimentation. As part of the overall process of producing empirical evidence, psychologists follow the steps of the scientific method. In a nutshell, these steps are: (1) creating testable questions, (2) designing a study to collect data, (3) analyzing the data to arrive at conclusions, and (4) reporting the results. (Don H. Hockenbury and Sandra E. Hockenbury, *Discovering Psychology*)

3. Four different types of organic molecules are found in large quantities of organisms. These four are carbohydrates (composed of sugars), lipids (nonpolar molecules, most of which contain fatty acids), proteins (composed of amino acids), and nucleic acids (composed of complex molecules known as nucleotides). (Helena Curtis and N. Sue Barnes, *Invitation to Biology*)

4. After the earthquake, the Oakland Bay Bridge was seriously damaged, and the legendary Santa Monica Freeway, one of the most heavily used roads in the United States, had to be closed. This necessitated great inconvenience to the residents in the San Francisco Bay metropolitan area. People had to find ingenious and different ways to get to work and get business done despite the disruption. In order to get the bridge repaired and the freeway reopened, a complicated array of different contractors needed to coordinate their efforts. By offering a collection of financial incentives to finish on target or prior to scheduled dates, the bridge and freeway were repaired and made usable again earlier than originally estimated. By comparison, the vast scheduling effort to open a new international airport to serve the Denver metropolitan area resulted in a series of announced openings and expensive delays when the scheduled dates could not be met. One of the sticking points was the development of an innovative baggage-handling system that was designed to speed travelers who started or ended their journeys in Denver or changed planes there. From the beginning, the baggage-handling facility caused trouble. Inadequate time had been scheduled for the development of the system, installing it, and testing it. For this project, the scheduling went awry! (Consortium for Mathematics and Its Applications, *For All Practical Purposes*)

    _____

5. Just as a camera flash captures the specific details of a scene on film, a flashbulb memory is thought to involve the recall of very precise details and images surrounding a significant, rare, or personally meaningful event. (Don H. Hockenbury and Sandra E. Hockenbury, *Discovering Psychology*)

    _____

. . . .

OBSERVING EXAMPLES

You have already learned how to identify the organizational pattern of examples. However, observing an author's examples will enable you to do more than simply recognize the organization of a reading selection. The examples themselves will help you to understand what the author is trying to say—especially when you analyze them in the context of all the examples in the reading.

Try to observe the examples in the following paragraph, from the reading on perceptual sets.

> ⑨   Everyday examples of perceptual set abound. In 1972, a British newspaper published genuine, unretouched photographs of a "monster" in Scotland's Loch Ness—"the most amazing pictures ever taken," stated the paper. But when Steuart Campbell approached the photos with a different perceptual set, he saw a curved tree trunk—very likely the same tree trunk others had seen in the water the day the photo was shot. Moreover, with this different perceptual set, viewers will notice that the object is floating motionless, without any water disturbance or wake around it—hardly what we would expect of a lively monster.

As you read this paragraph, you can observe that the author begins by referring to "everyday examples." Seeing the word *examples* tips you off that the author will illustrate his idea further with additional ones from everyday life. He uses the example of the Loch Ness "monster" and then provides still more examples in the next paragraph:

> Our perceptual set can influence what we hear as well as what we see. Witness the kindly airline pilot who, on a takeoff run, looked over at his depressed co-pilot and said, "Cheer up." The co-pilot heard the usual "Gear up" and promptly raised the wheels—before they had left the ground. When listening to rock music played backward, people often perceive an evil message *if* specifically told what to listen to. When observing presidential campaign debates, most Americans perceive their favorite candidate as being the better debater. Clearly, much of what we perceive comes not just from the world "out there" but also from what's behind our eyes and between our ears.

Notice that the second paragraph of "Perceptual Set" contains only one example, while the third paragraph includes three—about airline pilots, rock music, and presidential debates. In comprehending the third paragraph, you relate its three examples to the examples included in the first two paragraphs.

After reading more than one example of a concept, ask yourself the question "What do all these examples have in common?" Thinking about and then putting into words what traits the examples share will help you to understand the concept they illustrate. In the case of the reading on perceptual sets, all the examples show people whose preconceptions altered what they heard or saw—which is exactly how perceptual sets work.

Exercise 8-2

Underline the examples in each of the following paragraphs. Make sure to underline each example within a paragraph separately. The first one is done for you.

Example:

Today the two tenets underlying democracy are majority rule and the protection of basic rights for all citizens. **Majority rule** takes shape mainly through regular elections, though the exact type and timing of elections vary considerably from one nation to another. <u>In the United States the timing of elections is fixed by law—every four years, for example, for the presidency.</u> <u>In Great Britain the prime minister can call an election at any time during a five-year term.</u> (Lewis Lipsitz and David M. Speak, *American Democracy*)

1. Across place and time, children have thrived under various child-rearing systems. Upper-class British parents traditionally left routine caregiving to nannies, before sending their children off to boarding school. Their children generally grew up to be pillars of British society, just like their parents. In some preindustrial societies, babies spend the day on their mother's back—with lots of body contact but little face-to-face and language interaction. When the mother becomes pregnant, the toddler is weaned and handed over to someone else, often an older sibling. Today's North American parents give their children lots of cuddles and hugs—more so than at the beginning of this century. Although children do better when treated warmly than when treated coldly, such diversity in child-rearing cautions us against presuming that our culture's way is the only way to rear successful children. (David G. Myers, *Psychology*)

2. In a society as complex as ours, everyday problems such as providing services efficiently and on time require accurate planning of both people and machines. Take the example of a hospital in a major city. Around-the-clock scheduling of nurses and doctors must be provided to guarantee that people with particular expertise are available during each shift. The operating rooms must be scheduled in a manner flexible enough to deal with the emergencies. Equipment used for X-ray, CAT, or MRI scans must be scheduled for maximal efficiency. (Consortium for Mathematics and Its Applications, *For All Practical Purposes*)

3. Because choices range over every imaginable aspect of human experience, so does economics. Economists have investigated the nature of family life, the arts, education, crime, sports, job creation—the list is virtually endless because so much of our lives involves making choices. (Timothy Tregarthen and Libby Rittenberg, *Macroeconomics*)

4. Like art, music, or any other human creative activity, science makes use of intuition and experience. But the approach used by scientists to explore physical reality differs from other forms of intellectual endeavor in that it is based fundamentally on *observation, logic,* and *skepticism.* (William J. Kaufmann III and Roger A. Freedman, *Universe*)

5. The first people who lived in the Western Hemisphere were migrants from Asia. Some might have come by water, but most probably came by land. Strong archaeological evidence suggests that during the last Ice Age, which began about 30,000 years ago, small bands of hunters followed herds of game across a land bridge between Siberia and Alaska. A tale of the Tuscarora Indians, who lived in present-day North Carolina, tells of a famine in the old world and a journey over ice toward where "the sun rises," a trek that brought their ancestors to a lush forest with abundant food and game. Most anthropologists believe that this migratory stream continued for about 20,000 years, until the glaciers melted and the rising ocean waters submerged the land bridge. Then the people of the Western Hemisphere, who by that time had moved as far south as the tip of South America and as far east as the Atlantic coast of North America, were cut off from the rest of the world for 400 generations. (James A. Henretta, David Brody, and Lynn Dumenil, *America: A Concise History*)

OBSERVING DETAILS

When we observe details, we look at the elements, the bits and pieces of something. Details provide the specifics of a reading passage. They include information, numbers, facts, and examples. Look at the details in the following passage from *Macroeconomics*.

> The number of buyers affects the total quantity of a good or service that will be bought; in general, the greater the population, the greater the demand. Other demographic characteristics can affect demand as well. As the share of the population over age 65 increases, the demand for medical services, ocean cruises, and motor homes increases. The birth rate in the United States fell sharply between 1955 and 1975 but has gradually increased since then. That increase has raised the demand for such things as infant supplies, elementary school teachers, soccer coaches, and in-line skates. It caused the demand for higher education in the second half of the 1990s to increase and should continue to increase demand for the next several years. Demand can thus shift as a result of changes in both the number and characteristics of buyers.

In observing the details of this passage, it is helpful to note that the paragraph discusses the number of buyers and how that number affects the quantity of goods and services that will be bought. It is also helpful to note that the authors go on to provide examples of how other demographic characteristics affect demand by discussing the population over age sixty-five and the birthrate between 1955 and 1975. These two factors have a direct effect on the demands for certain things (infant supplies, elementary school teachers, soccer coaches) and the demand, overall, for higher education.

One strategy you can use to observe details is to underline them or list them as you read. Careful observation of the details a writer uses is essential for comprehending what a writer is saying. Like examples, all the details an author includes will add up to help you understand the main point more fully.

OBSERVING REPETITION

Writers repeat themselves for emphasis. They may state an idea at the beginning of a passage and restate it later, in the middle or at the end. They may express an idea in the same words each time, or they may vary the words used to convey their ideas.

One way to improve your reading comprehension is to be alert for repetition in a text. Look for words and phrases that recur. Look for slight variations in phrasing. Be observant too of exact repetition.

The author of "Perceptual Set" repeats the idea of the passage in different ways throughout the passage. After suggesting the main idea in the heading, he either repeats the words *perceptual set* or rephrases the idea using different words. Observing the use of such repetition and understanding the relationship between the repeated words and sentences aids your comprehension of the passage.

Look at this passage taken from the textbook *Family Relationships* by Betty Yorburg, which falls under the heading "Social Class":

> Our location in a particular **social class** affects every aspect of our lives every day of our lives. Membership in a social class, also known as **socioeconomic status,** is determined by three factors: income and property, years of education, and prestige of occupation. These three factors tend to work together, but not always. For example, drug dealers usually rank low on occupational prestige and years of education but high on income and property.

Looking for instances of repetition in this paragraph, you will observe that the author repeats the words *social class* or *socioeconomic status* three times. Also, after listing the three factors, "income and property, years of education, and prestige of occupation," the author repeats each of them in the context of her example. Observing these instances of repetition in this short paragraph, you can see that the author's main point is to define social class and show how it works.

Focusing on repetition while reading helps you focus on the author's most important points. Observing repeated examples, statements, and ideas in a passage helps you comprehend the writer's meaning. By annotating repetition in a reading selection or by listing the repeated elements, you also take an important step toward later study and review.

■ Using Writing to Develop Your Observation Skills

Have you ever noticed that when you write something about your reading you often notice more than when you don't? Or have you had the experience of picking up a pen or pencil as you read and jotting an occasional question or comment in the margins? If so, you probably had the experience of being more engaged in your reading. If not, it's time you tried a few writing techniques to help you read with greater comprehension.

Writing while reading makes you a more observant reader. Writing while you read keeps you alert as you await opportunities to underline passages and jot down observations. This alertness leads to a kind of active reading that can make reading less of a chore and more of a rewarding experience. Reading becomes more rewarding when you comprehend what you read and when you are actively engaged by it. Writing while you read can help increase both your reading comprehension and your engagement.

ANNOTATING

One useful form of writing while reading is **annotating.** Annotating is a method of marking what you read to highlight key words and sentences, major concepts, and important details and examples. Annotating your textbooks can help you in a number of ways. It can help you emphasize significant ideas about a subject. It can help you review and study because you have marked the essential information and ideas you need to learn. Compared to other forms of writing and note taking, annotating is quick and relatively easy.

Annotating includes underlining words, phrases, and sentences. It may take the form of highlighting passages with a marker. Annotating also involves writing notes around the passage you are reading. In annotating this book, for example, you might underline or highlight the second sentence of this section, which defines annotating. You might write numbers next to the ways annotating can help you as they are listed in the first paragraph. Or you might write a note in the margin next to this paragraph. Your note might provide a shorthand summary of the key points of this paragraph. You might write the words *underline, highlight,* and *jotting* in the margin to identify the ways you can annotate a reading selection.

When you annotate as you are reading, you may jot comments or questions in the margins. These comments and questions can be quite brief, sometimes only a single word. You might jot *Memorize!* or *key point* in the margin. Or you might express your disagreement with a *No!,* your reservations with a *Perhaps?,* or your approval with an *OK!* Annotations can also be brief phrases, even short sentences you jot in the side margins and on the top or bottom of a page.

Besides serving as reminders and expressing your personal reactions, your annotations should also help you comprehend and remember what you read. How much you annotate will vary with the kind of material you are reading, your purposes in reading it, and how much of it you are expected to remember. If you find yourself annotating nearly every sentence, you are probably annotating too much. If you annotate nothing on a page or in a section, you are probably annotating too little. If you annotate almost everything, the key points will not stand out. If you annotate hardly anything, you won't have much to refer to later when you review and study.

The most useful and effective annotations are often those made after you have skimmed a reading selection because during a quick first reading you gain an overview of the whole. You can use this sense of the whole to decide what is important and then annotate those things during your second reading.

Some readers create their own system of abbreviations when they annotate. They might use an asterisk (*), for example, or a star (☆) or a check (✔) to indicate a key concept. They might use a series of check marks for important sentences or sections. Or they might use abbreviations such as *Def.* to indicate a definition or *Ex.* for an example. Whether you use a system of symbols and abbreviations or you simply mark your reading materials with underlinings and jotted words or phrases, try to use annotation to read actively and to help you review and study.

Here is an example of a reading selection from the textbook *Family Relationships* using a system of symbols for annotations:

Alternative Family Forms In the United States today, large numbers of unmarried couples live together in heterosexual or homosexual relationships, with or without children. There is also a large variety of other nontraditional, sexually active groups, with single or multiple partners, married or unmarried, living in communes and elsewhere. These groups, too, define themselves as families. The growth and increasing acceptance (but not necessarily the approval) of these groups are reflected in the language—they are now called variant or *alternative family forms,* rather than pathological or deviant, as in the past.

There is a large and growing number of divorced or never-married single parents of many different ages and all economic circumstances. Vast numbers of remarried families and stepfamilies exist, whose problems are unique because the biological parent as well as the stepparent are both still living. In the past, death broke up most marriages; today, divorce does.

Here is the same passage annotated with words or phrases rather than symbols.

Alternative Family Forms In the United States today, large numbers of unmarried couples live together in heterosexual or homosexual relationships, with or without children. There is also a large variety of other (nontraditional,) sexually active groups, with (single) (or multiple partners,) married or unmarried, living in communes and elsewhere. These groups, too, define themselves as families. The growth and increasing acceptance (but not necessarily the approval) of these groups are reflected in the language—they are now called < variant or *alternative family forms*, rather than pathological or deviant, as in the past.

There is a large and (growing number of divorced or never-) (married single parents) of many different ages and all economic circumstances. Vast numbers of remarried families and stepfamilies exist, whose problems are unique because the biological parent as well as the stepparent are both still living. In the past, death broke up most marriages; today, (divorce) does.

diff. kinds of families

Really?

def.

more singles — why?

then —

now —

Exercise 8-3

Practice annotating the following selection, using some or all of the techniques you just read about.

Born in Pisa in 1170, Leonardo Pisano Bigollo has been known as "Fibonacci" for the past century and a half. This nickname, which refers to his descent from an ancestor named Bonaccio, is modern, and there is no evidence that he was known by it in his own time.

Leonardo was the greatest mathematician of the Middle Ages. His stated purpose in his book *Liber abbaci* (1201) was to introduce calculation with Hindu-Arabic numerals into Italy, to replace the Roman numerals then in use. Other books of his treated topics in geometry, algebra, and number theory. (Consortium for Mathematics and Its Applications, *For All Practical Purposes*)

LISTING

Another technique you can use to improve your comprehension is listing. In the same way that you list items to buy at the grocery store or you make a list of chores to do, you can list observations you make about your reading. These observations might concern the structure or organization of a passage, key words or sentences, details, examples, instances of repetition, or the kinds of information the passage includes.

Authors often use lists to highlight what is to come later in a passage or chapter. You can use lists when you read for later review when you study. In either case, lists can serve as structural cues.

Exercise 8-4

List the questions or examples included in the passage about perceptual sets on pages 226 and 229. The first one is done for you.

Example:

> *Is the image in the center picture of the following figure a man*
>
> *playing the saxophone or a woman's face?*

1. _____

2. _____

3. _____

4. _____

■ Making Connections

Now that you have practiced observation strategies for reading, the next step is to make connections among your observations. When you make connections, you identify relationships among details that you observe. You look for what your observations might have in common. You ask how your observations relate to one another.

As you make connections among observations, you discover how one example is related to another. You also discover how one paragraph is related to another, and you realize how one part of a passage is related to the other parts. In making these kinds of connections, you will more fully understand what the author says, and you will better understand how he or she organizes information.

IDENTIFYING RELATIONSHIPS

You observed that the pictures in the selection about perceptual sets could be interpreted in more than one way. You connected the set of pictures to the examples used later in the selection by observing that the middle picture of the first set and many of the examples could be interpreted in more than one way. You connected the author's use of the pictures and examples to his main idea. You also connected his concluding sentences to the examples he used in earlier sentences, and you identified the common link between his examples. To comprehend a writer's ideas, you consider how all the details you observe are related.

You can practice making connections as you read the following selection about sleep from the same textbook, *Exploring Psychology* by David G. Myers. While you read the passage, jot annotations as if you were preparing for a class discussion about sleep. You may wish to write a few questions about sleep. You may wish to note interesting or puzzling facts. You may wish to comment on the writer's examples.

Most of all, however, look for how the observations you make about the passage's details can be related to one another.

Why Do We Sleep?

Sleep commands roughly one-third of our lives. Deprived of it, we begin to feel terrible; our bodies yearn for it. You can know you are sleep-deprived—as many college students are—if most of the following are true: You need an alarm clock to shorten your natural sleep pattern; you feel sleepy while sitting in class or you lack vigor needed for peak performance; you collapse into sleep almost immediately after your head hits the pillow. How much sleep do you need? The answer is simple, says sleep researcher William Moorcroft: enough so you will not feel tired the next day. [1]

Obviously, we need sleep. But why? It seems an easy question to answer: Just keep people awake for several days and note how they deteriorate. If you were a subject in such an experiment, how do you think it would affect your body and mind? [2]

Of course, you would become terribly drowsy at times—especially during the hours when your biological clock programs you to sleep. But could lack of sleep physically damage you? Would it noticeably alter your biochemistry or body organs? Would you become emotionally disturbed? Intellectually disoriented?

3

The major effect, as fatigued college students know, is sleepiness, and sometimes a general malaise. Owing to modern light bulbs, TV, shift work, and social diversions, people today more than ever suffer from sleep patterns that thwart their having an energized feeling of well-being. Teenagers typically need 8 or 9 hours sleep but now average nearly 2 hours less sleep a night than their counterparts of 80 years ago. Many fill this need by using home room for their first siesta and after-lunch study hall for a slumber party. As sleep researcher William Dement laments, "The national sleep debt is larger and more important than the national debt."

4

Other effects are more subtle: impaired creativity and concentration, diminished immunity to disease, slight hand tremors, irritability, slowed performance, occasional misperceptions on monotonous tasks. With some tasks, such as truck driving and controlling air traffic, these effects can be devastating. "Rest. That's what I need is rest," said Eastern Airlines Captain James Reeves to the control tower on a September 1974 morning—30 minutes before crashing his airliner at low altitude, killing the crew and all 68 passengers. The *Exxon Valdez* oil spill; Union Carbide's Bhopal, India, disaster; and the Three Mile Island and Chernobyl nuclear accidents all occurred after midnight, when operators were likely to be drowsiest.

5

On short, highly motivating tasks, however, sleep deprivation has little effect. When 17-year-old Randy Gardner made his way into the *Guinness Book of World Records* by staying awake for 11 days, he at times had to keep moving to stay awake. Nevertheless, during his final night of sleeplessness, Gardner managed to beat researcher Dement 100 straight times in a pinball game. He then slept 15 hours and awoke feeling fine.

6

Why, then, must we sleep? We have few answers, but sleep may have evolved for at least two reasons: First, it hides us out of harm's way. Our ancestors were safer if asleep at night. Animals with the least reason to fear predation or the most need to graze tend to sleep less. For instance, elephants and horses sleep only 3 to 4 hours a day. Second, sleep helps us recuperate. It helps restore body tissues,

7

continued

especially those of the brain. As we sleep, our brain is actively repairing and reorganizing itself and consolidating memories. Our lowered body temperature during sleep also conserves energy for the daytime hours.

Sleep may also play a role in the growth process. During deep sleep, the pituitary gland releases a growth hormone. As adults grow older, they release less of this hormone, and they spend less time in deep sleep. These physiological discoveries are only beginning to solve the ongoing riddle of sleep. As researcher Dement deadpanned, "We have miles to go before we sleep."

8

Exercise 8-5

Make the following observations and connections based on the preceding reading. The first one is done for you.

Example:

What do the examples in paragraph 1 illustrate?

They illustrate ways to know if you are sleep-deprived.

1. What kinds of sentences make up paragraph 3?

   _____

   _____

2. Make two additional observations about the passage.

   _____

   _____

3. Explain the connection between the question in the title and the eight paragraphs about sleep.

   _____

   _____

4. Explain the connection between paragraph 4 and paragraph 3. How is paragraph 4 related to paragraph 3?

   _____

   _____

5. What is the relationship among the details of paragraphs 4 and 5? What is similar and different about the details in each paragraph?

   _____

   _____

6. How are paragraphs 7 and 8 connected? What is similar about the information they contain?

   _____

   _____

7. How are paragraphs 4–6 related to the concluding paragraphs, paragraphs 7 and 8? What is the focus of each group of paragraphs?

   _____

   _____

. . . .

PRACTICING MAKING CONNECTIONS

In reading the passage about sleep you probably connected what the author wrote to your own experience of sleep. In answering the questions in Exercise 8-5 you made connections among your observations about the details of the passage. You connected observations about the way the author's examples support his idea. You connected observations about his sentences, noting how, for example, he first asks questions and then answers them. You connected your observations about the information and facts provided in the middle of the passage (paragraphs 4–6) with the author's emphasis at the end (paragraphs 7 and 8). In making those kinds of connections among observations you were building your comprehension of the writer's ideas.

Here are some observations we can make about details in the passage "Why Do We Sleep?"

1. The passage contains information about sleep—how much people generally need, why we need sleep, and what happens when we don't get enough.
2. The author refers to psychological research studies done on sleep.
3. The passage is focused on a single question: "Why do we sleep?"

These observations about the details of the passage can be supplemented by observations we make about its structure.

4. The first three paragraphs form an introduction to the passage. They raise the questions that the remainder of the passage will answer.

5. The middle paragraphs (4–6) describe the effects of sleep deprivation.

6. Paragraph 4 contains different kinds of examples from those in paragraph 5.

7. The last two paragraphs describe the functions of sleep.

To fully comprehend the meaning of the passage, we make connections among our observations. Observation 4 identifies a connection among the first three paragraphs. Those paragraphs all serve to introduce the passage, to interest us in reading further. Observation 5 identifies a connection among the middle paragraphs (4–6). These paragraphs have one thing in common: They all concern the consequences of not getting enough sleep. Observation 6 identifies a connection between the last two paragraphs. Both paragraphs explain the role of sleep.

You can make even further connections about the structure of the passage. Observe, for example, how in the first three paragraphs the author addresses "you" directly. The observation that he is writing as if he is talking to the reader personally links the first three paragraphs. These three paragraphs thus form a cluster or unit that we have called an "introduction."

Observe what happens in paragraph 4. Here, as the author begins to cite research studies, he stops talking to "you" directly. Instead, he refers to studies done with teenagers, college students, and adults. These examples are connected by focusing on the effects of insufficient sleep.

As you read and make such observations, ask yourself just how the details you observe can be connected. These observations and connections help you see how the author organizes his material. Understanding the writer's organization helps you understand his ideas.

Reading the Parts

Cathy Young is a syndicated columnist who is known for her criticism of both liberals and conservatives. She is cofounder and vice president of the Women's Freedom Network. Her most recent book is *Ceasefire! Why Women and Men Must Join Forces to Achieve True Equality.* As you read this article from the *Detroit News* of March 8, 2000, try to recognize organization and structures, observe key words and key sentences, examples, and relationships. After reading each section and answering the questions that follow, move on to the next section. You will have a chance to read the entire article when you finish.

CATHY YOUNG

Trigger Guards Are Not Answer, but Moral Fiber Is

"Guns don't kill people, people kill people."   1

This National Rifle Association slogan has been widely treated   2
as a joke—as evidence of the folly and hypocrisy of gun fanatics.
And yet, looking at the terrible tragedy of 6-year-old Kayla Rolland,
shot to death by a first-grade classmate in Mount Morris Township,
it is hard not to think that the slogan has some truth to it.

Yes, it was a bullet from a .32-caliber revolver, which the boy   3
found under some laundry at home, that ended Kayla's life.
"Home" is a relative term; it was a flophouse full of illegal drugs,
stolen guns and grown-up criminals. If the boy, who had previously
stabbed a classmate with a pencil, had found a switchblade instead
of a gun, it's quite possible that Kayla would be just as dead.

Genesee County Prosecutor Arthur Busch has called the boy a   4
"victim of the drug culture and a home that is in chaos." This is a
child whose father has been in prison for most of the past 10 years,
and whose mother, a drug user convicted of abusing another son,
had dumped her two kids in a crack house after getting evicted
from her home.

In this case, even some pro–gun control commentators, such as   5
New York *Newsday* columnist Sheryl McCarthy, have sensed that
the problem runs deeper than lack of gun control.

1. From the title of this selection, "Trigger Guards Are Not Answer, but Moral Fiber Is," what conclusion can you draw about Cathy Young's stance on the issues of guns in American society?

   a. Cathy Young is against gun control but in support of moral development.

   b. Cathy Young is in favor of trigger guards.

   c. Cathy Young thinks that children should have more fiber in their diets.

   d. Cathy Young does not take a stance on gun control.

2. Young's inclusion of the detail in paragraph 3 that the boy who killed Kayla Rolland had "previously stabbed a classmate with a pencil" suggests that the boy was already violent and helps support her statement that

   a. "it is hard not to think that the slogan ['Guns don't kill people, people kill people'] has some truth to it."

   b. "This National Rifle Association slogan has been widely treated as a joke."

   c. "Yes, it was a bullet from a .32-caliber revolver, which the boy found under some laundry at home."

   d. "even some pro–gun control commentators . . . have sensed that the problem runs deeper than lack of gun control."

3. Young's use of the word *flophouse* in paragraph 3 connects with her characterization in paragraph 4 of the boy's home as a "crack house" to imply that

   a. the house was dirty.

   b. the boy's environment and upbringing influenced his behavior.

   c. Kayla Rolland lived in a better environment.

   d. drug dealers stayed away from the boy's home.

4. In paragraph 4 Young provides a quote from the prosecutor in which he calls the boy a "victim." What details does Young provide to support her inclusion of this comment?

   a. She provides details of the boy's educational record.

   b. She provides the boy's "rap" sheet.

   c. She provides details of the boy's mother and father and how they treated their children.

   d. She provides information related to the number of guns at the child's house.

5. Young's statement in paragraph 5 that "even some pro–gun control commentators . . . have sensed that the problem runs deeper than lack of gun control" helps support her conclusion that

    a. "Guns don't kill people, people kill people."

    b. "Trigger guards are not the answer, but moral fiber is."

    c. the boy was a "victim."

    d. "This National Rifle Association slogan has been widely treated as a joke."

Nonetheless, we have also heard the usual chorus of "How many more children have to die before we do something?" President Bill Clinton has lamented the failure by Congress to mandate child-safety trigger locks on all new handguns.   6

That may or may not be a good idea (depending on how much hindrance a lock would pose to an adult who needs to defend her/himself in an emergency), but such a law wouldn't have stopped any shooting involving any of the 65 million handguns that Americans already own. Besides, a thug like the 19-year-old drug dealer who had allegedly showed off the gun to the 6-year-old shooter could have easily disabled a trigger lock for convenience.   7

Ironically, in Sunday's *Washington Post,* Josh Sugarmann of the Violence Policy Center, a leading gun control advocacy group, ridiculed the notion of a trigger lock as the solution: "Considering the people who went in and out of that house, [this] expectation would strike most people as absurd on its face." What we need, Sugarmann argues, is to ban handguns. Well, considering the people who went in and out of that house, the expectation that any law could have kept it gun-free certainly strikes me as absurd on its face.   8

---

6. Cathy Young's inclusion of the statistic in paragraph 7 that 65 million handguns are already owned by Americans supports her conclusion that

    a. mandating child-safety trigger locks on all new handguns would not stop children from dying from gunshot wounds.

    b. there are too many guns available in the United States today.

    c. too many Americans don't use trigger locks anyway.

    d. Congress doesn't have a handle on the gun problem in America today.

7. Young provides a quote from Josh Sugarmann of the Violence Policy Center that states that handguns should be banned altogether. How does Sugarmann's statement connect to Young's statement that "considering the people who went in and out of that house [where the boy lived], the expectation that any law could have kept it gun-free certainly strikes me as absurd on its face"?

    a. Young is implying that the people who went "in and out of that house" already had many guns.

    b. Young is implying that the people who went "in and out of that house" have no regard for the law and can get guns anyway.

    c. Young is implying that the house was filled with guns anyway.

    d. Young is implying that Josh Sugarmann is on her side of the argument.

8. What is the stance of Josh Sugarmann of the Violence Policy Center on the issue of trigger locks?

    a. He disagrees with Cathy Young on the issue of trigger locks.

    b. He supports wholesale legalization of guns so that stricter laws can be put into effect.

    c. He "ridiculed the notion of a trigger lock as the solution."

    d. He thinks that there should be a congressional debate on the issue.

9. The words *trigger lock* or *lock* are repeated four times in paragraphs 6–8. Connecting this repetition with the repetition of *handguns,* you might conclude that

    a. only handguns require trigger locks.

    b. handguns never have trigger locks.

    c. there are too many handguns and too many trigger locks.

    d. both handguns and trigger locks are illegal.

10. In paragraph 6 Young explains that "President Clinton has lamented the failure by Congress to mandate child-safety trigger locks on all new handguns." This means that President Clinton

a.   supported the decision by Congress.

b.   had not heard about the decision by Congress.

c.   expressed disappointment with the decision by Congress.

d.   did not understand the decision by Congress.

After all, it was a crack house where drugs were routinely traded for guns. Drugs, in case the Violence Policy Center hasn't noticed, are already illegal and subject to what many believe are excessively draconian laws—which don't seem to have had much deterrent effect.   9

Predictably, Kayla's death has been the occasion for a lot of demagoguery about "the children." Clinton says that 13 children die from gunfire every day—without mentioning that this includes everyone under 19, and that 85 percent of the juvenile victims are over 16. Of course, these deaths are tragic, but an 18-year-old gang member is hardly a child.   10

In 1997, 630 children under 15 died from gun injuries—a considerable drop from the 1993 figure of 957 but still no reason to celebrate. But let's not forget that the same year, nearly 1,000 children drowned, more than 2,000 died in car accidents and more than 600 were murdered without firearms.   11

And here's something else to remember. The same day that the news of Kayla's shooting shocked the nation, murder charges were filed in Germany against three American teen-agers—children of soldiers stationed at a U.S. army base—who had killed two people and injured five. There wasn't a gun in the picture. The kids had been throwing rocks off a highway overpass.   12

When children without a moral center are intent on inflicting harm, they will find a way, guns or no guns.   13

11. When Cathy Young relates the story of three American teen-agers living in Germany who had killed two people and injured five by throwing rocks, she is supporting which of the following statements in paragraphs 9–13?

a.   "When children without a moral center are intent on inflicting harm, they will find a way, guns or no guns."

b.   "In 1997, 630 children under 15 died from gun injuries."

c.   ". . . 13 children die from gunfire every day."

d.   ". . . an 18-year-old gang member is hardly a child."

12. Young's statement that "Kayla's death has been the occasion for a lot of demagoguery [political posturing] about 'the children'" relates directly to which of the following statements from paragraphs 9–13?

    a. "The kids had been throwing rocks off a highway overpass."

    b. "Clinton says that 13 children die from gunfire every day—without mentioning that this includes everyone under 19, and that 85 percent of the juvenile victims are over 16."

    c. "Of course, these deaths are tragic, but an 18-year-old gang member is hardly a child."

    d. "When children without a moral center are intent on inflicting harm, they will find a way, guns or no guns."

13. In paragraph 11, Young cites statistics from 1997 that "630 children under 15 died from gun injuries, . . . nearly 1,000 children drowned, more than 2,000 died in car accidents and more than 600 were murdered without firearms." What point is she trying to emphasize by including those statistics?

    a. that more children were killed by guns in 1997 than drowned

    b. that more children died in car accidents than drowned in 1997

    c. that fewer children were murdered without firearms than with firearms

    d. that more children died from other causes—drowning, car accidents, and murder without firearms—in 1997 than were killed with firearms

14. According to Young, drugs are "subject to what many believe are excessively draconian laws." What does *draconian* mean?

    a. fair

    b. light, easy

    c. unfair, severe

    d. from the Old World

15. What point is Young trying to make when she mentions that "85 percent of the juvenile victims are over 16"?

    a. They are responsible for their own deaths.

    b. They should be allowed to own a gun.

    c. They are only children and don't know what they're doing.

    d. Clinton is being misleading when he refers to those over 16 as "children."

Reading the Whole

Now that you have read Cathy Young's essay in its parts and practiced making observations and connections, you are ready to read the whole essay, focusing more on your comprehension of her main point and how she makes it. As you read, continue to make observations about organization, structure, key words, key sentences, repetition, examples, and details, and continue to make connections among your observations. Most important, pay attention to all the arguments the author makes, and ask yourself if you are convinced.

CATHY YOUNG

Trigger Guards Are Not Answer, but Moral Fiber Is

"Guns don't kill people, people kill people." 1

This National Rifle Association slogan has been widely treated 2 as a joke—as evidence of the folly and hypocrisy of gun fanatics. And yet, looking at the terrible tragedy of 6-year-old Kayla Rolland, shot to death by a first-grade classmate in Mount Morris Township, it is hard not to think that the slogan has some truth to it.

Yes, it was a bullet from a .32-caliber revolver, which the boy 3 found under some laundry at home, that ended Kayla's life. "Home" is a relative term; it was a flophouse full of illegal drugs, stolen guns and grown-up criminals. If the boy, who had previously stabbed a classmate with a pencil, had found a switchblade instead of a gun, it's quite possible that Kayla would be just as dead.

Genesee County Prosecutor Arthur Busch has called the boy a 4 "victim of the drug culture and a home that is in chaos." This is a child whose father has been in prison for most of the past 10 years, and whose mother, a drug user convicted of abusing another son, had dumped her two kids in a crack house after getting evicted from her home.

In this case, even some pro–gun control commentators, such as 5 New York *Newsday* columnist Sheryl McCarthy, have sensed that the problem runs deeper than lack of gun control.

Nonetheless, we have also heard the usual chorus of "How 6 many more children have to die before we do something?" President Bill Clinton has lamented the failure by Congress to mandate child-safety trigger locks on all new handguns.

That may or may not be a good idea (depending on how much hindrance a lock would pose to an adult who needs to defend her/himself in an emergency), but such a law wouldn't have stopped any shooting involving any of the 65 million handguns that Americans already own. Besides, a thug like the 19-year-old drug dealer who had allegedly showed off the gun to the 6-year-old shooter could have easily disabled a trigger lock for convenience.

7

Ironically, in Sunday's *Washington Post,* Josh Sugarmann of the Violence Policy Center, a leading gun control advocacy group, ridiculed the notion of a trigger lock as the solution: "Considering the people who went in and out of that house, [this] expectation would strike most people as absurd on its face." What we need, Sugarmann argues, is to ban handguns. Well, considering the people who went in and out of that house, the expectation that any law could have kept it gun-free certainly strikes me as absurd on its face.

8

After all, it was a crack house where drugs were routinely traded for guns. Drugs, in case the Violence Policy Center hasn't noticed, are already illegal and subject to what many believe are excessively draconian laws—which don't seem to have had much deterrent effect.

9

Predictably, Kayla's death has been the occasion for a lot of demagoguery about "the children." Clinton says that 13 children die from gunfire every day—without mentioning that this includes everyone under 19, and that 85 percent of the juvenile victims are over 16. Of course, these deaths are tragic, but an 18-year-old gang member is hardly a child.

10

In 1997, 630 children under 15 died from gun injuries—a considerable drop from the 1993 figure of 957 but still no reason to celebrate. But let's not forget that the same year, nearly 1,000 children drowned, more than 2,000 died in car accidents and more than 600 were murdered without firearms.

11

And here's something else to remember. The same day that the news of Kayla's shooting shocked the nation, murder charges were filed in Germany against three American teen-agers—children of soldiers stationed at a U.S. army base—who had killed two people and injured five. There wasn't a gun in the picture. The kids had been throwing rocks off a highway overpass.

12

When children without a moral center are intent on inflicting harm, they will find a way, guns or no guns.

13

Integrated Skills

1. What is the author's response to the familiar saying "Guns don't kill people, people kill people"? Do you agree with her perspective? Why or why not?

2. Why does the author think child safety locks for guns are not an effective way of preventing children from killing other children?

3. Why does the author include information about drugs in this essay?

4. What examples of killings and deaths that occur without the use of guns does the author mention? Why does she mention those kinds of deaths?

5. Explain what the title of the reading selection means.

Reading Textbooks

Thematic Connections. You have just read Cathy Young's essay arguing that trigger locks are not the answer to violence against children in America. You may or may not agree with the points that Young makes, but you are probably aware that the issue is quite controversial. Underlying the often heated public discussion of trigger locks in America today is a larger debate about gun control. The question of how much the government can control gun use has its roots in a debate about the Second Amendment to the Constitution of the United States. This textbook reading, taken from *Practicing American Politics* by David V. Edwards and Allessandra Lippucci, addresses some of the core points of the debate. As you read, practice making observations and connections, and think about how discussions of political science can affect our everyday life.

Vocabulary Preview

bear (para. 1): to hold, keep (v.)
sophisticated (para. 2): advanced (adj.)

obsolete (para. 2): outdated (adj.)
administer (para. 4): to manage, supervise (v.)

The Politics of Language

Interpreting the Right
"to Keep and Bear Arms"

Both supporters and opponents of gun control claim that the Second Amendment is on their side. Their constitutional dispute is over the proper context in which to interpret "the right of the people to keep and bear Arms." The declaration of this right is preceded by the statement that a "well-regulated Militia" is "necessary to the security of a free State." 1

But what is a *militia*? In 1791, a militia consisted of free male citizens armed with muskets, rifles, and bayonets, whereas in the 1990s it consists of the National Guard units of the 50 states armed with sophisticated modern weapons. Gun-control advocates say that the amendment is obsolete (it is no longer *what is*) because it only authorizes "the people" as a body (a *militia*) to bear arms for the specific purpose of protecting society. The amendment does not, they claim, authorize individuals to carry weapons for any reason. Opponents of gun control, backed by the National Rifle Associa- 2 tion, claim that the "right of the people" in this amendment is meant to protect individuals, just as the rights in the First, Fourth, and Ninth Amendments are.

The Supreme Court has addressed this issue twice in this century. In 1939 it upheld the National Firearms Act of 1934, which required the registration of sawed-off shotguns on the grounds that this weapon bore no "reasonable relationship" to a well-regulated militia. The Court refused to review an Illinois case in which a town banned handguns in the home. The federal appeals court had upheld the law on grounds that the Second Amendment was a limitation on the federal government, not the states.

3

In 1997 the Court ruled 5–4 that Congress may not require states to help administer background checks on people seeking to purchase guns. The decision was a major victory for states' rights advocates and for opponents of gun control.

4

Thinking about the Textbook Selection
· ·

1. How is this textbook reading related to the newspaper article by Cathy Young about trigger guards on guns?

2. What is the Second Amendment to the United States Constitution all about?

3. How do supporters of gun control interpret the Second Amendment to the Constitution?

4. How do opponents of gun control interpret the Second Amendment?

5. Which group—gun control supporters or opponents—was happier with the 1997 Supreme Court ruling on guns? Why?

Reviewing

1. Identify three kinds of observations you can make about reading selections.

2. Explain how making these kinds of observations helps you comprehend what you read.

Recall /
Remember

3. Why is writing about a reading selection helpful? Identify two kinds of writing about your reading that you can do to help you understand what you read.

4. Why is it important to make connections among the details you notice when you read?

5. How does the use of repetition in a reading selection help you to observe details and make connections among them? Why is it important to notice and connect repeated details?

Chapter Summary

Throughout this chapter you have been practicing two essential steps of the reading process. You have been making observations about the details of a reading passage. You have also been relating those details, looking for connections among them.

By means of careful observation while reading, you have been laying the foundation for better reading comprehension. You have been observing different kinds of information writers include. You have observed how they use examples to illustrate their ideas. You have also observed how sentences at the ends of paragraphs and the ends of passages summarize, repeat, or restate the main idea.

Besides becoming a more observant reader of authors' details, you have become more observant about how authors organize their writing. Being able to identify the structure of a piece of writing is an important key to comprehending an author's meaning.

Making observations leads to asking questions about them. The key question concerns how those observations can be connected or related. You have practiced making connections among your observations. You have seen how writers use repetition. You have also identified different kinds of connections that occur in reading selections. These include connections between the examples in a paragraph or passage and connections between paragraphs or sections of a passage.

You have learned to ask the following questions as you read: How is this sentence (or paragraph or section) related to the one that goes before it? How is it related to the one that comes after it? Just as you develop an "observant frame of mind" for reading, you also develop a "connecting frame of mind." Both are essential for achieving greater comprehension of what you read.

In Chapter 9, you will be asked to take the next steps toward understanding what you read. These steps are making inferences and formulating conclusions. Both of these steps require additional kinds of thinking. These new steps too are necessary for success in achieving greater comprehension of what you read.

Making Inferences and Drawing Conclusions

Getting Ready   255

Learning the Skills   256

Applying the Skills
• Reading the Parts   277
• Reading the Whole   284
• Reading Textbooks   287

Reviewing   292

Getting Ready

In Chapter 8 you learned how to make observations about a reading selection and how to discover connections among your observations. In this chapter, you will learn how to build on those connections by making inferences and formulating conclusions.

An **inference** is an educated guess based on limited knowledge. It is a statement you make based on what you have observed. A **conclusion** is an interpretation based on all the inferences you've made. Inferences and conclusions are closely related. An inference is a kind of temporary "pre-conclusion" you make while reading. As you arrive at more inferences, you develop a more definite conclusion about the meaning and purpose of a reading passage. This conclusion is your understanding of the author's main idea.

This chapter will give you practice in making inferences and building upon those inferences to draw sound conclusions from your reading. You will also have a chance to use writing strategies to develop both skills.

Chapter Overview

Focusing
Questions

When you finish reading a selection, do you sometimes change your mind about what you think it means or says? Why?

How can you tell what an author thinks about the subject of a passage?

What do you look for in a passage when you have trouble comprehending what you read?

How do you decide what the meaning of a reading selection is?

Everyday
Reading

Outside your academic reading, you will have to make inferences and conclusions about all kinds of reading, from newspaper editorials to directions for assembling a new piece of furniture to health warnings on packages. Often, you successfully make inferences and conclusions about everyday reading without even noticing it. Perhaps the most common everyday reading that requires inferences and conclusions is advertisements: billboards, magazine advertisements, even some campus fliers. Consider, for example, the billboard for a particular brand of blue jeans that depicts a beautiful couple together. The text says, "Get together with our jeans." From the billboard, you are expected to *infer* that the couple is wearing those jeans; and you are expected to *conclude* that wearing those jeans will make you as happy as the couple in the photograph.

Find three printed advertisements and for each one list the inferences and the conclusions you think the writer expects you to make. Keep a copy of the advertisements to discuss them with your classmates.

Learning the Skills

■ **Developing Inferences** - educated guess

What do you do when you make an inference? Essentially, you make a little mental leap—an intellectual jump. You jump mentally or intellectually from what you know to what you don't know. This mental leap is based on the observations you make and the connections you discover among your observations. (For a review of making observations and connections, see Chapter 8.)

Inferences can be right or wrong. In observing someone unlocking a college classroom at 7 A.M., you might infer that the person is associated with the school and has the job of unlocking classrooms. This inference may or may not be correct. What other inferences might you make about this behavior?

Exercise 9-1

Make two inferences for each of the following examples. The first one is done for you.

Example:

The street is wet.

It has rained.

The street has been hosed down.

1. A cat is scratching at a door.

2. Your car won't start.

3. A friend's refrigerator is empty.

4. Your teacher is absent.

5. A friend doesn't show up at a party.

Get together with three or four of your classmates and compare the inferences you made for the items in Exercise 9-1. Chances are that at least some of your inferences will be different. Since inferences are only educated guesses based on your observations, they are only the beginning of the thinking process. The next step is figuring out which inferences are likely to be true. Making more observations and connections will help you to make more accurate inferences—knowing more makes your guesses better. You might have inferred from question 3 in Exercise 9-1, for example, that your friend's refrigerator is empty because he or she hasn't been to the grocery store recently. Perhaps your friend has been out of town. The truth is that from the information given, you cannot *know* exactly why the refrigerator is empty—you can only infer. However, if you observe party decorations around the house and dirty dishes on the countertops, you will be able to more accurately infer that the refrigerator is empty because your friend's party guests ate all the food. More observations help you to make more accurate inferences.

Exercise 9-2

The following imaginary scenario describes a couple, the Walkers, who live in your neighborhood. Imagine that you have made the following observations.

You haven't seen the Walkers either separately or together in more than a week, even though you are used to seeing them nearly every day. Newspapers are piled up by their door, their mailbox is overflowing, and some packages have been left on the porch.

The blinds are shut. Lights are on inside the house, but no lights are on outside. You have not seen their dog or cat in the past week either.

In connecting the observations, you will begin making inferences about the Walkers. List five inferences about the Walkers on the lines provided. Make each one as different from the others as possible, but make sure each one could be true.

Example:

 The Walkers are working very hard on a project and don't want to be

 interrupted.

1. _____

 _____

2. _____

_____

3. _____

_____

4. _____

_____

5. _____

_____

· ·

■ Reading Inferentially

The kind of inferences you made in Exercises 9-1 and 9-2 are everyday inferences. You make such inferences as a normal part of the thinking you do each day. The thinking process involved is the same for the inferences you make when you read. Making inferences during reading is essential to improving your ability to think. It is also essential for understanding the meaning of what you read.

When you make inferences during reading, you are reading inferentially. For example, if a psychological experiment is described as "a classic experiment," you infer that it is important. You might also infer that it is of historical interest or that it exemplifies a key aspect of psychology. You make these inferences based on the meaning of the word *classic*.

Reading inferentially also requires you to make sense of a text by building on your observations of particular details in the passage. For example, in reading about a psychological experiment, you may be given information such as the following:

a. Volunteers were put in a room for forty-eight hours where the lights were always on.

b. The volunteers were given no food during those forty-eight hours.

c. Experimenters placed sensory devices on the volunteers' heads during the experiment.

d. Experimenters did not allow the volunteers to talk with each other during the forty-eight hours of the experiment.

e. Volunteers were not allowed to read, listen to a radio, or watch television during the experiment.

As you were reading these facts about the experiment, you were probably developing inferences based on them. For example, you might have inferred that the experimenters were testing how well people can cope with silence or how well they adjust to the presence of others when they can't communicate with them. These inferences would be based on your prior experience, drawing not on your own participation in such an experiment but on your knowledge of how psychological experiments are conducted and your understanding of how people react when they cannot change their environment or when they must obey a strict set of rules.

What other inferences might you make about the experiment and about the people who volunteered for it? Ask yourself, for example, how the volunteers may have responded to the experiment. In making such inferences, consider how you might have responded.

■ Practicing Making Inferences

The rest of this chapter will follow a passage from a college science textbook, *Understanding Earth* by Frank Press and Raymond Siever, to illustrate how to make inferences and conclusions in your reading. The passage that follows is the first paragraph from the reading. To understand the passage about world population growth, you will need to begin by making inferences. As you read, think about what you might infer from the information provided in the paragraph. You will first need to make observations and then look for connections among your observations.

The world population of 5.5 billion in 1993 is expected to double by 2050. About 95 percent of this growth will occur in less developed countries (LDCs) where some 77 percent of Earth's inhabitants live. The developed countries, with only 23 percent of the world's population, produce 85 percent of the world's economic output and withdraw the majority of the minerals and fossil fuels from Earth's finite resources. These resources fuel industry and provide the basis for food, shelter, transportation, recreation, and all the other aspects of a high standard of living. The use of these resources is also responsible for a significant part of the pollution that has occurred.

In making inferences, you ask questions about the details of a passage and try to put together the details to make sense of them. By connecting details, you think about what they add up to—what they mean.

In doing *that* work, you make inferences. Use your observations and connections to lead toward your inferences.

Here are some observations, connections, and inferences we can make about this opening paragraph. By observing the detail that the population of 5.5 billion in 1993 is expected to double in a bit more than fifty years and then connecting it to the detail that using resources causes pollution, you can infer that a growing population will cause more environmental problems. By observing the detail that "95 percent of [the world's] growth will occur in less developed countries" and connecting it with your inference that environmental problems will increase, you can further infer that less developed countries will become worse off. Finally, by observing that more developed countries have more resources and less developed countries will have more problems, you might also infer that the less developed countries will need help dealing with the large population increase.

Here are a few other inferences you might make based on your observations of the paragraph and the connections among them:

- The developed countries are using up too many of the earth's resources.

- The developed countries might share more of their wealth with the poorer countries.

- The developed countries need to do something about the problem of pollution.

The facts and statistics given in the first paragraph provide the information necessary to make inferences about the next paragraph. Your inferences will come from the connections you discover between details you observe in both the first and second paragraphs.

Here is the second paragraph of the passage:

The world faces several dilemmas. How do we reduce the greenhouse gases, wastes, and other pollutants released by the developed nations without halting their economic growth? (Even a developed nation like the United States needs economic growth to provide the funds to solve some of its social problems.) How can we meet the legitimate aspirations of the LDCs for economic growth without adding to the load of pollutants borne by our planet? If the LDCs were to achieve the high standard of living of the developed nations and consume Earth's resources in the same manner, the load on the biosphere could not be sustained. Profound changes in the global

continued

environment would occur, and human health would be threatened. The world would suffer an irreversible loss of biodiversity with the large-scale destruction of plant and animal species. There would be political unrest and large-scale migrations of people. The population explosion in the LDCs compounds the problem.

This second paragraph develops the idea of the opening paragraph by identifying the expected population increase as a "problem" that will worsen several other world environmental problems. The paragraph explains some of those problems and suggests that readers consider how to solve them.

You might infer from this paragraph, however, that the problems of world population growth appear nearly impossible to solve. You might also infer that because the problems associated with world population growth are so urgent, serious measures must be taken to deal with them. You might infer also that those serious measures will have to be taken soon—almost immediately. Delays could make the problems even more difficult to solve.

These inferences follow one another in a kind of chain. They are based on the observations you make about the details provided in the paragraph. For example, the inference that it will be almost impossible to solve these problems is based on observation of the detail that creating economic growth in the LDCs will add to "the load of pollutants borne by our planet." If this increase in pollution occurs, other problems will follow. The authors state that if major steps are not taken soon to address the growth in world population, serious consequences could follow. The authors present the following consequences in sentences 6–8 of their second paragraph.

- The global environment will be changed.
- Human health will suffer.
- Animal and plant species will be destroyed.
- Political unrest will occur.
- Migrations of many people will result.

The authors offer these consequences as evidence to support their argument that the population explosion must be addressed immediately. But these consequences do not actually exist, at least not yet. They are predictions the authors make about what will happen if something is not done right away to solve the problem of world population growth. In fact, it is possible that these consequences will not actually occur. Furthermore, the authors do not provide evidence to persuade readers that their predictions will come true.

In reading the authors' predictions about future consequences, what inferences can you draw? You can infer that the authors are extremely concerned about the problem. You can infer that they believe strongly in the likelihood that these consequences will actually occur. You can infer these things from their urgent tone, which is established by their use of questions and by their listing of serious consequences one after another.

By making observations in these two paragraphs and making connections among them, you were able to make many inferences about the authors' main point—and about particular details and attitudes along the way.

Exercise 9-3

Read the following passage from the college astronomy text *Universe* by William J. Kaufmann III and Roger A. Freedman, and answer the questions by choosing the most appropriate inferences given. The first one is done for you.

Mars Attacks! Invaders from Mars! Martians, Go Home! Mars, the fourth planet from the Sun, has been the inspiration for many science-fiction films and novels about alien invasion. But why Mars? People have long speculated that life might exist there, because the red planet has many Earthlike characteristics. Around 1900 some astronomers claimed to have seen networks of linear features on the Martian surface, perhaps "canals" built by an advanced civilization. Seven decades later, spacecraft made many surprising discoveries about Mars—including an enormous volcano and a huge canyon—but found no canals and no signs of life. But life may have existed on Mars in the distant past. Spacecraft that landed on Mars, including the hugely successful Mars Pathfinder, found that water once flowed on this now-arid planet. And some scientists claim to have found fossil microorganisms within an unusual meteorite that came to Earth from Mars. Is there now, or was there ever, life on Mars? How much liquid water once existed on Mars? How active were the planet's volcanoes? We may have the answers to these questions soon, because we are now in a golden age of Martian exploration, during which a series of spacecraft will observe Mars from orbit while others land on the planet's surface.

Example:

Considering that "people have long speculated that life might exist" on Mars "because the red planet has many Earthlike characteristics," you can most reasonably infer which of the following?

a. that there never has been life on Mars

b. that red planets do not sustain life

c. that Earthlike characteristics are necessary for life

d. that Earth is a red planet also

1. Observing the detail that scientists found a volcano and a canyon on Mars, and connecting it to the observation that the scientists found no signs of life there, you can most reasonably infer which of the following?

a. that volcanoes and canyons aren't enough to show that life exists on Mars

b. that volcanoes and canyons might be made by Martian life

c. that no life forms could have created volcanoes and canyons

d. that signs of life cannot be found by scientists

2. Observing the author's use of the word *claimed* in the sentence "some astronomers claimed to have seen networks of linear features on the Martian surface" and connecting it to the detail that scientists "found no canals," you can most reasonably infer that

a. the linear features astronomers saw were canals.

b. astronomers actually did not see canals.

c. canals are not linear.

d. scientists did not find the canals.

3. Connecting the observation that "astronomers claimed to have seen networks of linear features on the Martian surface, perhaps 'canals' built by an advanced civilization" with the observation that spacecraft discovered "no canals and no signs of life," you can reasonably infer that

a. the canals were built by an advanced civilization.

b. the canals were built by spacecraft.

c. astronomers make better observations than do spacecraft.

d. canals might have indicated life on Mars.

4. Considering some scientists' claims that they have "found fossil microorganisms within an unusual meteorite" and that the meteorite "came to Earth from Mars," you can most reasonably infer which of the following?

    a. that the fossil microorganisms may have originally been on Mars

    b. that the fossil microorganisms did not come from Mars

    c. that the unusual meteorite came from somewhere other than Mars

    d. that the fossil microorganisms do not prove that life exists on Mars

5. Considering the observation that "water once flowed on this now-arid planet," you can reasonably infer that

    a. there is water on Mars.

    b. the water on Mars has dried up.

    c. water acts differently on Mars than on Earth.

    d. the water on Earth acts the same as the water on Mars.

- **Drawing <u>Conclusions</u>** — what overall selection means

A reader's conclusions make up an overall sense of what a reading selection means. Readers draw conclusions from their inferences as they read. After making some inferences, readers look for connections among them. The connections among inferences lead to conclusions.

This experience of building toward a conclusion while you read is part of the process of reading for comprehension. As an active, engaged reader, you seek connections not only among your observations but also among your inferences. Active readers continue making observations and connections even after they have begun making inferences. After they have made a few inferences, active readers will make connections among their inferences in a process that leads to conclusions about the writer's purpose and ideas.

During the process of reading a selection, you may find yourself adjusting your understanding of it. You might decide, for example, that some observations that seemed important at first are not so important as you read further into the passage. You might decide that some of your inferences, which seemed reasonable when you first made them, seem incorrect as you read further. This experience of changing your mind about the meaning of what you are reading even as you are reading it is also part of the process of understanding a reading selection.

Let's imagine that the passage about population growth from earlier in the chapter ended where we left off on page 262. What conclusions could you draw based on the inferences you have made so far?

Since most of the inferences you have made so far are about problems with world population growth, you might conclude that the authors are pessimistic, that is, that they are not very hopeful about the future. You might also conclude that the authors do not believe that workable solutions to the problems associated with population growth will be found or even seriously tried. You might even conclude that no realistic solutions for such a large and serious problem are possible at all.

These conclusions would be perfectly reasonable, considering what the authors say in these paragraphs. In reality, however, these paragraphs form only part of what the authors have written about the topic. In reading later paragraphs from their piece you might reconsider your conclusions. In their next paragraph, for example, the authors say something that sounds more optimistic about the future. The paragraph may require some vocabulary work, but as you work through it you will begin to make other observations, connections, and inferences to help you draw your conclusions.

> Is it possible to have *sustainable* economic growth in both the developed nations and the LDCs while still preserving the environment and biodiversity and recognizing the finiteness of Earth's resources? The stabilization of population growth and advances in science and technology might offer a solution. Here is how it could work.

In this paragraph, you observe that the authors ask a question in the first sentence. You also observe that they italicize one word, *sustainable.* This question and this italicized word provide cues that the authors have more to say about the relationship between economic development and population growth. Is it possible, they ask, to make economic growth for LDCs work with environmental concern? Their answer is contained in the sentence that follows the question. Perhaps, they seem to say, there is some hope of a solution to the problem after all.

By observing the use of conditional words like *might* and *could,* you can infer that the authors are more hopeful than it seemed from reading their first two paragraphs. Your observation of these conditional words might lead you to infer also that the authors do not want to claim too much. They are careful to be exact about their claim and do not exaggerate it or insist that it is positively the right claim. That is, they do not say that the balance *will* occur, but only that it is possible. Stabilizing population growth and advancing science and technology *might* do the job. They *could* work to help solve the problem.

In addition, you might infer that the authors want to persuade people to think about what "sustainable" growth might be. They do not provide examples to explain what sustainable growth is. But they do encourage readers to think about it. In their next paragraphs the authors explain how sustainable growth could work.

As an alert reader, you have noticed that the authors shifted their stance in this paragraph, and you have altered your understandings and made changes to your conclusions-in-progress.

The authors next provide a different kind of explanation. By observing their change of direction in the passage, you might realize that the authors have organized it according to a problem/solution structure. In the first two paragraphs they present a series of interrelated problems and imply that these problems may be impossible to solve. In the next paragraph the authors suggest that the problems can be solved after all, if population growth can be stabilized and if science and technology can be applied sensibly.

Your observation of the structure of the entire passage prepares you to expect more hopeful and positive ideas in what comes next. Here is the next paragraph of the passage:

> High rates of population growth are characteristic of societies in poverty, where women have low status and lack education and access to contraceptives and family planning services and there is high infant mortality. A cooperative world effort could be undertaken by political leaders of both the developed nations and the LDCs to address these problems democratically and with sensitivity to human rights.

In this paragraph the authors focus on the first part of the problem, high population growth. They identify some reasons high population growth occurs in less developed countries, and once more they say that a solution to this part of the problem *could* be found if world political leaders made a cooperative effort. Key words here are *cooperative* and *democratically*. A key phrase is "with sensitivity to human rights."

What can you infer from the authors' use of the words *cooperative* and *democratically*? What do you infer from their phrase "with sensitivity to human rights"? Each of these carries a positive or hopeful connotation. In observing them together in the paragraph you might infer that such a cooperative effort of world leaders of developed and less developed countries will actually occur. You might also infer that the authors believe solutions to the problems can be found—but only if they are approached *democratically*, with all participants working together.

Finally, in the last two paragraphs the authors discuss the other part of the possible solution, "science and technology." They say that modern advances in science and technology can help the world use its energy resources more efficiently and conserve them more wisely.

The single gravest threat to the environment is the use of energy. Science and technology can enable us to use fuels more efficiently in transportation, homes, and factories. Alternative energy sources—such as safe nuclear energy, solar and biomass energy, and other renewable sources—could be developed. Runoff of water contaminated by fertilizers and pesticides used in agriculture, a serious source of chemical pollution, could be eliminated. New crop species could be developed that need fewer artificial fertilizers and chemical pesticides. With new technology, industrial processes could be modified to produce little or no effluents. Recycling and substitution would reduce the demand for materials.

Only by addressing population growth *and* using Earth's resources wisely can the world avoid a calamity as serious as any humankind has ever faced.

With the last two paragraphs, the authors lead readers to draw a conclusion about the growth of world population, about energy use, and about the relationship between them. It is the conclusion that they themselves have drawn and that they urge readers to consider and to act upon. They present this conclusion succinctly in the final short paragraph that ends the selection. As is clear from the final paragraph, the authors think the problem of world population growth is so serious and the possible consequences of it are so drastic that they recommend that two things be done, not just one.

Throughout the discussion of the process of drawing conclusions you have seen that active readers modify their conclusions as they read, adjusting them as they make additional observations, establish new connections, and develop more or different inferences. Even the conclusions you reach at the end of a reading selection, however, do not have to be final. You can change your mind about your understanding of what you have read.

Sometimes you will change your mind about the meaning of a selection because when you read it a second or third time you observe details, make connections, and develop inferences that you missed on your first reading. You may also alter your conclusions about a reading selection after discussing it with others, who may understand it differently. Drawing conclusions about reading selections is a continuing process that occurs both while you read and later, when you think back over what you have read.

For example, in thinking about the last paragraph of the passage about world population growth, you might change your mind about the authors' optimism for avoiding environmental catastrophe. In their concluding paragraph the authors note that *only* by taking steps now and only by acting *wisely* can destructive consequences be avoided. You might not be sure just how much emphasis to place on those words. That decision influences your understanding of what you believe the authors really think about the problem.

But whatever you decide, you should come to your own conclusions about the problem they describe. Your conclusion might be less hopeful, more hopeful, or about as hopeful as the authors' conclusions seem to be. Notice that we say "seems to be" because what you think about the authors' idea is your own interpretation of what they say about the problem.

The conclusions you draw, therefore, might be tentative, or uncertain, rather than final or absolute. You can always think more about what a text or passage says or implies. You can change your mind about its meaning, just as you do with the inferences you make during reading. Your freedom to change the way you understand a reading selection and your responsibility as a reader to base your conclusions on connected inferences are part of what is meant by critical reading, which is the focus of the next chapter.

Exercise 9-4

. . . .

Read the following passages from textbooks and answer the questions by making the most reasonable conclusions based on the passage. The first one is done for you.

Example:

When we speak of "health care," we're speaking of the entire health-care industry. This industry produces services ranging from heart transplant operations to therapeutic massages; it produces goods ranging from X-ray machines to aspirin tablets. Clearly each of these goods and services is exchanged in a particular market. To assess the market forces affecting health care, we'll focus first on just one of these markets: the market for physician office visits. When you go to the doctor, you're part of the demand for these visits. Your doctor, by seeing you, is part of the supply. (Timothy Tregarthen and Libby Rittenberg, *Macroeconomics*)

From this passage, you can most reasonably conclude that

a. therapeutic massages require X-ray machines.

b. visiting the doctor is only a small part of the health care industry.

c. the goods and services of health care affect particular markets.

d. the health care industry is the most substantial part of doctor visits.

1. A **symbol** is a person, object, or event that suggests more than its literal meaning. This basic definition is simple enough, but the use of symbol in literature makes some students slightly nervous because they tend to regard it as a booby trap, a hidden device that can go off during a seemingly harmless class discussion. "I didn't see that when I was reading the story" is a frequently heard comment. This sort of surprise and recognition is both natural and common. Most readers go through a story for the first time getting their bearings, figuring out what is happening to whom and so on. Patterns and significant details often require a second or third reading before they become evident—before a symbol sheds light on a story. Then the details of a work may suddenly fit together, and its meaning may be reinforced, clarified, or enlarged by the symbol. Symbolic meanings are usually embedded in the texture of a story, but they are not "hidden"; instead, they are carefully placed. Reading between the lines (where there is nothing but space) is unneces-

sary. What is needed is a careful consideration of the elements of a story, a sensitivity to its language, and some common sense. (Michael Meyer, *The Bedford Introduction to Literature*)

From this passage, you can reasonably conclude

a.   that the author wants to make sure readers are not intimidated by symbols.

b.   that symbols are always hidden.

c.   that readers will understand symbols the first time they read a story.

d.   that the author doesn't like the use of symbols.

2.   All constitutions are essentially political documents conceived in power politics and shaped by compromises. Like the U.S. Constitution, however, every successful constitution eventually becomes as much a symbol as a document. Written interpretations of it resemble analysis of scripture; it comes to prescribe civic virtue and to legitimize good behavior, and an elaborate code of laws and customs builds up around it, presumably shaped by the needs of the day. It is easy to forget that a constitution originally arises as a political document. (Lewis Lipsitz and David M. Speak, *American Democracy*)

From this passage, you can infer that other countries have constitutions, and you can most reasonably conclude that

a.   the authors believe all countries with constitutions *should* regard them as seriously as scripture.

b.   other countries' constitutions are thought of by the people in those countries in many of the ways Americans think of the U.S. Constitution.

c.   all documents in every country are written interpretations of power politics.

d.   laws and customs do not have anything to do with the creation of constitutions.

3.   As a star evolves off the main sequence, various parts of the star either contract or expand. When this happens, the gases behave in much the same way as gases here on Earth when they are forced to compress or

are allowed to expand. (William J. Kaufman III and Roger A. Freedman, *Universe*)

From this passage, you can most reasonably conclude that

a. stars seldom contract or expand.

b. stars are always the same size and consistency.

c. there are no gases in outer space.

d. stars can change shape and consistency.

4. Another day, another headline. This one says, "Study Shows Aspirin Prevents Heart Attacks." We read on and learn that the study looked at 22,000 middle-aged doctors. Half took an aspirin every other day, and the other half took a dummy pill. In the aspirin group, 139 doctors suffered a heart attack. The dummy pill group had 239 heart attacks in the same period. Is that difference large enough to show that aspirin really does prevent heart attacks? (Consortium for Mathematics and Its Application, *For All Practical Purposes*)

From this passage, you can most reasonably conclude that

a. doctors have more heart attacks than the rest of the population.

b. the authors think that 22,000 doctors are not enough to study.

c. the difference in numbers of heart attacks may not be enough to show that aspirin prevents heart attacks.

d. dummy pills are as good as aspirin at preventing heart attacks.

5. When making each day's hundreds of tiny judgments and decisions—Is it worth the bother to take an umbrella? Can I trust this person? Should I shoot the basketball or pass to the player who's hot?—we seldom take the time and effort to reason systematically. Usually, we follow our intuition. After interviewing policymakers in government, business, and education, social psychologist Irving Janis concluded that they "often do not use a reflective problem-solving approach. How do they usually arrive at their decisions? If you ask, they are likely to tell you . . . they do it mostly by the *seat of their pants*." (David G. Myers, *Psychology*)

From this passage, you can most reasonably conclude that

a. policymakers in government, business, and education make decisions differently from the rest of the population.

b. Irving Janis uses a reflective problem-solving approach.

c. intuition and systematic reasoning are different.

d. tiny judgments and decisions are most often made systematically.

■ Writing to Aid Reading Comprehension

One thing that can increase your understanding of a text or passage is writing about it. One kind of writing that is very important for comprehension is **summarizing.** When you summarize a reading selection, you explain what the author says by choosing other language to convey your understanding of it. You put the author's ideas "into your own words." You do this to make sure that you comprehend the writer's main idea.

Summarizing a reading selection provides a kind of check that you really do understand what it says. When you have trouble summarizing it, you may be having problems understanding what it says.

Writing a summary of a reading selection is a way to clarify and emphasize the conclusions you draw from reading it. A summary, in effect, is a written version of the conclusions you draw from your reading.

A summary is a form of compression. It is shorter than the original passage. In a summary you extract or pull out the essential aspects—the central idea and key supporting details—of the passage.

Your summary can be as short as a single sentence or a single paragraph, or it can be as long as several paragraphs. The length of your summary depends, to some extent, on the length of the passage you are summarizing.

Here is one version of a brief summary of the reading passage on world population growth:

> In an article on the doubling of the world's population in the next fifty years, the authors suggest that drastic consequences will occur if two things are not done soon. They urge people to find ways of reducing population growth through family planning, and they suggest that a careful effort be made to preserve the world's resources.

Here is an example of a longer summary:

> A recent article about world population predicts that it will double in just over fifty years, creating disastrous consequences around the globe, but especially in poorer countries. The less developed countries of the world could experience a serious decline in the health of their people. They could also experience political unrest and large-scale migrations of their population. Other consequences would affect the world at large, including significant changes in the environment, resulting in destruction of many plant and animal species. The solution is to avoid the problem by controlling human population growth and by carefully conserving the earth's precious natural resources.

Notice that in both summaries the ideas of the article are expressed, but the authors' exact language—their phrases, sentences, and precise wording—is avoided. Usually when you summarize an author's work your goal is to put his or her ideas into your own words. There will be times, however, when you may wish to quote a few of the author's words directly as part of your summary. You will usually do this when you are writing a research paper or when you have a very special reason for quoting part of the text, for example because it is so memorably expressed that no summary will do justice to the author's words.

Guidelines for Writing a Summary

1. Read the text carefully, looking for the main idea and important supporting points.
2. Write a sentence that identifies the writer's main idea.
3. Write a few sentences that explain the key supporting points from different paragraphs or paragraph clusters.
4. Write a draft of your summary by putting together the sentences you wrote for steps 1–3, in the order you wrote them.
5. Revise your summary by adding transitional words and phrases to link your sentences. Add introductory and concluding sentences as necessary.

One way to build a summary that aids your reading comprehension is to write a single sentence that sums up the content of each paragraph in an article or a passage. You could try this with the article on world population growth, perhaps as another way to do Exercise 9-5.

You can use the guidelines on page 274 to help you.

Exercise 9-5

Read the following passage from the literature textbook *The Bedford Introduction to Literature* by Michael Meyer and write a summary on the lines provided.

Close reading is an essential and important means of appreciating the literary art of a text. This formalist approach to literature explores the subtle, complex relationships between how a work is constructed using elements such as plot, characterization, point of view, diction, metaphor, symbol, irony, and other literary techniques to create a coherent structure that contributes to a work's meaning. The formalist focuses on the text itself rather than the historical, political, economic, and other contexts of a text. A formalist reading of *The Scarlet Letter,* for example, is more likely to examine how the book is structured around a series of scenes in which the main characters appear on or near the town scaffold than to analyze how the text portrays the social and religious values of Nathaniel Hawthorne or of seventeenth-century Puritan New Englanders. Although recent literary criticism has continued to demonstrate the importance of close readings to discover how a text creates its effects on a reader, scholars also have made a sustained effort to place literary texts in their historical and cultural contexts.

Cultural critics, like literary historians, place literary works in the contexts of their times, but they do not restrict themselves to major historical moments or figures. Instead of focusing on, perhaps, Hawthorne's friendship with Herman Melville, a cultural critic might examine the relationship between Hawthorne's writing and popular contemporary domestic novels that are now obscure. Cultural critics might even examine the Classic Comic book version of *The Scarlet Letter* or one of its many film versions to gain insight into how our culture has reinterpreted Hawthorne's writing. The materials used by cultural critics are taken from both "high culture" and popular culture. A cultural critic's approach to James Joyce's work might include discussions of Dublin's saloons, political pamphlets, and Catholic sexual mores as well as connections to Ezra Pound or T. S. Eliot.

Write your summary here.

_____

_____

_____

_____

_____

_____

_____

_____

_____

_____

Reading the Parts

The following essay was written by David Gergen, a journalist and former member of the Nixon, Ford, Reagan, and Clinton administrations. The essay appeared in *U.S. News and World Report* on August 16, 1999. Gergen's most recent book is *Eyewitness to Power: The Essence of Leadership, Nixon to Clinton.* As you read, be aware of observations you can make and connections among them. Continue to make inferences, and begin to draw conclusions about Gergen's points. After reading each section and answering the questions that follow, move on to the next section. You will have a chance to read the entire essay when you finish.

DAVID GERGEN
Keeping the Flame Alive

1   From our modern vantage point, it is hard not to look down upon life a thousand years ago. C. S. Lewis called it the "snobbery of chronology," a natural tendency to believe that earlier peoples were shorter, dumber, and poorer. What could we possibly learn from them about today?

2   Life was indeed harsh back then. In the midst of our own Great Depression, [the economist] John Maynard Keynes was asked if we had ever seen anything like it before. "Yes," he replied, "it was called the Dark Ages, and it lasted 400 years." Western Europe in A.D. 1000 was just emerging from that shadow, and people still lived close to the edge, never certain when disaster would strike again.

3   Yet in the midst of hard times, the people of that era wrote a remarkable chapter in the human story. In England, as author Robert Lacey tells us, ploughmen developed a work ethic that became a basis for material success in the centuries that followed.

4   In place of the autocracies of other empires, they built social organizations that depended upon consent and cooperation, laying the foundations for democracy. Prayer and music flourished. And they developed a language that has become universal in our own age: Computer analysis of the English spoken today shows that the

100 most frequently used words are all of Anglo-Saxon origin. Without them, Winston Churchill would never have given roar to the lion. In short, says Lacey, their lives were "a veritable triumph of the human spirit."

1. In paragraphs 1–4, David Gergen refers to "life . . . back then," the Dark Ages, and the Anglo-Saxon culture in England. Considering these references and the question "What could we possibly learn from them about today?" what conclusion can you draw about the essay?

   a.   The author is not interested in history.

   b.   Gergen believes the past can teach us about the present.

   c.   Nothing can be learned from the past.

   d.   The author will be using fire imagery to make his point.

2. From the quotation at the beginning of paragraph 1, "From our modern vantage point, it is hard not to look down upon life a thousand years ago. C. S. Lewis called it the 'snobbery of chronology,'" it is reasonable to infer

   a.   that people in modern civilizations think they are unquestionably better than the people that came before them.

   b.   that the people of a thousand years ago were snobs.

   c.   that dumber, poorer peoples lived in the Dark Ages.

   d.   that modern people are approaching the Dark Ages.

3. Which of the following is not an example of the "material success in the centuries that followed" in paragraphs 1–4?

   a.   the work ethic that ploughmen developed

   b.   the prayer and music that flourished

   c.   the creation of fire

   d.   the development of the English language

4. What conclusion can you draw from the comparison of the Great Depression and the Dark Ages by John Maynard Keynes in paragraph 2 and the quote "In the midst of our own Great Depression, John Maynard Keynes was asked if we had ever seen anything like it before. 'Yes,' he replied, 'it was called the Dark Ages, and it lasted 400 years'"?

a.   Life was just as harsh during the Great Depression as it was in the Dark Ages.

b.   Keynes expected the Great Depression to last four hundred years, just like the Dark Ages.

c.   Keynes expected Americans to flourish in spite of hardship, just as people did after the Dark Ages.

d.   Keynes thought that people would live "close to the edge" for a long time, perhaps never emerging from the Great Depression.

5. Based on the examples given in paragraph 4—social organizations dependent on consent and cooperation, prayer and music flourishing, the development of a universal language—what conclusion can you draw from the Robert Lacey quote "their lives were 'a veritable triumph of the human spirit'"?

a.   that despite hard times, the ancient peoples were still able to create fire

b.   that despite hard times, people a thousand years ago flourished and laid the foundation for many things that we have today, like the concept of democracy, the English language, art, and music

c.   that despite hard times, the Dark Ages was fun

d.   that despite hard times, music was played

Keeping score. And that spirit spawned a rebirth of civilization itself. The late [art historian] Kenneth Clark recounts that in the Dark Ages, the ancient Greek and Roman traditions very nearly perished. But not long after the Dark Ages ended, around A.D. 1100, Western Europe experienced an extraordinary burst of energy, art, and technology. It was a leap forward seen only three or four times in history, and it was only possible because the people of the year 1000 had kept the human flame alive.   5

What to make of all this today? It's too easy to pass it off as mere historical curiosity. There's something that goes to the root of existence when one thinks about those who came before us, how they prevailed against the odds, and how well we match up. Our own scorecard is a lopsided one.   6

It's true that in the 20th century, we have fought off military threats at least as daunting as any posed by the Vikings. It's true as   7 well that in our own age, we have begun to master the means of production and have extended the frontiers of science and technology far beyond our imaginations. As the revolution in electronics gives way to a revolution in the molecular sciences, we could be on the edge of a new era of plenty.

6. In paragraph 5, the author writes, "The late Kenneth Clark recounts that in the Dark Ages, the ancient Greek and Roman traditions very nearly perished . . . [the leap forward seen around A.D. 1100] was only possible because the people of the year 1000 had kept the human flame alive." What conclusion can you draw about people in the Dark Ages from these two sentences?

   a. They were a hot-blooded people.

   b. They had a tremendous amount of spirit and courage and were able to withstand great hardship.

   c. They were able to keep fire going throughout the Dark Ages.

   d. They learned how to make fire.

7. In paragraph 6, what conclusion can you draw from the sentence "Our own scorecard is a lopsided one"? What can you infer about how the author thinks that modern people match up against the accomplishments of earlier people?

   a. The author thinks that we are about even with earlier people in terms of accomplishments.

   b. The author thinks that we are way behind earlier people in terms of technological development.

   c. The author thinks that earlier people achieved more and withstood greater hardship than we do today.

   d. The author has no opinion about how modern people match up.

8. In paragraph 7, the author writes, "It's true that in the 20th century, we have fought off military threats at least as daunting as any posed by the Vikings." What can you infer about the Vikings from this statement?

   a. They were fierce and aggressive in war and a threat to earlier people.

   b. They were a peace-loving people.

c. They roamed the land in search of food.

d. They fought wars on the open seas.

9. Reread paragraph 7, particularly the last sentence—"As the revolution in electronics gives way to a revolution in the molecular sciences, we could be on the edge of a new era of plenty." What inference can you make regarding the phrase "new era of plenty"?

a. There will be more television technology to choose from.

b. There will be great advancements in science that will lead to many new discoveries.

c. Technology will change the way we access information.

d. Technology will change the way we buy electronics.

10. Connecting Gergen's positive characterization of Dark Ages people in paragraph 5 with the list of accomplishments of twentieth-century people, you can infer that

a. Gergen believes that modern people will flourish as earlier people did.

b. Gergen thinks modern people are inferior to earlier people.

c. Gergen thinks we are in the Dark Ages.

d. Gergen hopes that new discoveries will be made about earlier accomplishments.

> But will future generations also look back and say that in the year 2000, there was a veritable triumph of the human spirit? Does the question even deserve an answer?
>
> Men and women today are haunted by a sense that in the midst of plenty, our lives seem barren. We are hungry for a greater nourishment of the soul. In the England of today, a businessman turned philosopher, Charles Handy, has won a widespread following with his writing. Capitalism, he argues, delivers the means but not the point of life. Now that we are satisfying our outer needs, we must pay more attention to those within—for beauty, spiritual growth, and human connection. "In Africa," Handy writes, "they say there are two hungers. . . . The lesser hunger is for the things that sustain life, the goods and services, and the money to pay for them, which we all need. The greater hunger is for an answer to the question 'why?,' for some understanding of what life is for."

8

9

In A.D. 1000, people could never truly satisfy their lesser hunger, but history suggests they were pretty good at fulfilling their greater one. Their lives were richer for it, and so were those that followed. A millennium later, our situation seems just the reverse. Is this really where we want to be? Or can we learn something from those poor folks, after all?

10

11. In paragraph 8, the author asks, "But will future generations also look back and say that in the year 2000, there was a veritable triumph of the human spirit? Does the question even deserve an answer?" What conclusion can you draw about what the author thinks the answer is to those two questions?

   a. The author has no answer to those questions and that is why he is asking them.

   b. The author thinks the answer is maybe.

   c. The author thinks the answer is no.

   d. The author thinks the answer is yes.

12. In paragraph 10, the author writes, "A millennium later, our situation seems just the reverse. Is this really where we want to be? Or can we learn something from those poor folks, after all?" When the author refers to "those poor folks," knowing that he quoted C. S. Lewis ("snobbery of chronology") in paragraph 1, what can you conclude about how he really feels about our forebears?

   a. He thinks that in terms of material wealth, we are better off.

   b. He thinks that in terms of spirit and the understanding of life, they were better off.

   c. He is just being sarcastic and has nothing to say about our forebears.

   d. He thinks that our forebears are just "poor folks."

13. In the context of what the author writes at the beginning of paragraph 9—"Men and women today are haunted by a sense that in the midst of plenty, our lives seem barren. We are hungry for a greater nourishment of the soul"—what can you infer about Charles Handy's writings?

   a. Handy's writings are about our forebears.

   b. Handy's writings are bleak and despairing.

    c.   Handy's writings touch on stories about the Vikings.

    d.   Handy's writings fulfill our need for a greater nourishment of the soul and touch on issues that help people feel like their lives are less barren.

14. From the statement in paragraph 10 "In A.D. 1000, people could never truly satisfy their lesser hunger," what can you infer about earlier people and the times in which they lived?

    a.   The people were not able to satisfy basic needs.

    b.   It rained a lot.

    c.   Earlier people felt sad a lot of the time.

    d.   Earlier people were at war a lot of the time.

15. In paragraph 10, when the author writes, "A millennium later, our situation seems just the reverse," what can you infer about how the author feels about modern people?

    a.   The author feels that we have more than enough to sustain us physically, but we need more spiritually.

    b.   The author thinks we have a long way to go in terms of developing technology.

    c.   The author feels modern people have more than enough food to eat.

    d.   The author thinks that not many people attend church.

Reading the Whole

Now that you have read David Gergen's essay in its parts, made observations, connections, inferences, and conclusions about each part, and answered questions, you are prepared to read the essay as a whole, practicing your skills on the entire essay. As you read, continue to make observations, connections, inferences, and conclusions, and pay attention to the ways all the parts fit together to help Gergen make his main point.

DAVID GERGEN

Keeping the Flame Alive

From our modern vantage point, it is hard not to look down upon life a thousand years ago. C. S. Lewis called it the "snobbery of chronology," a natural tendency to believe that earlier peoples were shorter, dumber, and poorer. What could we possibly learn from them about today?

Life was indeed harsh back then. In the midst of our own Great Depression, [the economist] John Maynard Keynes was asked if we had ever seen anything like it before. "Yes," he replied, "it was called the Dark Ages, and it lasted 400 years." Western Europe in A.D. 1000 was just emerging from that shadow, and people still lived close to the edge, never certain when disaster would strike again.

Yet in the midst of hard times, the people of that era wrote a remarkable chapter in the human story. In England, as author Robert Lacey tells us, ploughmen developed a work ethic that became a basis for material success in the centuries that followed.

In place of the autocracies of other empires, they built social organizations that depended upon consent and cooperation, laying the foundations for democracy. Prayer and music flourished. And they developed a language that has become universal in our own age: Computer analysis of the English spoken today shows that the 100 most frequently used words are all of Anglo-Saxon origin. Without them, Winston Churchill would never have given roar to the lion. In short, says Lacey, their lives were "a veritable triumph of the human spirit."

Keeping score. And that spirit spawned a rebirth of civilization itself. The late [art historian] Kenneth Clark recounts that in the Dark

1

2

3

4

5

Ages, the ancient Greek and Roman traditions very nearly perished. But not long after the Dark Ages ended, around A.D. 1100, Western Europe experienced an extraordinary burst of energy, art, and technology. It was a leap forward seen only three or four times in history, and it was only possible because the people of the year 1000 had kept the human flame alive.

What to make of all this today? It's too easy to pass it off as mere historical curiosity. There's something that goes to the root of existence when one thinks about those who came before us, how they prevailed against the odds, and how well we match up. Our own scorecard is a lopsided one.

It's true that in the 20th century, we have fought off military threats at least as daunting as any posed by the Vikings. It's true as well that in our own age, we have begun to master the means of production and have extended the frontiers of science and technology far beyond our imaginations. As the revolution in electronics gives way to a revolution in the molecular sciences, we could be on the edge of a new era of plenty.

But will future generations also look back and say that in the year 2000, there was a veritable triumph of the human spirit? Does the question even deserve an answer?

Men and women today are haunted by a sense that in the midst of plenty, our lives seem barren. We are hungry for a greater nourishment of the soul. In the England of today, a businessman turned philosopher, Charles Handy, has won a widespread following with his writing. Capitalism, he argues, delivers the means but not the point of life. Now that we are satisfying our outer needs, we must pay more attention to those within—for beauty, spiritual growth, and human connection. "In Africa," Handy writes, "they say there are two hungers. . . . The lesser hunger is for the things that sustain life, the goods and services, and the money to pay for them, which we all need. The greater hunger is for an answer to the question 'why?,' for some understanding of what life is for."

In A.D. 1000, people could never truly satisfy their lesser hunger, but history suggests they were pretty good at fulfilling their greater one. Their lives were richer for it, and so were those that followed. A millennium later, our situation seems just the reverse. Is this really where we want to be? Or can we learn something from those poor folks, after all?

Integrated Skills

1. What does the phrase "the snobbery of chronology" mean?

2. What accomplishments of the "Dark Ages" have affected how we live today?

3. What does the author suggest is different about people's lives in the year 2000 from the way people lived in the year 1000?

4. What do you think that those of us living in the twenty-first century might be able to learn from people who lived one thousand years ago? Why?

Reading Textbooks

Thematic Connections. You have just read David Gergen's essay about how the modern world relates to the past, and you have thought about how spiritual needs are sometimes answered even when physical needs are not. In his comparison, Gergen refers to the Dark Ages in Europe—also known as the Middle Ages—and how those Middle Ages emerged into a new age of flourishing art and science. He suggests that in modern times we have many physical comforts that people in the Middle Ages did not and asks if we in modern times will be able to flourish as well. However, Gergen does not specifically talk about what life was like for people in the Middle Ages. This passage, taken from the world history textbook *The Global Past* by Lanny B. Fields, Russell J. Barber, and Cheryl A. Riggs, will give you a better sense of what life was like back then. As you read, continue to make observations, connections, inferences, and conclusions. Compare the way you live today with how people lived in the Middle Ages, and think about Gergen's main question: Will we, with all the comforts of modern times, be able to produce the same kind of enlightened era that the Middle Ages produced?

Vocabulary Preview

urbanization (para. 1): the making of towns (n.)

commercialism (para. 1): methods of profit making (n.)

specialization (para. 2): skill in a particular field (n.)

negligence (para. 3): failure to provide care (n.)

ecclesiastical (para. 4): belonging to the Christian church (adj.)

jurisdiction (para. 4): authority to enforce laws (n.)

proliferated (para. 9): increased in number (v.)

Everyday Life

The general population of medieval Europe continued to rise until around the middle of the fourteenth century. City populations of 25,000 to 50,000 were not uncommon, and a few major centers, like Paris, could boast of populations around 100,000. Scholars estimate the entire European population by 1300 to have been about 70 to 80 million, an increase from the approximate total of around 26 million in 600. Although urbanization and commercialism grew

1

at a rapid pace from 1050 to 1300, most Europeans, like most peoples of the world, lived in rural areas. The mean family size in cities was 3.9 and in the country 4.8.

RURAL LIFE

Each manor consisted of the lord's manor-house, a village, fields, an orchard, and buildings for special tasks. Each farmer worked his own strips in the various fields as well as a portion of the lord's strips (see the accompanying map of a medieval manor). The produce from each strip was divided between the farmer and the lord according to each farmer's obligation. All produce from the lord's strips was retained by the lord. As time passed, occupational

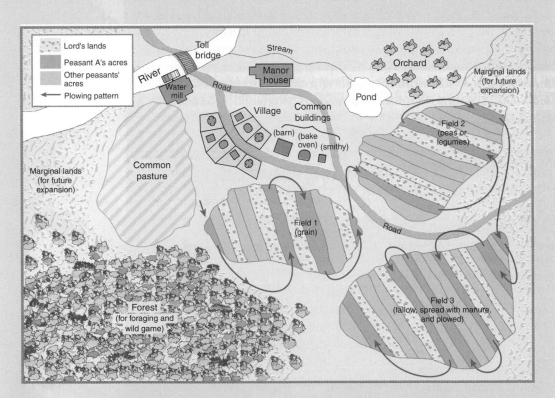

Medieval Manor.
Serf and peasant farmers tilled fields divided into long, alternating strips that made plowing easier by eliminating the need for tight turns with plow and oxen. Individual farmers often owned some animals and equipment, but more typically, almost everything on the manor belonged to the lord: the common bakery, the orchard, the pond or stream and the fish in it, the forage area, and everything else needed to work a self-sufficient farm. The marginal lands near the manor held wild game, but those who hunted without permission were charged with poaching. Each farmer had to pay the lord, in goods or in labor, for the use of any equipment or special service—even for picking apples from the orchard.

specialization increased on the manors; smiths, bakers, shepherds, and other artisan specialists worked full time at their occupations for the benefit of the entire manor population in exchange for other farmers tilling their strips.

The lords of the manor were also the lords of manorial law. Each lord held a manorial court where villagers could make complaints against their neighbors or where the lord could pronounce punishments or exact payments. Usual proceedings included complaints of negligence of required duties, charges of petty theft, and typical lord-villager transactions, as the following notations from a manor court demonstrate:

> Hugh Free appeared asking for clemency because his beast was caught in the lord's garden; Roger Pleader appeared with a suit against Nicholas Croke explaining that neither he nor his [kin] killed Nicholas's peacock; Gilbert Richard's son paid five shillings for a license to marry.

Some farmers lived as peasants in nonmanorial communal villages. The villages were small agrarian communities of several huts surrounded by fields not subject to feudal control. These villages often developed around secure locations, like castles, or in ecclesiastical districts where stone churches offered protection. Many such villages came under manorial jurisdiction during times of crisis. As in the manorial system, nonmanorial farming was a cooperative effort; tools, draft animals, and plows were too expensive for a single peasant to own. Law was established by a village council, and the necessity of mutual dependence gave incentive for quick settlement of disputes.

Many agricultural innovations and new technologies led to increased productivity and improved quality of life. The three-field system divided the land into three major field areas, where planting was done by rotation. Each season, farmers planted crops in two fields and let the other lie fallow, allowing nature to replenish the nutrients in its depleted soil. Careful planning and the spreading of manure helped to bolster the yield per acre, which in turn yielded surpluses. In addition, the introduction of new harnessing techniques, the heavy-wheeled plow, and iron plow tips resulted in increased cultivation in the heavy, rich soils of Europe. Water mills and windmills led to increased productivity. All of these factors increased the food supply and resulted in a healthier and growing population.

3

4

5

Villages and manors were successful only when families worked together for the benefit of all. Women and older children toiled alongside their husbands and fathers on the farms, and in their spare time children played with their toys: tops, play swords, wooden tricycles, and dolls. Everyday life consisted of rising early and laboring long hours tilling in the fields, tending animals, or working at any of the other myriad chores associated with farm life. Next to their huts, most farmers had small vegetable plots that required their attention after their village or manor obligations were complete.

Medieval women had varied employment. In order to supplement income, peasant women often hired out to other manors if laborers or maids were needed. Women, whether aristocratic or poor, were responsible for the preparation of food in the household. They also managed the household and cared for children, servants, and many of the family-owned animals. They frequently were the healers and midwives. Aristocratic women often ran the manors when their husbands and sons were absent because of feudal obligations. These women instructed the overseers on how to run the manors and kept the financial records, collecting rents and payments and procuring supplies not produced on the manor.

By the end of the Early Middle Ages in the eleventh century, many marginal lands were coming under development, trade towns were growing into cities, and most local economies were thriving. Economic growth was the result of new technologies that led to greater production on village communes and manors, and the surpluses for trade benefited both farmer and lord. The growing village and manorial populations often meant relocation for some peasants, because many villages and manors were landlocked by their neighbors and could not expand to accommodate the increasing numbers. Cultivation of marginal lands drew excess population from settled areas, and lords of new manors enticed laborers by establishing more liberal manorial conditions. Some lords had to ease their control to keep peasants and serfs from running away in search of better opportunities elsewhere.

URBAN LIFE

From around the twelfth to the fifteenth centuries, opportunities for employment proliferated. Many artisans from the village communities and manors relocated to the growing towns, particularly smiths, bakers, tanners, and others who could sell their goods or services. They joined merchants, who traded goods from as near as the manor down the lane to as far away as China.

Towns and cities that developed and prospered on feudal lands were given charters from the lords who held jurisdictional authority. The charters were essentially contracts of operation that spelled out the obligations of the towns and cities to the lord and the lord's responsibility to the town. Eventually, many towns extracted charters that gave them greater freedom. Usually the town was awarded the right of self-governance in exchange for yearly payments.   10

Town governance was organized around the guild system. Each profession, artisan or merchant, had a guild. The shoemaker guild, for instance, licensed, set prices, and generally regulated all shoemakers in the town. Shoemakers (like all artisans, bankers, and merchants) were located on the same streets: Shoemaker Street, Baker Street, and so on. Every shoemaker had to be a member of the guild, paying dues and performing guild responsibilities. Guilds permeated all aspects of urban life, from the workplace to recreation. They gave donations to churches, often paying for chapels, stained-glass windows, and upkeep. The building of a cathedral was usually a boon to a town, giving carpenters, stone-masons, cloth makers, candle makers, and many others employment for centuries. Guilds helped with funeral expenses and supported widows and orphans. Elected representatives, almost always the wealthy and influential from each guild, formed an urban council responsible for justice, trade laws, and negotiations with the lord. Towns and cities gained these freedoms sometimes in cooperation with investment-hungry lords and, at other times, through violent riots or with the help of mercenaries hired to fight for the town's cause.   11

Many women played important roles in the towns and cities. As mentioned earlier, some were artisans themselves. Some women found employment as goldsmiths, cloth makers, and various other professions that required periods of training and apprenticeship. Many a wife worked with her husband and continued the family business after his death, directing apprentices just as the husbands, the mastercraftsmen, had. These women inherited membership in the guilds. Single women also had the right to own property and establish businesses. By the thirteenth century, many aristocratic women and wealthy merchant women were engaged in long-distance trade ventures. One English woman lost her cargo to Spanish pirates; upon learning of her loss, she filed a lawsuit and gained royal permission to seize Spanish cargo at English ports until the loss was repaid.   12

Thinking about the Textbook Selection

1. Where did most people live during the Middle Ages—from A.D. 600 to 1300?

2. What was the manorial system? How did it work?

3. What was the three-field system? How did it work? Why was it used?

4. What responsibilities did women fulfill in medieval times? How do women's lives today compare with women's lives and work one thousand years ago?

5. Which kind of life and lifestyle do you prefer? Why?

Reviewing

Recall / Remember

1. What are inferences and why are they important for reading?
2. What do you do with inferences once you have made them?
3. Explain why the conclusions you draw about reading selections can be tentative—why, that is, you can change your mind about how you understand them.
4. What are some things that might influence a change in how you understand a reading selection?

Chapter Summary

In this chapter you have taken a major step in the direction of critical reading. You have continued the work you began in Chapter 8 with making observations about the details and structure of a text and making connections among your observations. You have practiced making inferences, connecting those inferences, and drawing conclusions based on them.

You have been introduced as well to the way active reading requires you to make adjustments and reconsider your observations, connections, and inferences in the process of reading. You have also been introduced to the pleasures and powers that derive from comprehending a reading selection and coming to your own conclusions about what it says and means.

The following chapters will give you additional practice in making inferences and drawing conclusions. Chapter 10 invites you to apply your knowledge of the reading process described in the last two chapters. In that chapter you will learn how to become a critical reader, one who evaluates reading selections and makes judgments about them.

Chapter 10

Getting Ready	295
Learning the Skills	296
Applying the Skills	
• Reading the Parts	315
• Reading the Whole	321
• Reading Textbooks	324
Reviewing	327

Becoming a Critical Reader

Getting Ready

Critical reading describes an active and thoughtful approach to what you read. The word *critical* indicates thinking carefully and evaluating what a writer says. As a critical reader, instead of accepting everything an author says, you think about it. You ask questions about it. You consider an author's ideas in light of your experience and your reading.

To become a critical reader you need to practice the reading techniques and strategies from previous chapters, especially making observations and connections (Chapter 8) and making inferences and drawing conclusions (Chapter 9). Critical reading builds on the understanding you gain from observing, connecting, inferring, and drawing conclusions from your reading. But critical reading goes beyond these to include other strategies as well, including the following:

1. Identifying an author's **purpose**
2. Determining an author's **point of view**
3. Distinguishing between **facts and opinions**
4. Recognizing and making **judgments**

Learning these four skills will help you develop your ability to read college-level material thoughtfully. You will also gain increased confidence in evaluating what you read.

Chapter Overview

Focusing
Questions

How does someone's tone change the way that person comes across? Think of an example.

What are some different purposes authors have for writing? How can you tell an author's purpose from reading his or her work?

How can you tell what an author's attitude is toward the subject he or she is writing about?

How do facts and opinions differ? Are all opinions equally valid and equally persuasive?

Why is making judgments about what you read important?

Everyday
Reading

In many of the things you read during the course of a day you will find opinions expressed. Posters and flyers, billboards, bumper stickers, and movie marquees all contain information that consists of facts, opinions, judgments, or a combination of them.

Find two examples of everyday reading, such as those identified here, and copy the examples in your notebook. Place check marks above the facts, underline the opinion words, and circle the judgment words. After you have worked through and completed this chapter, review your work. Did you find all of the facts, opinion words, and judgment words in these two examples?

Learning the Skills

■ Identifying an Author's Purpose

Authors have various reasons, or purposes, for writing. The following purposes are among the most important:

- To inform
- To explain
- To persuade
- To entertain

How can you determine an author's purpose? You do it by applying what you have learned in Chapters 8 and 9. You observe the details included in the text and make connections among them. Then, based on those observations and connections, you make inferences about what you think is the writer's purpose.

Among the most common purposes authors have for writing is to simply provide information. Authors write *to inform* their readers about historical events, political realities, scientific discoveries, sports exploits—and so on for every imaginable topic. It's very likely that for any topic you can think of, someone has written an informative article or book about it. The following passage is the opening paragraph of a *Newsweek* magazine article by Connie Leslie about why some students drop out of college, titled "You Can't High-Jump If the Bar Is Set Too Low." As you read the passage, think about why the author might have written it.

> The problem is familiar: black students are not faring well in college. The national dropout rate for African-Americans is nearly 70 percent, while for whites it's 40 percent. And the diagnosis is familiar too. Researchers have blamed everything from poverty and poor schools to a history of racism. But these explanations have been of little help in breaking the frustrating cycle of failure. Now there's a new idea, one that is shifting the intellectual discussion and offering some hope. Claude Steele, a professor of social psychology at Stanford University, calls it "stereotype vulnerability," which in simple terms means that if you, by word or deed, tell kids they're part of a group that can't succeed, they won't. "Over time," Steele told *Newsweek,* "the pressure from 'stereotype vulnerability' can push black students to stop identifying with achievement in school."

In this passage, Connie Leslie *informs* her audience about a national problem: that black students are dropping out of college at an alarming rate. She also informs her readers about an expert's explanation for this situation.

Authors also write *to explain* things to readers. Explanation is closely linked with providing information. Authors explain how to use information to achieve a desired result. Authors of self-help books explain how you can lead a more satisfying and fulfilling life by following their recommendations. The author of this book provides many explanations to help you understand how to become a more confident and competent reader.

Let's consider how the author of the article about black college dropouts explains that situation.

Steele argues that when blacks (or any other group) are confronted with a stereotype about their intellectual skills before they take tests, they tend to perform according to the stereotype. Change the expectations, however, and Steele finds that blacks score as high as white students taking the same test. Steele's famous, identical-twin brother, the conservative essayist Shelby Steele, is skeptical. But Charles Murray, who claimed in his controversial book *The Bell Curve* that genetics may explain racial group differences in intellectual performance, is intrigued. "It's interesting research," says Murray. "We certainly need something to help explain why blacks underperform relative to the predictions we've made from their test scores." Another black conservative, Boston University economist Glenn Loury, is more enthusiastic: "If I could invest in the idea of stereotype vulnerability, I would put some money on it. It's got legs."

In the first two sentences of the preceding paragraph, the author explains how groups perform according to expectations. Researcher Claude Steele argues that black students perform poorly on tests when teachers and others believe that they are incapable of performing well. However, Steele argues that when black students are not stereotyped as poor learners and test takers, they are more successful academically. In both cases, these students fulfill the expectations others have about them.

Here is the next paragraph in Leslie's article, which continues the explanation of the second paragraph. The paragraph also provides some information about Claude Steele and his research. Note that a paragraph (and an article overall) can include both information and explanation. In fact, this happens often, with information helping to provide the evidence or examples for the explanation.

Steele first detected stereotype vulnerability as a psychologist at the University of Michigan in 1987. He was studying the school's high dropout rate for blacks. "Black students know that the stereotypes about them raise questions about their intellectual ability. Quite beside any actual discriminatory treatment, they can feel that their intelligence is constantly and everywhere on trial—and all this at a tender age and on difficult proving ground," says Steele. Whether blacks believe the stereotype or not, the mere threat that they might be judged in terms of it—or fulfill it—can hurt their academic performance.

The next two paragraphs continue to inform as well as explain. As you read them, keep in mind that explanation is a kind of in-depth way to inform. Try to pay attention to which parts consist more of explanation and which are meant simply to inform.

> After he moved to Stanford in 1991, Steele received a federal grant to conduct a series of experiments on undergraduates. Groups of black and white students were given portions of the Graduate Record Exam. In a section asking for personal information, half the tests asked the student's race. The other half of the tests did not. What followed, says Steele, was astounding: blacks asked to identify their race scored lower than whites asked the same question; blacks not asked about race scored about the same as their white counterparts. In another experiment, when blacks were told that they were taking a test that would evaluate their intellectual skills, they scored below whites. Blacks who were told that the test was a laboratory problem-solving task that was not diagnostic of ability scored about the same as whites.
>
> Blacks aren't the only group that can suffer academically because of stereotypes. Steele and his colleagues found that the scores of female students dropped when they were told that men scored higher on a math test that they were about to take. When not told about the gender differences, women scored about the same as men. Steele's graduate students even saw similar preliminary results when white men were told that Asian-Americans generally performed very well on a given standardized test. The scores of the white males subsequently dropped.

In the last paragraph of the passage the writer's purpose is to *persuade* people to do something. Authors often write to persuade readers to believe what they themselves believe. Sometimes writers may wish to convince their readers to adopt a course of action—to send money to support a fund drive, for example. Writers may write to criticize an idea, to support it, or simply to celebrate something they believe is important.

> In the past, most colleges have tried to help blacks through remedial programs. The reason such programs fail, says Steele, is that they immediately confront blacks with the stereotype about their abilities. The solution: schools must change the environment on campus that black students face. "Challenging students works better than dumbing down their education," says Steele.

Exercise 10-1

Read the following passages and identify the author's purpose in each: to inform, to explain, to persuade, or to entertain. Underline the words and phrases that best convey the writer's purpose.

Example:

> More than ever, an education that emphasizes general problem-solving skills will be important. In a changing world, <u>education is the best preparation</u> for being able to adapt. As the economy shifts, people and societies who are appropriately educated will tend to do best. The premium that society pays for skills is going to climb, so my advice is to get a good formal education and then keep on learning. Acquire new interests and skills throughout your life. (Bill Gates, "Software Is My Life," *Newsweek*, November 27, 1995)

AUTHOR'S PURPOSE: *to persuade that education is important*

1. Allow me to make an outrageous assertion: of all the historic trails in the United States, the Camino Real was the most significant. It was the first European road in the nation, and for many years the longest in North America. Some of the earliest European settlers in what would become the United States used this trail. The first breeding horses, cattle and sheep entered the West via this trail. The wheel, gunpowder, written language, iron and Christianity first became established here via the Camino Real. But although it changed the nation's history, the Camino Real has languished in obscurity while other trails, arguably of lesser import (I am referring to the Oregon, California and Santa Fe trails), were celebrated in book, song and film. (Douglas Preston, "Camino Real," *Smithsonian*, November 1995)

AUTHOR'S PURPOSE: _____

2. Male listening style is often misinterpreted as inattentiveness or rudeness. Female style is often mistaken for encouragement or agreement. A woman continually reacting to perceived discourtesy can appear oversensitive or irrational to a male boss, client or colleague. A man contin-

ually assuming that female listeners have indicated agreement can appear arrogant or manipulative. Such perceptions damage careers. (Jayne Tear, "Men/Women Talking," *Wall Street Journal*, November 20, 1995)

AUTHOR'S PURPOSE: _____

3. Classical music: Just what do we mean by that? The ordinary meaning of *classical* is something old and established, and valued on that account. The term is applied to many kinds of music, as we know: Classic Jazz, Classic Rock, even Classic Rap. "Classical music" itself can be very old indeed; it covers the better part of two thousand years of music as practiced and heard in Europe and, more recently, America. You may also hear this music called "art music," or "Western music," or music of the Western tradition. (Joseph Kerman and Gary Tomlinson, *Listen*)

AUTHOR'S PURPOSE: _____

4. Although the repetition of words and phrases can be an effective means of creating rhythm in poetry, the more typical method consists of patterns of accented or unaccented syllables. Words contain syllables that are either stressed or unstressed. A **stress** (or **accent**) places more emphasis on one syllable than on another. We say "*syl*lable" not "syl*la*ble," "*em*phasis" not "em*pha*sis." We routinely stress syllables when we speak. "*Is* she con*tent* with the *con*tents of the *yel*low *pack*age?" To distinguish between two people we might say "Is *she* con*tent. . . ?*" In this way stress can be used to emphasize a particular word in a sentence. Poets often arrange words so that the desired meaning is suggested by the rhythm; hence, emphasis is controlled by the poet rather than left entirely to the reader. (Michael Meyer, *The Bedford Introduction to Literature*)

AUTHOR'S PURPOSE: _____

5. As we move beyond the Earth to explore other worlds, the first one we discover is our own Moon. The Moon is a familiar friend in the sky, so near to us that some of its surface features are readily visible to the naked eye. But the Moon is also a strange and alien place, with dramatic differences from our own Earth. A first glance shows that the Moon lacks an ocean and atmosphere. More careful examination

shows that it also lacks both an atmosphere and a magnetic field. Unlike the Earth's surface, the surface of the Moon has remained essentially unaltered for billions of years. Long ago, debris left over from the formation of the planets rained down on the Moon, extensively cratering its rocky surface. Broad plains, called maria, bear silent witness to vast lava flows that flooded the largest impact basins, then ceased forever. Today the Moon is devoid of the kind of geologic activity that we find on Earth. (William J. Kaufmann III and Roger A. Freedman, *Universe*)

AUTHOR'S PURPOSE: _____

■ Determining an Author's Point of View

An author's point of view is his or her position or stance on a topic. Expressing a point of view helps an author achieve his or her purpose. Authors express their points of view through the kinds of words they use and by the kinds of details they include in their writing.

There are three reasons why it is important to recognize an author's point of view when you read:

1. Identifying an author's point of view helps you understand the author's position on a topic.
2. Identifying an author's point of view helps you compare it with your own position.
3. Identifying an author's point of view may help you understand differences of opinion among authors on a topic.

As a critical reader, your recognition of an author's point of view enables you to actively engage the author. For example, you may agree with the author, disagree with the author, or wish to qualify what he or she says. By identifying an author's point of view, you become not merely a passive accepter of another's ideas and opinions, but someone with ideas and opinions of your own.

In the readings for your college courses, you will be exposed to many different topics with multiple points of view. Part of your responsibility as a student in those courses will be to understand the value of competing points of view and to make reasoned judgments about their strengths and weaknesses. The following short passage by Scott Russell Sanders reflects a point of view about dogs.

I know I've left my neighborhood when I can no longer hear the infernal dogs. Fenced up in backyards or chained to front porches, with only time on their paws, they devote themselves to barking. They protest the arrivals and celebrate the departures of milkman, mailwoman, butcher, baker, grocer, plumber, joggers, bicyclists, every soul that ventures down our street. They howl at ambulances and airplanes. They growl at school children. They bark at invisible, perhaps even metaphysical, provocations. No opera singer is more diligent at running the scales of outrage and grief.

You can determine Sanders's point of view in this passage by identifying words that convey his attitude toward dogs. In the first sentence, you find dogs described as "infernal," which means "hellish." In general you can determine a writer's point of view from observing modifiers — adjectives and adverbs — that describe the topic. You can also determine a writer's tone by observing the kinds of verbs he or she uses. Sanders says that dogs "protest," "howl," "growl," and "bark." At one point he writes that dogs "devote themselves to barking." Connecting these observations about the writer's words, you infer that he does not like dogs very much. The negative words he uses to refer to dogs convey his point of view about them.

As you read the next passage, from a *Newsweek* article titled "Who's a Hillbilly?" by Rebecca Thomas Kirkendall, reflect on how you might reevaluate your own point of view about the topic based on the author's argument and examples. Make some observations and connections about the writer's choice of words. Based on those observations and connections, make some inferences about the writer's point of view.

While growing up I was often surprised at the way television belittled "country" people. We weren't offended by the self-effacing humor of *The Andy Griffith Show* and *The Beverly Hillbillies* because, after all, Andy and Jed were the heroes of these shows, and through them we could comfortably laugh at ourselves. But as I learned about tolerance and discrimination in school, I wondered why stereotypes of our lifestyle went unexamined. Actors playing "country" people on TV were usually comic foils or objects of ridicule. Every sitcom seemed to have an episode where country cousins, wearing high-water britches and carrying patched suitcases,

continued

visited their city friends. And movies like *Deliverance* portrayed country people as backward and violent.

As a child I laughed at the exaggerated accents and dress, never imagining that viewers believed such nonsense. Li'l Abner and the folks on *Hee Haw* were amusing, but we on the farm knew that our work did not lend itself to bare feet, gingham bras, and revealing cutoff jeans.

Although our nation professes a growing commitment to cultural egalitarianism, we consistently oversimplify and misunderstand our rural culture. Since the 1960s, minority groups in America have fought for acknowledgment, appreciation and, above all, respect. But in our increasingly urban society, rural Americans have been unable to escape from the hillbilly stigma, which is frequently accompanied by labels like "white trash," "redneck," and "hayseed." These negative stereotypes are as unmerciful as they are unfounded.

Exercise 10-2

Determine the writer's point of view by answering the following questions. The first one is done for you.

Example:

List words used by the writer to identify herself as a country person.

our, we

1. List the words used to describe country people by others.

2. List the words used by the writer to describe other people's words for country people.

3. Write a couple of connections based on your observations.

4. Write a couple of inferences based on your connections.

_____

_____

_____

5. What is your conclusion about the writer's point of view?

_____

_____

_____

. . . .

Rebecca Thomas Kirkendall announces her topic in her title. When people refer to country people as "hillbillies," they do so to poke fun at them. Davis says that television "belittles" country people by promoting "stereotypes" about their lifestyle. She notes that TV makes country people "objects of ridicule," and she provides examples to illustrate her point.

The author extends and deepens her idea in her second paragraph by claiming that people in the United States "oversimplify" and "misunderstand" country people and their rural culture. She describes the term *hillbilly* as a "stigma," a painful mark of criticism. She also includes other stereotypical and biased terms some use for country people, such as *white trash, redneck,* and *hayseed.* The author considers these negative terms "unmerciful" and "unfounded," words that indicate her rejection of the "hillbilly" stereotype and her criticism of those who promote it.

■ Distinguishing between Facts and Opinions

A fact, for our purposes here, refers to an observation that can be verified. A fact is something that is always true. Evidence to support a fact is readily available. Writers often present facts as evidence to support their ideas. Those facts may appear as examples to illustrate ideas or to refer to events, collections of data, or information in written sources. Factual statements are based on observations that can be demonstrated to be true. As a critical reader, you will have to check each observation against other available experience and evidence to make sure it is true and is indeed a fact.

Facts and opinions are very different. Unlike facts, opinions express an attitude or a point of view *about* a fact or a set of facts. People have opinions about how welfare should be reformed, about whether citizens should be permitted to carry guns, about who is the best team in baseball. Opinions by themselves may be interesting to state, to hear, and to debate. But they are of little value unless they are supported with evidence in the form of facts, details, examples, reasons, and information.

It is a fact, for example, that traffic on a certain stretch of road slows to a standstill during rush hour on certain days. To say that a new road should be built to make traffic flow more easily would be to express an opinion. The opinion is arguable—that is, different people might have different opinions about how to deal with a traffic problem.

A statement of opinion cannot be completely proved or disproved the way a statement of fact can. Statements of opinion reflect the point of view of a speaker or a writer. For example, you may think college athletes should spend more time on their studies and less on their sports—or vice versa. Your opinion on this issue may reflect your point of view about the value of college sports in general. The evidence you use as support for your opinion might include such things as the money and/or the prestige athletic teams bring to the university. It might also include statistics about the graduation rates of NCAA athletes or about the ratio of college to professional athletes.

Critical readers distinguish between facts and opinions. They evaluate an author's opinions by considering how well those are supported by evidence in the form of facts, details, statistics, and other kinds of information. As a thoughtful critical reader, you are obliged to consider how well a writer's opinion is supported by facts.

One way to identify opinions is to be alert for words that indicate that an opinion is being expressed. Words and phrases such as the following often introduce an author's expression of an opinion.

INTRODUCTORY OPINION WORDS

apparently	it might be	one possibility is
in my view	it seems	perhaps
it appears	maybe	

Notice how these words also seem to qualify what a writer says. That is, the writer who introduces an idea or an opinion by saying "it appears" or "perhaps" is not insisting that he or she is right or that this idea or opinion is either the best or the only one that might be held.

Instead, such opinion words indicate that a writer recognizes that his or her opinion is one among others and that the ideas and opinions of other people (including readers) also have merit, even when they differ from those of the writer.

Exercise 10-3

In the space provided, mark each of the following statements either **F** for fact or **O** for opinion. The first one is done for you.

Example:

The Honda Accord is the best car on the road. ___O___

1. Computers are being used for business, education, and entertainment. _____

2. Computers are, perhaps, the most important invention of the twentieth century. _____

3. The arrival of computers in every American school will make books and libraries unnecessary. _____

4. Reading is a complex skill involving concentration, memory, and knowledge. _____

5. Reading might be the most important skill any student can learn. _____

6. The development of good reading habits will become increasingly harder for students since they are distracted by many forms of entertainment, including movies and television. _____

7. In my view the Internet should be restricted from presenting pornographic materials. _____

8. Others, however, believe that restricting access to the Internet in any way violates an American's constitutional right of free speech. _____

9. It seems that a few large and powerful companies will wind up controlling access to the Internet. _____

10. Whatever your opinion of the Internet and the World Wide Web, one thing is certain: both are here to stay. _____

. . . .

■ Recognizing and Making Judgments

Other words may convey a strong opinion by expressing a judgment, which indicates approval or disapproval. Judgment words are more insistent about the opinion expressed than the opinion words just presented. As a reader, recognizing judgment words will help you identify an author's point of view.

The following are a few commonly used judgment words.

STRONG JUDGMENT WORDS

good	weak	boring
bad	strong	tedious
better	successful	stunning
worse	splendid	magnificent
best	horrendous	dreadful
worst	fascinating	beautiful
mediocre		

Critical readers make inferences about what authors say from their use of such opinion and judgment words. These words help readers comprehend an author's attitude toward his or her subject. When you read such judgment words, you need to ask yourself why the writer expresses his or her viewpoint so strongly. You also need to look for evidence the writer uses to support his or her judgments.

Just because an author uses judgment words does not mean that you should not accept what he or she says. Rather, ask yourself whether the judgment words that express an author's approval or disapproval are supported by evidence in the form of facts, details, statistical data, examples, good reasons, and other kinds of information.

If a movie is described as "dreadful," look to see what the author found dreadful and why. If a presidential policy is described as "dangerous," look for evidence to support the author's point of view. If a statement about the causes of bulimia or the effects of ozone depletion is described as "true," "accurate," or "convincing," ask yourself what evidence the author presents to persuade you of that claim. If you find the evidence convincing, you may wish to remember it as useful information. You may also wish to link it in your mind or your notebook with the opinion or idea the evidence supports. If you find the evidence unconvincing, you should be able to say why it is unpersuasive. In addition, you should also try to find evidence that supports your contrary viewpoint.

Exercise 10-4

In the following sentences, circle the words that indicate a judgment. The first one is done for you.

Example:

Twelve years have passed since the (terrible) flood that wiped out the town.

1. The Boston Red Sox pitcher Pedro Martinez pitched a magnificent game on Tuesday night.

2. Nancy Lopez exhibited grace and generosity in congratulating the golfer who beat her in the tournament.

3. Many horror movies use similar boring film techniques.

4. Recent horror movies have not been nearly as successful in frightening people as previous films have been.

5. The most stunning views of the ocean are those from the road that runs along the cliff.

6. The worst violations of human freedom have been committed by political rulers of the twentieth century.

7. Although the overall orchestral performance was mediocre and occasionally weak, there were some strong and beautiful moments.

8. Five members of the orchestra were horribly late for the performance.

9. Walking is one of the most popular forms of exercise among the elderly.

10. Walking is the best form of exercise you can do on a daily basis.

. . . .

Sometimes expressions of fact may not be what they appear to be. A statement that seems to present facts may actually do something quite different. As you read the following statement, be aware of the words that convey the writer's judgment of the Beatles.

> The Beatles were the single most important musical phenomenon to emerge during the sixties. Their innovative music thrilled millions of fans, introduced radical changes in the popular music of the decade, and influenced countless major musical groups during the past thirty years.

Although this statement appears to report facts, it offers a judgment that expresses approval of the Beatles' music. The statement also offers an opinion that is unsupported by evidence. To know whether the Beatles actually were as important as the statement indicates, readers would have to be provided with facts such as that the Beatles attracted a vast amount of media attention, or that sales of Beatles albums far surpassed those of all other performers in either popular or classical music, or that the Beatles spawned a series of imitators, their music breaking new ground in harmony, ensemble playing, and lyrics. To support an opinion that the Beatles were as important as the statement indicates, the writer would have to provide facts. The writer could, for example, use as evidence the October 24, 1996, news report that nine million Beatles records were sold in 1996, more than in any previous year. Even then, however, the statement is still an opinion.

Be alert for expressions that seem to suggest that a fact is being presented. Authors sometimes present opinions disguised as facts. Expressions such as "the fact is" "the truth of the matter is" seem to be introducing facts. But such expressions might (and often do) introduce opinions.

Exercise 10-5

Read the following passages to identify the judgments expressed. Circle words and phrases that convey judgments. (You will disagree with some of the judgments the writers express. Consider how well each judgment is supported by evidence, and make up your own mind about the subject.) The first one is done for you.

Example:

> Both as reformers and as teachers northern women played a (major) role in education. From Maine to Wisconsin women (vigorously) supported the movement led by Horace Mann to increase the number of public elementary schools and improve their quality. As secretary of the newly created Massachusetts Board of Education from 1837 to 1848, Mann lengthened the school year; established teaching standards in reading, writing, and arithmetic; and (improved) instruction by recruiting (well-educated) women as teachers. The intellectual leader of the new corps of women educators was Catharine Beecher, who founded academies for young women in Hartford and Cincinnati. In a series of publications Beecher argued that "(energetic) and (benevolent) women" were the (best) qualified to impart moral and intellectual instruction to the young. By the 1850s most teachers were women both because school boards heeded Beecher's arguments and because women could be paid less than men. (James A. Henretta, David Brody, and Lynn Dumenil, *America: A Concise History*)

1. The chemical business is one of the dirtiest industries in the country. It put more toxic materials into surface waters than any other industry in 1998, the most recent year for which the Environmental Protection Agency has compiled data. It accounted for 77 percent of the underground injection of hazardous wastes. It was third over all — after metals mining and electric utilities — in emitting toxins to the environment. It released 320 million pounds of hazardous chemicals into the air, and more than 730 million total. No wonder the industry has an image problem. (Lila Guterman, "'Green Chemistry' Movement Seeks to Reduce Hazardous Byproducts of Chemical Processes," *The Chronicle of Higher Education*, August 4, 2000)

2. The United States may (or may not) need more immigrants—this is a subject of much disagreement. But we surely don't need more poor and unskilled immigrants, and Mexicans fall largely in this category. The stakes here transcend economics. Americans are justly proud of being a nation of immigrants. Peoples of many lands and customs have become American—which is different from what they were—even as they refashioned what it means to be American. By contrast, many Mexican immigrants have little desire to "join the American mainstream" precisely because their overriding motive for coming was economic and their homeland is so close. Their primary affection remains with Mexico. (Robert J. Samuelson, "The Limits of Immigration," *Newsweek,* July 24, 2000)

3. In the history of talk-show hosts, has a host ever talked more than Kathie Lee Gifford? Her dogs, her husband, her kids, her stretch marks—and that was all before the first commercial. Since the day she joined Regis Philbin on *The Morning Show,* Gifford has been off and running her mouth. She's made plenty of enemies. In a *TV Guide* poll, readers said Kathie Lee would be the first person they'd vote off the island on a celebrity version of *Survivor.* (Mark Peyser, "Why We'll Miss Kathie Lee," *Newsweek,* July 24, 2000)

4. It's been a year or so since Perry has had to "tear one down," as he says—disassemble a flawed wall he's built in order to do it over again. The Fridge is not what you could call a natural for this line of work. The man who must now climb scaffoldings as high as 50 feet has not exactly been wasting away since hanging up his worldwide football pants. (Austin Murphy, "Chillin' with the Fridge," *Sports Illustrated,* July 31, 2000)

5. ABC News correspondent John Stossel should be fired for calling organic food no safer than regular food in a pair of *20/20* reports, an environmental group said yesterday. (Donna Petrozzello, "Inner Tube: Environmental Group Calls for Stossel's Head," *New York Daily News,* August 2, 2000)

Becoming a critical reader involves practice and determination. You will need to use all your reading skills together at once, especially making observations, connections, inferences, and conclusions, to fully understand a piece of writing and how you feel about what it says. Use the following chart, which summarizes the guidelines for critical reading.

Guidelines for Critical Reading

- Identify the author's purpose—to inform, explain, entertain, persuade, or a combination of these.

- Determine an author's perspective or point of view—his or her attitude toward the topic.

- Be alert for introductory opinion words (p. 306).

- Be alert for strong judgment words (p. 308).

- Distinguish carefully between fact and opinion.

- Identify the writer's judgments.

- Base your own judgments on the writer's use of evidence to support his or her idea.

Applying the Skills

Reading the Parts

The following essay, written by student Abbie Gibbs, was originally published in Oklahoma State University's student newspaper, *The Daily O'Collegian*. Gibbs was a senior when she wrote the essay in February 1998. After you read each part of the essay, answer the questions that follow. As you read, pay particular attention to the author's purpose and point of view. Make observations about Gibbs's use of facts, opinions, and judgment words. You will have a chance to read the whole essay when you finish.

ABBIE GIBBS
Witnessing Execution

Watching a man prepare to die and gasp for his last breath is something I never thought I would volunteer to witness. But Friday I put my name in a box, in some perhaps morbid hope of being chosen to witness an execution. My name was the last one drawn. I was told I was going to be the second college student in Oklahoma to witness an execution. My apprehension increased every time an official from the prison asked me if I was sure I wanted to do this. Was I ready? They wanted to know. [1]

I and eleven other media witnesses were loaded into a van and driven to the prison. It was dark and silent, and there was a heavy low-lying fog surrounding the prison. I couldn't change my mind, but at this point I wished that I could. We were escorted into the prison, searched, and frisked. All around us were cement walls, iron bars, and mechanical doors. It was silent. Prison guards led us to a small library and told us to wait until they were ready. Some of the reporters talked and joked. For some, this was their fourth or fifth execution. [2]

I knew that somewhere in the building where I waited there was a man preparing for his last minutes on earth. I can't comprehend what it must feel like to be able to count the minutes until you will be dead. I couldn't comprehend what he must be feeling. However, I also can't imagine what it must feel like to lose my sister or mother to a senseless murder. [3]

1. Which statement best describes Abbie Gibbs's point of view toward seeing the execution?

    a. Gibbs thinks the experience will be exciting.

    b. Gibbs feels apprehensive about the experience.

    c. Gibbs does not want to see the execution.

    d. You cannot tell Gibbs's point of view toward seeing the execution.

2. Which of Gibbs's statements expresses an opinion?

    a. But Friday I put my name in a box.

    b. I was told I was going to be the second college student in Oklahoma to witness an execution.

    c. We were escorted into the prison.

    d. It was dark and silent, and there was a heavy low-lying fog surrounding the prison.

3. Which of the boldface words in the following statements expresses a judgment?

    a. Watching a man prepare to die and **gasp** for his last breath is something I never thought I would volunteer to witness.

    b. But Friday I put my name in a box, in some perhaps **morbid** hope of being chosen to witness an execution.

    c. I and eleven other media **witnesses** were loaded into a van and driven to the prison.

    d. We were **escorted** into the prison, searched, and frisked.

4. Which of the following statements expresses a fact?

    a. Watching a man prepare to die was something Gibbs always thought she would do one day.

    b. Gibbs's apprehension decreased every time an official from the prison asked her if she was sure she wanted to witness the execution.

    c. Gibbs was confident that she was ready for the experience of witnessing an execution.

    d. Prison guards led Gibbs and the other media witnesses to a small library.

5. Which of the following best characterizes Abbie Gibbs's purpose for writing the first three paragraphs?

   a. to entertain readers with an amusing story

   b. to explain how people witness an execution

   c. to inform readers of an event in her life

   d. to persuade readers that she witnessed an execution

I've always been in favor of the death penalty, and witnessing an execution did not change my mind. I thought it might, but it didn't. Perhaps because Michael Edward Long wanted to die: He seemed almost eager. After guards escorted us through the prison to the small witnessing room, we sat down shoulder to shoulder, about seven feet from the window looking into the execution room. The blinds on the window were closed. We waited and watched as Long's sister and other acquaintances filed into the room and sat in the front row. The blinds were opened, and Long lay in front of us strapped to a table with intravenous lines in both arms. He had a peaceful expression on his face. He was almost smiling. He told a happy religious parable as his last statement and told us all to accept Jesus into our lives. He never said he was sorry or asked the victims' families for forgiveness. Long gasped and moaned and shook as life left his body. I just sat and stared. I felt no emotions of sadness or fear. It didn't seem real to me. I didn't think about the fact that Long would not wake up in the morning.

4

6. Which of Abbie Gibbs's statements from the first sentences of paragraph 4 expresses an opinion?

   a. After guards escorted us through the prison to the small witnessing room, we sat down shoulder to shoulder, about seven feet from the window looking into the execution room.

   b. I've always been in favor of the death penalty, and witnessing an execution did not change my mind.

   c. The blinds on the window were closed.

   d. We waited and watched as Long's sister and other acquaintances filed into the room and sat in the front row.

7. Which of Gibbs's statements from the last sentences of paragraph 4 expresses a fact?

    a. He had a peaceful expression on his face.

    b. I felt no emotions of sadness or fear.

    c. The blinds were opened, and Long lay in front of us strapped to a table with intravenous lines in both arms.

    d. It didn't seem real to me.

8. Which of the following boldface words reveals a judgment?

    a. I thought it **might,** but it didn't.

    b. We sat down shoulder to shoulder, **about** seven feet from the window looking into the execution room.

    c. He had a **peaceful** expression on his face.

    d. I felt no **emotions** of sadness or fear.

9. Which statement best describes Abbie Gibbs's point of view about witnessing the execution?

    a. Gibbs thinks the execution is horrific.

    b. Gibbs feels no emotion in response to Long's execution.

    c. Gibbs enjoys the execution.

    d. Gibbs thinks the death penalty should be abolished.

10. What is the purpose of paragraph 4?

    a. to entertain readers with the story of the execution

    b. to explain how execution works

    c. to inform readers about what happened and how she felt about it

    d. to persuade readers to feel sympathy for Long

> I left the execution viewing room. I left the prison. I waited for the overwhelming emotions I imagined I would feel after watching a man lose his life, but they never came. I was focused on doing my job—writing a news story—and thought the emotions would come after that, but they didn't. I was exhausted. I thought they would come after sleep, but they didn't. I wondered why the emotions didn't come.
>
> 5

> Then I realized, behind me in the execution viewing room, 6
> behind a darkly tinted glass, sat a group of people. Maybe the
> mother of the murdered woman was there, maybe the father of the
> murdered child was watching, maybe someone who lost a sister or
> a best friend. That's why the emotions hadn't hit me: There were
> none. I felt no emotion for this man who took two innocent lives.
> The victims did not get to request a last meal. They did not get to
> say their goodbyes. They did not get to make their peace. Long
> deserved to lose his life, and as he did not express any remorse for
> his victims, I express no remorse for him.

11. Which statement best describes Abbie Gibbs's purpose in paragraphs 5 and 6?

    a. to inform readers about prison life

    b. to persuade readers that Long deserved no sympathy

    c. to entertain readers

    d. to explain how she wrote her news story

12. Which of the following statements best describes Gibbs's point of view toward the execution she witnessed as expressed in paragraphs 5 and 6?

    a. Gibbs believes that the execution she witnessed had no meaning.

    b. As a result of witnessing the execution, Gibbs believes that the death penalty should be abolished.

    c. Gibbs believes that Long deserved to die.

    d. Gibbs believes that *this* execution should never have happened.

13. Which of the following of Gibbs's statements from paragraphs 5 and 6 is an expression of a fact?

    a. Maybe the mother of the murdered woman was there.

    b. I felt no emotion for this man.

    c. Long deserved to lose his life.

    d. I left the execution viewing room.

14. Which of the following statements from paragraphs 5 and 6 expresses an opinion?

    a. I left the prison.

    b. I waited for the overwhelming emotions.

    c. Long deserved to lose his life.

    d. They did not get to say their goodbyes.

15. Which of the boldface words expresses a judgment?

    a. I waited for the **overwhelming** emotions I imagined I would feel.

    b. I was **focused** on doing my job.

    c. I **wondered** why the emotions didn't come.

    d. That's why the **emotions** hadn't hit me.

Reading the Whole

Now that you have read Abbie Gibbs's essay "Witnessing Execution" in its parts and identified the author's purpose and point of view, as well as her use of facts, opinions, and judgment words, you'll be better prepared to read the essay in its entirety. As you read the whole essay, continue to apply the skills of critical reading, paying attention to the main point that Gibbs makes about her particular experience and the death penalty in general. As you read—and then again when you have finished the essay—ask yourself how *you* feel about what she is saying.

ABBIE GIBBS
Witnessing Execution

Watching a man prepare to die and gasp for his last breath is something I never thought I would volunteer to witness. But Friday I put my name in a box, in some perhaps morbid hope of being chosen to witness an execution. My name was the last one drawn. I was told I was going to be the second college student in Oklahoma to witness an execution. My apprehension increased every time an official from the prison asked me if I was sure I wanted to do this. Was I ready? They wanted to know.   1

I and eleven other media witnesses were loaded into a van and driven to the prison. It was dark and silent, and there was a heavy low-lying fog surrounding the prison. I couldn't change my mind, but at this point I wished that I could. We were escorted into the prison, searched, and frisked. All around us were cement walls, iron bars, and mechanical doors. It was silent. Prison guards led us to a small library and told us to wait until they were ready. Some of the reporters talked and joked. For some, this was their fourth or fifth execution.   2

I knew that somewhere in the building where I waited there was a man preparing for his last minutes on earth. I can't comprehend what it must feel like to be able to count the minutes until you will be dead. I couldn't comprehend what he must be feeling. However, I also can't imagine what it must feel like to lose my sister or mother to a senseless murder.   3

I've always been in favor of the death penalty, and witnessing an execution did not change my mind. I thought it might, but it didn't.   4

Perhaps because Michael Edward Long wanted to die: He seemed almost eager. After guards escorted us through the prison to the small witnessing room, we sat down shoulder to shoulder, about seven feet from the window looking into the execution room. The blinds on the window were closed. We waited and watched as Long's sister and other acquaintances filed into the room and sat in the front row. The blinds were opened, and Long lay in front of us strapped to a table with intravenous lines in both arms. He had a peaceful expression on his face. He was almost smiling. He told a happy religious parable as his last statement and told us all to accept Jesus into our lives. He never said he was sorry or asked the victims' families for forgiveness. Long gasped and moaned and shook as life left his body. I just sat and stared. I felt no emotions of sadness or fear. It didn't seem real to me. I didn't think about the fact that Long would not wake up in the morning.

I left the execution viewing room. I left the prison. I waited for 5 the overwhelming emotions I imagined I would feel after watching a man lose his life, but they never came. I was focused on doing my job—writing a news story—and thought the emotions would come after that, but they didn't. I was exhausted. I thought they would come after sleep, but they didn't. I wondered why the emotions didn't come.

Then I realized, behind me in the execution viewing room, 6 behind a darkly tinted glass, sat a group of people. Maybe the mother of the murdered woman was there, maybe the father of the murdered child was watching, maybe someone who lost a sister or a best friend. That's why the emotions hadn't hit me: There were none. I felt no emotion for this man who took two innocent lives. The victims did not get to request a last meal. They did not get to say their goodbyes. They did not get to make their peace. Long deserved to lose his life, and as he did not express any remorse for his victims, I express no remorse for him.

Integrated Skills

1. Do you think you could witness someone's execution? Why or why not? If you could, how do you think you might react?

2. Why is the writer surprised by her reaction to witnessing the execution? What is her response? Why doesn't she respond as she expected to?

3. What does the writer think of the death penalty? Why?

4. What do you think of the death penalty? Explain whether you think the death penalty should be used and under what circumstances.

Reading Textbooks

Thematic Connections. You've just read about the death penalty from a single person's perspective. But a number of questions remain unanswered. Why, for example, do some societies make use of capital punishment while others don't? Where do your individual opinions come from? The following selection, taken from the textbook *Psychology* by David G. Myers, addresses some of these topics. As you read, think about how the passage answers questions you may have had while reading Abbie Gibbs's essay "Witnessing Execution." Also be sure to pay attention to the author's tone, point of view, facts presented, and opinions. In the end, ask yourself how *you* feel — as a critical reader — about the subject.

Vocabulary Preview

postmodernism (para. 1): modern viewpoint (n.)

biases (para. 1): unfair preferences (n.)

desegregation (para. 3): the end of separation of racial groups (n.)

deterrent (para. 6): something that discourages behavior (n.)

Thinking Critically about the Death Penalty
When Beliefs Collide with Psychological Science

An influential modern viewpoint, ironically called *postmodernism,* questions scientific objectivity. Rather than mirroring the real world, say postmodernists, scientific concepts are socially constructed fictions. "Intelligence," for instance, is a concept we created and defined. Because personal values guide theory and research, truth becomes personal and subjective. (What behaviors shall we call "intelligent"?) In questing for truth, we cannot help but follow our hunches, our biases, our cultural bent. [1]

Psychological scientists agree that many important questions lie beyond the reach of science. And they agree that personal beliefs often shape perceptions. But they also believe that there is a real world out there, and that we advance truth by checking our hunches against it. Madame Curie did not just construct the concept of radium, she *discovered* radium. It really exists. In the social sciences, pure objectivity, like pure selflessness, may be unattainable, but should we not pursue it as an ideal? Better to humble ourselves before reliable evidence than to cling to our presumptions. [2]

Letting go of presumptions is what the U.S. Supreme Court did, after considering pertinent social science evidence before deciding to disallow five-member juries and to end school segregation. These decisions in turn helped inspire hundreds of studies that researchers hoped might similarly inform future judicial decisions. Recently, however, the Court has joined postmodernists in discounting social science research. In deciding whether the death penalty falls under the Constitution's ban on "cruel and unusual punishment," the Court wrestled with whether society defines execution as cruel and unusual, whether courts inflict the penalty arbitrarily, whether they apply it with racial bias, and whether execution deters crime more than all other available punishments. The social science answers to each of these questions, note psychologists Mark Costanzo and Craig Haney and Deana Logan, could hardly be clearer. On two issues—the fairness of the death penalty and its effectiveness—the Court has disregarded social science research.

3

IS THE DEATH PENALTY FAIR?

Should it be permissible to execute a person with mental retardation—someone having the mental age of a 6½-year-old, as in one case? Attitudes toward capital punishment tend to follow legal practice, and thus are now mostly favorable in the United States and opposed in most other nations (as readers in Canada, Western Europe, Australia, New Zealand, and most of South America will recognize). Nevertheless, public opinion surveys show Americans to be overwhelmingly opposed to executing people with mental retardation. Some justices have dismissed such surveys, preferring to trust state legislation and jury decisions as indicators of public attitudes. However, studies show that those eligible to serve as jurors in capital punishment cases—those who accept the death penalty—are unrepresentative of the greater population. Compared with people excluded by virtue of their qualms about capital punishment, those chosen are less likely to be minorities and women. They are more likely to believe prosecution arguments, and they are more conviction-prone.

4

The Court has accepted social science evidence that a 15-year-old is too immature emotionally and too vulnerable to peer pressure for the death penalty to be appropriate. Yet, without explanation, it ignored the same body of evidence when deciding that a 16-year-

5

old, and even someone with the mental ability of a 6½-year-old, could be executed.

DOES THE DEATH PENALTY WORK— DOES IT DETER CRIME?

The evidence is impressively consistent: States with a death penalty do not have lower homicide rates. Their rates have not dropped after instituting the death penalty. And homicide has not risen when states abandoned the death penalty. People committing a crime of passion don't pause to calculate the consequences (and, if they did, would likely consider life in a prison cell an ample deterrent). But no matter, the Court persists in deciding that 16-year-olds and adults with the mental abilities of 6½-year-olds have sufficient judgment and perspective to be executable, that admitting only jurors who accept the death penalty provides a fair and representative jury of one's peers, and that "the death penalty undoubtedly is a significant deterrent."

6

Thinking about the Textbook Selection

1. What do people mean when they say that concepts such as "intelligence" are socially constructed fictions?

2. Why does the author mention Madame Curie? What purpose does Madame Curie serve for the writer?

3. What is the author's view of a law that allows for execution of mentally retarded people? Do you agree or disagree with the author's view? Why?

4. Does the author think that the death penalty is fair? Do you? Why or why not?

5. Does the author think that the death penalty is effective in deterring crime? Do you? Why or why not?

Reviewing

1. What is "critical" reading? Why is it important to develop habits of a critical reader?

2. Identify two aspects of critical reading and explain why they are important for becoming a critical reader.

3. Explain the difference between a fact and an opinion.

4. What is the difference between an opinion and a judgment?

5. Explain how some statements of opinion or judgment might be made to look like statements of fact.

Chapter Summary

In this chapter you have learned to identify an author's purpose in writing. Observing the words writers use clues you in to their intentions, such as to inform, to persuade, to explain, or to entertain. Understanding a writer's purpose is basic to understanding his or her point of view or attitude toward the topic being discussed.

You also worked on distinguishing facts from opinions, by attending carefully to a writer's choice of language. Even more important than being able to identify a writer's opinions is making a judgment—forming your own opinion—about how well the writer supports his or her point of view with evidence. In addition, you learned from your work in this chapter that writers may use judgment words, which convey their opinions, often strongly.

This chapter builds on the earlier ones in requiring you to read carefully in order to comprehend an author's meaning. It goes beyond the previous chapters in encouraging you to read critically, that is, to come to a judgment about how well writers present information or persuade you that their opinions are well supported. In the next two chapters you will continue to practice the critical reading skills you have been developing in this one. You will have a chance to continue to develop these and other reading skills on textbook materials, including visuals.

Chapter 11

Getting Ready   329

Learning the Skills   330

Applying the Skills
- Reading the Parts   355
- Reading the Whole   362
- Reading Textbooks   366

Reviewing   369

Skimming, Scanning, and Understanding the Parts of a Book

Getting Ready

You may often find yourself reading for different purposes. You read the daily newspaper for information about a basketball game or other sports event. You read magazines for articles and stories about subjects that interest you. You read your car manual for information about how to maintain it. You read a cookbook to follow a recipe for vegetable lasagne. And you consult books for information as well, particularly when you need to "look something up," an address or phone number, for example. And, of course, you read the textbooks assigned for your courses.

This chapter includes information on how to use a book's table of contents and index to look things up. It gives you a chance to practice two techniques for previewing reading material: **skimming** and **scanning.**

Chapter Overview

How can you determine whether a book contains the type of information you are looking for?

When you want to know something specific in a book, **how** do you find it?

Focusing Questions

Do you ever preview something you'll be reading by looking it over before actually reading it?

How do you find specific information without reading a whole article or passage?

Everyday Reading

For one day, keep a list of all of the different things you read. Your list will probably include a newspaper or two, your textbooks, several advertisements, and maybe a magazine.

Once you have compiled your list, think about why you did each individual reading. Were you looking for information? Were you reading for enjoyment? Next to each entry, write your purpose for reading.

On another day, skim the following and jot down the overall idea of the selection:

- One article from the local news section of your newspaper
- The first page of a chapter you have not read in one of your textbooks
- An article from one of your favorite magazines

Learning the Skills

■ Skimming a Reading Selection

Skimming is a form of quick reading. In your everyday life you have opportunities to skim reading material quickly and efficiently. In reading posters and notices printed on your campus, for example, you can use skimming to quickly get a sense of what they announce. In reading junk mail and catalogs that appear in your mailbox, you can skim to see if anything is worth looking at more closely. There are several reasons for skimming:

- To look for only what is useful in a particular reading
- To get the overall idea or gain an overview of a reading selection
- To see what the reading selection contains
- To review a reading selection, perhaps by focusing on its highlights or key point

Your goal when skimming is to read the essential parts and acquire a sense of the author's purpose and idea. Follow the guidelines on page 331 when skimming an article or a chapter of a book.

Guidelines for Skimming

1. **Consider the title.** The title identifies the topic of the selection. It may also indicate the author's intended audience.

2. **Look for a subtitle or title heading.** Both of these provide additional, more specific information about the selection's topic.

3. **Glance at headings and subheadings.** These provide a breakdown of the topic discussed in the selection.

4. **Read the opening paragraph.** The first paragraph of a selection introduces the topic in some detail and often identifies the author's main idea.

5. **Read the first and last sentences of the remaining paragraphs.** These sentences usually contain the main point of each paragraph. They also identify connections among the selection's information and ideas.

6. **Look for boldface or italicized words.** Key words identify important concepts, which are generally illustrated and defined.

7. **Look at pictures, maps, charts, drawings, diagrams, or cartoons, and read the legend or caption for each.** The legend or caption explains each visual. A selection's visual information sometimes summarizes its written content. (You will learn more about visuals in Chapter 12.)

8. **Read the concluding paragraph.** This last paragraph typically wraps up the selection by summarizing the main idea or by providing ways to think about its importance.

Exercise 11-1

Answer the following questions by skimming the reading selection that follows the questions. The reading is from an earth science textbook. Use the skimming techniques described in the table above. First read each question and then skim the reading to find the answer. Then move on to the next question and do the same. The first answer is filled in for you as an example.

Example:

What does the title tell you about the selection?

that the reading will discuss principles of ecology

1. What information does the heading below the title provide?

    _____

    _____

2. Which words appear in boldface? Define two of them.

    _____

    _____

    _____

    _____

3. What point is made in the second paragraph of the passage?

    WAYs Species relate to these enviromt

    _____

4. What point is made in the concluding paragraph of the passage?

    _____

    _____

5. Identify key points from three additional paragraphs.

    _____

    _____

    _____

    _____

Principles of Ecology

Ecology is the study of the factors that govern the distribution and ₁
abundance of organisms in natural environments. Some of these factors
are conditions of the physical environment, and others are modes of
interaction between species.

A Species' Position in Its Environment

The way a species relates to its environment defines its **ecologic niche.** ₂
The niche requirements of a species include particular nutrients or food
resources and particular physical and chemical conditions. Some species
have much broader niches than others. Before human interference, for

example, the species that includes grizzlies and brown bears ranged over most of Europe, Asia, and western North America, eating everything from deer and rodents to fishes, insects, and berries. The sloth bear, in contrast, has a narrow niche. It is restricted to Southeast Asia, feeding mainly on insects, for which its peglike teeth are specialized, and on fruits. The ecologic niches of many other closely related species present similar contrasts.

We speak of the way a species lives within its niche as a **life habit.** A   3
species' life habit is its mode of life—the way it obtains nutrients or food, the way it reproduces, and the way it stations itself within the environment or moves about.

Every species is restricted in its natural occurrence by certain envi-   4
ronmental conditions. Among the most important of these **limiting factors** are physical and chemical conditions. Most ferns, for example, live only under moist conditions, whereas cactuses require dry habitats. The

salt content of water is an important limiting factor for species that live in the ocean. Few starfishes and sea urchins, for example, can live in lagoons or bays where normal ocean water is diluted by fresh water from rivers.

Almost every species shares part of its environment with other   5
species. Thus, for many species, **competition** with other species—or the process in which two or more species vie for an environmental resource that is in limited supply—is a limiting factor as well. Among the resources for which species commonly compete are food and living space.

Often two species that live in similar ways cannot coexist in an environment because one species competes more effectively, thereby excluding the other. Plants that grow in soil, for example, often compete for water and nutrients in that soil; as a result, plant species living close together often have roots that penetrate the soil to different depths.

Predation, or the eating of one species by another, is another limit-   6
ing factor. An especially effective predator can prevent another species from occupying a habitat altogether.

. . . .

Did you notice how the boldface letters at the start of the passage in Exercise 11-1 indicate the title and overall topic: **Principles of Ecology?** And did you also notice how the heading "A Species' Position in Its

Environment" provides the topic of that passage? Both the overall topic and the heading help orient you—direct you—to what you will read about in the selection.

The boldface words in the paragraphs—*ecology, life habit,* and *competition,* for example—are key terms that the textbook authors define for you. You can use the techniques of learning vocabulary through context clues (see Chapter 2) to determine the meanings of these important terms.

The first paragraph of the selection explains what ecology is. The last paragraph explains how predators (animals that eat other animals) are important for ecology. And the middle four paragraphs explain other key aspects of ecology, such as how an animal species' "life habit" is limited by "competition" from other animal species.

Exercise 11-2

Answer the following questions by skimming the reading selection that follows the questions. The reading is from the health textbook *Access to Health* by Rebecca J. Donatelle and Lorraine G. Davis. Use the skimming techniques described in the table on page 331. First read each question and then skim the reading to find the answer. Then move on to the next question and do the same.

1. What do you learn from the title?

_____

_____

2. What is emphasized by the two major headings?

_____

_____

3. What kind of information is printed in italics? Why?

_____

_____

4. What is the central concern of the opening paragraph?

_____

_____

5. What kind of information is included in the final paragraph?

_____

_____

Stress and the College Student

College-related stress may seem to be caused only by the pressure to   1
excel in the academic arena. In fact, college students experience numerous distressors, including changes caused by being away from home for
the first time, possible climatic differences between home and school
environments, pressure to make friends in a new and perhaps intimidating setting, the feeling of anonymity imposed by large classes, and pressures related to time management.

Some students are stressed by athletic team requirements, dormi-   2
tory food, roommate habits, expectations of peers, questions about personal values and beliefs, relationship problems, fraternity or sorority
demands, or financial worries. For older students, worries about not
being able to compete with 18-year-olds may also be distressful.

Managing Your Reactions to Distress

Distressors can consist of typical everyday happenings or larger cat-   3
astrophic events. The cumulative effects of multiple daily stresses may
be just as damaging as a single catastrophic event. Although standing in
line for an hour to buy books may not make you sick, finding that your
parked car has been damaged, and that your roommate has invited
guests when you wanted some time alone, and that there is a pile of
dirty dishes in the sink waiting for you may add up to more than a "bad
day." These seemingly minor stressors added together over extended
periods of time may have serious consequences.

Regardless of the type of distressor, the first step is to examine the   4
problem thoroughly. Often we cannot change the requirements at our
college, unexpected distressors, or accidents. Inevitably, we will be stuck
in classes that bore us and for which we find no application in real life.
We feel powerless when a loved one has died. The facts themselves cannot be changed. Only our reactions can be changed.

After recognizing a distressor, you need to examine the situation.   5
Can the circumstances be altered in any way to reduce the amount of

distress you are experiencing, or must you change your behavior and reactions to reduce distress? If five term papers from five different courses are due during the semester, you know you cannot change your professor's mind. You can, however, begin those papers early, spacing them out over a period of time to avoid the last-minute rush. If your boss is vague about directions for assignments, you cannot change the boss. You can, however, ask the boss to clarify in writing the things that are expected of you.

Changing your responses requires practice and emotional control. If your roommate is habitually messy, you can choose among several responses. You can express your anger by yelling, you can pick up the mess and leave a nasty note, or you can diffuse the situation with humor. The first response is not always the best response. Asking yourself "What is to be gained from my (anger, note-writing, humor, moving out)?" is the next step. In changing your responses to stressful situations, act mentally to change attitudes or physically combat the physical effects of stress.   6

Examine your emotions as you experience them to determine whether they arise from irrational beliefs. For example, the stress you feel in speaking in front of a class often produces anxiety and fear. A rational fear would be a fear of making mistakes, forgetting your speech, or doing a poor job and receiving a lower grade than you hoped for. An irrational fear would be the fear that everyone in the class thinks you are stupid, and if you do poorly, they will dislike you even more. Allowing your irrational fear to control you could cause you to panic, become easily frustrated, and fail. Recognizing that everyone in your class is probably nervous, your speech really does not determine your competence, and you do not need the approval of others will help you adopt a more positive response to the situation.   7

Changing the Way You Think

Once you realize that some of your thoughts may be irrational or overreactive, making a conscious effort to reframe or change the way you've been thinking and focus on more positive ways of thinking is a key element of stress management. Specific actions you might take include: 8

- *Worry constructively*—Don't waste time and energy worrying about things you can't change or things that may never happen.
- *Look at life as being fluid*—If you expect change and accept that change is a natural part of living and growing, the jolt of change may have a much smaller impact.
- *Consider alternatives*—Remember that there is seldom only one right or appropriate action. Anticipating options in advance will help you plan for change and adjust more rapidly if circumstances change.
- *Moderate expectations*—Aim high, but be realistic based on your circumstances and motivation.
- *Weed out trivia*—Don't sweat the small stuff, and remember that most of it is . . . small stuff.
- *Don't rush into action*—Think before you act.

Additional actions to reduce stress include aerobic exercise, relaxation techniques (deep breathing and meditation to name a few), hypnosis, massage therapy, biofeedback, better nutrition, and finding support groups (friends, family, co-workers, professors, clergy, and dorm supervisors). If this type of support is not available to you, most colleges and universities provide counseling services at no cost for short-term crises. When university services are not available, or if you are concerned about confidentiality, most communities offer low-cost counseling through mental health clinics. 9

Exercise 11-3
. . . .

Answer the following questions by skimming the reading selection that follows the questions. The reading is from the business textbook *Exploring the World of Business* by Kenneth Blanchard, Charles Schewe, Robert Nelson, and Alexander Hiam. Use the skimming techniques in the table on page 331. First read each question and then skim the reading to find the answer. Then move on to the next question and do the same.

1. What do you learn from the title?

    _____

    _____

2. What is emphasized by the major headings?

   _____

3. What is the function of the first paragraph?

   _____

   _____

4. What is the key point of the first paragraph?

   _____

   _____

5. Excluding headings, what words appear in boldface? Define two of them.

   _____

   _____

   _____

   _____

   _____

   _____

The Functions of Business

To perform its work, a business must engage in a wide range of 1
activities. Employees are hired, materials purchased and transported, information acquired and analyzed. Every business is unique and performs its work for its customers in unique ways. But businesses have many similarities as well, because all must perform six basic functions. These functions are described below, and each one is covered in a Part of this book.

Business Formation

Every business was started by someone, who had to name it and 2
decide upon its structure. And as a business grows, its form must constantly be monitored and updated to reflect needs and opportunities. This function, forming the business, is ongoing because businesses, like people, need to grow and change. A business is like a house that is con-

stantly under construction. New offices may be opened in new countries or old factories at home closed down. At other times, a business will buy or merge with another in order to take on a new, more useful form. Many students will be involved in starting up or growing a business during their careers.

Management

What work should be done, when and how, and by whom? Where 3
should people be located to do their work most efficiently? These sorts of questions are answered daily by managers, the people who supervise other people's work. **Management** means accomplishing organizational goals through people and other resources. Management is therefore responsible for all the other functions and people in the business. In addition, management is responsible for the production processes of a business, such as Toyota's factories, AT&T's telephone services, and Goya's canning plants. **Production** is the transformation of resources into goods or services that customers value. The cost and quality of such processes in large part determine how well the business meets customer needs, how much customers buy, and therefore how much profit the business makes (or how well it accomplishes its social mission). College students who major in management may work for a business or start their own companies.

Human Resources

People, the company's human resources, are at the heart of every 4
business, whether it's a small home-based business or a huge company operating around the world. Goya Foods employs 1,800 people, which sounds like a lot until you compare it with a *really* big company. AT&T, for example, employs 274,000 people, some of whom work as far away from its New York headquarters as the People's Republic of China. Many businesses have separate human resources or personnel departments that help hire and motivate employees. When you apply for a job, your first contact may be a human resources manager. Specialized courses in human resources will prepare you to work in this field.

Marketing

Marketing is the process of creating, pricing, promoting, and dis- 5
tributing ideas, goods, and services to create exchanges that satisfy the

customer and the business. Marketing helps the business find a customer need and fill it. The goals of the marketing function are to please customers by finding out what they want and need, to help the business develop and produce it, to bring it to the attention of customers, and to make it available for purchase. Many students also take marketing courses or major in the subject. Entry-level marketing jobs in sales, advertising, customer research, and other areas of marketing are common first jobs for business graduates.

Control Systems

Many businesses use computerized systems to collect, store, and analyze information about their internal operations and the world beyond their doors. **Controlling** is the process of monitoring and evaluating activities to ensure that objectives are being achieved. Control systems enable managers to make better decisions—to set objectives, establish and implement policies, evaluate employee performance and take action to improve performance, and adjust to the changing business environment. **Accounting** is the process of collecting, summarizing, and reporting financial information for decision making. Students who train to become accountants may work within a business or in specialized accounting firms that service other businesses. Accounting, which tracks the financial life of the organization, is part of a business's larger **information systems,** which collect, process, store, and disseminate information in support of decision making, control, and analysis. Students who become experts in information management enjoy the challenge of actually improving the way the business runs.

6

Financial Management

Businesses raise money either by borrowing it or by attracting new owners who buy a share of the business. This money is then used to invest in new equipment, hire more employees, or obtain other resources needed to maintain and grow the business. The money businesses raise and earn must be managed day to day. **Financial management** is the function of obtaining funds, managing the day-to-day flow of funds, and committing funds for long-term expenditures. Students who go on to study finance might work in the finance department of a business or in one of the many financial service firms that help businesses and individuals manage their money, such as a bank or insurance firm.

7

■ Scanning a Reading Selection

Like skimming, **scanning** is a quick way of finding information. Scanning is useful for searching for specific information when you have a particular question in mind. The techniques of scanning complement and support those of skimming, which are useful for previewing a selection and for reviewing its content.

Scanning is particularly useful for finding specific information in a passage when no index or table of contents is available. Scanning is a type of quick reading—a form of searching. You may be searching through the classified ads of a newspaper for a particular type of used car. You may be searching for the football broadcast times in your area. You may be searching for a fact, detail, or statistic to complete a report. In these and many other reading situations, scanning can help you find the information you need.

Use the following guidelines to scan efficiently and effectively.

Guidelines for Scanning

1. **Scan with specific questions in mind.** Write out your questions. Convert your search into the answer to a question.

2. **Look at the selection's organization.** If headings are included, note them. Copy down headings and subheadings in your notebook. Look for other breaks in the text that signal shifts of focus. If there are no breaks, look for signal words at the beginnings of paragraphs—transitional words such as *another instance, also, in addition, instead, on the other hand, a second reason,* and so on.

3. **Search methodically.** Look first in one part of the selection, then in another. Search the beginning and end, then the middle of the selection.

4. **Check yourself once you find what you are looking for.** Once you've found the information you are looking for, you will need to make sure it is accurate and useful. Perform a check by reading the context—the surrounding sentences—carefully.

Apply the guidelines for scanning to the following passage from a book titled *Sport in Contemporary Society* by D. Stanley Eitzen. Without reading the entire selection, search for answers to these questions:

- How is sport a microcosm (a model) of society?
- How important are sports in American culture?

Sport is a microcosm of society. If we know how sport is organized, the type of games played, the way winners and losers are treated, the type and amount of compensation given the participants, and the way rules are enforced, then we surely also know a great deal about the larger society in which it exists. Conversely, if we know the values of a society, the type of economy, the way minority groups are treated, and the political structure, then we would also have important clues about how sport in that society is likely organized.

The United States, for example, is a capitalistic society. It is not surprising, then, that in the corporate sport that dominates, American athletes are treated as property. In the professional ranks they are bought and sold. At the college level players once enrolled are unable to switch teams without waiting for a year. Even in youth sports, players are drafted and become the "property" of a given team.

Capitalism is also evident as team owners "carpetbag," i.e., move teams to more lucrative markets. At the same time these owners insist that the cities subsidize the construction of new stadiums, thereby making their franchises more profitable. The players, too, appear to have more loyalty to money than to their teams or fans.

Americans are highly competitive. This is easily seen at work, at school, in dating, and in sport. Persons are evaluated not on their intrinsic worth but on the criterion of achievement. As Sage has written, "Sports have consented to measure the results of sports efforts in terms of performance and product—the terms which prevail in the factory and department store."

Athletes are expected to deny self and sacrifice for the needs of the sponsoring organization. This requires, foremost, an acquiescence to authority. The coach is the ultimate authority, and the players must obey. This is the way bureaucracies operate, and American society is highly bureaucratic whether it be in government, school, church, or business. As Paul Hoch has stated, "In football, like business . . . every pattern of movement on the field is increasingly being brought under the control of a group of nonplaying managerial technocrats who sit up in the stands . . . with their headphones and dictate offenses, defenses, special plays, substitutions, and so forth to the players below."

Thus, American sport, like American society, is authoritarian, bureaucratic, and product-oriented. Winning is everything. Athletes use drugs to enhance their performances artificially in order to

> succeed. Coaches teach their athletes to bend the rules (to feign a foul, to hold without getting caught) in order to win. Even at America's most prestigious universities, coaches offer illegal inducements to athletes to attend their school. And, as long as they win, the administrators at these offending schools usually look the other way. After all, the object is to win, and this mentality permeates sport as it does politics and the business world.

Did you observe the organization of the passage? In this passage there are six paragraphs, but no heads or subheads.

Did you search the beginning, ending, and middle, in that order? What does each paragraph tell you about sports? The first paragraph emphasizes connections between a society's social and political values and its organization of sports. The last paragraph links sports to business as well as politics. It also identifies three elements that link these areas: all are authoritarian, bureaucratic, and product-oriented.

Did you notice how the middle of the selection provides examples and evidence to clarify and support these ideas? In scanning the selection you could have omitted the middle paragraphs.

Did you find the answers to the questions in the first and last paragraphs?

- Sport is a microcosm of American society in reflecting its values and its organization.
- Sport is tremendously important in American culture, sharing important connections with politics and with business.

Exercise 11-4
. . . .

Each of the following passages begins with a question or questions. Read each question and scan the passage that follows to find the answer. Write your answer on the lines provided. Questions 3, 4, and 5 can all be answered by scanning the reading that follows them. The first one is done for you.

Example:

What fish does the state of Massachusetts warn residents not to eat?

all freshwater fish statewide except for fish that are raised in captivity

and released in stocking programs

In a far-reaching warning about mercury contamination, Massachu- 1
setts public health officials yesterday urged young women and children
under age 12 to stop eating most fish from the state's lakes and streams
as well as some types of seafood.

The state has long warned that the meat of some freshwater fish 2
contains toxic mercury, but until yesterday, officials had simply urged
caution in eating fish from water bodies with high mercury levels. Now,
the "do not eat" warning applies to all freshwater fish statewide except
for fish that are raised in captivity and released in stocking programs.

The advisory for the first time warns against eating some saltwater 3
fish, previously believed to be relatively free of mercury contamination.
Shark, swordfish, king mackerel, tilefish, and tuna (one of the most
popular fish served as sushi) are all listed as saltwater fish to avoid.
(Mac Daniel, "Mercury Levels in Fish Rising," *Boston Globe,* July 24,
2001)

1. Why do female dolphins form "playpens" around their offspring?

   _____

   _____

Within the community, dolphins have a tendency to associate with 1
members of the same sex and age, except in the case of females and
young calves. Mothers and offspring form some of the tightest bonds in
the community, remaining together until the calf is weaned between the
ages of three and four years.

Indeed, like chimpanzees, sons and daughters may often closely 2
associate with their mothers years after weaning. Wells [researching as
far away as Florida] reports that he has watched older offspring return
to their mother's side for the birth of a sibling. "They seem to want to
check out the new arrival," says Wells.

Female dolphins with calves are extremely cooperative. The moth- 3
ers will often form "playpens" around youngsters and allow them to
interact within the protective enclave. Episodes of "baby-sitting" are also
common, where one female will watch another's calf while the mother
is occupied elsewhere. (William Booth, "The Social Lives of Dolphins")

2. Who manufactures the Frisbee?

_____

Each summer, they fill the skies with aerobatic wonder. Above 1
beaches, parks, picnic areas, and just about any open space, they are like
flocks of oddly shaped birds feathered in plastic, metal, cloth, or wood.

Whether soaring or diving, dashing or fluttering, zipping away or 2
coming back, millions of throwing toys in diverse shapes, sizes, and colors go aloft each day as testimony to human fascination with flight and
competition.

The insatiable appetite for things that fly continuously prods engi- 3
neers and designers to develop new disks, rings, boomerangs, and
winged things that push the limits of performance and curiosity.

Designers look for new ways to manipulate the physical properties 4
that dictate flight characteristics. By experimenting with often subtle
design changes, they attempt to control lift, drag, spin, angular mo-
mentum, torque, and other forces that influence how and why an object
flies.

For example, Alan Adler, a veteran designer who in the mid-1980s 5
developed a ring that holds the 1,257-foot distance record for a thrown
object, says adding a small lip and a concave edge to a disk greatly
increases its stability in flight. And Eric Darnell, a boomerang designer,
says his patented three-wing Y-shaped design is easier to control and
catch than the traditional two-blade, L-shaped arrangement.

Some of the newer devices push the limits of toy aeronautics and 6
puzzle even the experts on how or why they fly. Increasingly, flight toys
depend upon precision design and manufacturing tolerances within a
few thousandths of an inch to seemingly defy physics and fly better than
their predecessors.

These days, the venerable Frisbee-brand flying disk, made by the 7
Wham-O Manufacturing Company, which was recently acquired by the
toy giant Mattel Inc., and its numerous clones vie for flying time with
exotic boomerangs, footballs with fins, flying cylinders, rings that sail
hundreds of feet at a toss, and all manner of gliding and soaring objects.

"People like to throw things and watch them fly," says Kyle Burk, 8
an advertising executive and former flying-disk-throwing champion

from Mission Viejo, Calif., who has become a self-styled "flying toy historian" with a collection of hundreds of flying objects that go back more than 40 years. "If it flies, skips, or hops, if it has any aerodynamic properties at all, people are fascinated with it. It's something very basic in humans." (Warren E. Leary, "Lift, Drag, and Torque," *New York Times,* June 20, 1995)

3. What is an ecologic community?

   _____

   _____

4. What is the difference between flora and fauna?

   _____

   _____

5. What is the difference between a food chain and a food web?

   _____

   _____

Communities of Organisms

Populations of several species living together in a habitat form an 1 **ecologic community.** In most ecologic communities, some species feed on others. The foundation of such systems consists of organisms called **producers,** which are plants or plant-like organisms that manufacture their own food from raw materials in the environment. In contrast, animals and animal-like organisms, known as **consumers,** feed on other organisms. Consumers that feed on producers are known as **herbivores,** and consumers that feed on other consumers are known as **carnivores.** Terrestrial herbivores include such diverse groups as rabbits, cows, pigeons, garden slugs, and leaf-chewing insects. Terrestrial carnivores include weasels, foxes, lions, and ladybugs.

The organisms of a community and the physical environment they 2 occupy constitute an **ecosystem.** Ecosystems come in all sizes, and some encompass many communities. Earth and all the forms of life that inhabit it represent an ecosystem, but so does a tiny droplet of water that is inhabited by only a few microscopic organisms. Obviously, then, large ecosystems can be divided into many smaller ecosystems, and the size of the ecosystem that is treated in a particular ecologic study depends on the type of research that is being conducted. The animals of an ecosystem are collectively referred to as a **fauna** and the plants as a **flora.** A flora and a fauna living together constitute a **biota.**

One of the most important attributes of an ecosystem is the flow of 3 energy and materials through it. When herbivores eat plants, they incorporate into their own tissue part of the food that these plants have synthesized. Carnivores assimilate the tissue of herbivores in much the same way. In most ecosystems, carnivores that eat herbivores are eaten in turn by other carnivores; in fact, several levels of carnivores are often present in an ecosystem. An entire sequence of this kind, from producer to top carnivore, constitutes a **food chain.** Because most carnivores feed on animals smaller than themselves, the body sizes of carnivores often increase toward the top of a food chain.

Simple food chains—sequences in which a single species occupies 4 each level—are uncommon in nature. Most ecosystems are characterized by **food webs,** in which several species occupy each level. Most species below the top carnivore level serve as food for more than one consumer species. Similarly, most consumer species feed on more than one kind of prey.

Exercise 11-5

· ·

The reading selection in this exercise is from the psychology textbook *Discovering Psychology* by Don H. Hockenbury and Sandra E. Hockenbury. It is longer than the selections that you have scanned so far. Read the following questions and use your scanning techniques on the reading to answer them. The first question is answered for you.

Example:

When were drugs developed to help control the symptoms of serious psychological disorders?

in the 1950s and 1960s

1. What is the definition of *biological psychology, cognitive psychology,* and *cross-cultural psychology?*

   _____

   _____

   _____

   _____

2. What was one important factor in the cognitive revolution?

   _____

   _____

3. What is *social loafing?*

   _____

   _____

4. List some of the signal or transition words used to denote shifts of focus in the paragraphs.

   _____

   _____

Psychology Today

Since the 1960s, several approaches have emerged as important influ- 1
ences on contemporary psychology, including biological, cognitive, and
cross-cultural psychology.

Contemporary Trends in Psychology

Biological psychology emphasizes studying the physical bases of 2
human and animal behavior. Several factors have contributed to the
growth of biological psychology in the last few decades. For example,
during the late 1950s and early 1960s, drugs were developed that
helped control the symptoms of serious psychological disorders. The
relative success of these new drugs led psychologists to focus on the
important interaction between biological factors and human behavior.
Equally important were later technological advances that allowed psychologists and other researchers to study the structures of the intact
brain such as the CAT scan, PET scan, and MRI. Gradually, the com-

plex functions of the brain were beginning to be unraveled, producing new understandings about the biological bases of memory, learning, emotions, mental disorders, and other aspects of human behavior.

The 1960s also witnessed a return to the study of mental processes 3 and their influence on behavior, a development that is often called "the cognitive revolution" because it represented a break from traditional behaviorism. The new field of *cognitive psychology* focused once again on the important role of mental processes in how people process information, develop language, solve problems, and think.

One important factor in the cognitive revolution was the develop- 4 ment of the first computers in the 1950s. Computers gave psychologists a new model for conceptualizing human mental processes. Like a computer, human thinking, memory, and perception could be understood in terms of an "information processing" model.

More recently, psychologists began to take a closer look at how 5 cultural factors influence patterns of behavior. By the late 1980s, *cross-cultural psychology* had emerged in full force as large numbers of psychologists began studying the diversity of human behavior in different cultural settings and countries. In the process, some well-established psychological findings that were thought to be universal turned out not to be so.

For example, one well-established psychological finding was that 6 people will exert more effort on a task when working alone than when working as part of a group, a phenomenon called *social loafing*. Social loafing was originally demonstrated during the 1970s, and it has been a common finding in many psychological studies conducted with American and European subjects. But when the similar studies were conducted with Chinese participants in Taiwan during the 1980s, the exact *opposite* was found to be true. Chinese participants worked harder on a task when they were part of a group than when they were working alone.

As it turned out, such findings were just the tip of the iceberg. Today, 7 psychologists have become very sensitive to the influence of cultural and ethnic factors on behavior. We have included "Culture and Human Behavior" boxes throughout this textbook to help sensitize you, as well, to the influence of culture on behavior — including your own.

■ Understanding the Parts of a Textbook

Just as you skim and scan for information in everyday life by looking things up in the yellow pages, in manuals and cookbooks, you skim and scan for information for your college courses. To become an efficient reader, it is helpful to know the different parts of a book, what each contains, and how it can help you in your reading and study.

Two parts of a book especially important for finding information are the table of contents and the index. A book's table of contents and index can give you a sense of the book's contents and its range and depth of coverage. You can use these resources to determine whether a book will be useful, such as when you are researching a paper or a project.

THE TABLE OF CONTENTS

A **table of contents** is usually located at the beginning of the book. The table of contents lists the titles of a book's chapters. Most textbooks, including this one, also list chapter headings, subheadings, and other elements of the book. The table of contents provides an overview of the topics each chapter covers. The headings and subheadings identify more specifically each chapter's contents.

For example, in this book's table of contents—at the beginning of the book on page xi—the title of Chapter 2, "Learning Vocabulary from Context Clues," is followed by the beginning features, Chapter Overview, Focusing Questions, and Everyday Reading. The chapter's main headings, Restatement Context Clues, Example Context Clues, Contrast Context Clues, and General Context Clues, tell you each topic covered in the chapter.

The headings and subheadings in the table of contents of a textbook make it easy for readers to locate information. One way you can make textbook headings work for you is to have some questions in mind when you look at a table of contents. You can then decide which chapters and sections are more likely to help answer your questions.

Exercise 11-6

Use the table of contents of this book to answer the following questions. The first question is answered for you.

Example:

Which chapter contains a reading by Ben Krull?

Chapter 5

1. In which chapter are implied main ideas discussed?

   _____

2. In which chapter are inferences explained?

   _____

3. What chapter introduces the concept of active reading?

   _____

4. What patterns of organization are discussed in this book?

   _____

   _____

5. Name one aspect of critical reading.

   _____

· ·

THE INDEX

An **index**—usually located in the back of a book—lists, in alphabetical order, the topics discussed in a book. A book's index is much more detailed than its table of contents. An index also provides references to individual pages, whereas a table of contents usually indicates only on what page a chapter or topic begins. In addition, an index often lists entries for a topic under the topic heading.

The index for *Putting It Together* can be found on the inside of the book's back cover. Turn to it and look for the entry for "context clues." You will see that to learn or review example context clues, you would turn to page 30. The index directs you to the pages that have the information you need.

Exercise 11-7

· ·

Use the index inside this book's back cover to answer the following questions. The first one is done for you.

Example:

   On what page can you find information about graphs?
   page 373
   _____

1. On what page is cause and effect discussed? _____

2. Where would you look to learn about supporting paragraphs? _____

3. Where are prefixes and suffixes discussed? _____

4. Where can you read about pie charts? _____

5. Where can you learn about unstated main ideas? _____ _____

· ·

OTHER PARTS OF A BOOK

In addition to a table of contents and an index, a book may also include one or more of the following: a preface, an introduction, a glossary, an appendix, and a bibliography. College textbooks typically include all these features. Here is a description of what you can expect to find in each.

- **Preface.** A preface explains the author's reasons for writing the book. It may also include an overview of the book's contents and the author's goals. Some prefaces for college textbooks may include a section written "to the instructor" and another written "to the student."

- **Introduction.** A book's introduction identifies and explains the author's central ideas—the basic issue or concern of the book. It may also provide background information for understanding the book. Like a preface, an introduction appears at the beginning of a book.

- **Glossary.** A glossary is an alphabetical list of terms that occur in the book. The terms are accompanied by definitions and sometimes also by examples or by page references to examples. Glossaries are especially important for introductory college textbooks.

- **Appendix.** An appendix adds something extra to a book—for example, related information that did not fit easily into the book's chapters. Often appendices provide data in the form of charts, graphs, or statistics. Many college textbooks include appendices; other books assigned for college courses, especially in science and social science, may contain them as well.

- **Bibliography.** A book's bibliography identifies books and other sources the author consulted in writing the book. The sources are printed in alphabetical order, along with information including the name of the publisher and the place and date of publication. College textbooks and many other books assigned in college courses include bibliographies, sometimes under headings such as "Works Cited" or "Additional Readings" or "Sources."

Exercise 11-8

Using the table of contents and index for one of your other textbooks, indicate or identify the following on the lines provided.

1. the book's major parts

2. the titles of the chapters within one of those parts

3. whether the book includes an introduction, preface, or both

4. whether the book includes an appendix, glossary, or both

5. an important topic (one with many subdivisions) beginning with the letter *a, b,* or *c* and subtopics for the topic

Exercise 11-9

Choose a different textbook and answer the following questions.

1. What is its title (and subtitle) and what do they indicate?

    _____

    _____

    _____

2. What does the table of contents reveal about the book's organization?

    _____

    _____

    _____

3. What ideas are identified in the preface?

    _____

    _____

    _____

4. Does the book contain a glossary? If so, what kind?

    _____

    _____

    _____

5. Does the book contain a bibliography or list of sources? How is this list organized?

    _____

    _____

    _____

Applying the Skills

Reading the Parts

Mark Trahant, the author of this article, is a member of Idaho's Shoshone-Bannock tribe and is chairman of the Robert C. Maynard Institute for Journalism Education. Trahant wrote this article for MSNBC.com on April 19, 2001. The essay is longer than many other of the essays in *Putting It Together,* but you won't have to read every word of it at first, since this is your chance to apply what you've learned about skimming and scanning. To begin, simply skim each part of the essay and answer the questions that follow. In some cases you will have to skim the section again or scan it quickly in order to answer the questions. After you have skimmed and scanned each part of the essay and answered the questions that follow, you will have a chance to reread the entire selection as a whole.

MARK TRAHANT
Every Symbol Tells a Story

1   Americans are a people who cling to symbols. Most symbols, like Old Glory, are cues to tell a story. We see a flag and tell a friend about a holiday or some other warm memory. Others see a flag and recall a past war or some other test of our freedom. I see the flag and hear the poetry of the First Amendment; a respect for differences as a core national principle.

2   The American Flag is an important symbol in Indian country, too. I have always been amazed at how many flags I see at powwows: Sewn into beaded belt buckles, draped across floats in Indian parades, or even woven onto the back of a fancy-dancer's clothing. Each powwow begins with Grand Entry where the American Flag leads a formal procession of dancers wearing full regalia into an arena.

3   Perhaps this attachment to the flag is extraordinary because it would be understandable if American Indians rejected it; it would be so easy to point to generations of injustice and say "not this symbol." Yet the stories told about the flag are as important in the Native American community as in general society. Past injustice does not matter — nor does any current dispute with government or society.

I recall my first use of the flag. I was about 8 or 9 years old and had entered a youth parade during a tribal fair. I decked out my bike in red, white, and blue crepe paper, wore an Army helmet, and placed a flag on the back of my bike.

4

The symbol worked. The judges gave me $5 and a first-place prize.

5

I think the flag still works as a symbol because the story it tells crosses generations: it contains a narrative for young and old. A symbol with a history—including adventure, glory—and, yes, tragedy. But also a story with a promise, chapters yet to be written about an evolving democracy, something better ahead.

6

1. Consider the title of the selection, "Every Symbol Tells a Story," and scan the first paragraph. What do you think the main topic of the selection will be?

   a. Old Glory

   b. the First Amendment

   c. symbols

   d. Americans

2. Scan the first three paragraphs of the selection. What is the main idea of these paragraphs?

   a. the connection between Native Americans and the American flag

   b. what Native Americans do at a powwow

   c. past injustices against Native Americans by the American government

   d. how the American flag is worn by Native Americans

3. Scan paragraphs 4–6 of the selection and identify the author's ethnic heritage.

   a. He is Italian American.

   b. He is Irish American

   c. He is a Muslim Indian.

   d. He is Native American.

4. Scan paragraphs 1–6 of the selection. What was the author's first use of the flag as a symbol?

   a. The author wore the American flag to the beach as a swimsuit.

   b. The author burned the flag at a Native American rally.

c. The author placed the flag on the back of his bike at a youth parade.

d. The author used the flag to cover his head on a hot day.

5. Scan paragraphs 1–6. How would you describe the author's point of view about the flag as a symbol and its future as a symbol?

a. Trahant thinks the American flag is an inadequate symbol for the future.

b. Trahant believes the American flag is a hopeful symbol for the future.

c. Trahant believes the American flag is a symbol more of the past than the future.

d. Trahant wishes the American flag were not used as a form of protest.

THE POWER TO HURT

Not all symbols meet that test. Some symbols are only about the past. They remind us about a day that is no more, one that will never be again.   7

Such is the case with the Native American images and mascots used by schools and professional sports franchises. We see an image of a smiling, buck-toothed face of some mythical chief advertising a Cleveland baseball franchise. Or a football team named "Redskins," a word once used to describe the bounty paid for dead Indian bodies.   8

There will come a time—perhaps soon—when we will look back on this controversy and ask: "How could this ever have been so? How could one people violate simple principles of common sense, courtesy and respect for one segment of society?"   9

BOTTOM-LINE PRESSURES

It may be economics that forces teams—big professional sports organizations and hometown high school players—to change their names. Two years ago, the U.S. Patent and Trademark office opted not to renew trademark protection for the Washington Redskins. That office decided the team name violated a federal law that no trademark shall be registered "which may disparage" people, institutions, beliefs, or national symbols, "or bring them into contempt or disrepute."   10

This decision is on appeal, but its portent is powerful. If the Washington Redskins—or any other team—cannot protect the use of its franchise in the market, then the name will change; new names will sprout up as fast as logo-embroidered caps. 11

The U.S. Civil Rights Commission is the latest group to investigate—and it also reached the inevitable and logical conclusion. The time has come, the commission says, for this controversy to fade into history. "The Commission believes that the use of Native American images and nicknames in school is insensitive and should be avoided. 12

"It is particularly disturbing that Native American references are still to be found in educational institutions, whether elementary, secondary or post-secondary. Schools are places where diverse groups of people come together to learn not only the 'Three Rs,' but also how to interact respectfully with people from different cultures." 13

The statement asks that we consider what kind of environments we're creating in schools for all our citizens. "Children at the elementary and secondary level usually have no choice about which school they should attend," the commission said. And at the college level, imagine a Native American trying to get an education when the fight over a symbol flames intense and often base emotions. 14

6. Skim paragraphs 7–14 and notice particularly the use of the headings, "The Power to Hurt" and "Bottom-Line Pressures." Based on your scanning of the paragraphs and the heads, what do you think the main idea of paragraphs 7–14 is?

   a. the misuse of symbols and the economic pressures that affect them

   b. children in elementary and secondary school

   c. professional sport teams' economics

   d. the power of symbols

7. Scan paragraphs 7–11. Which professional sports team is used as an example to show the outdated use of Native American nicknames and mascots?

   a. the Buffalo Bills

   b. the Atlanta Braves

   c. the Washington Redskins

   d. the Cleveland Browns

8. Scan paragraphs 7–11 again. In what paragraph does the author provide a definition for the once-used word *redskin*?

   a. 7

   b. 8

   c. 9

   d. 10

9. Scan paragraphs 7–14. What is the definition of a "redskin," as stated by the author?

   a. someone with red skin

   b. Native American hostage

   c. bounty paid for dead Indian bodies

   d. wampum

10. Scan paragraphs 7–14. Which of the following is *not* a quote used to support the author's main idea?

   a. "I recall my first use of the flag."

   b. "The Commission believes that the use of Native American images and nicknames in school is insensitive and should be avoided."

   c. "Schools are places where diverse groups of people come together to learn not only the 'three Rs,' but also how to interact respectfully with people from different cultures."

   d. "Children at the elementary and secondary level usually have no choice about which school they should attend."

NORTH DAKOTA'S DILEMMA

Such is the case in North Dakota, where the state university must choose between an Indian mascot and millions of dollars. If the Indian mascot disappears—so will support from some prominent alumni. On the other hand, the American Indian Movement says it will disrupt graduation ceremonies this spring, unless the name is dropped.

The line is drawn because so many alumni cling to past notions about honoring native people. Even when Native Americans disagree. Worse yet, the commission says, the symbols are plain wrong. "Even those that purport to be positive are romantic stereotypes that give a distorted view of the past. These false portrayals prevent non-Native Americans from understanding the true historical and cultural experiences of American Indians."

AN AMERICAN STORY

This controversy is about all of us—not just American Indians who are disrespected in sports. The same cultural differences are found in Mississippi where a state flag with the Confederate bars and stars draws on different stories for different people. To some it represents some past glory; others only see injustice. But the flag will one day change because the stories told are only about that state's past, not its future.   17

The fight over symbols boils down to the choice between cultural manifest destiny and respect for all. It's inevitable because there's only one direction that will satisfy the country's changing demographics as well as our core principles. There's only one answer that will allow us to become the country we want to be.   18

One by one, schools are moving ahead, reaching the inevitable and logical conclusion that mascots must go. Some are doing this by keeping their names, but stripping away the native imagery. Professional basketball's Golden State Warriors long ago figured this solution out. Or some like Miami University of Ohio shift from Redskins to Redhawks—creating new stories to tell.   19

How long will it take for our nation to embrace the symbols that represent experiences we all share? What symbols do we choose—and what stories do we want to tell? Stories of inclusion or exclusion? Our symbols can build upon images that give us hope for the future; especially those that help some kid win $5 riding in a parade.   20

11. Skim paragraph 15. Consider the heading, "North Dakota's Dilemma." What is North Dakota's dilemma, according to the author?

   a. The state university must close due to pressure from Native Americans.

   b. The state university must choose between an Indian mascot and millions of dollars.

   c. North Dakota must abandon the tradition of graduation ceremonies to appease a group of Native Americans.

   d. Certain songs cannot be played at graduation ceremonies or Native Americans will march in protest.

12. Scan paragraphs 15–20. Which professional sports team does the author use as an example of a team that stripped away native imagery?

    a. Washington Redskins

    b. Cleveland Cavaliers

    c. Golden State Warriors

    d. Oakland Raiders

13. Scan paragraph 20, paying particular attention to the last sentence, "Our symbols can build upon images that give us hope for the future; especially those that help some kid win $5 riding in a parade." To whom is the author referring? If necessary, skim the entire passage to answer the question.

    a. The author is referring to the owner of the Washington Redskins.

    b. The author is referring to the center of the Golden State Warriors.

    c. The author is referring to himself.

    d. The author is referring to any Native American child who has been to a parade.

14. Scan paragraphs 15–20 again. How does the U.S. Civil Rights Commission feel about Native American symbols used as mascots, references, or nicknames?

    a. It supports some use of the imagery.

    b. It feels that "the symbols are plain wrong."

    c. It thinks the symbols "represent true historical and cultural experiences of American Indians."

    d. The commission did not comment on the use of symbols.

15. Scan paragraphs 15–20 to discern which school changed its mascot's name from the Redskins to the Redhawks in deference to Native Americans.

    a. Miami University of Ohio

    b. Florida State University

    c. University of Miami Ohio

    d. Jacksonville Community College

Reading the Whole

Now that you have skimmed and scanned Mark Trahant's essay "Every Symbol Tells a Story" in its parts, you'll be better prepared to read it again—this time in its entirety. As you read, recall what you learned about the essay from skimming and scanning its parts. Notice how the headings organize the author's main point and provide quick hints for what follows. Pay attention to the subtleties of what Trahant is saying, and, most important, think about what ways your experience skimming and scanning was different from your experience reading the essay all the way through. What points did you miss when you were skimming and scanning? What information did you pick up when you read the essay thoroughly that you didn't need for a general overview? Under what circumstances would you need to skim or scan the essay, and when would you prefer to read it?

MARK TRAHANT

Every Symbol Tells a Story

Americans are a people who cling to symbols. Most symbols, like Old Glory, are cues to tell a story. We see a flag and tell a friend about a holiday or some other warm memory. Others see a flag and recall a past war or some other test of our freedom. I see the flag and hear the poetry of the First Amendment; a respect for differences as a core national principle. 1

The American Flag is an important symbol in Indian country, too. I have always been amazed at how many flags I see at powwows: Sewn into beaded belt buckles, draped across floats in Indian parades, or even woven onto the back of a fancy-dancer's clothing. Each powwow begins with Grand Entry where the American Flag leads a formal procession of dancers wearing full regalia into an arena. 2

Perhaps this attachment to the flag is extraordinary because it would be understandable if American Indians rejected it; it would be so easy to point to generations of injustice and say "not this symbol." Yet the stories told about the flag are as important in the Native American community as in general society. Past injustice does not matter—nor does any current dispute with government or society. 3

I recall my first use of the flag. I was about 8 or 9 years old and had entered a youth parade during a tribal fair. I decked out my 4 bike in red, white, and blue crepe paper, wore an Army helmet, and placed a flag on the back of my bike.

The symbol worked. The judges gave me $5 and a first-place prize.   5

I think the flag still works as a symbol because the story it tells   6 crosses generations: it contains a narrative for young and old. A symbol with a history—including adventure, glory—and, yes, tragedy. But also a story with a promise, chapters yet to be written about an evolving democracy, something better ahead.

THE POWER TO HURT

Not all symbols meet that test. Some symbols are only about the   7 past. They remind us about a day that is no more, one that will never be again.

Such is the case with the Native American images and mascots   8 used by schools and professional sports franchises. We see an image of a smiling, buck-toothed face of some mythical chief advertising a Cleveland baseball franchise. Or a football team named "Red-skins," a word once used to describe the bounty paid for dead Indian bodies.

There will come a time—perhaps soon—when we will look   9 back on this controversy and ask: "How could this ever have been so? How could one people violate simple principles of common sense, courtesy and respect for one segment of society?"

BOTTOM-LINE PRESSURES

It may be economics that forces teams—big professional sports   10 organizations and hometown high school players—to change their names. Two years ago, the U.S. Patent and Trademark office opted not to renew trademark protection for the Washington Redskins. That office decided the team name violated a federal law that no trademark shall be registered "which may disparage" people, institutions, beliefs, or national symbols, "or bring them into contempt or disrepute."

This decision is on appeal, but its portent is powerful. If the   11 Washington Redskins—or any other team—cannot protect the use of its franchise in the market, then the name will change; new names will sprout up as fast as logo-embroidered caps.

The U.S. Civil Rights Commission is the latest group to investi-   12 gate—and it also reached the inevitable and logical conclusion. The time has come, the commission says, for this controversy to fade into history. "The Commission believes that the use of Native

American images and nicknames in school is insensitive and should be avoided.

"It is particularly disturbing that Native American references are still to be found in educational institutions, whether elementary, secondary or post-secondary. Schools are places where diverse groups of people come together to learn not only the 'Three Rs,' but also how to interact respectfully with people from different cultures." 13

The statement asks that we consider what kind of environments we're creating in schools for all our citizens. "Children at the elementary and secondary level usually have no choice about which school they should attend," the commission said. And at the college level, imagine a Native American trying to get an education when the fight over a symbol flames intense and often base emotions. 14

NORTH DAKOTA'S DILEMMA

Such is the case in North Dakota, where the state university must choose between an Indian mascot and millions of dollars. If the Indian mascot disappears — so will support from some prominent alumni. On the other hand, the American Indian Movement says it will disrupt graduation ceremonies this spring, unless the name is dropped. 15

The line is drawn because so many alumni cling to past notions about honoring native people. Even when Native Americans disagree. Worse yet, the commission says, the symbols are plain wrong. "Even those that purport to be positive are romantic stereotypes that give a distorted view of the past. These false portrayals prevent non-Native Americans from understanding the true historical and cultural experiences of American Indians." 16

AN AMERICAN STORY

This controversy is about all of us — not just American Indians who are disrespected in sports. The same cultural differences are found in Mississippi where a state flag with the Confederate bars and stars draws on different stories for different people. To some it represents some past glory; others only see injustice. But the flag will one day change because the stories told are only about that state's past, not its future. 17

The fight over symbols boils down to the choice between cultural manifest destiny and respect for all. It's inevitable because there's only 18 one direction that will satisfy the country's changing demographics as well as our core principles. There's only one answer that will allow us to become the country we want to be.

One by one, schools are moving ahead, reaching the inevitable and logical conclusion that mascots must go. Some are doing this by keeping their names, but stripping away the native imagery. Professional basketball's Golden State Warriors long ago figured this solution out. Or some like Miami University of Ohio shift from Redskins to Redhawks—creating new stories to tell.   19

How long will it take for our nation to embrace the symbols that represent experiences we all share? What symbols do we choose—and what stories do we want to tell? Stories of inclusion or exclusion? Our symbols can build upon images that give us hope for the future; especially those that help some kid win $5 riding in a parade.   20

Integrated Skills

1. Why does the author think the American flag "still works as a symbol"?

2. List some other symbols the author discusses. What is the author's point about how these symbols work and what they symbolize?

3. How might economics "force teams—big professional sports organizations and hometown high school players—to change their names"?

4. What other symbols can you think of that the author might consider to be "only about the past"?

5. Do you agree with the author's assessment of symbols in sports and on flags? Why or why not?

Reading Textbooks

Thematic Connections. You have just read Mark Trahant's essay "Every Symbol Tells a Story" about the controversies surrounding certain symbols—particularly those that depict Native Americans in sports organizations. In the essay, Trahant contrasts such symbols with the American flag, suggesting that Native American images look toward the past and highlight negative stereotypes of Native Americans. However, Trahant only mentions the history of the stereotypes in passing. The following textbook passage, taken from the American history book *The American Promise* by James L. Roark, Michael P. Johnson, Patricia Cline Cohen, Sarah Stage, Alan Lawson, and Susan M. Hartmann, discusses a very early historical depiction of Native Americans. As you read the textbook passage, think about what it tells you about Trahant's main point. Pay particular attention to the misunderstanding that led the native people of San Salvador to be renamed by Columbus, and begin to draw your own conclusions about how such a misunderstanding might have contributed to the symbols Trahant discusses.

Vocabulary Preview

surmise (para. 4): to conclude on limited evidence (v.)

contrary (para. 4): opposite (n.)

perceptions (para. 5): the results of observation or discernment (n.)

1   A half hour before sunrise on August 3, 1492, Christopher Columbus commanded three ships to catch the tide out of a harbor in southern Spain and sail west. Just over two months later, in the predawn moonlight of October 12, 1492, Columbus glimpsed an island on the western horizon. At last, he believed, he had found what he had been looking for—the western end of a route across the Atlantic Ocean to Japan, China, and India. At daybreak, Columbus could see people on the shore who had spotted his ships. He rowed ashore and, as the curious islanders crowded around, he claimed possession of the land for Ferdinand and Isabella, king and queen of Spain, who had sponsored his voyage. He named the island San Salvador, in honor of the Savior, Jesus Christ.

2   A day or two afterward, Columbus described that first encounter with the inhabitants of San Salvador in an extensive diary he kept during his voyage. He called these people Indians, assuming that

their island lay somewhere in the East Indies near Japan or China. The Indians were not dressed in the finery Columbus expected. "All of them go around as naked as their mothers bore them; and the women also," he observed. Their skin color was "neither black nor white." They were not familiar with the Spaniards' weapons. "I showed them swords," Columbus wrote, "and they took them by the edge and through ignorance cut themselves." This first encounter led Columbus to conclude, "They should be good and intelligent servants, for I see that they say very quickly everything that is said to them; and I believe that they would become Christians very easily, for it seemed to me that they had no religion."

The people Columbus called Indians called themselves Tainos, which to them meant "good" or "noble." They inhabited most of the islands Columbus visited on his first voyage, as had their ancestors for more than two centuries. The Tainos were an agricultural people who grew cassava, a nutritious root, as well as sweet potatoes, corn, cotton, tobacco, and other crops. To fish and to travel from island to island, they built canoes from hollowed-out logs. The Tainos worshiped gods they called *zemis,* the spirits of ancestors and of natural objects like trees and stones. They made effigies of *zemis* and performed rituals to honor them. "It seemed to me that they were a people very poor in everything," Columbus wrote. But the Tainos mined gold in small quantities, enough to catch the eye of Columbus and his men.

What the Tainos thought about Spaniards we can only surmise. At first, Columbus believed that the Tainos thought he and his men came from heaven. After six weeks of contact, Columbus concluded that in fact he did not understand Tainos. Late in November 1492, he wrote that "the people of these lands do not understand me nor do I, nor anyone else that I have with me, them. And many times I understand one thing said by these Indians . . . for another, its contrary."

The confused communication between Europeans and Tainos suggests how different, how strange, each group seemed to the other. Columbus's perceptions of Tainos were shaped by European ideas, attitudes, and expectations, just as Tainos' perceptions of Europeans must have been colored by their own culture. Yet the word that Columbus coined for the Tainos—*Indians,* a word that originated in a colossal misunderstanding—hinted at the direction of the future. To Europeans, *Indians* came to mean all native inhabitants of the New World, the name they gave to the lands in the

Western Hemisphere. After 1492 the perceptions, the cultures, and even the diseases of Europeans began to exert a transforming influence on the New World and its peoples.

Long before 1492, certain Europeans restlessly expanded the limits of the world known to them. Their efforts made possible Columbus's encounter with the Tainos. In turn, Columbus's landfall in the Caribbean changed the history not only of the Tainos, but also of Europe and the rest of the world. Beginning in 1492, the promise of the New World lured more and more Europeans to venture their lives and fortunes on the western shores of the Atlantic, a promise realized largely at the expense of New World peoples like Tainos.

6

Thinking about the Textbook Selection

1. What was Christopher Columbus looking for as he sailed from Europe? What did he find?

2. Who sponsored Columbus's voyage, and why did he name the island he landed on "San Salvador"?

3. Why did Columbus call the inhabitants of San Salvador "Indians"?

4. Why did Columbus think that the Tainos would be good servants?

5. Identify two mistaken notions that Columbus had about the Tainos.

6. Why did the Tainos and the Europeans not understand each other very well?

7. What effect did the Europeans have on the Tainos? Why?

Reviewing

1. What is skimming? List the guidelines for skimming a book or article.
2. When is skimming more useful than reading a book or article?
3. What is scanning? List the guidelines for scanning a book or article.
4. When is scanning more useful than reading a book or article?
5. Identify the major parts of a book, and explain how you can use them to see what the book contains.

In this chapter you learned the techniques for skimming and scanning for information. You can use skimming, a form of quick reading, to gain an overview of the contents of an article or a chapter of a book. Skimming can be an effective way of prereading to help you prepare to read the passage and to better understand it after you have finished reading. Scanning, or searching for specific information, is particularly useful when you are answering a question or when reviewing material for a test or class discussion.

In this chapter you also learned the parts of a book and how to use them. The table of contents, usually located at the front of the book, lists the important subjects the book covers and gives page numbers where you can find them. The table of contents is usually listed in the order that the material appears. A book's index also lists the book's important subjects and page numbers. However, an index usually appears at the back of the book, is listed alphabetically, and includes more detail. You also learned several other parts of a book and how to use them.

Getting Ready	371
Learning the Skills	372
Applying the Skills	
• Reading the Parts	397
• Reading the Whole	404
• Reading Textbooks	408
Reviewing	410

Developing Visual Literacy

Getting Ready

Chapter Overview

Just as you can improve your reading comprehension, you can improve your ability to comprehend **visual materials.** Learning to read and understand visual materials will help you better understand the texts that include these visual materials. Understanding visual materials can also improve your ability to "see" the meaning of information and ideas explained in newspapers and magazines about current events and contemporary life.

Visuals, or **graphics,** serve the following important purposes:

- They clarify and illustrate key concepts.
- They summarize complex discussions in the written text.
- They provide additional information and examples.
- They add interest to written explanations and information.

Because graphics serve these important purposes, learning to understand them will help you in other ways. For example, you will be better able to study a textbook chapter when you review for an exam. You will reinforce the skills you developed in reading written texts as you identify the main idea of visual materials and make connections and establish relationships among their details, making inferences and drawing conclusions based on the information they provide.

Which of your books contains the most graphics? Why do you think this is the case?

How can graphics help you understand concepts and processes described in your textbooks?

How can graphics help you understand the information in newspapers, magazines, and Web sites?

Everyday
Reading

Many things you read in everyday life use visual materials, or graphics, to illustrate the ideas presented in the reading. Magazine articles use visual materials, as do the advertisements that appear among the articles. Newspapers, cookbooks, and even instructions for preparing some pre-packaged foods all use visuals.

Browse through your local newspaper and take note of how visuals—photographs, drawings, maps, and charts—are used to make the accompanying text clearer to the reader. Find three articles that use different kinds of visuals to make their point and describe how each visual helps to illustrate what the writing communicates. What information exactly does each visual illustrate? Why?

Learning the Skills

■ Types of Graphics

Many types of graphics can accompany written material. In a single text-book alone, you may find photographs, maps, diagrams, charts, graphs, and tables that help illustrate what the textbook is teaching. Understanding the differences among different types of graphic material is the first step in understanding how that material helps illustrate the writing. The following list includes eight major types of visual materials you might find in your reading and a brief description of how they are often used.

- **Photographs** are used to attract a reader's attention, to create visual appeal, to illustrate objects, or to convey impressions of people and places.

- **Maps** show geographical areas, such as countries or cities. Maps also depict topographical features such as mountains and deserts.

- **Diagrams** show the elements or parts of a system or a sequence of events.

- **Charts** visualize the lines of responsibility in an institution, or they portray the direction of a process, as with flowcharts.
- **Graphs** use elements like circles, bars, and lines to display information. Graphics depict the relationship between two or more things, such as between two variables.
- **Tables** provide information so that it can be easily accessed. Especially useful for comparing data, tables present information in columns or rows.
- **Cartoons** often comment on topics, events, and people—often in a humorous way.
- **Fine art** (painting and sculpture) may be used for various purposes, for example to portray a person or a group, to depict a historical or mythological event, or to depict an image of a deity.

Since graphics vary widely in form, appearance, and purpose, it is advisable to approach reading them systematically. Use the following guidelines, adapting them to the particular types of graphics you encounter in your reading.

Guidelines for Reading Graphics

1. Read the title and subtitle. The title and subtitle tell you what the graphic is about—its topic.
2. Read the caption or legend written beside or beneath the graphic. The caption or legend provides specific information about the content of the graphic.
3. Observe how the information in the graphic is organized—as a table, chart, map, and so on.
4. Observe the graphic's scale or units of measurement—whether its numbers represent thousands, for example, or percentages.
5. Determine the trend(s), pattern(s), and relationship(s) the graphic is designed to show. Look for connections among its data.
6. Read any explanatory notes (footnotes) the graphic includes. Notes might provide information about how the data represented in the graphic were collected or whether information is incomplete.
7. Check the source(s) of the information the graphic includes.
8. Make inferences and draw conclusions from the information or concepts presented in the graphic. Think about the significance of what the graphic shows.
9. Relate the graphic to the written text.

PHOTOGRAPHS

Photographs are among the most commonly found types of visual material. A photograph in a newspaper or magazine story can make the events, people, and things discussed more vivid and meaningful. For example, while a news story can discuss dollar damages from a hurricane or quote its victims, a photograph can actually show the devastation. Photographs in newspapers and magazines make us familiar with everything from leaders of distant countries to new products. In textbooks, photographs create visual interest and direct readers' attention to important facts, issues, and ideas.

In an American history textbook, for example, you can expect to find photographs that depict key people, places, and events involved in shaping the course of American life and culture. You might expect to see an image from the civil rights movement of the 1960s, perhaps a picture of Martin Luther King Jr. making a speech before a rally or leading a demonstration protesting racial inequality.

Figure 12.1 is a picture of the legendary boxer Joe Louis standing amid a crowd of children in Harlem, in New York City. The 1949 photograph shows Louis enjoying his status as one of the first African American cultural icons in the United States. The short exercise that follows the photograph will help you understand how the photograph works.

Figure 12.1

Exercise 12-1

Answer the following questions based on Figure 12.1.

1. What observations can you make about the people in the picture, and what inferences can you draw from those observations?

    _____

    _____

    _____

    _____

2. What aspects of the topic of culture do you think an article accompanied by this picture might discuss?

    _____

    _____

    _____

Here is another photograph, this one from a textbook on American government. The caption explains the picture's significance.

Figure 12.2

Borne up by an alliance of diverse ethnic and racial groups that he called "the Rainbow Coalition," Rev. Jesse Jackson campaigned for the Democratic presidential nomination in 1984 and 1988. He and his family acknowledged a standing ovation after he addressed the 1988 Democratic convention.

Exercise 12-2

. . . .

Answer the following questions with regard to Figure 12.2.

1. How does the picture reflect the text of the accompanying caption?

    _____

    _____

    _____

2. What section of a book on American government might include such a picture? Why?

    _____

    _____

    _____

. . . .

MAPS

Maps depict physical locations and geographical areas. Geography books include maps that depict land masses and bodies of water. Some maps are topographical, which means they show differences in elevation of the land as hills or mountains, plains, or deserts. Other maps may depict changes or trends—in weather patterns, for example, or in population density.

History books also tend to include many maps. A chapter on the American Civil War, for example, might have maps that show some of the following:

- the Union and Confederate states
- the railroad lines in the North and the South
- the locations of major battles
- the terrain of particular battle sites, such as Gettysburg

The map on page 377, taken from the textbook *America's History* by James A. Henretta, David Brody, Susan Ware, and Marilynn S. Johnston, shows how the Union took over more and more Confederate territory each year of the war.

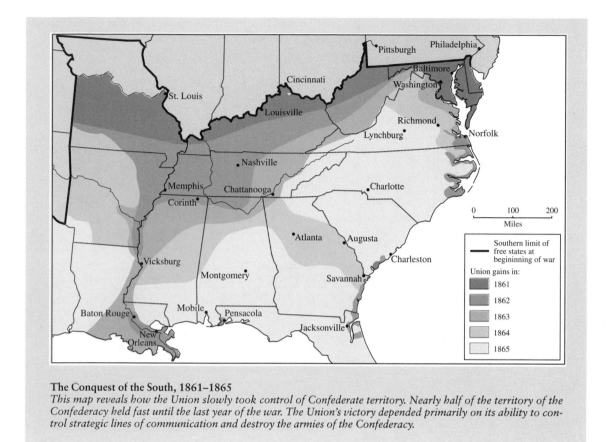

The Conquest of the South, 1861–1865
This map reveals how the Union slowly took control of Confederate territory. Nearly half of the territory of the Confederacy held fast until the last year of the war. The Union's victory depended primarily on its ability to control strategic lines of communication and destroy the armies of the Confederacy.

Figure 12.3

Exercise 12-3

Answer the following questions about the map shown in Figure 12.3.

1. What is the purpose of the map?

    _____

2. Which year did the Union gain the most territory?

    _____

Here is a map of the United States that indicates the ten fastest growing states during the years 1990 to 1995.

Figure 12.4

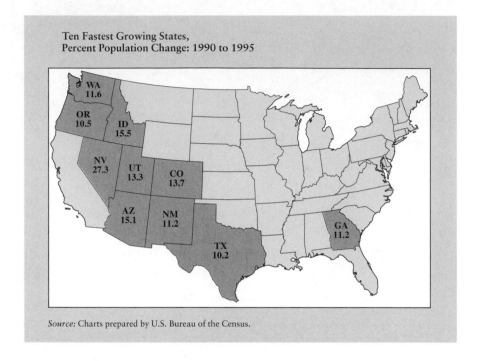

Ten Fastest Growing States,
Percent Population Change: 1990 to 1995

Source: Charts prepared by U.S. Bureau of the Census.

Exercise 12-4

. . . .

After studying Figure 12.4, answer the following questions.

1. Which state had the fastest rate of growth from 1990 to 1995?

   _____

2. Which parts of the country had the most population growth?

   _____

. . . .

DIAGRAMS

Diagrams are drawings that show an object or a process by labeling its parts or its steps. In a biology textbook, for example, you find labeled diagrams of organ systems of animals and plants. Figure 12.5, taken from the book *Psychology* by David Myers, depicts the human endocrine glands and their locations in the body.

Figure 12.5

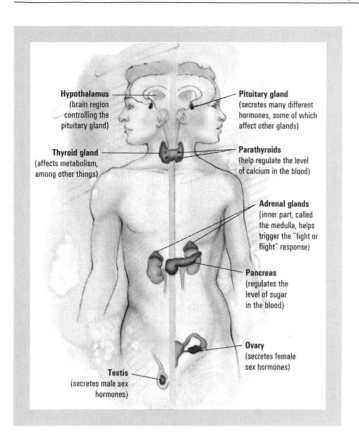

Exercise 12-5

Answer the following questions based on Figure 12.5.

1. Which endocrine glands are located in the head, which in the neck and throat, and which in the mid-body?

_____

_____

2. Write a paragraph explaining how this diagram might be used to illustrate a process.

_____

_____

_____

_____

_____

The following diagram from the geology textbook *Understanding Earth* by Frank Press and Raymond Siever shows how eruptions from volcanoes affected the earth's atmosphere. Water expelled from volcanoes was released into the oceans and the air, its oxygen supplemented by that produced by plants during photosynthesis.

Figure 12.6

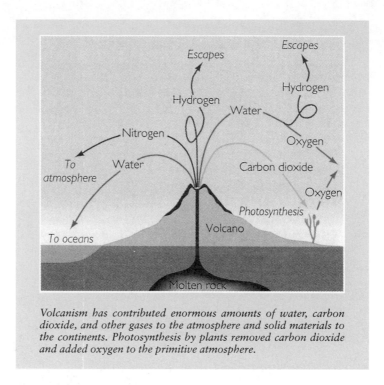

Volcanism has contributed enormous amounts of water, carbon dioxide, and other gases to the atmosphere and solid materials to the continents. Photosynthesis by plants removed carbon dioxide and added oxygen to the primitive atmosphere.

Exercise 12-6

Write a paragraph explaining the process described in Figure 12.6.

_____

_____

_____

_____

_____

_____

CHARTS

Three popular types of charts found in textbooks and in business materials are flowcharts, organizational charts, and pie charts.

Flowcharts. Flowcharts typically show how a process occurs or how a procedure works. They are useful for laying out the stages of a process or the steps of a procedure. Flowcharts include lines or arrows that indicate the direction, or flow, of the process portrayed. Flowcharts are often used to summarize the accompanying text. For this reason, they are particularly useful for review and study.

The following flowchart from the textbook *Psychology* by David Myers describes the steps involved in applying the scientific method. It also includes a specific example. Begin reading the flowchart at the top right. Follow the direction of the arrows through each successive step until they loop back to the first or top stage of the process. The circular portrayal indicates that the process recurs, or happens again, with each of the stages repeated.

Figure 12.7

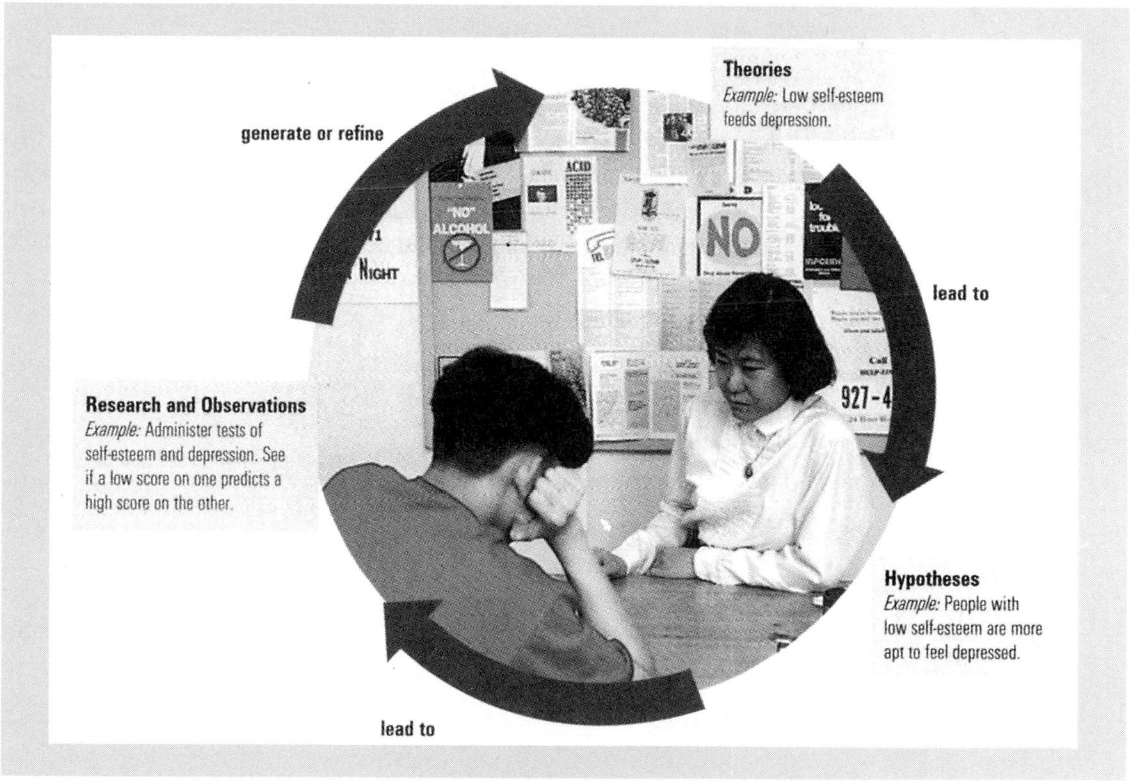

generate or refine

Theories
Example: Low self-esteem feeds depression.

lead to

Research and Observations
Example: Administer tests of self-esteem and depression. See if a low score on one predicts a high score on the other.

Hypotheses
Example: People with low self-esteem are more apt to feel depressed.

lead to

Exercise 12-7

Answer the following questions based on Figure 12.7.

1. Why do you think the flowchart includes the element of repetition?

   _____

   _____

2. How do the caption and headings in the flowchart help you understand what it represents?

   _____

   _____

   _____

Organizational Charts. Organizational charts show the structure and hierarchy of an organization, such as a corporation or a university. You will find organizational charts in business textbooks, in magazines devoted to business topics, and in corporate publications. Organizational charts are often used to show lines of authority—who reports to whom—as illustrated by the chart shown in Figure 12.8, which is from the textbook *Exploring the World of Business* by Kenneth Blanchard, Charles Schewe, Robert Nelson, and Alexander Hiam.

Exercise 12-8

Answer the following questions based on Figure 12.8.

1. What individual or group has the most authority in the corporation?

   _____

2. Which group has authority over the CEO? Which group has authority over the board of directors?

   _____

Figure 12.8

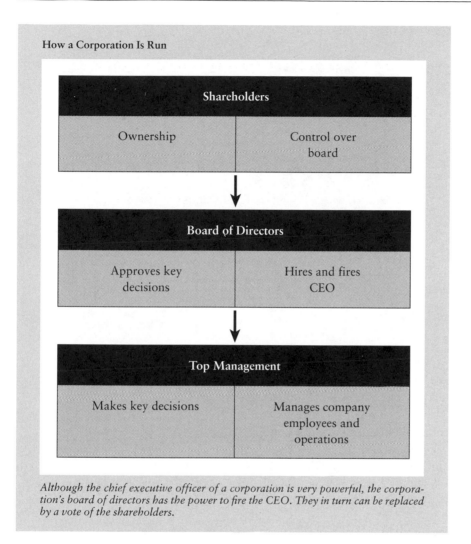

How a Corporation Is Run

Although the chief executive officer of a corporation is very powerful, the corporation's board of directors has the power to fire the CEO. They in turn can be replaced by a vote of the shareholders.

Pie Charts (Pie Graphs). Pie charts, also called pie graphs (and sometimes circle graphs), get their name from their shape. The circle of a pie chart or graph is "cut" into sectors, sliced by lines converging in the center. Each section represents one part of the pie. Pie charts show the relative size or importance of the various elements represented by the sectors.

The pie chart in Figure 12.9 on page 384 shows the types of taxes collected by state governments, in percentages, for 1994. Notice how exactly half of all state taxes came from sales and gross receipts, while the remaining half of the tax pie came from different types of taxes.

Figure 12.9

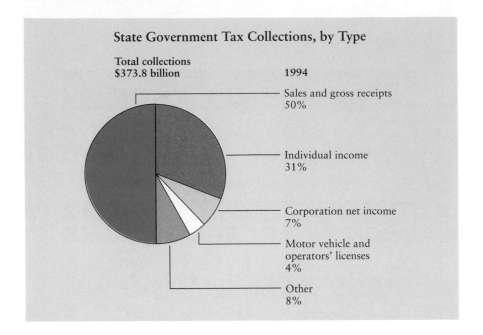

Many times textbooks, newspapers, and magazines that include pie charts or graphs will include multiple pie charts for comparative purposes. The pie chart in Figure 12.9 was printed with another, which represented the same kind of state government tax collections, but for 1970.

Figure 12.10

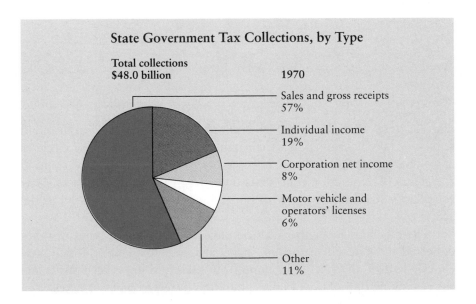

Exercise 12-9

After comparing the data presented in the two pie charts in Figures 12.9 and 12.10, answer the following questions.

1. What happened to state sales taxes as a percentage of the whole tax pie between 1970 and 1994?

    _____

2. What happened to corporation taxes as a percentage of the entire net income during that period?

    _____

3. In what segment or sector did the biggest change occur?

    _____

4. What explanation might you offer for these changes?

    _____

    _____

    _____

GRAPHS

The two most common types of graphs are bar graphs and line graphs.

Bar Graphs. Bar graphs are used to compare amounts or quantities. Most often they show differences between the items the graph describes. The bar graph from *America's History* in Figure 12.11 on page 386 shows how in 1860, at the start of the Civil War, the economy of the North was much stronger than that of the South.

Exercise 12-10

After studying Figure 12.11, answer the following questions.

1. According to the graph, in what area did the North have its greatest advantage over the South?

    _____

Figure 12.11

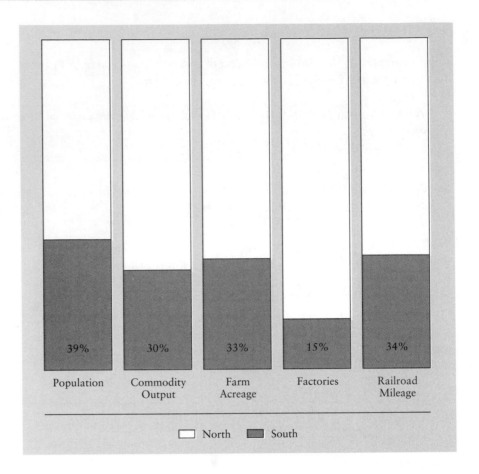

| Population | Commodity Output | Farm Acreage | Factories | Railroad Mileage |

39%   30%   33%   15%   34%

☐ North   ■ South

2. In what area was the South least at a disadvantage?

_____

. . . .

Some bar graphs make comparisons among multiple elements. The bar graph in Figure 12.12, for example, compares participation in sports activities for males and females, while showing the percentage of participation in the ten most popular sports activities. Notice how this graph, from *The American Almanac, 1996–1997,* is arranged horizontally, with its shaded bars running across the page, rather than up and down as in Figure 12.11.

Figure 12.12

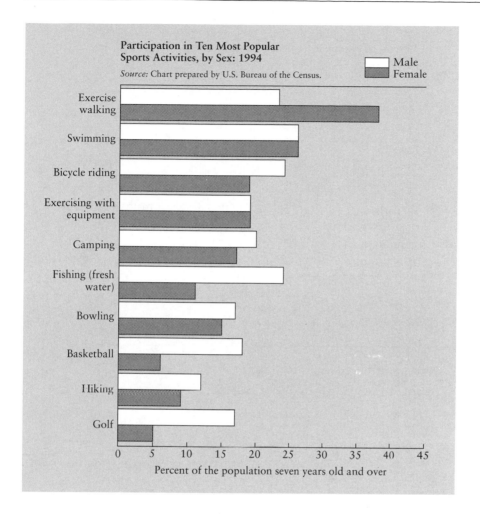

Participation in Ten Most Popular
Sports Activities, by Sex: 1994

Source: Chart prepared by U.S. Bureau of the Census.

Percent of the population seven years old and over

Exercise 12-11

After studying Figure 12.12, answer the following questions.

1. Which two sports activities show the greatest similarities in participation by males and females?

   _____

2. Which sports activities show the greatest difference in male and female participation?

   _____

3. What do you think some other, less popular sports might show in terms of comparing male and female participation? Consider, for example, football, tennis, and wrestling.

_____

_____

_____

Line Graphs. Line graphs (also called linear graphs) are plotted or drawn on a horizontal and a vertical axis. Each axis represents a variable, or an item that varies in relation to the other. The line (or lines) of the graph allows viewers to compare the two items. Figure 12.13, taken

Figure 12.13

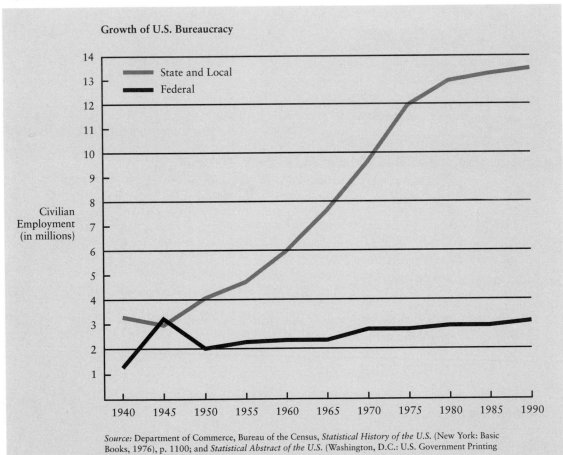

Growth of U.S. Bureaucracy

Source: Department of Commerce, Bureau of the Census, _Statistical History of the U.S._ (New York: Basic Books, 1976), p. 1100; and _Statistical Abstract of the U.S._ (Washington, D.C.: U.S. Government Printing Office, 1991), p. 329.

from the textbook *Politics in a Changing World* by Marcus Ethridge and Howard Handelman, shows the change in the number of state and local government workers as compared with federal workers from 1940 to 1990. The vertical axis represents the number of civilian workers in millions, ranging from a little less than 1 million to nearly 14 million workers. The horizontal axis represents the years from 1940 to 1990 marked in five-year intervals.

Exercise 12-12

After studying Figure 12.13, answer the following questions.

1. Which group of workers increased most between 1940 and 1990?

    _____

2. What prediction can you make about the number of workers in each group for the year 2000?

    _____

Some line graphs include many lines identifying a number of variables. The line graph in Figure 12.14 on page 390 shows consumers' use of various types of media from 1989 to 1999. Notice that the last few years are based on projections rather than actual data.

Exercise 12-13

Answer the following questions based on studying Figure 12.14.

1. Which types of media are people spending increasing amounts of time using? Which types of media are people spending less time on?

    _____

    _____

2. Which media appear to be remaining stable in terms of how often people use them?

    _____

Figure 12.14

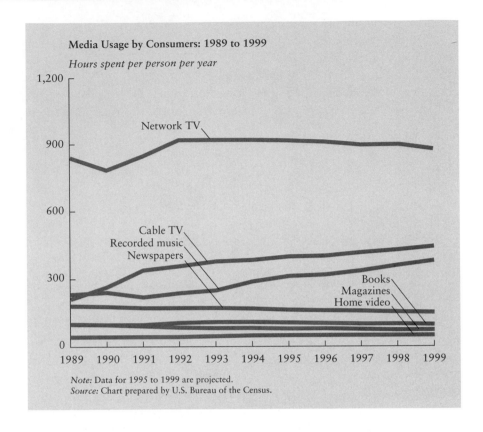

Media Usage by Consumers: 1989 to 1999

Hours spent per person per year

Network TV

Cable TV
Recorded music
Newspapers

Books
Magazines
Home video

1989 1990 1991 1992 1993 1994 1995 1996 1997 1998 1999

Note: Data for 1995 to 1999 are projected.
Source: Chart prepared by U.S. Bureau of the Census.

3. What projection would you make for network TV as compared with cable TV usage for the year 2010?

_____

_____

. . . .

TABLES

Tables present complex information so that it can be more easily under-stood. They compress a lot of information into a small amount of space. For this reason of efficiency and for their visual clarity, tables commonly present large amounts of data.

Tables contain information organized in rows and columns. Some tables contain only two columns; others have many columns. The table in Figure 12.15 comes from the college textbook *America's History.* As

Figure 12.15

Ten Largest Cities by Population, 1870 and 1910

1870		1910	
City	*Population*	*City*	*Population*
1. New York	942,292	New York	4,766,883
2. Philadelphia	674,022	Chicago	2,185,283
3. Brooklyn*	419,921	Philadelphia	1,549,008
4. St. Louis	310,864	St. Louis	687,029
5. Chicago	298,977	Boston	670,585
6. Baltimore	267,354	Cleveland	560,663
7. Boston	250,526	Baltimore	558,485
8. Cincinnati	216,239	Pittsburgh	533,905
9. New Orleans	191,418	Detroit	465,766
10. San Francisco	149,473	Buffalo	423,715

* Brooklyn was consolidated with New York in 1898.

Source: U.S. Census data.

its title indicates, the table gives the ten largest American cities by population for the years 1870 and 1910. For each year the table lists the cities in size order with a second column to the right of each city listing its population.

Exercise 12-14

Answer the following questions based on Figure 12.15.

1. What might you infer from the changes in the population of the ten largest American cities between 1870 and 1910?

2. Why do you think some cities dropped off the list and others were added in 1910? That is, why do you think some cities gained population at a faster rate than others?

Unemployment Rate, 1995

Race and age	Women[1]	Men[1]
All races:	5.6	5.6
16 to 19 years	16.1	18.4
20 years and over	4.9	4.8
White	4.8	4.9
16 to 19 years	13.4	15.6
20 years and over	4.3	4.3
Minority races:	10.1	9.9
16 to 19 years	29.1	30.8
20 years and over	8.8	8.2

1. Annual averages. *Source:* Bureau of Labor Statistics, Department of Labor.

Unemployment Rate in the Civilian Labor Force

Year	Unemployment rate	Year	Unemployment rate
1920	5.2	1984	7.5
1928	4.2	1986	7.0
1930	8.7	1987	6.2
1932	23.6	1988	5.4
1934	21.7	1989	5.3
1936	16.9	1990	5.5
1938	19.0	1991	6.7
1940	14.6	1992	7.4
1942	4.7	1993	6.8
1944	1.2	1994	6.1
1946	3.9	1995	5.6
1948	3.8	Jan.	5.7
1950	5.3	Feb.	5.4
1952	3.0	March	5.5
1954	5.5	April	5.7
1956	4.1	May	5.6
1958	6.8	June	5.6
1960	5.5	July	5.7
1962	5.5	Aug.	5.6
1964	5.2	Sept.	5.6
1966	3.8	Oct.	5.5
1968	3.6	Nov.	5.6
1970	4.9	Dec.	5.6
1972	5.6	1996	
1974	5.6	Jan.	5.8
1976	7.7	Feb.	5.5
1978	6.0	March	5.6
1980	7.1	April	5.4
1982	9.7	May	5.6

NOTE: Estimates prior to 1940 are based on sources other than direct enumeration. *Source:* Department of Labor, Bureau of Labor Statistics.

Figure 12.16

Exercise 12-15

. . . .

Answer the following questions based on the tables in Figure 12.16.

1. What do you notice about the rate of unemployment in the United States for the 1930s? Why do you think there is a sudden change between 1930 and 1932, and again between 1940 and 1942?

    _____

    _____

    _____

2. How might you explain the very low unemployment rate in 1944—the lowest recorded rate in U.S. history?

    _____

    _____

    _____

3. What observations and inferences can you make from the data about the 1995 unemployment rates for men and women, white and minority workers?

    _____

    _____

    _____

. . . .

■ Understanding Text and Graphics Together

In reading graphic visual materials in your textbooks, you'll need to connect not only the visual part of the graphic and its caption but also the entire graphic with the written text it illustrates or supplements.

When you read a textbook that includes visual materials and written text, use the guidelines on page 394.

Keep in mind that the graphic materials included in college textbooks are visual aids, that is, a supplementary visual means to present information and concepts. Although you can never grasp a book's central ideas by looking at its visuals, you can use the graphics in a textbook

---

Guidelines for Linking Graphics and Written Text

- Preview the chapter by looking through it for graphics.

- Read the graphics and their accompanying captions to gain a preliminary overview.

- Read the textbook written material until you come to a reference to a graphic, often "see Figure X."

- Look at the graphic and read its caption.

- Think about the relation between the visual material and the written explanation.

- Return to your reading of the written text, moving back and forth between it and any visual materials it directs you to look at.

---

to help you do several things: (1) zero in on key ideas and concepts; (2) preview a chapter or section; (3) review a chapter or section.

Visual aids in textbooks perform a valuable function by enabling readers to "see" the material in another format. Graphics also provide visual aid for readers by summarizing essential information and concepts. In addition, graphic visual aids sometimes provide additional or supplementary material, which is not specifically discussed in the text.

Exercise 12-16

With a small group of classmates, work on one of the following activities, each of which invites you to create a form of visual aid or graphic. Write a caption for your graphic.

A. Make a map of the classroom, showing where people sit and where the instructor locates himself or herself.
   OR
   Make a map showing the geographical location(s) people in the class commute from.

B. Make a pie chart or graph showing the breakdown of academic majors among you and your classmates.

C. Make a bar graph that shows the ethnic background or ancestry of people in the class.

Exercise 12-17

Select a graphic from one of your textbooks and write a description of what the graphic describes, clarifies, or explains. Use your own words rather than the language of the textbook.

_____

_____

_____

_____

_____

Exercise 12-18

For a chapter in one of your textbooks, make a visual graphic to show the topics discussed in it and their relation to one another. You may wish to use a diagram, a chart, a map, or some other form of visual aid. Accompany your graphic with brief written explanations for each section, part, or element.

Reading the Parts

The following essay, "Erectus Afloat" by Robert Kunzig, is reprinted from the January 1999 issue of the science magazine *Discover*. Kunzig, the European editor of the magazine, is also the author of two acclaimed books about ocean science, *The Restless Sea: Exploring the World Beneath the Waves* and *Mapping the Deep: The Extraordinary Story of Ocean Science*. He is the winner of the American Association for the Advancement of Science's Westinghouse Science Journalism Award and the American Geophysical Union's Walter Sullivan Award for Excellence in Science Journalism. This essay, divided into three parts, includes two maps and a photograph. As you read the essay in its parts and answer the questions that follow each part, pay special attention to how the illustrations relate to the text. How do they add information? What information do they add? Once you have read a section and answered its questions, move on to the next section. You will have a chance to reread the entire essay when you finish.

ROBERT KUNZIG
Erectus Afloat

What kind of brain does it take to build a boat and steer it across 15 miles of choppy seas and strong currents? Could a chimp do it? Not likely. Could human ancestors—*Homo erectus*, to be precise—have done it 800,000 years ago, which is about 750,000 years earlier than any previous evidence of watercraft? Mike Morwood thinks so. This past year the Australian archeologist from the University of New England in New South Wales reported what he considers proof that *Homo erectus* once set watercraft to breakers on the beaches of Indonesia. 1

The evidence comes from the island of Flores, several hundred miles and several deep straits east of Java, the previous southeastern limit of *Homo erectus*'s range. There, Morwood and his Indonesian and Australian colleagues have found more than a dozen stones that they say are tools—flakes and choppers for working wood or 2 animal carcasses. Although their published drawings of the stones are inconclusive, Morwood says the stones themselves show clear evidence of the sharp edges, cracks, and microscopic striations that stone acquires only from being smacked around by a hominid (as opposed to, say, being rolled around in a river).

1. What country is the archeologist Mike Morwood from?

   a. Wales

   b. the United States

   c. Australia

   d. Indonesia

2. What are *Homo erectus*?

   a. chimps

   b. rounded stones

   c. human ancestors

   d. special watercraft

3. Based on the observation of the "sharp edges, cracks, and microscopic striations [scratches]" of the stones, what have Morwood and his colleagues inferred?

   a. that the stones were "rolled around in a river"

   b. that the stones were used as tools

   c. that the stones were used by animal carcasses

   d. that the published drawings of the stones are inconclusive

4. What is special about the location of the stones that Morwood has found?

   a. They come from Java.

   b. They were found several hundred miles away from where *Homo erectus* were previously known to live.

   c. They were within the previous southeastern limit of *Homo erectus*'s range.

   d. They were several hundred miles away from the breakers on the beaches of Indonesia.

5. What conclusion has Mike Morwood drawn from the evidence
   he has gathered?

   a.   that *Homo erectus* probably never traveled very far

   b.   that chimps may have traveled by boat

   c.   that *Homo erectus* may have traveled by boat

   d.   that New South Wales was inhabited by *Homo erectus*

The tool layer, say the researchers, dates to 800,000 years ago. *Homo erectus* had long since reached Java by then—on foot. During the ice ages, sea level was sometimes so low that Java was connected to the Asian mainland. But between Java and Flores lie three straits too deep to have dried out during glacial periods, one of which was more than 15 miles wide. "It's a pretty formidable water crossing," Morwood says. "The vast majority of animals didn't make it." But early humans did.

3

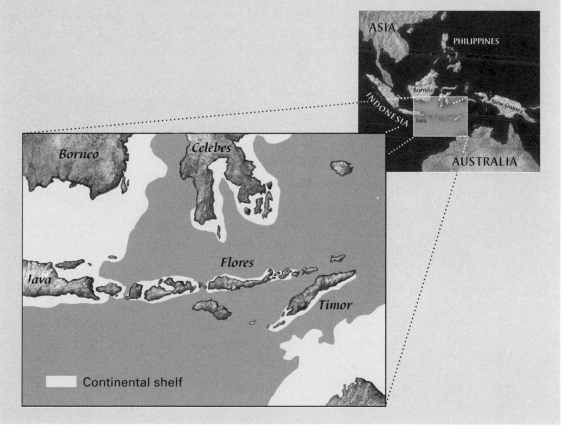

Presumably they didn't swim. Nor does Morwood think they 4
could have crossed the straits in any significant numbers by accident, hanging on to logs or crude rafts. "I think you need directed
watercraft," he says. "You'd have to have some means of steering,
and some means of propulsion. If you try to put a few logs together
and jump on it, you're probably going to die."

6. Based on general context clues, what is the "tool layer" the
author refers to in paragraph 3?

   a. the layer of earth where the stone tools were found in the
archeological dig

   b. one of the layers of water between the islands

   c. the layer of ice left over from the glaciers

   d. one of the layers connecting Java to the Asian mainland

7. Based on the context of the sentence "But between Java and
Flores lie three straits too deep to have dried out during glacial
periods" and on the map that follows paragraph 3, what are
straits?

   a. islands

   b. narrow channels of water

   c. parts of the Asian mainland

   d. glacial periods

8. How do the two maps relate?

   a. The larger map shows a part of the smaller map in more
detail.

   b. The smaller map shows part of the larger map in more
detail.

   c. The smaller map shows this area of the world 800,000
years ago and the larger shows it today.

   d. The larger map shows this area of the world 800,000 years
ago and the smaller shows it today.

9. According to the larger map, how many straits are there in total
between Java and Flores?

   a. 3   c. 9

   b. 2   d. 4

10. According to the maps, what island is immediately south of Borneo?

 a. Philippines   c. Celebes

 b. New Guinea   d. Java

Until now the earliest evidence of boats has been the presence of   5
modern humans in Australia between 40,000 and 60,000 years ago.
To make such a voyage, it has been argued, requires quintessentially
modern skills—not just technical ones but the ability to plan, to
work as a group, even to talk. Setting sail from Timor to Australia,
over the horizon and into the unknown, may still seem qualitatively
different and more human than hopping from one Indonesian
island to the next, as *Homo erectus* appears to have done. But Morwood sees the difference as one of degree. "We're not dealing with
glorified chimpanzees here," he says. "We're dealing with a species
that has many of the characteristics of modern people."

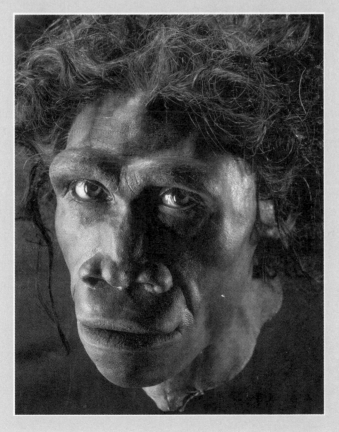

11. In paragraph 5, the author notes, "Until now the earliest evidence of boats has been the presence of modern humans in Australia between 40,000 and 60,000 years ago." From the author's use of the phrase "until now," you can conclude that

    a. the author believes the stones on Flores are new evidence of boats.

    b. *Homo erectus* is the closest human ancestor.

    c. during the ice age, it was possible to cross from Java to Flores.

    d. chimpanzees may have traveled by boat.

12. In paragraph 5, the author states, "Setting sail from Timor to Australia, over the horizon and into the unknown, may still seem qualitatively different and more human than hopping from one Indonesian island to the next, as *Homo erectus* appears to have done." What does "hopping from one Indonesian island to the next" refer to?

    a. the trip from Java to Flores

    b. the trip from the Asian mainland to Java

    c. the trip from Timor to Australia

    d. the trip from Borneo to Java

13. Why might sailing from Timor to Australia seem "qualitatively different and more human than hopping from one Indonesian island to the next"?

    a. because it is farther and "into the unknown"

    b. because it requires planning and working together

    c. because "glorified chimpanzees" could do it

    d. because the Indonesian islands are "over the horizon" from one another

14. Based on the context of the essay, the photograph after paragraph 5 is most likely of

    a. a model of *Homo erectus*

    b. an advanced chimpanzee

    c. the scientist Mike Morwood

    d. the first man to travel from Timor to Australia

15. Which of the following is most likely a reason for including the photograph?

   a. to show the resemblance of *Homo erectus* to *Homo habilis*

   b. We may have a better understanding of our ancestors if we see how much they looked like modern-day humans.

   c. The model shows that *Homo erectus* may have had the "quintessentially modern skills" that a trip by boat would require.

   d. to illustrate how *Homo erectus* looked like "glorified chimpanzees"

Reading the Whole

Now that you have read Robert Kunzig's "Erectus Afloat" in its parts and have studied the maps and answered questions about the photograph, you will be better prepared to read the whole essay. As you reread, continue to think about how the visual materials relate to one another and to the text. Think specifically about what important information the illustrations add that is left out of the text. Finally, pay particular attention to what Morwood and his colleagues found, where they found it, and how the observations they made led to inferences and then to conclusions. At the end of the essay, ask yourself whether you think they have sufficient evidence to support their conclusions. What else might you want to know to be able to draw your own conclusions? What other illustrations might help?

ROBERT KUNZIG

Erectus Afloat

What kind of brain does it take to build a boat and steer it across 15 miles of choppy seas and strong currents? Could a chimp do it? Not likely. Could human ancestors—*Homo erectus,* to be precise—have done it 800,000 years ago, which is about 750,000 years earlier than any previous evidence of watercraft? Mike Morwood thinks so. This past year the Australian archeologist from the University of New England in New South Wales reported what he considers proof that *Homo erectus* once set watercraft to breakers on the beaches of Indonesia. 1

The evidence comes from the island of Flores, several hundred miles and several deep straits east of Java, the previous southeastern limit of *Homo erectus*'s range. There, Morwood and his Indonesian and Australian colleagues have found more than a dozen stones that they say are tools—flakes and choppers for working wood or animal carcasses. Although their published drawings of the stones are inconclusive, Morwood says the stones themselves show clear evidence of the sharp edges, cracks, and microscopic striations that stone acquires only from being smacked around by a hominid (as opposed to, say, being rolled around in a river). 2

The tool layer, say the researchers, dates to 800,000 years ago. *Homo erectus* had long since reached Java by then—on foot. During 3

the ice ages, sea level was sometimes so low that Java was connected to the Asian mainland. But between Java and Flores lie three
straits too deep to have dried out during glacial periods, one of
which was more than 15 miles wide. "It's a pretty formidable water
crossing," Morwood says. "The vast majority of animals didn't
make it." But early humans did.

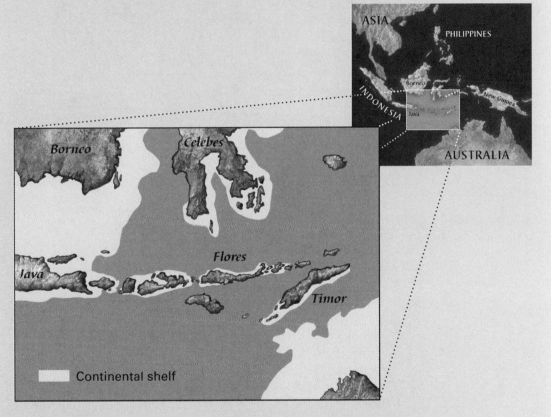

Presumably they didn't swim. Nor does Morwood think they
could have crossed the straits in any significant numbers by accident, hanging on to logs or crude rafts. "I think you need directed
watercraft," he says. "You'd have to have some means of steering,
and some means of propulsion. If you try to put a few logs together
and jump on it, you're probably going to die."

Until now the earliest evidence of boats has been the presence of
modern humans in Australia between 40,000 and 60,000 years ago.
To make such a voyage, it has been argued, requires quintessentially
modern skills—not just technical ones but the ability to plan, to

4

5

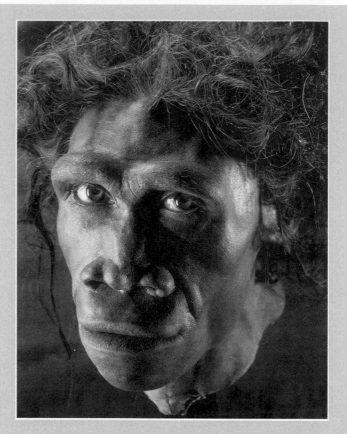

work as a group, even to talk. Setting sail from Timor to Australia, over the horizon and into the unknown, may still seem qualitatively different and more human than hopping from one Indonesian island to the next, as *Homo erectus* appears to have done. But Morwood sees the difference as one of degree. "We're not dealing with glorified chimpanzees here," he says. "We're dealing with a species that has many of the characteristics of modern people."

Integrated Skills

1. Write a paragraph that describes how the presence of stone tools on the island of Flores led researchers to believe that *Homo erectus* had traveled by boat earlier than previously thought. Be sure to trace the researchers' train of thought.

2. What does Morwood's conclusion suggest about the minds of *Homo erectus*? Why?

3. Based on the essay, how does Morwood's discovery change the understanding of when, where, and how humans developed?

4. List two other illustrations that would help you understand Morwood's discovery and its importance.

Reading Textbooks

You have just read Robert Kunzig's article from *Discovery* magazine on a potentially important discovery. Kunzig reports the findings of archeologist Mike Morwood that suggest early ancestors of human beings, *Homo erectus,* traveled by boat 750,000 years earlier than had been previously thought. Morwood's conclusion, like much of science, is formed from a very carefully considered inference which is, in turn, based on certain observations and connections that Morwood made. The following passage, taken from Chapter 27 of the biology textbook *Inquiry into Life* by Sylvia S. Mader, shows how the same kinds of reasoning have been used in the related field of biogeography. The passage discusses ways in which scientists understand the distribution of different kinds of life throughout the world. As you read it, think about the similarities between Morwood's reasoning and that of the scientists who draw conclusions about biogeography. Finally, consider what the conclusions about biogeography can tell you about Morwood's conclusions.

Vocabulary Preview

hypothesis (para. 1): tentative assumption made for the sake of argument (n.)

plausible (para. 2): appearing worthy of belief (adj.)

anatomically (para. 2): with respect to structural makeup (adv.)

Geography and Evolutionary Relationships

Biogeography is the study of the distribution of plants and animals throughout the world. Such distributions are consistent with the hypothesis that related forms evolve in one locale and then spread out into other regions. For example, there are no rabbits in South America because rabbits originated somewhere else and they had no means to reach South America. 1

Physical factors, such as the location of continents, often determine where a population can spread. For example, at one time in the history of the earth, South America, Antarctica, and Australia were all connected (fig. 27.2). Marsupials (pouched mammals) arose at 2 this time and today are found in both South America and Australia. When Australia separated and drifted away, the marsupials diversified into many different forms suited to specific environments. These observations support common descent. It is quite plausible that a particular line of descent in a particular geographical region could give rise to many forms, each adapted to a different environment. We recognize that these many forms are related because they are anatomically similar. In this example, all the animals are marsupials and none are placental mammals (animals in which development occurs in the uterus).

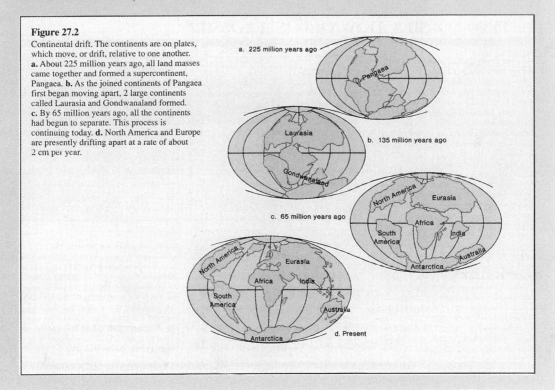

Figure 27.2
Continental drift. The continents are on plates, which move, or drift, relative to one another. **a.** About 225 million years ago, all land masses came together and formed a supercontinent, Pangaea. **b.** As the joined continents of Pangaea first began moving apart, 2 large continents called Laurasia and Gondwanaland formed. **c.** By 65 million years ago, all the continents had begun to separate. This process is continuing today. **d.** North America and Europe are presently drifting apart at a rate of about 2 cm per year.

Thinking about the Textbook Selection

1. What is biogeography, and what is its relation to evolution?

2. Why are there no rabbits in South America?

3. What is one factor that determines where human populations can spread?

4. What is continental drift, and how does the illustration help you understand that concept?

5. Explain what you see as you look at part a of the figure, then part b, part c, and finally part d.

Reviewing

Recall / Remember

1. What are some of the purposes of graphics? How can they be helpful to you as a reader?

2. Identify four common types of graphics, and explain what kinds of information they provide and how they visualize that information.

3. What is a caption, and why is it important to read the captions that accompany graphics?

4. In addition to reading a graphic's caption, what else should you read? Why?

Chapter Summary

In this chapter you have focused on how authors use visual materials, or graphics, to present important information, ideas, and concepts. You have seen how graphics summarize information, illustrate processes, and clarify concepts. Photographs enhance written text by providing visual images for readers to respond to, sometimes emotionally. Maps portray many kinds of physical details of geography and topography as well as identifying locations. Diagrams show the parts of a structure and their relation to the whole. Charts represent organizational structures and present visually the steps in a sequence or process. Graphs depict relationships among two or more items or variables. Tables classify information by presenting it in columns and rows so that it is easily accessed and understood.

Although the types of graphics discussed in this chapter are not the only types you will encounter, they are the most common and the most important. For all forms of graphics, remember to read the caption if there is one and relate it to the visual part of the graphic. Assure yourself that you understand the connection between the graphic and the written explanation in the text that the graphic explains or illustrates. You will gain additional practice in reading graphics (and in skimming and scanning) in the following chapter, which describes how to read an entire textbook chapter. You will also have an opportunity to relate different kinds of graphics to the chapter's written text.

Chapter 13

Getting Ready	413
Learning the Skills	415
Applying the Skills • Reading Textbooks	425
Reviewing	461

Reading a Textbook Chapter

Getting Ready

This chapter applies what you have learned about reading to reading chapters in your college textbooks. It will help you understand the features and elements of your textbooks so you can read them more confidently.

Chapter **Overview**

As you have already discovered, a textbook differs from other kinds of books because it is specifically designed for study. A college textbook is typically written to introduce and define terms, explain and illustrate concepts, and demonstrate how to apply them in understanding the subject the textbook discusses. Textbooks are designed to be clear so that readers understand their content. Textbook authors try to be both informative and supportive in presenting their material.

You have already read excerpts from textbooks in previous chapters. This chapter includes an entire chapter from a textbook on the subject of interpersonal communication. The selection focuses on personal relationships. We will work through the major elements of the textbook chapter so you can practice skills you have already learned. Working through this final chapter will bring together your reading skills, including understanding vocabulary, finding the main idea and supporting details, identifying patterns of organization, making observations and connections, developing inferences and drawing conclusions, understanding visual elements, and using techniques of critical reading.

Focusing Questions

What is the first thing you do when you begin a reading assignment in one of your college textbooks?

Do you survey the chapter, quickly looking over its contents?

Do you skim the headings and subheadings in the chapter?

Do you look at the visual aids it contains, especially any pictures?

Do you read the captions that accompany diagrams, charts, tables, pictures, and other visual aids?

Do you read with a pen in hand, ready to annotate and jot quick notes?

What is the last thing you do when you complete a reading assignment?

Everyday Reading

The kind of reading in everyday life most similar to textbook reading may be reading manuals that accompany products you use. You may need to read the manual for your car or the manual for operating your VCR. You may read the manual for using a computer or printer, or you may read manuals associated with compact disc and tape players, portable phones, or electrical appliances, such as microwave ovens.

Take a look at one of these manuals to see what elements of textbook organization and textbook teaching they include. Look, for example, at the table of contents to see how it lists topics. Look at the way it places material in boxes or otherwise emphasizes key bits of information. Skim the manual to check whether it includes other textbook features, such as headings and subheadings, lists, questions, and the like.

Find a manual most similar to a textbook and make an outline of it, listing the parts it has in common with a textbook.

Learning the Skills

■ Preparing to Read a Textbook

Even before you begin reading a textbook, you should acquaint yourself with it. Look through the book to see how many chapters it contains, how long the chapters are, what kinds of headings and visual materials it includes. Look to see if there is a chapter introduction, a chapter conclusion or summary, and exercises or assignments. Try to get a feel for the topics the textbook covers and the way information is presented about those topics. Are key terms in italics or boldface? Are chapter headings and subheadings written as phrases, sentences, or questions? Does the textbook include information in the margins?

You can use the techniques of skimming and scanning to answer these preliminary questions as you acquaint yourself with a textbook. We will practice skimming and scanning the textbook chapter selection included in this chapter a bit later.

Another thing you can do before reading a textbook is to check the assignment. Does the assignment require you to read the entire chapter or only part of it? How long is the assignment? Assess how much time you will need to read it thoroughly. You may decide to divide the chapter into sections and read each section in a different reading and study session. Does the assignment require you to take notes or make an outline? Does it require you to answer questions or write responses to exercises? You might wish to ask your instructor these questions or others, such as when the textbook assignment should be completed. Check with your instructor about any questions you have about the textbook assignment.

■ Textbook Elements

Most textbook chapters contain three types of elements, which you should notice when you survey a chapter:

- Preliminary elements
- Body elements
- Concluding elements

PRELIMINARY ELEMENTS

Preliminary elements are found at the beginning of the chapter. These elements often include the chapter title, chapter overview or chapter introduction, and chapter objectives. We will briefly discuss each of these introductory textbook elements.

Chapter title. The title of the chapter provides a clue to its content. You can gain a quick sense of the chapter's central concern from its title. The title of the sample chapter on pages 427–460, for example, "Developing and Maintaining Relationships," tells you what that chapter is about. As you read the sample chapter, ask yourself how its different parts explain or illustrate the topic identified in the title.

Chapter overview or chapter introduction. A chapter overview or introduction provides a quick summary of its contents. The chapter you are reading right now (as well as the other chapters in *Putting It Together*) includes such an overview summary immediately after the title. You can use a chapter overview or introduction to study by taking notes on it and by using both it and your notes for review.

Chapter outline. Some books also contain an outline of the major topics of the chapter in their order of appearance. The outline maps the overall organization of the chapter. The sample chapter "Developing and Maintaining Relationships" contains such an outline. You can use this outline when you study by reviewing the subtopics it includes.

Chapter objectives. Some textbooks also contain a list of goals for reading the chapter. These goals identify what you should learn upon reading and studying the chapter. Chapter objectives can be framed as a list, a series of questions, or a paragraph. The chapter objectives may be indicated by different titles, such as "Looking Ahead" or "Chapter Goals." The key goals of each chapter in *Putting It Together* are included in the Chapter Overview.

BODY ELEMENTS

Body elements are found throughout a textbook chapter, following the preliminary elements. The most important body element of a textbook is the text itself. Other body elements include textbook features such as lists, visual materials, exercises, and boxes. These and other body elements such as headings and subheadings are used to divide parts of the chapter. The body elements may also shift the focus from one part of a chapter's topic to another.

Body elements present the information and the ideas of the chapter and provide examples or illustrations. Because body elements often highlight key issues and concepts and often summarize them, they make good study aids. You can use body elements for review when you study. In *Putting It Together,* the body elements include the text describing the skills and strategies of college reading, examples of readings, exercises, boxes, lists, and sometimes visual materials, or graphics.

Lists. Lists can appear in a textbook chapter in different ways. Sometimes a list is simply presented as a string of items in a sentence, as in the last sentence of the previous paragraph. Sometimes a list of items is set off from the text to make those items easy to see. (Look back at the bulleted list of items on p. 415). Items in a list presented vertically (down the page) tend to be highlighted.

Lists in textbooks can be a simple collection of items to learn. Some lists are organized as sequenced steps or stages. For example, a sequence of steps for reading comprehension (discussed in Chapters 8 and 9) could be listed like this:

STEPS TO READING COMPREHENSION

1. Make observations about the details of a reading passage.
2. Connect the details, looking for relationships among them.
3. Make inferences on the basis of the related details you find.
4. Draw conclusions based on your observations, connections, and inferences.

This list can be shortened and the numbers eliminated. In fact, many textbooks provide lists with brief contents. The list of steps will not always be numbered. Here is an example of a shorter list, one without numbers for each item.

STEPS TO READING COMPREHENSION

- Make observations.
- Establish connections.
- Make inferences.
- Draw conclusions.

Boxes. Boxes include text or graphics separated from the main body of the chapter's text. The material included in a box is self-contained. That is, you should read it as a separate section. However, it is important that you relate the information presented in the box to the information included in the main body of text.

Boxed material is often set off in a different typeface or in a different background color from the rest of the chapter. Boxes contain information that clarifies key issues and ideas in the chapter. This information may include summaries of key ideas, case studies, interviews, applications, or other things. In this book, you will find boxes that list steps or guidelines for doing certain tasks, such as the box "Guidelines for Critical Reading" on page 313.

Exercises. One textbook element sometimes appears as a body element and sometimes as a concluding element: exercises. The exercises in a textbook chapter provide an important way for you to check your understanding of the chapter's content.

Exercises can take a number of different forms:

- multiple choice, fill-in-the-blank, matching, or true/false questions
- discussion questions in which you are required to respond to a question by discussing your answer with your classmates
- writing assignments that ask you to respond to a question by creating a written response

You should do any exercises your instructor assigns. When you do not understand a particular exercise item, you should ask for clarification from the instructor. If that is not possible, you can check with a classmate.

It is a good idea to do exercises even when they are not assigned. Working through the exercises in a textbook chapter provides you with a sense of how well you understand the chapter material. Doing the chapter exercises also reinforces what you learn from reading, studying, and taking notes on the chapter.

CONCLUDING ELEMENTS

At the end of a college textbook chapter, you might find a summary of the chapter, a list of questions for discussion, or a list of references for further reading. These **concluding elements** can help you review the chapter for study. They can also help you preview the chapter when you are preparing to read it for the first time. Previewing a chapter's concluding elements gives you another way to gain a sense of the chapter's goals and key ideas.

Exercise 13-1

Answer the following questions about your college textbooks this semester. Use a different textbook for each question.

1. Select one of your college textbooks and look through the chapter titles. Write out the titles of five chapters, and next to each chapter title, briefly identify the topic of the chapter and what kinds of issues you expect the chapter to cover.

    a. CHAPTER TITLE: _____

    TOPIC: _____

    ISSUES IN THE CHAPTER: _____

    _____

    b. CHAPTER TITLE: _____

    TOPIC: _____

    ISSUES IN THE CHAPTER: _____

    _____

    c. CHAPTER TITLE: _____

    TOPIC: _____

    ISSUES IN THE CHAPTER: _____

    _____

    d. CHAPTER TITLE: _____

    TOPIC: _____

    ISSUES IN THE CHAPTER: _____

    _____

    e. CHAPTER TITLE: _____

    TOPIC: _____

    ISSUES IN THE CHAPTER: _____

    _____

2. Select one of your textbooks that includes a chapter overview or chapter introduction. Make a list of the key points the chapter overview or introduction includes.

    _____

    _____

    _____

    _____

3. For one chapter of a textbook that does not include chapter goals or focusing questions, write three of your own goals or questions for the chapter. Try to select a chapter that you have not yet read.

   a. _____

   b. _____

   c. _____

4. Find three lists in three different textbooks. Write the titles of the lists on the lines below, and indicate the titles of the chapters where you found them.

   a. LIST TITLE: _____

      CHAPTER TITLE: _____

   b. LIST TITLE: _____

      CHAPTER TITLE: _____

   c. LIST TITLE: _____

      CHAPTER TITLE: _____

5. Find three boxes in three different textbooks. Write the titles of the boxes on the lines below, and explain how the boxed material relates to the surrounding text. Does it illustrate or explain a concept? Does it provide a particular example?

   a. BOX TITLE: _____

      HOW IT RELATES: _____

      _____

      _____

   b. BOX TITLE: _____

      HOW IT RELATES: _____

      _____

   c. BOX TITLE: _____

      HOW IT RELATES: _____

      _____

■ Reading/Writing Connection

When you study a textbook chapter, it is necessary that you understand how the chapter connects with the instructor's lectures and with class-work for the course. If you know, for example, that an instructor arranges lectures according to the organization of the textbook chapters, you can use the textbook chapters and your lecture notes to reinforce one another.

You might decide to read a textbook chapter *before* the instructor lectures on that chapter's topic. If you take notes on the chapter, you could then have an outline of the professor's lecture as you listen to it. You could add lecture notes to your reading notes.

You could also read or reread a textbook chapter *after* you take notes in class on the lecture on that chapter's topic. In that case reading and taking notes on the chapter would help you review the key points the instructor presented in the class lecture.

You will find that reading a chapter before a lecture helps you to listen better in class. It also enables you to ask good questions and to understand the instructor's responses because you already have a base of knowledge about the topic. You will also discover that rereading a chapter after a lecture can clarify your understanding of what was said in class.

In both cases, it is important to write down the main ideas and some examples of supporting details. You can also write out key questions to help you focus on the essentials.

■ Skimming the Sample Chapter

In skimming the sample chapter on relationships (beginning on p. 427) you may notice that the authors use three types of preliminary elements: (1) a numbered list of objectives; (2) an imaginary situation about two roommates; and (3) a brief, untitled opening paragraph.

The objectives are designed to alert you to what you should learn in your reading and study of the chapter. The imaginary situation is meant to engage your interest in the chapter's ideas by applying them to an everyday situation related to your experience. The introductory paragraph connects the sample chapter with the larger topic of the book: competent communication.

Your skimming of the chapter should have alerted you to the following body elements:

- Major headings, such as "Relational Knowledge" and "Expectations"
- Subheadings, such as "Interpersonal Attraction" and "Physical Proximity"
- Exercises, such as "Determining Your Own List of Costs and Rewards"
- Marginal annotations that define terms and explain figures
- Figures that visually illustrate particular concepts

Recognizing these chapter elements is necessary for comprehending the content of the chapter. You can use the subheadings under each major heading as a way to review the key issues for each of the major headings. For example, the second major heading of the chapter is "Expectations." The three subheadings under this head are "Expectations about Relationships," "Expectations about Relational Patterns," and "Violated Expectations." In reading and reviewing the chapter you will see that each of these three subtopics includes an idea about how expectations play different roles in interpersonal relationships.

In reading the chapter you should either write answers to the exercises or read through the exercises and think about how you would answer the questions they contain. Doing the exercises enables you to become more actively engaged in reading and studying the chapter. Doing the exercises carefully also increases your chances of learning the chapter's contents and remembering it when tested.

The marginal annotations and the figures both provide additional study aids to help you master the contents of the chapter. Read the annotations carefully to ensure that you understand the definitions they include. Study the figures attentively to be sure you understand what they portray. If you do not understand a definition or a figure, ask your instructor for clarification. You can also review the annotations and figures to review the highlights of the chapter's content.

The end of the chapter contains two concluding elements:

1. a review summary of the chapter's central ideas
2. a set of five discussion questions based on the case of the roommates Bruce and Saleh that was introduced at the beginning of the chapter

The review summary identifies once more the key concepts of the chapter. The discussion questions invite you to apply what you have learned.

■ Finding the Main Idea and Comprehending the Chapter

In reading a textbook chapter you will almost always find more than one main idea. Try to find the main idea of each of the chapter's major sections. Consider the main idea individually for the sections on relational knowledge (p. 428), relational development (p. 428), expectations (p. 432), costs and rewards (p. 435), reducing uncertainty (p. 436), stages of a relationship (p. 439), types of relationships (p. 452), and competent relationships (p. 457). For the parts that contain subsections, consider the main ideas individually of each of the subsections. In deciding on the main idea of the section "Stages of a Relationship," you should also find the main idea for the following subsections: the initial stage, the exploratory stage, the intensification stage, the stable stage, the decline stage, relational repair, the termination stage, and reconciliation.

In the section on the intensification stage (p. 441), the main idea is that intensification of a relationship moves it to a new level, one that begins to involve greater intimacy than before. During the intensification stage, partners' expectations about each other change. They may begin to confide in one another and to spend less time simply acquiring information about each other than sharing experiences and enjoying each other's company.

In finding the main idea of the larger section of which "The Intensification Stage" is a part, it is important to relate the main idea of the individual subsections to one another. For example, what we just said about the main idea of the subsection "The Intensification Stage" should be linked with the main idea of the other subsections on the "Stages of a Relationship." Especially important for linking to the main idea of "The Intensification Stage" are the subsections that come immediately before and after it: "The Exploratory Stage" and "The Stable Stage."

This kind of careful focusing on main ideas in the chapter's parts is crucial to comprehending the chapter as a whole. In discovering the main idea of each part you will also be applying what you learned in Chapters 8 and 9—about making observations and connections and developing inferences and conclusions.

The observations you make about the structure of the chapter are crucial to your comprehension of it. Your observations about the headings and subheadings, along with the content within them, help you identify the authors' main ideas. The connections you make among your observations about the chapter's details, examples, and structure prepare you to infer what the authors want you to learn about personal relationships. You infer from their end-of-chapter summary, for example, what the main ideas of the chapter are. From reading that summary after studying the chapter, you may conclude that you should test your understanding of the chapter's details by referring to each of the main ideas listed in the summary.

Among the connected observations you make and the conclusions you draw from your inferences are those made from the visuals included in the chapter. In looking at the cartoon about Cathy on page 442, for example, you relate what you infer from reading it to the text's discussion of love relationships. In looking at the table of relational stages, you infer that personal relationships are complex and that they can be developed, diminished, extended, and terminated in different ways at different times in the relationship's development. Your observations about each visual figure lead you to make inferences about it and to relate it to your understanding of the chapter as a whole.

Applying the Skills

Reading Textbooks

Unlike the other chapters in *Putting It Together,* the textbook reading in Chapter 13 is an entire chapter from a textbook. Taken from the book *Competent Communication* by Dan O'Hair, Gustav W. Friedrich, John M. Wiemann, and Mary Wiemann, the chapter discusses a subject many of us take for granted, developing and maintaining relationships. As you read the textbook selection, take note of all the different parts of the chapter and be aware of how the information is organized. What features of the book present material, and what other features help you understand that material and put it into context? Annotate the chapter as you read and pay attention to how your own ideas grow as you go through the chapter—that is, pay attention to your own *learning* and how the chapter helps you with that. Approach the chapter as if you were in a communications course. Read it as if you were going to be tested on the material, and, most important, read it to learn the material. It may turn out to be useful to you both in school and in your everyday life outside of school.

Vocabulary Preview

competence (p. 428): an ability to do something (n.)

obsession (p. 429): an excessive preoccupation (n.)

proximity (p. 429): nearness (n.)

alleviating (p. 430): relieving, lessening (v.)

chronic (p. 430): habitual; prolonged; continuing for a long time (adj.)

formulate (p. 430): develop and express (v.)

compatible (p. 431): agreeable; existing together harmoniously (adj.)

negotiation (p. 431): the process of arranging for something through discussion and compromise (n.)

idealistic (p. 432): placing standards of perfection or excellence before practical considerations (adj.)

straitlaced (p. 432): excessively strict, uptight (adj.)

extrinsic (p. 436): external; coming from outside (adj.)

intrinsic (p. 436): internal; coming from inside (adj.)

proactive (p. 437): acting in anticipation of future problems (adj.)

exploratory (p. 439): investigative, analytical; relating to the act of studying (adj.)

intensification (p. 439): the process of becoming stronger or more deeply felt (n.)

demeanor (p. 439): look or countenance (n.)

accumulated (p. 441): gathered, piled up (v.)

volatile (p. 441): easily excited; quickly changeable (adj.)

reciprocal (p. 442): mutual; given to or felt by each toward one another (adj.)

erosion (p. 446): wearing down; gradually diminishing (n.)

platonic (p. 448): spiritual, without sexual desire (adj.)

terminating (p. 450): ending (v.)

vitality (p. 450): energy, liveliness (n.)

stagnant (p. 450): without motion or change (adj.)

reconciliation (p. 452): restoration to harmony (n.)

rejuvenate (p. 452): give new vigor to; reenergize (v.)

Assesing textbook
outline

427 -   458

Developing and Maintaining Relationships

●BJECTIVES

After reading this chapter, you should be able to:

1. Identify the goals and motivations people have in developing relationships.

2. Describe how expectations affect communication in interpersonal relationships.

3. Explain how relational knowledge affects interpersonal communication.

4. Explain the costs and rewards of relationships.

5. List three strategies that people use to reduce uncertainty about their relational partners.

6. Discuss the various stages of relational development.

7. Describe six characteristics of friendship.

8. Identify at least three ways to improve family relationships.

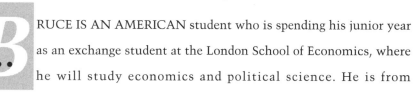

RUCE IS AN AMERICAN student who is spending his junior year as an exchange student at the London School of Economics, where he will study economics and political science. He is from Minnesota, and he recently completed 2 years as an economics major at the University of Minnesota. Bruce's interests are his Macintosh computer and sports, especially soccer. His roommate for the year is Saleh, who is also a new exchange student. Saleh's home is in Riyadh, Saudi Arabia's royal capital and largest city, located in the east central part of the Arabian peninsula. Saleh will also study economics and political science. His outside interests include both sports and the arts, especially classical music and theater. As you read through this chapter, consider how its content might apply to the situation of Bruce and Saleh.

INTERPERSONAL COMMUNICATION

The process of two or three people exchanging messages in order to share meaning, create understanding, and develop relationships.

As you may recall from the model of communicative competence, relationships play a central role in determining the type of communication that is most effective and appropriate. In turn, competent **interpersonal communication** permits more meaningful relationships to develop. Each of you is involved in a number of relationships of different levels of importance. There is no guaranteed plan for a perfect relationship. However, by understanding how relationships form and disengage and what components make up a relationship, you may better understand your own relationships.

◆ Relational Knowledge

RELATIONAL SCHEMAS

Information used to interpret messages received in a relationship.

Relational knowledge is the information you gain through your experiences in relationships. This knowledge greatly influences your behavior, communication style, perceptions, and self-concept. As your relationships grow and develop, you begin to form theories about how others will act, feel, and think in response to your actions. As you recall from Chapter 2, these hypotheses are referred to as *schemas*, and they guide your processing of information. **Relational schemas** are the bits and pieces of information that you use to interpret the messages you receive in a relationship.[1] Jay has never had a serious girlfriend and considers himself unlucky in love. Whenever Jay has attempted a serious relationship, he has been told that he is immature, insensitive, and incapable of maintaining an adult relationship. Jay and Lesley have gone out a few times, but Jay will not pursue a serious relationship with Lesley because he fears rejection. Jay's previous experiences have formed a schema that stops him from initiating any serious relationship.

RELATIONAL HISTORY

The sum of the "objective" events in a relationship and the shared experiences of relational partners; also, the set of thoughts, perceptions, and impressions one has formed about one's previous relational partners.

Relational history also plays an important role in relational knowledge. **Relational history** is the set of thoughts, perceptions, and impressions you have formed about current or previous relational partners. If you hold positive views about a former partner and later run into that person again, you will react differently than if your history were more negative. For example, Isabella has always focused on what she wants in life. She has worked in the county hospital since her volunteering days during high school and has become very knowledgeable in her field. Louise, the head nurse in pediatrics, first met Isabella as a candy striper and knows that Isabella recently obtained an LVN (licensed vocational nurse) degree. Louise's relational history of Isabella helped Louise nominate Isabella for the RN (registered nurse) college scholarship. As this example shows, remembering things about a relational partner contributes to your overall impression, adding to your relational schema about that person.

◆ Goals and Motivations for Relationship Development

Why do you enter into relationships with certain individuals and not with others? The goals and motivations behind the initiation and development of relationships vary. Expectations play a big role in why you enter into relationships, why you have relationships with certain people, and why some relationships continue to develop while others do not. However, there are yet other influences that lead you to form relationships.

Interpersonal Attraction

What attracts you to certain individuals? Their looks? Their personality? Their sense of humor? Why is it that two people who are very similar may not be attractive to each other? It is not always easy to explain why some people are attracted to others. Two people might be attracted to the same individual for completely different reasons. For instance, Jeremy and Connie both met Shellee at a community Fourth of July picnic. Both were attracted to her because of a "special quality" they saw in her. To Jeremy, Shellee was special because she had lived in Colón, Panama, where he had grown up. In contrast, the special quality that Connie admired was Shellee's satirical sense of humor.

Physical attractiveness is a special kind of interpersonal attraction. Western society places great emphasis on having a pleasant physical appearance. Of course, looks aren't everything, but they do play an important role in attracting others, especially in the early stages of a relationship. In fact, keeping up your physical appearance by eating healthful foods, working out, and getting adequate sleep has become an obsession in the 1990s. What is more, television and fashion magazines keep you up to date on current styles so that your clothing can always be "in." Plastic surgery and cosmetic dental work, once options chosen mainly by the wealthy, are now widely used to achieve the look people want.

Physical Proximity

Long-distance relationships are difficult to maintain simply because of lack of proximity. Although some would argue that "absence makes the heart grow fonder," it can also be said, "out of sight, out of mind." Julie and Moya had a relationship that seemed very successful. They were good friends and had many similar interests. When Moya graduated and moved away, however, the relationship quickly diminished. At first, the two would talk almost every day, but after only a few weeks they became involved in their own activities and their talks grew less frequent. Eventually, they spoke every once in a while but not on a regular basis. As so often happens, they made new friends and entered into new relationships.

Julie and Moya's story is possible in all types of relationships, including friendships, work relationships, and romantic relationships. The simple fact is that people who have frequent, regular contact are more likely to develop and maintain a relationship than are individuals who see one another less regularly. As proof, think for a moment about your current relationships. How many of these formed because of frequent contact? No doubt, you will find that you formed most of your relationships with roommates, classmates, teammates, co-workers, and neighbors because of frequent interaction.

Alleviating Loneliness

What Stimulates You about Relationships?

How do you feel when someone you don't know well takes a special interest in you? Is intellectual, emotional, or physical stimulation most important to you? How does your need for stimulation change as your relationships develop and grow?

Humans feel a natural need for companionship. Between 10 and 20 percent of the population is estimated to experience chronic loneliness, which can result in severe psychological problems.[2] Such problems as anxiety, stress, depression, alcoholism, drug abuse, and poor health have all been tied to loneliness. Most people, however, are lonely only from time to time, and that is when they seek out relationships with other people. A person who feels lonely tends to see a relationship as a logical answer to the problem. A relationship can act as a security blanket, helping to ward off the chill of loneliness. Do you know people who form friendships for no apparent reason other than to escape loneliness?

Stimulation

People have an innate need for stimulation, as is readily evident in the popularity of television and movies. The interaction between two people, however, provides a unique kind of stimulation because it occurs on a personal level. This stimulation is intellectual as well as emotional and physical.

At an *intellectual level*, stimulation has many guises. For example, it stems from conversations about topics of shared interest, especially current events, movies, books, and societal issues. Such conversations help people explore issues and formulate their opinions about them. On a different level, because people have *emotions*, they naturally feel a need for emotional stimulation. This need is best filled by a person who can mutually benefit from emotional gratification. The bond created between two people in a relationship, then, provides an opportunity for them to express their emotions.

Physical stimulation is yet another form. Humans love to touch and be touched. You probably know people who touch while they talk or kiss and hug "hello" and "goodbye" after every encounter. Physical stimulation can

Relational partners can provide intellectual, emotional, and physical stimulation for each other.

be a pleasurable, healthy, and natural part of relationships—as long as it does not interfere with other relational goals.

Achieving Goals

Some people enter into relationships to achieve certain goals. For example, if you have dreamed all your life about doing public service work overseas, you might seek relationships with influential people in that field. Similarly, if you are looking to advance your career, you might try to develop relationships with your superiors and co-workers. Often, your initial motivation for developing a relationship with a particular individual is to see what that person can do for you or how he or she can help you. Of course, the other person will have goals that may or may not be compatible with your own. Therefore, the negotiation of mutual or compatible goals is an important process in relationships.

Goals and Motivations in Intercultural Relationships

Are your relationships with people from other cultures and co-cultures different from your intracultural relationships? Consider two of your important relationships—both business or both social—for comparison, one with a partner from a culture other than yours and one with a partner from your own culture. For each relationship, answer the following questions; then compare your answers for the two relationships.

1. What were your goals and motivations in developing the relationship?
2. What did you believe to be the goals and motivations of your partner?
3. Did your goals and motivations seem compatible with your partner's? What factors led you to choose this partner?
4. Describe your relationship now. Has it developed as you expected? Did you encounter any obstacles? If so, how did you and your partner respond? Describe your progress toward achieving your goals. Describe how your goals and motivations have changed, if at all, as the relationship has developed.

From your answers to these questions, you can make some observations about the role of cultural differences in your relationships. Are cultural differences an important factor in relational development? Research shows that people do not view the relationship process any differently simply because a person is from another culture.* Rather, the main issue is how *similar* the other person seems to you. Intercultural relationships are as strongly grounded in perceived similarity as are intracultural relationships.

*W. B. Gudykunst (1985), An exploratory comparison of close intracultural and intercultural friendships, *Communication Quarterly*, 33, 270–283.

◆ Expectations

Recall from Chapter 1 that the model of communicative competence gives expectations a central position in forming the proper messages. How much do your expectations affect your relationships? Whenever people enter into a relationship, they form ideas as to what they think will or should happen. As the relationship develops, these ideas will change and some new ideas may form. Expectations have a way of influencing how people act and feel toward others. You may form expectations not only about the individual with whom you have a relationship but also about the relationship itself.

Expectations about Relationships

Many people have idealistic notions about relationships. "Once I have this friend," or "once I get married, I'll have it made." It is not unusual to develop expectations about relationships without having particular individuals in mind. Even before relationships begin, you form expectations about future partners. Friends, families, novels, and the media offer many models for you to choose from. Some people may prefer relationships that are intense but last only a short period of time, whereas others prefer intellectual, long-lasting relationships. Every person has strong individual expectations based on relational knowledge and personal tastes and preferences.

Expectations about Relational Partners

When you meet people for the first time, it does not take long for your initial impression to be set in stone, and only after a great deal of interaction will your initial opinion change. When people meet for the first time, they form expectations about each other, as David and Anthony did.

DAVID   When I first met Anthony, I thought he seemed a little conservative and straitlaced. He acted as if going out and having a good time were against the law. He seemed to think that I was wild and out of control. Little did I know that we would become best friends just a short time later.

ANTHONY   I thought David was a real jerk the first time I met him. He seemed so full of himself and acted as if his only goal in life was to go out and get drunk every night. I never would have believed it if someone had told me that we would become friends.

Unrealistic expectations can create problems in a relationship. Unrealistic expectations may arise because of what society says is important in a relationship. Society can give the impression that in a "good" relationship conflict will not arise.

How realistic is this couple?

JOANNIE   Being in love means we'll never fight.

STEPHEN   I know, it's great. You know I'll never make you mad.

What Are Your Expectations for Relationships?

Do you expect romantic relationships to be long and meaningful? Do you tolerate the idea of short, relatively meaningless relationships? Have you started a relationship knowing that it would probably end in hurt feelings? How would you characterize the ideal relationship? How do your expectations influence your communication? Can you explain how relational expectations affect the communicative competence model?

Unrealistic expectations produce a great deal of unnecessary stress because such expectations are hardly ever met. As a result, people sometimes dismiss relationships that might have ultimately been beneficial.

Realistic expectations can help prevent the development of potentially unsuccessful relationships. Yasar has a strong Muslim background and considers religion an important part of his life. Rachel is Jewish and has had very little exposure to the Muslim religion. The two are considering dating, but Yasar thinks that their religious differences are too great to overcome. He feels that Rachel will never be able to meet his expectations concerning religion. Yasar's expectations have prevented him from entering into a relationship that would probably not succeed.

Violated Expectations

The following story shows what can happen when one person in a relationship does not adhere to the expectations of the other. Roberto and Carol had been dating for two months, seeing each other every Friday and Saturday night and on Wednesday afternoons. Although they had occasionally discussed dating each other exclusively, they had not made a formal agreement to that effect. Roberto went out of town for several days and told Carol that he did not expect to return until after the weekend. But Roberto finished his trip early and arrived back in town on Friday night. On his way home, he decided to go by Carol's house to ask her out for Saturday night. He was stunned to learn that Carol was entertaining another man at her house. Roberto had formed certain expectations about his relationship with Carol, and now those expectations had, in essence, been violated. He was hurt and sad that Carol would "cheat on him."

Was Carol wrong to violate Roberto's expectations? What do you do if things do not turn out as you had hoped they would? Why are some people willing to ignore some expectancy violations, whereas others deal with unmet expectations severely? The difference probably has to do with the kind of relationship and the individuals involved. The more important a relationship or individual is to you, the more you will allow violations. You may think that maintaining a relationship with an individual is more

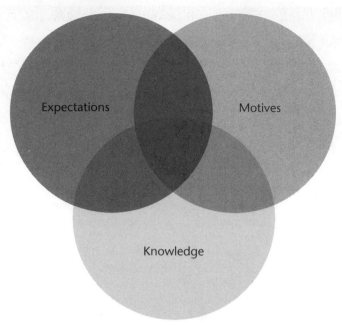

FIGURE 7.1
Knowledge, motives, and expectations affect one another as a relationship develops.

important than having your expectations met, or perhaps you may alter your expectations. Many people enter into relationships expecting a fairy-tale ending, but they soon realize that life seldom follows that kind of story line. To continue a relationship, then, you generally have to revise your expectations. Or, you may discover that the relationship or person is less important than your expectations.

Knowledge, Motives, and Expectations

When you consider knowledge, motives, and expectations together, it becomes clearer how relationships begin, develop, grow, and maybe even deteriorate (see Figure 7.1). You initiate a relationship because of your goals and motives (loneliness, stimulation, etc.), and then you form expectations about the person and the relationship based on your level of relational knowledge. This knowledge changes as you interact with your partner and your inter-actions modify your expectations, which in turn affect your motives for being in the relationship. Relationships are highly dynamic, requiring a continuous assessment of these three elements. As you study the process of relationship development, you will gain a better understanding of the dynamic and evolving nature of these elements.

How Do You Handle Expectations?

When was the last time someone violated your relational expectations? Were you too optimistic in your predictions? Too pessimistic? How do you avoid making expectations that are too high or too low?

*D*etermining Your Own List of Costs and Rewards

Consider the following list of traits and behaviors and decide which are most important to you as relational rewards and costs. Write "R1" in the blank for items that you consider primary (very important) rewards, "R2" for those you view as secondary rewards (nice to have), and "R3" for rewards that are relatively unimportant to you. Write "C1" before items that you consider primary (very important) costs, "C2" before those you view as secondary costs, and "C3" before costs that are relatively unimportant to you.

_____ Laughs at my jokes

_____ Is affectionate

_____ Is physically attractive

_____ Fits in with my friends

_____ Fits in with my family

_____ Tells inappropriate jokes

_____ Refuses to share emotions

_____ Ignores my feelings

_____ Is career oriented

_____ Wears clothes I dislike

_____ Has views about religion different from mine

_____ Has views about children similar to mine

_____ Has an exciting personality

Do you notice a pattern? Are traits or behaviors in certain areas (e.g., appearance, emotional expressiveness) particularly important to you?

◆ Costs and Rewards

Every relationship produces advantages and disadvantages for the relational partners. In a widely cited book, *Social Penetration Theory*, Altman and Taylor suggest that relationships begin, develop, grow, and deteriorate based on the rewards and costs that come from the interaction of the two relational partners.[3] *Rewards* are those relational elements that you feel good about, whereas *costs* are those that annoy you. For example, negative expectancy violations are costs, and warm companionship is a reward. When people believe the rewards outweigh the costs, they will most likely find the relationship beneficial and will work to make sure it continues. A person

EXTRINSIC REWARDS

Benefits gained from association with another person, including new opportunities and contacts.

INSTRUMENTAL REWARDS

Rewards that relational partners give to each other, including material benefits.

INTRINSIC REWARDS

Benefits that result from an exchange of intimacy.

who thinks that the costs are greater than the rewards will most likely not attempt to develop that particular relationship.

Three categories of rewards are available to relational partners. **Extrinsic rewards** are gained purely from association with another person. These types of rewards range from new opportunities, to "contacts" that may later be useful, to a perceived higher social status. A struggling actor trying to become a star may become involved with a director in show business who can help his career. **Instrumental rewards** are those that relational partners give to one another—for example, a basic exchange of goods for services. Two people may decide to live together because one can provide appliances and furniture and the other can provide a steady income to pay the rent. **Intrinsic rewards** result from an exchange of intimacy.[4] People looking for these types of rewards are interested in each other for personal reasons. For example, two people who are working out at the local gym may be physically attracted to each other. They may meet later for drinks and eventually develop an intimate relationship.

◆ Strategies for Reducing Uncertainty

According to the uncertainty reduction theory developed by Berger and Calabrese, when two people meet, their main focus is on decreasing the uncertainty that lies between them.[5] Early in a relationship, uncertainty acts as a double-edged sword, creating both excitement and frustration. In a new romantic relationship, for example, the excitement comes from the mystery, which pumps your heart a little harder, stirs the butterflies in your stomach, and moistens your palms. The frustrations stem from expectancy violations, hurt feelings, and insecurity. In any type of relationship, three factors explain your motivation for reducing uncertainty. First, if you believe that developing a relationship with a particular person will benefit you in some way, you will be more motivated to secure a level of certainty with that person. Second, if you believe that you will have frequent contact with that person in the future, you will want to reduce any uncertainty you may have. Finally, if the person acts in a manner that is unexpected or not considered "normal," you will want to reduce uncertainty to help you better understand his or her behavior.

The best way to reduce uncertainty is to obtain information about a person that is unique to that individual. In this way, you will know that person at a more intimate level. Uncertainty reduction allows you to predict your relational partners with more accuracy, which in turn makes you feel more comfortable in developing your relationships even further. You will never know everything about your partner. But the more you understand, the more likely you will be able to have a fulfilling relationship with that person.

How do you reduce this uncertainty? As with many things in your life, when you are uncertain you seek information. Once you have sufficient information about your partner, you will be able to make educated predictions about that person. Predictions help you determine what the partner will say and how he or she will react or feel in particular situations. From the beginning stages of a relationship, partners make predictions about one another and the relationship. As the partners get to know each other—as there is less uncertainty between the two—their predictions will more often be correct. Information-seeking behaviors can take three forms: monitoring, proactive, and indirect.

Monitoring Strategies

When Rob wants to learn more about Deanne, he takes advantage of an opportunity to observe her as she talks with her friends in the hallway before class. He learns that she laughs frequently, that she likes to touch her friends on the shoulder when she is talking to them, and that her friends like her a lot. This type of information seeking, monitoring, is useful to Rob because it allows him to observe Deanne in her everyday settings and to obtain knowledge about her as a potential relational partner. Of course, watching Deanne talking to friends gives Rob only a small picture of what she is really like, so he may want to observe her in different settings. If he knows that she attends the public relations club, for example, he may go to one of their meetings to see Deanne in action again. Monitoring strategies allow you to observe people as they communicate with others. Do they seem like people you would want to know better? Is their behavior like that of people you enjoy being with?

Sometimes just observing others as they go about their business does not give you all the information you need. You may want to see people in situations that interest you. Rob, for instance, may want to know how Deanne would act around his friends, so he asks her out and they go to a party where his friends will be. In this way, he can monitor her behavior in a situation that is important to him.

Proactive Strategies

Proactive strategies let you obtain information about a person more directly. Rob is acquainted with one of Deanne's friends, Eduardo, and calls him up to ask some questions about Deanne. Rob finds out that Deanne is not dating anyone exclusively right now, that she loves Mexican food, and that she goes to aerobics classes on Monday and Wednesday afternoons. Of course, Rob is aware that Eduardo might tell Deanne that he called and asked about her, but Rob thinks it is worth the risk. Besides, he reasons, it wouldn't hurt for Deanne to learn of his interest in her from a third party.

A more forthright method is direct questioning of the person you are interested in. Sometimes referred to as *interactive strategy*, this technique increases your chances of learning what you really want to know about a person and shows the person you are interested. Both purposes increase your opportunities to reduce uncertainty.

ROB   [Talking with Deanne in the student union] Are you going to stay in Seattle after you graduate?

DEANNE   [Thinking, "Hmm, he must really be interested in me"] I really haven't decided yet. The job market looks pretty bleak. What about you?

ROB   [Thinking, "Good, she wants to know about me too"] Well, I'm hoping my uncle can use me at his firm. Have you thought about graduate school?

DEANNE   Yeah, but I'll have to retake the GRE to get into grad school here.

Obviously, direct questioning is helpful in reducing uncertainty, but it also entails risks. If you ask questions that are forward or inappropriate, you may do more harm than good.

ROB   Do you plan to have kids after you marry?

DEANNE   [Thinking, "Hey, slow down, Speedy"] I don't know. Hey, isn't that Richard over there? I need to talk to him. See you later.

An even riskier proactive strategy is self-disclosure. As you recall from Chapter 3, self-disclosure is revealing personal information that would otherwise remain hidden from others. How does self-disclosure function as information seeking? Quite often, recipients of self-disclosure counter with personal information of their own, either out of a sense of obligation or because they see this as an opportunity to exchange information. The risk comes when self-disclosure is not reciprocated. If you self-disclose and the other person elects not to reciprocate, that individual has an information advantage over you. On the other hand, self-disclosure is an excellent way for two people to reduce uncertainty, for it is one of the most direct means of exchanging information.

ROB   I've always felt uncomfortable about long-term relationships.

DEANNE   Really? Me, too. Although I'm willing to give the right person a chance to change my mind.

Indirect Strategies

When monitoring strategies cannot provide specific information and proactive strategies are too direct or risky, a third alternative is available: indirect strategies. These techniques can help you obtain information from a relational partner without directly asking for it. They are used when issues are too sensitive to bring into the open or when the relationship may not be ready for a full-blown discussion of some topics.

Secret tests is an indirect strategy used in learning about your partner that involves searching for information in a roundabout manner. This approach is especially useful when you are trying to determine what a partner thinks about the relationship. Examples are *jealousy* tests (making a partner jealous to see his or her reaction), *self-putdowns* (making self-deprecating remarks in the hope that your partner will correct you), and *forced choice* (giving the partner an ultimatum to decide between you and someone else).[6] Yvonne and Igor have been dating for about 3 months and seem to be developing a good relationship. They have not talked yet about the relationship or their feelings for each other. Yvonne is beginning to wonder whether Igor has serious plans for their relationship or if he is just having fun but not taking the relationship as seriously as she is. When they go to a party one night, Yvonne spends a great deal of time talking to Jack. She stands close to him and touches him several times as she speaks to him. While talking with Jack, Yvonne is constantly observing Igor to see his reaction to her behavior. This is an example of a jealousy test; it serves to decrease the uncertainty the partners might have about one another. Once uncertainty is reduced, they can make better predictions as to what the other will do, say, think, and feel.

◆ Stages of a Relationship

How do relationships develop? Although each relationship is unique, most relationships go through certain stages. These stages are graphically presented in the model of relational development, Figure 7.2 [page 440]. Expectations, motives, and relational knowledge constitute one part of the model. As you know, these elements affect the relational partners' perceptions of each other and the relationship. Changes in any of these elements can significantly affect what happens to a relationship. Rewards and costs also play a role in the process. If rewards exceed costs, you are more likely to proceed in a relationship; if costs overwhelm rewards, relational decline can result. Uncertainty reduction is a key feature of this model because gaining information about a relational partner will affect expectations, motives, and knowledge as well as costs and rewards.

Examine Figure 7.2 carefully. As you will see, there are six possible stages of relational development. It is important to note that not all relationships experience each of these stages, particularly the last two, decline and exit. Assume that all relationships start with an initial stage. Many will proceed to an exploratory phase; some of these relationships will go on to intensification, and some of those will become stable. If at any point in the process costs exceed rewards, relational decline may result. If relational partners are willing to work at the relationship, repair strategies may be attempted, moving the relationship back to one of its previous stages. If relational decline has reached a "point of no return," termination strategies may be used to exit the relationship altogether.[7] We will now discuss the six stages in some detail.

The Initial Stage

When you begin a relationship, you are probably uncertain about your potential partner. Your expectations and knowledge are based on general information gained from the partner's appearance, demeanor, and behavior.

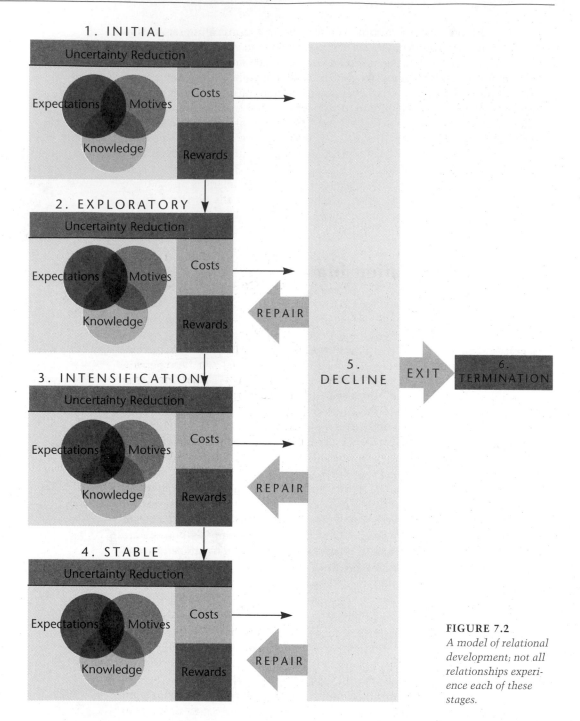

FIGURE 7.2
A model of relational development; not all relationships experience each of these stages.

After some contact with the person, you may begin to form impressions that confirm or modify your knowledge, expectations, and motives for being in the relationship. Positive impressions (assessments) translate into rewards, whereas negative impressions are perceived as costs. If costs seem to outweigh rewards, the relationship will probably end at this point. If enough rewards are present, the relationship will move to the exploratory stage.

The Exploratory Stage

The exploratory stage, true to its name, involves a great deal of information seeking. It assumes that both relational partners want to reduce uncertainty. Monitoring, proactive, and indirect strategies are used in this stage, so that enough relational knowledge is accumulated to make further assessments. In the exploratory stage, relational partners are still hesitant to delve into highly intimate topics; they are still testing the relationship. As information is exchanged, expectations, knowledge, and motives are reassessed, and rewards and costs are reexamined. If costs exceed rewards, relational decline is likely; if rewards are abundant, the next stage further intensifies the relationship.

The Intensification Stage

By the time relational partners reach this stage, they have made an investment in each other and can afford to intensify their relationship. This is especially evident in the means they use to reduce uncertainty further. Instead of seeking personal information about each other, the partners are more likely to focus on the relationship. This is especially true if the relationship is a romantic one. Intensification reflects a desire to move the relationship to a new level. Both relational partners realize that their expectations, motives, and knowledge are different from those in the earlier stages, so they assess rewards and costs along new lines. For example, two friends who are intensifying their relationship will know not to hold unrealistic expectations because their relational knowledge has grown. They may even develop new motives for being in the relationship. In the earlier stages, they may have valued companionship, but now they value their partner's trust more than anything else. Rewards and costs may change as well. It is in the intensification stage that relational intimacy or closeness may be felt for the first time.

The Stable Stage

By the time partners have reached the stable stage, their relationship is no longer volatile or temporary. Relational partners now have a great deal of knowledge about one another, their expectations are accurate and realistic, and they feel comfortable with their motives for being in the relationship. Uncertainty reduction is not a major issue in this phase unless events in the lives of the relational partners change. Perceptions of rewards and costs become more stable, providing a measure of predictability in the relationship. This is not to

cathy®

by Cathy Guisewite

How can you recognize the exploratory stage of a relationship?

say that relationships don't continue to evolve, for in order for relationships to enjoy stability, they must continue to interest the partners.

Wilmot characterizes stable relationships in the following three ways: "(a) relationships stabilize because the participants reach some minimal agreement on what they want from the relationship, (b) relationships can stabilize at differing levels of intimacy, and (c) a stabilized relationship still has areas of change occurring in it."[8] The concept of intimacy is worth considering in more detail.

Intimacy is a special aspect of relational development that is found in the stable phase.[9] **Intimacy** is a deep understanding of another person and is one of the highest levels that a relationship can aspire to. One popular misconception about intimacy is that it is usually sexual. On the contrary, intimacy is not restricted to romantic relationships. As noted earlier, it can occur between parent and child, best friends, and colleagues; even adversaries can enjoy intimacy if they have a deep understanding of one another.

Once partners have achieved a satisfactory level of intimacy, they must continuously work to sustain that intimacy. Many strategies can be used to maintain intimacy, but this section suggests the following ones.

INTIMACY

A deep understanding of another person; one of the highest levels that a relationship can aspire to.

> *Reciprocal self-disclosure and trust* If individuals think that they can completely trust their partners and their partners have complete trust in them, then they are more likely to self-disclose private and personal matters and create a greater sense of intimacy. Marissa thinks that Natalie trusts her because whenever she discloses something personal, Natalie responds and often follows up with a self-disclosure of her own.

> *Supportive interchanges* If you feel confident that your partner supports you 100 percent, you will most likely feel a greater closeness or intimacy. In order to give supportive interchanges, you should be aware

of your partner's successes and improvements, give frequent approval of his or her activities, and avoid expressing disapproval.[10]

Commitment talk Relationships sustain intimacy when the partners feel an involvement and use commitment talk. The rejection of competitors, a willingness to resolve any problems in order to maintain the relationship, and an acceptance of personal responsibility for the relationship are just some of the ways that partners exchange commitment talk.[11]

Enchantment People can deliberately be enchanting in order to sustain intimacy. In the beginning, relationships are exciting and full of surprises. Later, this newness can wear off and leave the partners feeling as though every day were the same. To help maintain intimacy, partners can be playful, mysterious, or unpredictable. Intimacy is unique in each relationship, and how you and your partner sustain intimacy is also unique. No matter which strategies you use, you should remember that an intimate relationship requires continuous maintenance.

A Definition of Love. Love expresses a wide range of feelings, from deep passion for another person to great fondness for a favorite dessert. Saying "I love you" seems to have lost some of its emphasis and does not appear to have the definite meaning it once did.

Love generally involves an exclusive kind of relationship. The relationship of people who claim to be "in love" is supposed to be different from any other relationship either might have. Love has been described as a permanent

The pressure on young adults to find a romantic partner remains a strong force in contemporary society.

LOVE

A deep affection for and attraction to another person; generally involves a relationship that is more exclusive than friendship.

relationship with deep emotional ties—one that is passionate and intense. However, that is the fairy-tale version. For this section, we define **love** as a deep affection for and attraction to another person.

Types of Love. Have you ever thought that love can be different for different people? Do you experience different types of love depending on who the person is? The Canadian psychologist J. A. Lee conducted extensive research with the goal of placing different types of love into categories.[12] His research, which involved hundreds of people, revealed six different types of love.

Eros—beauty and sexuality Sex is the most important aspect of erotic love. This type of relationship is quite intense, both emotionally and physically. The focus is on beauty and attractiveness more than on qualities such as intelligence and sense of humor.

Ludus—entertainment and excitement Ludus means *play* in Latin, and the ludic lover views love as a game. Ludic love does not require great commitment or feeling, for it lacks passion and intensity. It lasts only as long as the partners find each other entertaining or fun. When things begin to dull, new partners are found. The casual dating of many different people is a prime example of ludus.

Storge—peacefulness and slowness Storge is a type of love that lacks passion and excitement. It develops over an extended period of time and often begins in friendship. Storgic lovers may have difficulty pinpointing the precise moment when they knew they were in love. For them, falling in love was a gradual process; they didn't realize it had happened until much later. Storgic lovers often share common interests and activities but rarely disclose any feelings about their relationship.

Pragma—practicality and tradition In Greek, *pragma* means *life work*. Pragmatic lovers are extremely logical and practical in seeking a companion. They want a long-term relationship with an individual who shares their goals in life. If a person wants a relationship that does not require much time or effort, then he or she will search for a mate who is looking for the same things. Pragmatic relationships seem to last longer than any of the others, perhaps because both parties enter with realistic expectations—"with open eyes."

Mania—elation and depression This is the love that is often referred to as "romantic love." It exhibits extreme feelings, ranging from high excitement and passion to deep depression. Manic lovers are often so concerned with the thought of losing their mate that they are unable to enjoy the relationship. Mania love is characteristically intense, obsessive, desperate, and painful. Manic relationships often appear out of control; the partners act impulsively and often get hurt. Mania love is full of excitement and intensity, but it reaches a peak and then quickly fades away.

Agape—compassion and selflessness In this type of love, the individual gives willingly and expects nothing in return. This type of lover can care for others without close ties; a deep relationship is not necessary for agapic love to develop. The agapic lover always wants the other to be happy, even if it results in his or her own pain or unhappiness.

No map of the road of love has ever been prepared; only trial and error, along with the passing of time and experience, will help you in your love relationships. Nonetheless, Goss and O'Hair give several helpful hints on how you may establish *effective love*.[13]

1. Develop insight into and empathy for a partner's concept of love.

2. Analyze your own and your partner's expectations of love.

3. Accept the fact that, even though two people have different concepts of love, neither owns the truth.

4. Be flexible. Adapt the way you show love to meet a partner's image of loving behavior.

5. Recall what you said or did to show loving feelings in the early stages of the relationship.

6. Notice what your partner does to make you feel loved.

Paths to Stable Relationships. Maintaining successful relationships requires a great deal of effort. Partners must gain an understanding of their individual relationship, work within its limits, and utilize its strengths. You can try to achieve stable relationships by adopting the following behaviors.

Be understanding. Try to understand how your partner views the world. Empathize with his or her fears, pain, and dreams. It is important to be supportive. Do not judge these concerns. Aim only to understand in order to communicate more effectively with your partner. Show that you care.

Reveal your feelings. Reveal yourself cautiously. It may be detrimental to self-disclose too much. Knowledge of past acts or certain feelings may harm the relationship if disclosed at the wrong time. Consider how the knowledge will affect your partner's actions and feelings; use good judgment. Still, self-disclosure is an essential part of a relationship. It strengthens the bond between relational partners.

Be flexible. Recognize that people and relationships naturally change and that these changes must be handled. Often, conscious change is necessary on the part of one or both of the relational partners. Thus, an understanding that change is natural and essential is crucial.

Be accommodating. Conflict naturally occurs. Relational partners who accept this reality and proceed in conflict situations with the right intentions will benefit greatly. Proceed with the goal of reaching a compromise instead of winning the argument; otherwise, one or both partners may get hurt. Conflict can be healthy, but when approached incorrectly it can be very detrimental.

Don't demand too much. Be realistic in your expectations of your partner and of the relationship. Do not compare your relationship with other

Thinking about Love

How many times have you experienced the types of love outlined here? Can you add any new categories? Is love always different for every person, or are some qualities common to many types of love? If so, what are some of these qualities?

*L*ove on the Move

Joyce and Jim, who were introduced by common friends, have been dating for 6 months. Joyce has told Jim on several occasions that she loves him and wants them to be together forever. Jim is thrilled to hear this and always reciprocates Joyce's sentiments and feelings. The fact of the matter is that, although Joyce does love Jim, she knows full well that her career will cause her to move soon. Jim owns a thriving business in the community where they both live, and all of his family, including his ex-wife and three children, live near him. Joyce knows that Jim would never move with her. Even though she knows they will break up in a few months, Joyce continues to discuss their future, including marriage, with Jim. Joyce fears that Jim would look elsewhere for a relationship if he knew about her impending move, and she wants to maintain the relationship as long as she is in town.

Is Joyce using unethical communication to maintain her relationship with Jim? If so, does the fact that she really loves him make her behavior less unethical? Would it be unethical for Jim to find another relationship if he thought Joyce were moving? Should ethics always come before love?

relationships that you perceive to be better than your own. Actually, most relationships experience the same kinds of trouble that your own does. Therefore, do not set your expectations too high.

The Decline Stage

Relationship decline, the erosion that occurs over time to some relationships, has several causes. Although no two relationships are the same, the causes of relationship decline share some similarities. As you observed in Figure 7.2, relational decline results when costs exceed rewards and relational partners put less effort into the relationship. Three factors in the costs/rewards evaluation typically lead to relational decline: (1) uncertainty events, (2) unmet expectations, and (3) interference (family, work, timing, money, etc.).

Uncertainty Events. Events or behavioral patterns that cause uncertainty in a relationship are called **uncertainty events**. Uncertainty events leave one or both partners wondering about the cause of the events and their significance for the relationship. Planalp and Honeycutt studied these events and found several factors that cause uncertainty in a relationship:[14]

- Competing relationships, either dating relationships or platonic ones
- An unexplained loss of closeness
- A change in sexual behavior

UNCERTAINTY EVENTS

Events that cause uncertainty in a relationship (e.g., a competing relationship, an unexplained loss of closeness, deception, or an unexplained change in the personality of one partner).

- Deception or betrayal of confidence
- An unexplained change in personality or values

These events or changes may be sudden and very noticeable, or they may be subtle and escape immediate attention.

Unmet Expectations. The way two people interact is greatly influenced by their expectations for the relationship and their perceptions of each other's expectations. These expectations range from where the relationship is going in general to very specific expectations about how the other person will react to a certain situation.

Dissatisfaction with a relationship often begins when a gap forms between a person's expectations about a relationship and the actual course the relationship is taking. This is often the result of differences between the partners' respective expectations. Susannah and Jiro were friends for 2 years while they were business majors at the same university. Upon graduation, Susannah went to work at a stock brokerage. When another job opened at the firm, Jiro expressed interest in it to Susannah. Although she encouraged Jiro to apply, Susannah felt uneasy mixing friendship and work and did not recommend Jiro for the position. Jiro expected Susannah, as a friend, to help him get the job. When she went against Jiro's expectations, he decided to end their friendship.

Interference. Many obstacles may crop up in a relationship, interfering with its growth. Timing, third-party relationships, the family or friends of one partner, and problems with work or money can all contribute to the decline of a relationship.

The amount of involvement within a particular relationship can influence the timing of the breakup. The great majority of relational breakups (71.1 percent) occur during the spring and summer months, from April to September. Research has also found that the degree of involvement in the relationship plays a part in determining when to end it.[15] Relational partners who were more emotionally involved broke up during the school year, while less involved partners ended their relationship during vacation time.

Often a relationship fails to meet a person's needs, and when this happens, that person may seek fulfillment outside of the relationship. A third party may not necessarily be a competing romantic interest; it may be a friend or family member. Whoever it is, however, that person fulfills a need that the relational partner cannot, making the presence of the partner unnecessary. When Natalie refused to go to the golf course with Carl while he played, Carl invited another friend, Katherine, to play. The two enjoyed playing golf together, and their golf games soon became a regular occurrence. Although Natalie herself was responsible for this situation, she became extremely jealous of Carl and Katherine's relationship. When she told Carl that she did not think it was right for him to play golf with another woman instead of his girlfriend, Carl did not understand why Natalie was so upset. After all, his relationship with Katherine was strictly

Causes of Unmet Expectations

Unmet expectations can result from personality differences, uncompromising attitudes, differing levels of sexual attraction and enjoyment, or lost romance. What other causes can you cite?

platonic, and he had asked Natalie to play golf before he had ever contacted Katherine. Although the relationship between Carl and Katherine was a friendship based on a hobby both enjoyed, Natalie found this third-party relationship threatening.

Often problems develop within a relationship because of differences between one partner and the family or friends of the other partner. These problems often result from personal differences or differences in value systems, leading to disapproval shown by the family or friends of the relational partner. This may cause problems as the partner "caught in the middle" tries to reconcile the competing views and decide what to do. When Rosa and Charles announced that they were getting married, their families were pleased. Rosa's Mexican heritage taught her that the groom's family was responsible for the bulk of the wedding expenses, whereas Charles's American culture led him to believe that the bride's family carried the load. As plans for the wedding began to take shape, each family had its own ideas of exactly how everything should be and who should bear most of the costs. Both Rosa and Charles felt caught between the two families. When the disagreement between the families continued, Rosa and Charles decided to elope. They felt that was the only way their relationship could survive the family interference.

Problems associated with work occur on many levels. Two of the most common complaints made about relational partners are that they spend too much time at work or "bring the office home." At issue here is time spent on one's job in proportion to time spent with the relational partner or family. A perception that more time is spent on one's job may lead to the belief that the job is more important than the partner or family.

Work also causes problems when it clashes with expectations and values. Career-oriented females with children may be viewed as neglectful and uncaring, whereas career-focused males with children are seen as ambitious providers. There are many opinions about quality time versus quantity of time. One question that is often raised about this issue is: How many professionals say on their death beds, "I wish I'd worked more!"?

Money is a major issue in most relationships. DeVito notes that one-fourth to one-third of all couples rank it among their most troublesome problems. He also states that it is the close connection between money and power that makes it such a thorny issue. For example, the person who makes more money usually has the final say about the purchase of expensive items and about many other financial decisions. Money also causes problems because couples naturally argue about how it is to be spent in general. Another reason why money may contribute to difficulties is that the partners often view money differently because of upbringing, spending habits, and gender.[16]

Relational Repair

The warning signs of a relationship in decline are often pretty obvious. An argument may get out of hand or a situation may cause misunderstandings that could have been corrected. One person may feel that not enough effort has been exerted; or the partners may simply "give up." Whatever the

Why do you think financial problems are frequently a cause of relational decline?

reason for the decline, some people will have a desire to repair the relationship. Duck suggests the following repair tactics:[17]

- Improve communication.
- Bring out the partner's positive side.
- Focus on the positive aspects of the relationship.
- Reinterpret the behavior of the partner as positive and well intentioned.
- Reduce negativity toward the partner and adopt a more balanced view.
- Reevaluate the attractiveness and unattractiveness of alternative relationships and alternative partners.
- Enlist the support of others in order to hold the relationship together.

In order to repair their relationship, partners have to decrease the amount of disagreement in their interactions. They must focus on the relationship itself and not on the source of a particular argument. Next, the partners may need to improve the quality of their communication. Some relational partners need to work on their listening skills and strive to understand the other person's perspective. Like all communication, thinking about what you are about to say is also very important because words spoken harshly are not easily forgotten. Another repair tactic is for the relational partners to display the attractive qualities that sparked the relationship in the first place. The partners may also try to increase their intimacy, by making more self-disclosures and spending quality time with one another.[18]

Applying the Model of Relational Development

Find a married couple whom you know, but are not related to, and ask them to describe how their relationship developed. Show the couple the model of relational development (Figure 7.2) and ask them how relevant the model is to their relationship.

Repair tactics used during the final stages of termination will most likely involve one of three approaches: the use of persons outside the relationship to help hold the relationship together; social support from friends; and an accounting to others of why the relationship ended.

The Termination Stage

Every relationship is influenced by unique situations and circumstances, but it is still possible to make some generalizations. Davis identifies two general reasons for terminating relationships.[19]

The first reason he notes is *passing away*, which is characterized by the gradual fading of a relationship. The relationship loses its vitality perhaps because of another intimate or because of jealousy over the time one partner spends in activities not associated with the other partner. Also, the time available for interaction may have decreased. As a result, communication and intimacy may have declined, leading to a separation of attitudes between the partners. A relationship may also pass away because the partners simply do not continue making the effort needed to maintain an intimate relationship. This leads to a stagnant relationship and a decrease in communication.

Davis also identifies the situation of *sudden death*, which refers to an unexpected ending that comes suddenly. Here the partners may terminate a relationship that one or both of them have desired to end for some time. Feelings that were once present may have died. Nonetheless, the partners may have continued the relationship because of circumstances external to the relationship, such as the years invested together or the presence of children.

If only one partner wishes to terminate a relationship, he or she may suddenly act on this desire after a long period of uncertainty. The partner seeking an end to the relationship may previously have allowed it to drag on in response to alternating good and bad phases or to the efforts of the other partner to maintain the relationship. Whatever the reason, the dissatisfied partner, once resolved to terminate the relationship, will do so quickly and "move on."

Sudden relationship death may also occur when one partner, perceiving that a relationship is moving too fast, requests a slowdown. If this request is not met, the person may react by terminating the relationship altogether. A relationship may also be ended by isolated occurrences, such as a single argument that goes too far or a unique misunderstanding that ends an otherwise smoothly running relationship. Finally, a partner may violate some implicit or explicit rule of interaction that both had adopted earlier. For example, one partner decides not to attend an official holiday celebration with the partner's family, instead opting to visit a childhood friend in another state. This action may cause the other partner to be angry enough to end the relationship.

Strategies for Terminating a Relationship. As we mentioned earlier, the circumstances present in each relationship are different; accordingly, termination strategies also vary. Several common methods of terminating romantic relationships are listed in Table 7.1. Which of these strategies have worked for

TABLE 7.1 ROMANTIC RELATIONAL TERMINATION STRATEGIES

STRATEGY	TACTICS	EXAMPLE
Positive-tone messages	Fairness	"It wouldn't be right to go on acting like we're in love when I know I am not!"
	Compromise	"I still care about you. We can still see each other occasionally."
	Fatalism	"Destiny would never let us go on for very long in this relationship."
Deescalation	Promise of friendship	"We can still be friends."
	Implied possible reconciliation	"We need time alone; maybe that will rekindle our feelings for each other."
	Blaming relationship	"It's not your fault, but this relationship is bogging us down."
	Appeal to independence	"We don't need to be tied down right now."
Withdrawal/ avoidance	Avoid contact with the person as much as possible.	"I don't think I'll be able to see you this weekend."
Justification	Emphasize positive consequences of disengaging	"It's better for you and me to see other people since we've changed so much."
	Emphasize negative consequences of not disengaging	"We will miss too many opportunities if we don't see other people."
Negative identity management	Emphasize enjoyment of life	"Life is too short to spend with just one person right now."
	Nonnegotiation	"I need to see other people—period!"

Source: Adapted from D. J. Canary & M. J. Cody (1994), *Interpersonal communication: A goals-based approach* (New York: St. Martin's Press), pp. 266–268.

you in the past? How could you use some of these strategies more effectively in the future?

Effects of Termination. The termination of serious or lengthy relationships can be both traumatic and stressful. A great deal of research has been done on the tactics individuals use to cope with a breakup. Harvey, Orbuch, and Weber, for example, have devised a model that focuses on psychological needs, communication, and post-termination mental health.[20] According to this model, after a traumatic experience, individuals experience a natural need to explain fully what happened. Months or even years may be needed to complete this process because so much information, so many details, and so much potential for second-guessing have built up. This accounting process consists of forming a detailed, coherent story about the relationship, what happened, when, why, and with what consequences. In addition, emotional consequences must be dealt with when a relationship is terminated. Both partners will experience some type of emotion in regard to the ending of their relationship. Feelings of distress, unhappiness, and disappointment are common. The relational partner who initiated the breakup may experience guilt, while the other partner may feel angry and depressed.

Reconciliation

Reconciliation is a repair strategy that goes the extra mile. It signals that one relational partner wants to rekindle an extinguished relationship. Reconciling a relationship entails a lot of risk because the other person may have no interest in a "second chance." It takes a lot of guts and initiative for someone to risk another dose of rejection and humiliation. Nonetheless, some people will launch headfirst into a series of strategies designed to rejuvenate a relationship. Other people may carefully consider the options available and construct a message that will appeal to an ex-partner.

Relationships that are begun anew may turn out in several different ways. The relationship may be strengthened by the termination and subsequent reconciliation. In this case, the partners are sure of their goals for the relationship and their feelings about each other. In other cases, old issues may not be settled and may resurface, causing the same troubles or resulting in intensified disagreement and strife. There is no way to say with any certainty how a reconciliation attempt will turn out.

I ◆ Types of Relationships

There are as many different types of relationships as there are individuals who make up these relationships. Some common relationships are those between co-workers, between doctors and patients, and between salespeople and clients. However, this section is concerned primarily with two important types: friendship and family.

FRIENDSHIP

A relationship between two or more people that is perceived as mutually satisfying, productive, and beneficial.

A Friendship

1) **Friendship** is a relationship between two or more people that is perceived as mutually satisfying, productive, and beneficial. Everyone has a personal opinion as to what important qualities a friend should have.

Characteristics of Friendship. In spite of individual differences as to what constitutes friendship, agreement seems to have been reached on six characteristics: availability, caring, honesty, confidentiality, loyalty, and empathy.[21]

What good would a friend be who was never available to spend time with you? People want friends to make time for them and be accessible. If the parties in a relationship seldom interact with each other, the relationship often deteriorates or loses its closeness. Do your close friends make time for you even when they are busy? You may often make friends through your activities, classes, or work. You want to have common interests and activities with your friends. What would two people do together if they had absolutely nothing in common? Usually, these shared activities mean the difference between being acquaintances and being friends.

You want your friends to care about you. Even if something in your life is of no great importance to them, you want and expect them to care about what happens because it's important to you. Your friends do not have to agree with the choices or events in your life, but they need to care about them. If an individual were to ignore you, have no regard for your feelings, and genuinely seem not to care about what happened to you, you would not identify that person as your friend.

Honesty is a virtue that is vital in all relationships. You want your friends to be open and honest with you. When a relational partner deceives you, the deception tends to decrease the degree of closeness that the two of you shared. Sometimes your friends may have to be "brutally honest" and tell you things that you would rather not hear. You have to accept this honesty as constructive criticism and remember that, although you may not like what you are hearing, you may need to hear it and hearing it from a friend may actually be best.

You want confidentiality from your friends. In other words, you want to be sure that what you disclose to your friends will not end up in the *National Inquirer* tomorrow. What you share with your friends may seem meaningless and trivial to them but may be extremely personal to you. You want to be able to trust your friends and know that they will not share your deepest, darkest secrets with others.

A friend who can be loyal in even the worst of times is a lifelong friend. Have you ever had a friend who was extremely nice and supportive to your face, but the minute you left the room tore you and your reputation to shreds? A true friend is one who is loyal and would never allow others to degrade you without standing up for you or at least letting it be known that he or she did not agree with what was being said.

You expect some degree of empathy from your friends. **Empathy** is the understanding one has of another's experience. You want your friends to be able to see particular circumstances as you do and perhaps walk in your shoes. Even if they have never shared the same experiences, you expect friends to try to empathize with you.

In 1979, *Psychology Today* conducted a survey that confirmed these friendship qualities.[22] When the respondents were asked what they felt was

EMPATHY

The understanding one has of another's experience.

the most important quality in a friend, the most often mentioned quality was that of keeping confidences. Trust seemed to be a major issue in all friendships. Along with trust came loyalty; people want to believe that their friends will stick by them come what may. The importance of warmth and affection rounded out the top three qualities mentioned.

Types of Friendship. Even though the six characteristics we have discussed may seem to apply to all friendships, it is important to understand that there are different types of friendship. Reisman identifies three types: reciprocity, receptivity, and association.[23]

RECIPROCITY

A type of friendship that involves self-surrender, loyalty, mutual respect, affection, and support, and in which the partners give and take equally and share responsibility for maintaining the relationship.

Reciprocity is an ideal type of friendship in that it is composed of characteristics such as self-surrender, loyalty, mutual respect, affection, and support. Each individual in a reciprocal friendship equally gives and takes, and each person shares the responsibility of maintaining the relationship. Mike and Russell have been best friends as long as they can remember. The two met when they were in first grade and eventually ended up sharing an apartment together. They help one another in any way they can, and they find spending time with one another to be enjoyable and beneficial. They feel they can trust one another, and they are always comfortable when they are together. Clearly, Mike and Russell's friendship is one of reciprocity.

RECEPTIVITY

A type of friendship in which one partner is the primary giver and the other is the primary taker.

In **receptivity** there is a definite imbalance in the giving and taking, with one partner being the primary giver and the other the primary taker. However, this is not always a bad arrangement. The needs of each person can be met through the particular roles played. This type of friendship often develops between individuals of different status, as the following example illustrates. Dan is a teaching assistant for a class that Mark is taking. Mark is on the baseball team, and traveling causes him to miss several classes. Mark must meet with Dan every time he misses a class to get the information he needs, and through their frequent meetings the two have become friends. Mark is using Dan's access to information, and Dan is not receiving anything comparable from Mark in return, yet they still value each other's friendship.

ASSOCIATION

A type of friendship that develops through frequent contact; more an acquaintance than a true friendship.

Association might be seen as a relationship with an acquaintance rather than as a true friendship. An associative friendship is most likely to develop between people who have frequent contact, such as co-workers, classmates, or neighbors. Holly and Susan are in three classes together, and throughout the semester the two have become friends. Even though they do not do anything together outside class, they still consider each other friends.

Family

Whom do you consider your family? Whether it's your immediate family of father, mother, sisters, and brothers, or perhaps a more extended family including your grandparents, aunts, uncles, and cousins, you have relational and blood ties to other people whom you call family. Although families at times can be major sources of stress and difficulty, they can also provide some of your greatest joys. Definitions of family range anywhere from all the people living in the same household to all those claiming descent from the same ancestor. For the purposes of this section, Nass and McDonald's definition is used.[24] They define a **family** as "a social group having specified roles and statuses (e.g., husband, wife, father, mother, son, daughter) with ties of blood, marriage, or adoption who usually share a common residence and cooperate economically."

Family members do a number of things that require competent communication. Since families provide much of the nurturing humans require in life, many of the family members' interactions are in support of one another. Healthy families strive for effective communication in ensuring mental, intellectual, and emotional growth; promoting family ties; and helping each other to succeed in their goals. It is through communication that families generate their strengths. The following section outlines the communication functions of family members.[25]

Functions of Families. At the time of birth, a human infant is unable to care for him- or herself; a family is needed to ensure the infant's survival. The family fulfills needs such as food, shelter, clothing, and basic caretaking. Without the family, infants and most young children would be helpless. Older family members also require care. As more people live longer, their need for daily care increases. Whether older adults live within the household of an offspring, as in an extended family, or live elsewhere, their care usually falls to the family. Competent communication may be more difficult with older adults, but it is still very important at this stage of family development.

Long before children enter school, they begin to learn important basic lessons. They learn about the differences between humans and animals, honesty and dishonesty, niceness and meanness, and so on. The family helps children to discover what is appropriate behavior. Many of the beliefs and values you hold are shaped and influenced by your family through a process

FAMILY

A social group whose members are related by blood, marriage, or adoption; have specified roles (e.g., husband, wife, son, mother) and statuses; and usually share a common residence and cooperate economically.

The family is the first and most important agent for developing a person's values, beliefs, and customs.

*F*amily Functions in the Media and Your Life

Watch a recent movie or an episode of a television program depicting a family. You can even select one of your favorite sitcom programs. List the various functions the "media family" demonstrates. How effective are the members' communication styles in serving the family functions? Now describe how your own family performs these same functions. Is the media family unrealistic in its portrayal of family life? What lessons can be learned from the media about communicating effectively within families?

of observation and cultivation. Younger family members watch parents and older siblings as they interact with others in various contexts, learning how to handle themselves and other people in social situations. Family members encourage social skills in younger children through instructive and corrective communication practices.

Many families engage in activities that they enjoy doing together. Sports, working in the yard, or just lounging together on a lazy Sunday afternoon provide recreational opportunities for family members. Recreation also gives family members a chance to interact with one another in different contexts. For example, watching an otherwise quiet son become enthusiastic and cheer at a football game reveals a communication style seldom seen by his family members. Finally, recreational time can greatly influence the closeness of the family.

The family is the medium through which family customs or basic cultural guidelines can be passed from one generation to the next. Children learn different ideas from a variety of sources—games, books, television, and the like—but the family can be helpful in explaining these ideas and introducing different concepts. Children tend to imitate their parents and other family members; many children will arrange their homes like the one they grew up in, buy the same brands their parents did, or even vote for the same political candidates. When family members tell stories about their parents, grandparents, and great grandparents, younger members get a sense of history and pride about the family lineage and want to help perpetuate family strength. In this way, transmission becomes an important communication function for many families.

Improving Family Relations. Just about every family could improve the relationships among its members. Today, families face a host of communication challenges as they attempt to succeed in their busy lives. It takes a great deal of effort to ensure that family members use their relationships to maximum benefit. Here are several recommendations that will help enrich family relationships through competent communication.

Put yourself in their place. To understand what family members are feeling or experiencing, you must show some degree of empathy, not just sympathy. Try to grasp how others feel, even if your own experiences are different.

Let others know how you feel. Family members must be able to tell or show one another how they are feeling. If one member is hurt and angry about something that happened at school, the others will not know exactly what is wrong unless they are told. If the hurt individual keeps this feeling to him- or herself and just acts mad and upset, others may perceive that this anger is directed toward something they did. It is important to allow others to know what is happening.

Be flexible. Relationships are constantly developing and moving from one stage to another, and relationships within a family are no exception. As each member grows and develops, so will the relationships with others. For example, a daughter in a family may be extremely close to her father at the age of 10, but at the age of 16 she may become significantly closer to her mother. The parents must recognize this change as normal and must not see it as a failing on their part.

Fight fairly. Conflict is present in all relationships and sometimes more so in families. Family members need to learn how to fight fairly without unnecessarily hurting the feelings of someone who does not deserve it. Fighting fairly means listening to the other person and at least attempting to understand the other person's point of view. Fighting fairly also means that family members do not hit below the belt or gang up on one another. Families must recognize the importance of compromise and understand that there does not always have to be a definite winner and loser.

Give as much as you take. Individuals need to recognize when they are demanding too much of the other members of the family. Everyone has times when they are allowed to take more than they are giving, but there are also times when people must give more than they take. Be reasonable. Remember, how would you like it if other family members made excessive demands on you?

◆ Competent Relationships

Many experts on television and in self-help books seem to think that there is a simple formula for producing a long and happy relationship. As any happy couple will tell you, however, their relationship took a lot of time and understanding to build. One popular analogy is that a relationship is like a house that you must build from the ground up. A solid foundation is required for a solid, secure house, just as a solid foundation is needed for a solid, lasting relationship. A competent relationship is based on three main components: the characteristics of each relational partner, the relationship itself, and each partner's own relational history.

According to the model of communicative competence, each relational partner brings a unique set of personal characteristics to a relationship, including behaviors, communication styles, values, cultural identity, perceptions, memories, and attributions. Although each partner must contribute to the relationship in these areas, each must also continue to develop these same areas in his or her own self-concept and perceptions of the world. From these perceptions, you can develop realistic expectations of your partner, your relationship, and yourself in the relationship. These perceptions and values, then, are the tools that help make the relationship work.

Two types of expectations are inherent in every relationship: current expectations and future expectations. *Current expectations* and goals are often developed through daily interactions and conversations with relational partners. In contrast, expectations for the future are not discussed on a daily basis. Often *future expectations* are considered internally and given a great deal of thought before they are actually stated. The expression of expectations can give the relationship a clearer direction and set of goals, assuming both partners agree on the direction to take.

Each individual also brings his or her own relational history into the relationship. This can be both a benefit and a hindrance. Although you should learn from your mistakes, you may often find yourself dwelling on the past and concentrating too much on not repeating the mistakes you made in a previous relationship rather than enjoying the current relationship as it develops.

Every component that has been mentioned is greatly influenced by the culture in which it exists: A culture or society establishes the "dos and don'ts." The culture sets up the standards of what a "normal" relationship should be like, and often, if a relationship does not fit into society's mold, the partners may feel it is unsuccessful.

*T*he Case of Bruce and Saleh

At the beginning of this chapter we met Bruce and Saleh, two new foreign exchange students at the London School of Economics who will be roommates for the year. Bruce is American and Saleh is from Saudi Arabia. Think about their relationship from the perspective of this chapter as you consider the following questions.

- Which of the goals and motivations for relationship development are likely to be most relevant?

- Are expectations likely to play a major role in the development of Bruce and Saleh's relationship? Explain.

- What strategies for reducing uncertainty would you recommend to them?

- What stages of relationship would you predict for Bruce and Saleh?

- What type of friendship do you think will develop between them? What might be some characteristics of their friendship?

REVIEW

This chapter focuses on developing, maintaining, and repairing or possibly ending relationships with other people.

- Relational knowledge, goals and motivations, and relational expectations are the preliminary processes that determine how and why people develop relationships.

- The influences in forming relationships are interpersonal attraction, physical proximity, alleviation of loneliness, stimulation, and achievement of goals.

- Rewards are those aspects of a relationship that are valued. Three categories of rewards are extrinsic, instrumental, and intrinsic.

- If costs, or burdens to a relationship, exceed rewards, the relationship will not develop and be maintained as well as one that enjoys a higher percentage of rewards.

- Uncertainty reduction helps relational partners understand one another better. You can reduce uncertainty through monitoring, proactive, and indirect strategies.

- As you reduce uncertainty, your ability to predict your relational partner is enhanced, facilitating the development of intimacy.

- The model of interpersonal relationship development was proposed to explain the stages that relationships can go through.

- Relationships begin in the initiation stage, when acquaintances are formed. Subsequent stages of development are the exploratory, intensification, and stable phases, all of which are dependent on uncertainty reduction and assessments of rewards and costs.

- As a relationship develops, evaluations and modifications are made by relational partners in the areas of relational knowledge, motives and goals, and expectations. As these change with time and relational maturity, so too can costs and rewards change. If a relationship declines and cannot be repaired, termination strategies may be used to exit the relationship.

- Friendships and families are important types of relationships. Friendships include a number of qualities, such as availability, caring, honesty, confidentiality, loyalty, and empathy.

- Families serve several important social and communication functions, including provision of care, socialization, recreational needs, and transmission of culture.

CHAPTER 7
DEVELOPING AND MAINTAINING RELATIONSHIPS

[1]S. Planalp (1985), Relational schemata: a test of alternative forms of relational knowledge as guides to communication, *Human Communications Research, 12*(1), 3–29.

[2]R. A. Bell (1985), Conversational involvement and loneliness, *Communication Monographs, 52,* 218–235.

[3]I. Altman & D. Taylor (1973), Social penetration theory, New York: Holt, Rinehart & Winston.

[4]J. Rempel, J. Holmes, & M. Zanna (1985), Trust in close relationships, *Journal of Personality and Social Psychology, 49,* 95–112.

[5]C. Berger & R. Calabrese (1975), Some explorations in initial interaction and beyond: Toward a developmental theory of interpersonal communication, *Human Communication Research, 1,* 100.

[6]L. Baxter & W. Wilmot (1984), Secret tests: Social strategies for acquiring information about the state of the relationship, *Human Communication Research, 11,* 171–201.

[7]This model is based on the following research: G. Miller & M. Steinberg (1975), *Between people,* Palo Alto, CA: Science Research Associates; Altman & Taylor (1973); M. L. Knapp & A. L. Vangelisti (1992), *Interpersonal communication and human relationships* (2nd ed.), Boston: Allyn & Bacon.

[8]W. Wilmot (1981), Relationship stages: Initiation and stabilization. In J. Civikly (Ed.), *Contexts of communication,* New York: Holt, Rinehart & Winston.

[9]Knapp & Vangelisti (1992).

[10]E. Goffman (1971), *Relations in public,* New York: Harper & Row.

[11]Knapp & Vangelisti (1992).

[12]J. A. Lee (1973), *The colors of love: An exploration of the ways of loving,* Don Mills, Ontario: New Press; S. S. Hendrick & C. Hendrick (1992), *Liking, loving, and relating.* Pacific Grove, CA: Brooks/Cole.

[13]B. Goss & D. O'Hair (1988), *Communicating in interpersonal relationships,* New York: Macmillan.

[14]S. Planalp & J. Honeycutt (1985), Events that increase uncertainty in personal relationships, *Human Communication Research, 11,* 593–604.

[15]C. Hill, Z. Rubion, & L. A. Peplau (1976), Breakups before marriage: The end of 103 affairs, *Journal of Social Issues, 32,* 147–168.

[16]P. Blumstein & P. Schwartz (1983), *American couples: Money, work, sex,* New York: Morrow.

[17]S. W. Duck (1984), A perspective on the repair of personal relationships: Repair of what, when? In S. W. Duck (Ed.), *Personal relationships 5: Repairing personal relationships,* New York: Macmillan.

[18]Blumstein & Schwartz (1983).

[19]M. S. Davis (1973), *Intimate relations,* New York: Free Press, pp. 245–283.

[20]J. H. Harvey, T. L. Orbuch, & A. L. Weber (1990), A social psychological model of account-making in response to severe stress, *Journal of Language and Social Psychology, 9,* 191–207; J. H. Harvey, G. Agostinelli, & A. L. Weber (1989), Account-making and the formation of expectations about close relationships, in C. Hendrick (Ed.), *Close relationships,* Newbury Park, CA: Sage; J. H. Harvey, A. L. Weber, K. S. Galvin, H. C. Huszti, & N. N. Garnick (1986), Attribution in the termination of close relationships: A special focus on the account, in R. Gilmour & S. W. Duck (Eds.), *The emerging field of personal relationships,* Hillsdale, NJ: Lawrence Erlbaum; J. H. Harvey, A. L. Weber, & T. L. Orbuch (1190), *Interpersonal accounts: A social psychological perspective,* Cambridge, MA: Basil Blackwell.

[21]J. C. Pearson & B. H. Spitzberg (1990), *Interpersonal communication: Concepts, components, and contexts* (2nd ed.), Dubuque, IA: Wm. C. Brown.

[22]M. Parlee (1979), The friendship bond, *Psychology Today, 13*(10), 43–54, 113.

[23]J. Reisman (1979), *Anatomy of friendship,* Lexington, MA: Lexis Publishers.

[24]G. D. Nass & G. W. McDonald (1982), *Marriage and the family,* New York: Random House.

[25]S. Trenholm & A. Jensen (1988), *Interpersonal communication,* Belmont, CA: Wadsworth.

Thinking about the Textbook Selection

Answer the following questions about Chapter 7, "Developing and Maintaining Relationships," from *Competent Communication*.

1. Why do you think the authors begin the chapter by focusing on the roommates Bruce and Saleh?

2. Why do the authors link "relational communication"—the topic of this chapter—with "competent communication"—the topic of their book overall?

3. How would you explain the point of the *Cathy* cartoon?

4. What are the four goals people have in developing relationships?

5. Give an example of each of these four goals.

Reviewing

1. Why is it important to preview a textbook before actually beginning to read it?

2. What are some things you can do in prereading a textbook or a textbook chapter?

3. What preliminary elements are typically included in textbooks? Choose one and explain how it can aid your reading comprehension.

4. What body elements are usually included in textbooks? Choose one and explain how it can aid your reading comprehension.

5. What concluding elements are often included in textbooks? Choose one and explain how it can aid your reading comprehension.

6. What visual elements are included in textbooks? Choose one and explain how it can aid your reading comprehension.

**Recall /
Remember**

In this chapter you have practiced the reading strategies explained throughout this book. You have learned how to approach your college textbooks for careful reading and study. You have used vocabulary strategies to learn new terms, and you have used your skills to understand an

**Chapter
Summary**

author's main ideas. You have also made observations, connected them, drawn inferences from them, and arrived at conclusions that reflect your understanding of the chapter. Your application of critical reading strategies has led you to consider how far you agree or disagree with the authors' explanation of personal relationships. Based on your experience, your observations of others, and your reading and general knowledge, you may agree with some of what the authors propose and disagree with other parts of their analysis. Your application of critical reading strategies has helped you understand the authors' point of view as well as evaluate the persuasiveness of their ideas.

In employing the reading strategies you have learned throughout this book to the sample textbook chapter, you should gain confidence that you can master college textbook material. Your confidence in being able to do this comes from the competence you have achieved in developing your reading skills. This competence and confidence improve not only your reading and study habits but also your ability to succeed in your academic work. In addition, you can apply your reading and study strategies to the reading you do in your everyday life and to the reading and study requirements you face at work.

An Anthology of Readings

BILL COSBY

How to Read Faster

"How to Read Faster" was written by Bill Cosby for *The Power of the Printed Word Program* in 1979. Cosby, best known for his stand-up comedy acts and numerous television roles, received a Ph.D. in education and is the author of the best-selling books *Fatherhood* and *Time Flies.* In this essay, Cosby breaks down the reading process and offers three techniques to help students read more quickly, yet comprehensively—previewing, skimming, and clustering. With humor and charm, Cosby endorses regular reading habits, whether the material is classic literature or comic books.

Vocabulary Preview

efficiently (para. 10): effectively with the least amount of work (adv.)

nonfiction (para. 13): based on fact (adj.)

successive (para. 15): following in order (adj.)

1   When I was a kid in Philadelphia, I must have read every comic book ever published. (There were fewer of them then than there are now.)

2   I zipped through all of them in a couple of days, then reread the good ones until the next issues arrived.

3   Yes indeed, when I was a kid, the reading game was a snap.

4   But as I got older, my eyeballs must have slowed down or something! I mean, comic books started to pile up faster than my brother Russell and I could read them!

It wasn't until much later, when I was getting my doctorate, I realized it wasn't my eyeballs that were to blame. Thank goodness. They're still moving as well as ever.

The problem is, there's too much to read these days, and too little time to read every word of it.

Now, mind you, I still read comic books. In addition to contracts, novels, and newspapers. Screenplays, tax returns and correspondence. Even textbooks about how people read. And which techniques help people read more in less time.

I'll let you in on a little secret. There are hundreds of techniques you could learn to help you read faster. But I know of 3 that are especially good.

And if I can learn them, so can you—and you can put them to use *immediately.*

They are commonsense, practical ways to get the meaning from printed words quickly and efficiently. So you'll have time to enjoy your comic books, have a good laugh with Mark Twain or a good cry with *War and Peace.* Ready?

Okay. The first two ways can help you get through tons of reading material—fast—*without reading every word.*

They'll give you the *overall meaning* of what you're reading. And let you cut out an awful lot of *unnecessary* reading.

1. PREVIEW—IF IT'S LONG AND HARD

Previewing is especially useful for getting a general idea of heavy reading like long magazine or newspaper articles, business reports, and nonfiction books.

It can give you as much as half the comprehension in as little as one tenth the time. For example, you should be able to preview eight or ten 100-page reports in an hour. After previewing, you'll be able to decide which reports (or which *parts* of which reports) are worth a closer look.

Here's how to preview: Read the entire first two paragraphs of whatever you've chosen. Next read only the *first sentence* of each successive paragraph. Then read the entire last two paragraphs.

Previewing doesn't give you all the details. But it does keep you from spending time on things you don't really want—or need—to read.

Notice that previewing gives you a quick, overall view of *long, unfamiliar* material. For short, light reading, there's a better technique.

2. SKIM—IF IT'S SHORT AND SIMPLE

Skimming is a good way to get a general idea of light reading— like popular magazines or the sports and entertainment sections of the paper.   18

You should be able to skim a weekly popular magazine or the second section of your daily paper in less than *half* the time it takes you to read it now.   19

Skimming is also a great way to review material you've read before.   20

Here's how to skim: Think of your eyes as magnets. Force them to move fast. Sweep them across each and every line of type. Pick up *only a few key words in each line*.   21

Everybody skims differently.   22

You and I may not pick up exactly the same words when we skim the same piece, but we'll both get a pretty similar idea of what it's all about.   23

To show you how it works, I circled the words I picked out when I skimmed the following story. Try it. It shouldn't take you more than 10 seconds.   24

My brother Russell thinks monsters live in
our bedroom closet at night. But I told him he is crazy.
    "Go and check then," he said.
    I didn't want to. Russell said I was chicken.
    "Am not," I said.
    "Are so," he said.
    So I told him the monsters were going to eat him at midnight.
He started to cry. My Dad came in and told the monsters
to beat it. Then he told us to go to sleep.
    "If I hear any more about monsters," he said, "I'll spank
you."
    We went to sleep fast. And you know something?
They never did come back.

Skimming can give you a very good *idea* of this story in about half the words—and in *less* than half the time it'd take to read every word.   25

So far, you've seen that previewing and skimming can give you a *general idea* about content—fast. But neither technique can promise   26 more than 50 percent comprehension, because you aren't reading all the words. (Nobody gets something for nothing in the reading game.)

To *read faster and understand most*—if not all—of what you read, you need to know a third technique.   27

3. CLUSTER—TO INCREASE SPEED *AND* COMPREHENSION

Most of us learned to read by looking at each word in a sentence—*one at a time*.   28

Like this: 29

My—brother—Russell—thinks—monsters...

You probably still read this way sometimes, especially when the words are difficult. Or when the words have an extra-special meaning—as in a poem, a Shakespearean play, or a contract. And that's O.K.   30

But word-by-word reading is a rotten way to read faster. It actually *cuts down* on your speed.   31

Clustering trains you to look at *groups* of words instead of one at a time—to increase your speed enormously. For most of us, clustering is a *totally different way of seeing what we read.*   32

Here's how to cluster: Train your eyes to see *all* the words in clusters of up to 3 or 4 words at a glance.   33

Here's how I'd cluster the story we just skimmed: 34

(My brother Russell)(thinks monsters)(live in)
(our bedroom closet)(at night.)(But I told him)(he is crazy.)
("Go and)(check then,")(he said.)
(I didn't want to,)(Russell said)(I was chicken.)
("Am not,")(I said.)
("Are so,")(he said.)
(So I told him)(the monsters)(were going to)(eat him)(at midnight.)
(He started to cry.)(My Dad came in)(and told the monsters)
(to beat it.)(Then he told us)(to go)(to sleep.)
("If I hear)(any more about)(monsters," he said,)("I'll spank you.")
(We went)(to sleep fast.)(And you)(know something?)
(They never did)(come back.)

Learning to read clusters is not something your eyes do naturally. It takes constant practice.   35

Here's how to go about it: Pick something light to read. Read it as fast as you can. Concentrate on seeing 3 to 4 words at once rather than one word at a time. Then reread the piece at your normal speed to see what you missed the first time.

36

Try a second piece. First cluster, then reread to see what you missed in this one.

37

When you can read in clusters without missing much the first time, your speed has increased. Practice 15 minutes every day and you might pick up the technique in a week or so. (But don't be disappointed if it takes longer. Clustering *everything* takes time and practice.)

38

So now you have 3 ways to help you read faster. **Preview** to cut down on unnecessary heavy reading. **Skim** to get a quick, general idea of light reading. And **cluster** to increase your speed *and* comprehension.

39

With enough practice, you'll be able to handle *more* reading at school or work — and at home — *in less time.* You should even have enough time to read your favorite comic books — **and** *War and Peace*!

40

Thinking about the Selection

. . . .

1. Use context clues to determine the meaning of *comprehension* (paragraph 14).

2. Use word analysis to determine the meaning of *correspondence* (paragraph 7).

3. What is Cosby's main idea in this piece?

4. What is the author's purpose?

5. Why do you think he begins by talking about reading comic books?

6. What are three techniques he proposes for learning to read faster?

7. What kinds of materials does he recommend for previewing? Why?

8. What kinds of materials does he recommend for skimming? Why?

9. Do you agree that reading faster is something worth learning? Why or why not?

10. Did you find this piece interesting or engaging? Why or why not?

AMY DICKINSON

When Mommy or Daddy Dates

Amy Dickinson wrote "When Mommy or Daddy Dates" for *Time* magazine in July 2001. She generally writes articles concerning family and relationship issues. She reported on the Littleton massacre and has done a number of radio commentaries for *All Things Considered* on National Public Radio. In "When Mommy or Daddy Dates," Dickinson addresses the difficulties of single-parent dating. The article makes light of the awkwardness single parents are subjected to when dating and ends with an air of optimism.

Vocabulary Preview

Cremora (para. 1): a nondairy creamer (n.)

forge (para. 2): establish (v.)

reflexively (para. 2): automatically, without thinking (adv.)

figuratively (para. 4): not literally or actually (adv.)

refrain (para. 4): hold off (v.)

1   Dating the second time around can be awkward and painful, especially when you're reduced to asking your three-year-old, "Do these pants make Mommy look fat?" I'd like to blame my dates, of course, but their only crime is that they show up. I'm the one with the problem. I have become ridiculously picky and demanding—I once rejected a guy just because he used Cremora in his coffee.

2   Raising children alone and trying to forge a new relationship with another adult are at opposite ends of the spectrum of human experience. Any mother who has reflexively reached over and cut her date's meal into toddler-size pieces knows she has a long distance to travel between Happy Meals and nights of passionate abandon. And fathers who hire a baby sitter in order to get out for an occasional blind date—aware they will have to pay twice for the evening—realize that being "out there" isn't as free or easy as it was the last time they were single.

3   Those of us single parents who date inevitably carry the burden of our previous experiences, and the ex-spouses and kids in our lives can make it feel as if a whole crowd of people is looking over our shoulder. The stakes can seem impossibly high as we wrestle with a very natural instinct to build a new nuclear family. We want to improve on the family that failed and reclaim that hopeful picture of husband, wife and kids we once had in our head.

Given all these complexities, it's a triumph for any of us ever to leave the house. But that's exactly what we need to do, actually and figuratively. Lois Nightingale, a clinical psychologist in Yorba Linda, Calif., notes that dating is an adult experience and advises parents to leave their children out of it. She recommends against bringing a casual date home to spend the night. In fact, she suggests that parents refrain from introducing their dates to their children until a firm relationship has been established, if only to protect the kids from prematurely developing an attachment to another adult. This may be the one thing I've done right as a dating parent; I've never involved my daughter in my romantic misadventures. The policy has paid off, I think, since she still seems to have a favorable opinion of me. But then, I use real cream.

4

Thinking about the Selection

1. What can you guess about the meaning of *spectrum* (paragraph 2) from its context?

2. Use word analysis to determine the meaning of *inevitably* (paragraph 3).

3. Identify the topic sentence in each paragraph.

4. What point is made in the topic sentence of each paragraph?

5. What is the main idea of the essay?

6. What supporting details does the author include to support the main idea?

7. How is the essay organized? What pattern of organization does the author use?

8. What is the author's purpose in this essay?

9. What does the author mean when she writes in paragraph 3 that "kids . . . can make it feel as if a whole crowd of people is looking over our shoulder"?

10. Did you find the essay engaging? Interesting? Why or why not? To what extent can you relate to the experience the author describes?

ROBERT H. FRANK

The Downside of Hearing Whoopi at the Mall

This essay, "The Downside of Hearing Whoopi at the Mall," was written by Robert H. Frank for the *New York Times,* on August 7, 2001. Frank, who is currently a professor of economics at Cornell University, has served as chief economist for the Civil Aeronautics Board and was a fellow at the Center for Advanced Study in the Behavioral Sciences. He has published numerous articles on price and wage discrimination, public utility pricing, and other topics and has written a number of books on human behavior. He received the Critic's Choice Award and appeared on both the *New York Times* Notable Books list and *Business Week* Ten Best list for 1995. In this essay, Frank discusses the new technology of "voice cloning," the process of replicating a celebrity's voice for use in advertisements. He predicts an enormous market for this technology but argues that only a small portion of the population will benefit from the profits.

Vocabulary Preview

facsimile (para. 2): an imitation (n.)
archival (para. 2): stored away in an archive (adj.)

voice cloning (para. 3): a reproduced imitation of a person's voice (n.)

1   In the early 1980's, a friend's wife paid a voice impersonator to tape the greeting for her husband's answering machine as a gift. "Well, John's just not home at the moment," the tape began, in a voice eerily like former President Ronald Reagan's. "But if you'll leave your name and number, Nancy or I will have him get back to you as soon as possible." Last week AT&T announced a breakthrough in synthesized speech software that will put many voice impersonators out of business.

2   The new approach uses fragments of sounds culled from recordings of a subject's voice to recreate speech from printed text. In time, this software will render a lifelike facsimile of someone's voice saying things that he or she never actually said. Archival recordings will even make it possible to reproduce the voices of people long dead. Assuming that AT&T perfects its process and that people retain rights to their own voices, who will be the ultimate winners and losers?

3   Voice cloning is just one of many technologies that expand the market reach of the economy's most able performers. These technologies

increase our national wealth, but they also cause it to be distributed far more unequally. The invention of movies, for example, enabled a small cadre of highly talented stars to displace thousands of less talented stage actors in local theaters.

The new synthetic voices will replace the voices currently used in applications like car navigation systems and message systems, and clones of celebrity voices will be used in radio and television commercials.

4

The voices of noncelebrities will not command high prices, since there is a large number of people who could supply the voice templates for them. Still, the technology will make it possible to use only the best voices for these purposes. People with less perfect voices who are now in this line of work will be displaced. This is a net gain, since we will get announcements of higher quality and the displaced people will be freed up for other useful tasks, but most of them will probably earn less, since for most of them a recording job was their best option.

5

The changes from celebrity voice cloning promise to be more sweeping. Increasingly, advertisers are using the voices of celebrities in national radio and television commercials. So far, however, the expense of taping messages specifically tailored to each location has mostly excluded these voices from local commercials. Voice cloning will change that. The voices announcing this week's sales at neighborhood supermarkets, for example, could soon be those not of unknown local employees, but of, say, Tom Hanks or Whoopi Goldberg.

6

Some celebrities command far more viewer attention than others. That explains why sponsors pay someone like Michael Jordan as much as $40 million a year while most celebrities are of little or no value in the endorsement market. No one yet knows whose voices will prove most effective. But once the winners are identified, intensive bidding to acquire rights to their voice templates will begin.

7

In short, voice cloning, like other similar technologies, will create a winner-take-all market—one in which even small differences in performance give rise to large differences in economic reward. Technologies like this one have been rapidly transforming the American economic landscape: authors of the best tax-advice software have displaced thousands of local tax accountants, and the best Internet auction site has displaced thousands of local retailers. In countless arenas this phenomenon of duplication and distribution enables the best performers to serve ever broader markets.

8

Since cloning frees up resources while giving us services of higher quality, society benefits. But the downside is that the monetary value of these gains is distributed so unequally. The spread of winner-take-all markets helps explain why almost all recent gains in income and wealth have gone to a relatively small number of people atop the economic pyramid.

9

In the 2000 presidential campaign, Al Gore was unable to persuade a sufficiently large majority of American voters that tax cuts for top earners make little sense in such an economy. But once AT&T clones Franklin Delano Roosevelt's eloquent baritone, Democratic strategists will have a new weapon. In our era of sharply rising inequality, would Mr. Bush's razor-thin margin have withstood an updated series of F.D.R.'s fireside chats questioning the wisdom of massive tax cuts for the wealthy?

10

Thinking about the Selection

1. Use word analysis to determine the meaning of *impersonator* and *synthesized* (paragraph 1).

2. Use context clues to determine the meaning of *culled* (paragraph 2) and *option* (paragraph 5).

3. Identify the topic sentence of any two paragraphs.

4. What point is made in each of these topic sentences?

5. What is the main idea of the reading selection?

6. What supporting details and examples does the author use to support this idea?

7. How is the reading selection organized?

8. What is the author's purpose?

9. What are some of the consequences of voice cloning? What will result from its use?

10. Do you think using voices of celebrities in the ways the author describes will be a good thing? Why or why not?

ELLEN GOODMAN

The Suspected Shopper

"The Suspected Shopper" was written by Ellen Goodman for the *Boston Globe* in 1981. Goodman was a Nieman fellow at Harvard University and two years later began writing a column for the *Boston Globe,* which was syndicated by the Washington Post Writers Group. Currently, her Pulitzer Prize–winning column, "At Large," appears in more than 440 newspapers across the country. She also has written a book, *Turning Points,* which addresses issues of social change. Goodman has received numerous awards, including the American Society of Newspaper Editors Distinguished Writing Award, the Hubert H. Humphrey Civil Rights Award, the President's Award from the National Women's Political Caucus, and the American Woman Award. "The Suspected Shopper" addresses the issue of increased security in department stores and the distrust of merchants owing to a rise in theft. The article explores the consumer's feelings of resentment and embarrassment as a reaction to security precautions and the injustice of treating the public as potential criminals.

Vocabulary Preview

venture (para. 5): to risk; walk cautiously out (v.)

gyrations (para. 7): circular or side-to-side movements (n.)

belatedly (para. 8): in an overdue manner (adv.)

errant (para. 10): straying outside the proper bounds (adj.)

1   It is Saturday, Shopping Saturday, as it's called by the merchants who spread their wares like plush welcome mats across the pages of my newspaper.

2   But the real market I discover is a different, less eager place than the one I read about. On this Shopping Saturday I don't find welcomes, I find warnings and wariness.

3   At the first store, a bold sign of the times confronts me: SHOPLIFTERS WILL BE PROSECUTED TO THE FULL EXTENT OF THE LAW.

4   At the second store, instead of a greeter, I find a doorkeeper. It is his job, his duty, to bar my entrance. To pass, I must give up the shopping bag on my arm. I check it in and check it out.

5   At the third store, I venture as far as the dressing room. Here I meet another worker paid to protect the merchandise rather than to

sell it. The guard of this dressing room counts the number of items I carry in and will count the number of items I carry out.

In the mirror, a long, white, plastic security tag juts out from the blouse tucked into the skirt. I try futilely to pat it down along my left hip, try futilely to zip the skirt.

Finally, during these strange gyrations, a thought seeps through years of dulled consciousness, layers of denial. Something has happened to the relationship between shops and shoppers. I no longer feel like a woman in search of a shirt. I feel like an enemy at Checkpoint Charlie.

I finally, belatedly, realize that I am treated less like a customer these days and more like a criminal. And I hate it. This change happened gradually, and understandably. Security rose in tandem with theft. The defenses of the shopkeepers went up, step by step, with the offenses of the thieves.

But now as the weapons escalate, it's the average consumer, the innocent bystander, who is hit by friendly fire.

I don't remember the first time an errant security tag buzzed at the doorway, the first time I saw a camera eye in a dress department. I accepted it as part of the price of living in a tight honesty market.

In the supermarket, they began to insist on a mug shot before they would cash my check. I tried not to take it personally. At the drugstore, the cashier began to staple my bags closed. And I tried not to take it personally.

Now, these experiences have accumulated until I feel routinely treated like a suspect. At the jewelry store, the door is unlocked only for those who pass judgment. In the junior department, the suede pants are permanently attached to the hangers. In the gift shop, the cases are only opened with a key.

I am not surprised anymore, but I am finally aware of just how unpleasant it is to be dealt with as guilty until we prove our innocence. Anyplace we are not known, we are not trusted. The old slogan, "Let the Consumer Beware," has been replaced with a new slogan: "Beware of the Consumer."

It is no fun to be Belgium in the war between sales and security. Thievery has changed the atmosphere of the marketplace. Merchant distrust has spread through the ventilation system of a whole business, a whole city, and it infects all of us.

At the cashier counter today, with my shirt in hand, I the Accused stand quietly while the saleswoman takes my credit card. I watch her round up the usual suspicions. In front of my face, without a hint of embarrassment, she checks my charge number against the list of stolen credit vehicles. While I stand there, she calls the clearinghouse of bad debtors.

Having passed both tests, I am instructed to add my name, address, serial number to the bottom of the charge. She checks one signature against another, the picture against the person. Only then does she release the shirt into my custody.   16

And so this Shopping Saturday I take home six ounces of silk and a load of resentment.   17

Thinking about the Selection

1. Using context clues, determine the meaning of *futilely* in paragraph 6.

2. Use word analysis to determine the meaning of *wariness* in paragraph 2.

3. The main idea in this essay is delayed, rather than appearing in the first paragraph. Where does the author express the main idea of her essay? What is the main idea?

4. What details in the beginning of the essay—before the main idea is stated—support the author's main idea?

5. What details after the main idea support it?

6. What pattern of organization does Goodman use? How many examples does she provide to support the main idea?

7. To what extent have you experienced the kind of problem Goodman describes?

8. What does Goodman think about the many different ways stores check up on their customers?

9. What conclusion does Goodman draw from her shopping experience?

10. What would you say to Goodman or what would you ask her if you could speak with her about this essay? Why?

DANA HAWKINS

Lawsuits Spur Rise in Employee Monitoring

The article "Lawsuits Spur Rise in Employee Monitoring" was written by Dana Hawkins, senior editor of *U.S. News and World Report.* Hawkins has recently received the John Bartlow Martin Award for Public Interest Magazine Journalism and is known for her aggressive investigating abilities. This article addresses the increasing number of companies monitoring their employees' e-mails and computer files to avoid employee misconduct lawsuits. Hawkins explores the legal, ethical, and moral ramifications of this practice.

Vocabulary Preview

collaboration (para. 3): cooperation (n.)

subpoena (para. 3): a legal document ordering the receiver to appear in court (n.)

allegedly (para. 5): presumably (adv.)

1   In case you haven't heard, your company is probably peeking at your E-mail, computer files, and Internet surfing log. But why? Are employers concerned about productivity, worried about workers spilling company secrets, or are they just plain nosy? The answer may be all of the above. But the No. 1 reason for monitoring these days is to avoid the hot lights and high costs of courtroom drama. Companies say they need protection against lawsuits, and surveillance software and other tools that allow them to snoop are becoming less expensive and easier to use.

2   At the same time, some legal experts are taking a contrarian view. They don't believe that companies are always entitled to rummage through workers' E-mails and files for information, which can be used to fire employees at will.

3   A survey of 435 major U.S. firms, to be released this week by the American Management Association, in collaboration with the ePolicy Institute and *U.S. News & World Report,* examines why these companies are monitoring workers. Of the firms surveyed, almost 10 percent report having received a subpoena for employee E-mail. Nearly one third of the largest companies say they've been subpoenaed, and also report firing employees for sending sexually suggestive or otherwise inappropriate E-mails. One quarter of the firms surveyed say they perform key word or phrase searches, usually looking for sexual or scatological language.

The motivation is clear: "Almost every workplace lawsuit today, especially a sexual harassment case, has an E-mail component," says Nancy Flynn, executive director of the ePolicy Institute, which develops E-mail and Internet policies for employers. The survey also found that barely half of firms require staff to acknowledge, in writing, that they understand the company's computer-use policy, which is often vague and buried in an employee handbook.

4

The rise in monitoring and the resultant firings have paralleled the increased reliance on technology in the workplace over recent years. The new Electronic Policies and Practices Survey is a follow-up to the AMA's annual look at employee surveillance, released last spring. That report had found that more than 75 percent of major U.S. firms record and review their workers' communications— double the 1997 figure. Last June, at least 20 state employees in South Dakota were fired or disciplined for allegedly burning job time surfing sports, shopping, and porn sites. An investigation of the 100 workers who visited the most Web sites during a three-week period revealed thousands of inappropriate hits, says a spokesman for the governor's office.

5

E-mail as evidence. Employees are asking why they are so often kept in the dark about when and how their computers are searched. Some workers fired from the *New York Times*'s business office and more recently at Computer Associates International say that although they received offensive E-mail, they did not send it. Both companies dispute the claims. Some employees also say they weren't shown the evidence against them. "We didn't want to bring pornography into the employee meetings, because it's not appropriate," says Deborah Coughlin, a spokesperson for CAI. Giving workers a chance to respond to such accusations can make a big difference. Officials in South Dakota say when they discussed the reports with workers, one was cleared because he successfully argued that he wasn't even in the office when his computer recorded a substantial number of visits to questionable Web sites.

6

James M. Rosenbaum, chief judge of the U.S. District Court in Minneapolis, is challenging the conventional wisdom that businesses own not only the computers that employees use but also the personal messages, unfinished drafts, and other thoughts that they casually type into them. In a recent essay published in the *Green Bag*, a law review, Judge Rosenbaum proposes that investigations of workers' computers be handled like other legal searches. Compa-

7

nies should have probable cause, searches must be limited in scope, and employees need to be given prior notice and allowed to be present during the search, he argues. "I'll bet you all the money in the world I can go into your computer and find a basis to fire you," says Rosenbaum. "Computers never forget, which would be terrific if humans were perfect, but they aren't."

Thinking about the Selection

1. Use context clues to determine the meaning of *rummage* (paragraph 2) and *scatological* (paragraph 3).

2. Use word analysis to determine the meaning of *contrarian* (paragraph 2).

3. Identify the topic sentences in any two paragraphs.

4. What is the main point of each of those topic sentences?

5. What is the main idea of the article overall?

6. What details and examples does the author provide to support the main idea?

7. How is the article organized?

8. What is the author's purpose?

9. Identify two quotations used in the article and explain what function they serve in the article.

10. Do you think that companies should monitor (or snoop around) their employees' e-mail? Why or why not?

DOUGLAS McCOLLAM
The Bull Shark

The article "The Bull Shark" was written for *Slate* magazine in July 2001 by Douglas McCollam, a senior reporter at *American Lawyer* magazine. McCollam discusses the recent increase in shark attacks and gives a detailed description of the bull shark. He also points out that the attacks are due to an increase in the number of bathers, rather than an increase in the number of sharks or unprecedented aggressiveness.

Vocabulary Preview

lapsed (para. 1): fell (v.)

contemplating (para. 2): thinking about (v.)

MO (para. 2): *modus operandi,* method of operation (n.)

bovine (para. 3): like a cow or a bull (adj.)

pugnacious (para. 4): aggressive (adj.)

penchant (para. 4): tendency; inclination (n.)

spate (para. 8): increased number (n.)

1   On July 6, as 8-year-old Jessie Arbogast waded in about 2 feet of water along Florida's Gulf Islands National Seashore, a 7-foot-long bull shark ambushed him, tearing off his right arm and a chunk of his right leg. The attack came so near to shore that Jessie's uncle and another beachgoer were able to grab the shark and drag it onto land where park rangers shot it, pried its mouth open, and retrieved the severed arm. The boy almost bled to death and lapsed into a coma. Surgeons reattached the limb, and though Jessie is showing signs of coming to, doctors say it's too soon to know if he'll make a full recovery.

2   Earlier that day, just a few miles away, I was standing on the dock of my family's house contemplating a swim. I can't claim a premonition, but something made me hesitate. Call it a flash of anxiety. A thought of how the once benign waters of the Florida Panhandle have seemed a little less inviting this past year. Last summer, not far from the scene of the Arbogast attack, a bull shark ripped the swimming platform off a 22-foot speed boat. The same week, bull sharks mauled a group of triathletes as they trained 15 miles down the coast. Chuck Anderson, a 44-year-old school assistant principal, lost his right hand and much of his arm and barely made it to

shore as the sharks trailed him. Less than two months later Thadeus Kubinski, a retired businessman living near Tampa Bay, was attacked by a bull shark when he jumped off his backyard dock into five feet of water. His stunned wife ran to call 911. Kubinski died before help arrived. As I finished this story, the Associated Press reports that a man surfing just down the beach from the scene of the Arbogast attack was bitten while sitting on his board. He was taken to the same hospital, but his condition did not appear serious. The culprit wasn't identified, but the attack fit the bull shark's MO.

Chances are you've never heard of the bull shark. That's not a [3] surprise. It doesn't enjoy the fearsome reputation or star power of other man-eaters. Its hide is dull gray. It's about as streamlined as a backhoe, its beady eyes are set far forward on a thick snout, giving it a top-heavy, somewhat bovine appearance (hence the name). Hardly the stuff of Hollywood legends. Like your quiet next-door neighbor, the bull shark seems an unlikely killer. Still, many experts consider it the most dangerous shark in the world. And if you think you can avoid it this summer by sticking to the shallow water, or even back bays and estuaries, think again. As its recent victims found out, the bull shark is liable to turn up anywhere.

Contrary to popular perception, only three kinds of sharks con- [4] sistently attack humans: the great white of *Jaws* fame; the tiger shark, bane of Hawaiian surfers; and the bull shark. Whites and tigers are well known and feared: The majestic bruisers often exceed 15 feet in length and weigh a ton or more. Bull sharks are comparative runts, usually measuring 7 to 10 feet and topping out at between 400 and 500 pounds. But their size is a poor indicator of their lethality. The bull's pugnacious disposition and penchant for sudden attacks in seemingly safe surroundings make it the pit bull of the shark family.

All sharks sometimes venture close to shore, but bull sharks are [5] the only killers that like to hang out in water where your feet touch bottom. They inhabit temperate seas throughout the world, and their domestic range extends from the southern coast of Massachusetts to the Florida Keys and around the Gulf of Mexico. They are far less common in the cold-water currents of the West Coast, the domain of the great white. More alarmingly, bull sharks can't be counted on to keep to the ocean. They are the only shark, and one of the few creatures of any kind, that can live in either salt or fresh water. Though they normally prefer tropical and subtropical seas, bull sharks have been found in the Mississippi River above New Orleans and have attacked bathers in the Ganges and the Amazon. Lake Nicaragua was thought to have a unique species of freshwater shark until it was discovered that the beasts were bull sharks swimming upstream from the Caribbean, braving the rapids on the San Juan river like salmon coming home to spawn. Many researchers think a bull was the legendary "Jersey man-eater," the shark that killed several swimmers in Mattawan Creek in 1916 and inspired Peter Benchley to write *Jaws*. However, Michael Capuzzo's recent best seller about the attacks, *Close to Shore*, fingers a juvenile great white.

The bull shark possesses an indiscriminate palate: It will eat just about anything—other sharks, dolphins, and porpoises. (That stuff about dolphins meaning there aren't sharks around? Forget it.) Compared to their cousins the tiger and blue sharks—whose large, dark, disc of an eye make them such efficient sight hunters—the bull shark is as blind as Magoo. They often hunt in murky waters where visual acuity is less of a factor. Like all sharks, they command a keen sense of smell and can detect erratic movements from long distances. When zeroing in on prey, bulls use either a "bump and bite" technique to investigate the target or a more deadly rush attack where it delivers maximum damage immediately. As its stout build is complemented by disproportionally large jaws and teeth, the bull's bite is a deadly, shredding, vise.

6

The ubiquity of the plain-jane bull sharks lead some to assume they are a local species. In Africa they are often called the Zambezi shark. In India, the Ganges shark. In Australia, shovelnose, slipway grey, and Swan River sharks. In other parts of the world they go by square-nose, cub, or Van Rooyen's shark. By whatever name, bulls are known as an accomplished ambush predator. Since so many of its attacks occur in remote regions and are attributed to local fauna, the global total of bull shark attacks is difficult to calculate.

7

Despite the recent spate of incidents, shark attack remains a freak accident. Though it's often reported that the number of attacks worldwide is up sharply, the rate of attack has remained more or less constant. There are just more people in the water. To lessen your chance of attack, avoid brightly colored clothes or jewelry in the water; don't swim near dawn or dusk (when Jessie Arbogast was attacked); stay away from schooling bait fish; and, stay out of the water when you are bleeding.

8

I grew up swimming on the stretch of beach where Jessie was   9
attacked. My friends and I would tow rafts out to the edge of deep
water to dive for sand dollars and go spear fishing along the jetties
and sandbars. We never thought much about sharks, and in all
those years I never laid eyes on one, unless it was being hauled in to
a boat or weighed in at a dock. The sharks were always there of
course, just out of sight. But we knew they never did anything to
people. Almost never.

That old certitude seemed far away as I stood alone on my dock   10
staring down into the water with visions of Thadeus Kubinski and
Chuck Anderson flashing in my head. My jitters were irrational, I
knew. Worrying about being attacked by a shark every time you
swim in the ocean is like worrying about being struck by lighting
every time you run in the park: It happens, but c'mon, you still take
the run. Then, just as I was laughing off my anxiety and ready to
jump, a local fisherman's words about sharks and where you find
them came back to me:

Three feet long;
Or three feet between the eyes.
Thirty miles out;
Or as far as you can throw a baseball.
You never know.

I turned around and went upstairs.   11

Thinking about the Selection

1. Use context clues to determine the meaning of *benign* (paragraph 2), *estuaries* (paragraph 3), *indiscriminate* (paragraph 6), and *ubiquity* (paragraph 7).

2. Use word analysis to determine the meaning of *premonition* (paragraph 2), *triathletes* (paragraph 2), and *disproportionally* (paragraph 6).

3. This article begins with two paragraphs that describe stories about bull shark attacks. Where does the author explain his thesis or main idea? What is the author's main idea?

4. Identify the topic sentences in paragraphs 4, 5, and 6.

5. What details does the author include to support the topic sentence of paragraph 4?

6. How does the bull shark differ from the tiger shark and the great white shark?

7. Why does the author call the bull shark the "pit bull of the shark family" (paragraph 4)?

8. What is the author's point of view about bull sharks?

9. What is the author's purpose in writing this article?

10. Did you find the article engaging? Why or why not?

SUSANNAH MEADOWS

The Water of the Moment

"The Water of the Moment" was written by Susannah Meadows for *Newsweek* in July 2001. Meadows is the general editor of *Newsweek*'s Periscope section. Prior to that position, she worked at *GQ* magazine. In this article, Meadows provides statistical data on the growing popularity of bottled water. She also discusses the lengths to which Americans are willing to go, or pay, to get imported bottled water.

Vocabulary Preview

guzzled (para. 1): swallowed quickly in large gulps (v.)

eminence (para. 2): high position of importance (n.)

collaborated (para. 2): worked together closely (v.)

quench (para. 4): satisfy (v.)

infatuation (para. 5): all-absorbing passion (n.)

1   Even though American water is some of the cleanest on tap, bottled water is the country's fastest-growing drink. At the current pace, the amount of bottled water guzzled is on track to outdo milk, beer and coffee. By 2004 only soft-drink consumption will exceed the volume of bottled water Americans gulp down. Even Coke and Pepsi have jumped in, each spending millions launching competing water brands (Dasani and Aquafina). But it gets better: the current bottle of choice, before it wets the lips of celebrities and foodies, is shipped 5,500 miles across the Pacific ocean, from the Fiji Islands. Superchef Jean-Georges Vongerichten says Fiji Natural Artesian Water is lighter and more neutral-tasting than other water. But he doesn't cook with it as often as he'd like because it's too expensive. "I wish I had a well connected to Fiji."

2   Even more remarkable than its eminence are the logistics of shipping water from paradise. Turns out the distinctive square shape of the bottle was designed to save shipping costs as well as look cool. Square bottles simply use space in cargo holds more efficiently. Fiji's chairman, Canadian-born David Gilmour, collaborated with HMG Worldwide, the creator of L'Eggs pantyhose's egg-shaped packaging, to create the bottle's practical good looks.

3   The water is bottled at an eight-month-old plant built right on top of the source — ancient rainwater sandwiched between layers of

volcanic rock—use of which is leased from the government of Fiji for a percentage of the water's sales. Every week a container ship from Auckland, New Zealand, swings by Fiji on its way to the West Coast. The elegant bottles share space onboard with "grinding" beef bound for fast-food chain Carl's Junior and frozen tuna headed for a Bumble Bee factory. After two unrefrigerated weeks at sea, the water is unloaded in L.A.

Back in Fiji, where the tap water can make you sick, some natives marvel at the lengths Americans go to quench their thirst. "We just sort of laugh at it," says Elisapeci Tamanisau of the Fiji Trade and Investments Board. But that doesn't make Fijians any less happy about the jobs and publicity the company's brought to them. Gilmour founded the company in 1996, borrowing geologists from his gold business to tap the Fiji source. Since then the brand has ridden high on word of mouth born at his exclusive thatch-roof resort in Fiji, the Wakaya Club, which reportedly sheltered Tom Cruise just last week. After Pierce Brosnan's stay, the distinctive bottle showed up mid sex scene in his film *The Thomas Crown Affair*.

4

Not even recent studies debunking the purity of bottled water can derail the American infatuation with the product. Fiji water has used the research to its advantage. When HMG focus groups found that people were most concerned with making sure their bottled water was clean and pure, the package designers slapped a map of Fiji on the back of the bottle. The drawing of the stranded little islands is meant to illustrate their safe distance from the contamination of other lands. Now, however, another remote island is providing some new competition. Coming soon from the lower left corner of the map is Cape Grim bottled Tasmanian rainwater. Even Fiji may have a devil of a time beating back such a delicacy.

5

Thinking about the Selection

1. Use context clues to determine the meaning of *debunking* and *derail* in paragraph 5.

2. Use word analysis to determine the meaning of *consumption* (paragraph 1) and *contamination* (paragraph 5).

3. What is the topic sentence of each paragraph?

4. What is the main point of each paragraph?

5. What details are used to support the topic sentence of each paragraph?

6. What is the overall topic of the essay, and what is its thesis or main idea?

7. How is the essay organized?

8. What is the writer's purpose?

9. What points of view are expressed by the two people quoted in the essay—in paragraphs 1 and 4?

10. What do you think about bottled water? Do you buy it and drink it? Why or why not?

MIKI MEEK

You Can't Hide Those Lying Eyes in Tampa

Miki Meek wrote the article "You Can't Hide Those Lying Eyes in Tampa" for *U.S. News and World Report* in August 2001. She has also reported on politics, immigration, and education. As a student, Meek wrote for Brigham Young University's student newspaper, *The Daily Universe*. She won the 2000 Mark of Excellence Award from the Society of Professional Journalists. In this article, Meek discusses the use of television cameras to monitor public activity as a means of fighting crime. As she explores the pros and cons, she provides the opinions of both supporters and opponents.

Vocabulary Preview

pedestrians (para. 1): walkers (n.)
felons (para. 1): criminals (n.)
virtual (para. 3): not physically real (adj.)

trumped (para. 6): outdone or surpassed (v.)
thermal (para. 6): heat-sensing (adj.)

1   It's a typical day in Tampa: hot with lots of sunshine. As always, pedestrians flood the city's entertainment district, window-shopping and slipping into bars like the Green Iguana that line the colorful streets. What's not typical are the cameras scanning their every move: In July, the city installed 36 cameras in this high-crime part of town designed to randomly pluck wanted felons and missing kids out of the street crowds. But not everyone's smiling about this real-life version of *The Truman Show,* which has sparked a growing debate over privacy rights versus public safety.

2   "Our comings and goings are none of the government's damned business," growls House Majority Leader Dick Armey, R-Texas, who has called for congressional hearings into the use of the crime-fighting cameras. "It seems to me that we are taking a step that is a step too far."

3   Armey and other opponents like Randall Marshall, director of Florida's American Civil Liberties Union, charge that the cameras, which are strapped to utility poles, violate residents' privacy rights by putting folks not under suspicion in a "virtual lineup." Critics also say their use violates the Fourth Amendment, which prohibits unreasonable searches and seizures. Not so, say supporters, who

insist this is a constitutional and cutting-edge way of nabbing criminals and finding missing persons. "This is no different than a police officer standing on a street corner with a handful of wanted pictures, except for that it's more accurate and stops trouble faster," says Bill Todd, a Tampa detective who's in charge of the project. Todd says Tampa police first used face scanners at January's Super Bowl, where they picked 19 petty criminals out of 100,000 fans.

Tampa is the first city to install the controversial cameras; Virginia Beach, Va., has applied for a $150,000 state grant for a similar system. And many other cities are keeping an eye on Tampa—and the heated constitutional debate—to determine whether they should invest in such scanners, which utilize face-recognition technology to identify missing and wanted persons.

So how does the system work? Computers at police headquarters break down facial images of people captured on camera into 80 reference points such as the distance between the eyes and nose. An alarm goes off if the system matches 14 of those points with an image in its database; an officer then decides whether there are enough similarities to alert a cop on patrol to make an arrest. Nonmatching images are erased from the system.

Better to know? "Wouldn't you want to know if a murderer or rapist is sitting next to you while you're eating a sandwich? I would," says Joseph Atick, president and CEO of Visionics Corp., the maker of the face-scanning technology being used in Tampa. In 1998, his company installed the same system in the London Borough of Newham, England; the crime rate there dropped by 44 percent from 1998 to 2000. But the ACLU's Marshall says knowing may be trumped by privacy concerns. "The expectation of privacy can't simply depend on the technology available at any given moment," he says. The Supreme Court ruled last month in a marijuana case that police must obtain a search warrant before using thermal imagers to monitor activities inside a home. Kevin Watson of the Law Enforcement Alliance of America says that the ruling could set a precedent for police who use high-tech surveillance gadgets such as face scanners.

There's also a debate brewing over how, and whether, face-scanning data should be retained, disclosed, and sold or shared with third parties. Democratic California State Sen. Debra Bowen is currently crafting legislation that would require police in her state to obtain warrants before using face scanners and would bar them from sharing the data with third parties. Otherwise, she warns, cities could end up in court like San Diego, where 290 motorists are now challenging tickets they received after being snapped running red lights by cameras.

Says John Woodward of the Rand corporation: "It's a classic issue—an emerging technology that has the potential for great good and for great evil."

8

Thinking about the Selection

1. Use context to determine the meaning of *pluck* (paragraph 1) and *nabbing* (paragraph 3).

2. Use word analysis to determine the meaning of *controversial* (paragraph 4).

3. What is the topic sentence of each paragraph?

4. What is the main point of each paragraph?

5. What details are used to support the topic sentence of each paragraph?

6. What is the overall topic of the essay, and what is its thesis or main idea?

7. How does the writer organize this essay?

8. What is the writer's purpose?

9. Which words indicate the writer's point of view on the privacy issue?

10. What is your opinion about the use of street cameras? Do you think this emerging technology has more potential for good or more potential for harm? Why?

A. M. ROSENTHAL

The Way She Died

A. M. Rosenthal wrote the article "The Way She Died" for the March 15, 1994, issue of the *New York Times*. Rosenthal is an international journalist, columnist, and former executive editor of the *Times*. He was recently recognized for educating the public about the plight of the Tibetan people. He has also received numerous awards including the Light of Truth Award and the Pulitzer Prize. In this article, Rosenthal recalls a murder story in which thirty-eight bystanders watched a man repeatedly stab a woman to death. The attack lasted for a half hour, yet no one helped the victim or even called the police. The article explores the bystanders' apathy and the public's reaction to the story.

Vocabulary Preview

apathy (para. 4): lack of interest or caring (n.)

unctuous (para. 15): smug (adj.)

She died on the street, near her house in Queens, stabbed to death in the early morning of March 13, 1964. It wasn't much of a story; an editor in the *New York Times* newsroom held up a thumb and forefinger, meaning keep it short. 1

Four paragraphs appeared, written by a young police reporter. Even in the newsroom they were barely noticed. But two weeks later Catherine Genovese's name became known around the world. 2

For 30 years now, the half-hour before she died of her wounds have been studied in classes from grade school to universities, dissected in graduate seminars and related in church sermons, all in the search for some meaning. 3

A few days after the murder, I had lunch with Police Commissioner Michael Joseph Murphy. I was metropolitan editor of the *Times* then and we had talked occasionally about public apathy toward crime. 4

That day, at Emil's, near City Hall, he told me a story that made him shake his head. We checked it out, and on March 17 a story by Martin Gansberg appeared on the front page. It began: 5

"For more than half an hour, 38 respectable, law-abiding citizens in Queens watched a killer stalk and stab a woman in three separate attacks in Kew Gardens. 6

"Twice the sound of their voices and the glow of their bedroom lights interrupted him and frightened him off. Each time he returned, sought her out and stabbed her again. Not one person telephoned the police during the assault; one witness called after the woman was dead."   7

If any of the 38 witnesses had called during the first attack, the police said, Catherine Genovese, 28 years old, might have been saved.   8

When reporters talked to the witnesses, some said they did not want to get involved. One man said he was tired. Most, asked why they had done nothing, just said, "I don't know."   9

Later, some of the witnesses and their neighbors became angry. They told the reporters it was unfair how they kept writing about Austin Street, where Catherine Genovese died, and how they were giving the neighborhood a bad name, go away.   10

Reporters then consulted "experts." Mostly the answers were what you would expect—blahblahblah. A theologian said blah-blah maybe the city was "depersonalized." Then he said: "Don't quote me." That was the only funny thing that happened.   11

The police arrested a man called Winston Moseley. He was convicted, and received a life sentence. He is in the Green Haven correctional institution in Dutchess County, New York.   12

But how could it happen—38 witnesses keeping silent while Catherine Genovese died? I get letters, some of them from children studying the Genovese case in fifth or sixth grade. A teacher wrote that her children wept when they heard the story.   13

Sometimes I write to the children that maybe the fact that Catherine Genovese is remembered will mean that fewer people will turn away.   14

That's unctuous nonsense. It is difficult to say to the children—no, her death has not helped diminish apathy. But that is what I believe. In our city and country, there is more violence, more apathy toward it, not less.   15

For a while after Catherine Genovese died, reporters came up with a string of "apathy" stories. Ten years ago, when we printed a story about neighbors doing nothing during a courtyard shooting, the reporter mentioned her name.   16

But the thing is, "apathy" is not really news anymore. Every week, sometimes often in one week, somebody gets murdered before witnesses in our city—an execution on a drug corner, or death in a drive-by splatter of bullets.   17

When I see the scene in my mind, I know that there must have been lots of witnesses—in the streets, or watching from windows.   18

But the thought that they walked away or pulled their heads in does not startle me anymore. I take it for granted. If I were still an editor I would probably not bother to send reporters to search out witnesses, it seems so commonplace now, silent witness.   19

These years, when I think of how excited we all got about the story of neighbors who refused to get involved while a woman was killed, and how everybody was startled that it could actually happen, that time seems very distant, almost naive.   20

But how can you write that to children who cry at the memory of Catherine Genovese, and the manner of her dying?   21

Thinking about the Selection

1. Use word analysis to determine the meaning of *dissected* (paragraph 3).

2. Use context clues to determine the meaning of *stalk* (paragraph 6).

3. What is the importance and the effect of the headline for Rosenthal's piece?

4. Identify the topic sentence of any two paragraphs.

5. Identify the main point of any two paragraphs.

6. Select two details that are especially effective and meaningful. Explain why.

7. What is the overall point the writer is making in this article?

8. What is the writer's point of view toward the neighbors? How do you know?

9. Did you find this piece interesting? Engaging? Why or why not?

10. If you could ask the author of this article one question, what would it be? Why?

MICHAEL UTLEY

My Personal Bolt of Lightning

"My Personal Bolt of Lightning" was originally written for the *New York Times* in August 2001 by Michael Utley, an amateur golfer on leave from his position as vice president at UBS PaineWebber. In the article, he gives a personal account of being struck by lightning and warns readers of the threat. The incident injured his brain so severely that he was forced to relearn basic motor skills.

Vocabulary Preview

charred (para. 1): burned, blackened (adj.)
C.P.R. (para. 4): cardiopulmonary resuscitation, a lifesaving technique used to stimulate the heart and lungs when a person is near death (n.)
disseminates (para. 10): distributes (v.)

1   I never believed that I could be in danger on a golf course—until I was struck by lightning on one last year. What I learned that spring day is that lightning is an underrated killer that fries minds and turns bodies into charred shells.

2   I was playing in a charity golf tournament on Cape Cod. The sky was clear when our foursome joined in a shotgun start—players on every hole teeing off at the same time. My group was just finishing at the 10th hole when a horn, the signal for a storm threat, began blaring. We rushed toward our carts, heading for the clubhouse, but we were still far out on the course when I was struck. My life changed in seconds.

3   I understand the strike had a halo effect. The other players heard a loud bang and saw me stumble to the ground. They say smoke came from my body. The charge hit my head and lower body and then exited through my feet. My shoes flew off.

4   For a long 10 minutes, my golfing partners performed C.P.R., forcing life into me. At one point my friends thought I was dead—I had stopped breathing. I "died" a second time in the ambulance.

5   I remember none of this. A few days later I woke up in intensive care, but I didn't recover my memory for more than a month. Now, more than a year later, I am still working at rehabilitation from the physical disabilities I was left with.

6   It is our cultural habit not to take lightning seriously. Winning the lottery jackpot or finding the perfect husband is said to be

"about as likely as getting struck by lighting"—which is meant to convey that there's virtually no chance at all. Most Americans consider thunderstorms minor, if dramatic, inconveniences. Traffic keeps moving and outdoor games go on, despite the thunder, until pelting rain arrives. But while my experience may not be common, it's not freakish, either—and I invite casual risk takers to consider its severity.

Over the past 30 years, an average of 73 people a year have been killed by lightning in the United States, according to the National Weather Service, and about 300 are struck each year and survive. Since victims of lightning don't die from burns, but from cardiac arrest, it was my good fortune that one of my golfing buddies had just completed a refresher course in C.P.R. But still my body was profoundly shocked and my brain was damaged—and this is typical. 7

At 49, I am relearning basic motor skills—how to eat, shave, dress, walk down a hall without bumping into walls. I can't toss my little girl in the air. Sometimes the pain in my damaged nerves is intense. 8

I don't like the effect on my family. The people I most love are now caregivers. Insurers have told me that I will probably continue to need medical care—when I applied for long-term disability insurance, I received a letter stating I had been turned down "due to your medical history of lightning strike." 9

There are organized efforts to warn people about lightning. The National Oceanic and Atmospheric Administration issues alerts and disseminates the relevant advice: Go indoors at the first rumbling of thunder; stay clear of trees, water, wire objects and heavy equipment; don't use the telephone during a storm. The PGA Tour requires that a meteorologist be present at every event, to stop play when there's danger of lightning. 10

Yet I suspect most people are still as unaware of this particular danger as I used to be. More Americans are killed by lightning each year than by hurricanes or tornadoes—and many more than are killed by sharks. You'd never know this, however, from news coverage or even from popular lore. 11

Perhaps it is only natural that the press concentrates on dangers that threaten many people at once, and that stories are told and retold of events with many witnesses. Deaths and injuries from lightning are isolated and far-flung—easy to overlook or ignore. Unless, of course, you have been a victim. 12

Thinking about the Selection

1. Use context clues to determine the meaning of *shotgun start* (paragraph 2).

2. Use word analysis to determine the meaning of *meteorologist* (paragraph 10).

3. What is the thesis statement or main point of the essay?

4. What kind of support does the writer provide for his thesis or main idea?

5. What specific details does the author use to describe the effects of being struck by lightning?

6. What is the author's purpose in writing this essay?

7. Why does the author include statistics? What purpose do those numbers serve?

8. How did the author survive being struck by lightning? What aftereffects did he experience?

9. Did you find this essay interesting? Why or why not?

10. What do you think of the author's advice about protecting yourself when lightning strikes?

Using a College Dictionary

In the same way that a library is important to the intellectual life of a college, so is your college dictionary central to your academic work. If you have not already done so, you need to acquire a good college-level dictionary that includes between 150,000 to 200,000 words. One of the following would be fine in either a book or a CD-ROM version:

> *The American Heritage College Dictionary.* 4th ed. Boston: Houghton Mifflin, 2002.
>
> *Random House Webster's College Dictionary.* 2nd rev. ed. New York: Random House, 2000.
>
> *Webster's New World College Dictionary.* 4th ed. New York: Hungry Minds, 1999.

■ Getting Acquainted with Your Dictionary

A dictionary is a mini-library of information, a mini-encyclopedia of knowledge. It includes information about history and geography, brief biographical identification of historical figures, and the names of country and state capitals. It typically includes weights and measures and a list of the world's currencies. However, dictionaries mostly contain information about words, including spelling, pronunciation, part of speech, meaning, and origin (also called *etymology*).

Usually dictionaries consist of a section for each letter of the alphabet; within each section, the words beginning with that letter are listed alphabetically. The entry for each word generally begins with the word itself, divided into its syllables, which are usually separated by a small dot. Following the word is a pronunciation guide that uses symbols to show how the word is spoken. After this guide is a notation listing which part of speech the word is (noun, verb, adjective, and so on). The word's definitions usually follow and are followed in turn by a notation that tells about the word's origin. Look at the following sample entry for the word *marmoset,* taken from the *American Heritage College Dictionary.*

> **mar•mo•set** (mär′mə-sĕt′, -zĕt′) *n.* Any of various small, clawed monkeys of the genera *Callithrix* and *Cebuella* of the American tropics, having tufted ears and long tails. [ME *marmusette,* a small monkey < OFr. *marmouset,* grotesque figurine, alteration of *marmotte,* marmot. See MARMOT.]

In this definition, you may not recognize every symbol, but you can see the different parts of the entry. This appendix will help you understand these symbols and parts of dictionary definitions and will help you learn to use them as well.

■ Spelling

If you can't spell a word, how can you look it up? It's a logical question, and there are three good answers. First, of course, is that you often look up unfamiliar words that you encounter when you read, so the spelling is right in front of you. Second, problems with the spelling of words rarely involve their first three or four letters, which are all you usually need to find a word in the dictionary. Third, when a word has a complicated or unusual spelling, you can usually guess one or two different ways it might be spelled and try them both. Some words beginning with the *f* sound, for example, begin with *ph;* some words beginning with the *s* sound begin with *c,* and so on. Use what you already know about spelling rules in general, and in most cases you will be able to find the word.

The dictionary provides the correct spelling of words in English, as well as many commonly used foreign words and expressions such as *laissez-faire* and *faux pas.* It also indicates alternative spellings when more than one is acceptable. The word *marshal,* for example, can also be spelled *marshall.* When two spellings are indicated, often one is preferred. This preferred spelling is usually given first.

In addition, the dictionary will also indicate British spellings for words such as *color* (British: *colour*); *reflection* (British: *reflexion*); and *realize* (British: *realise*).

■ Pronunciation

One of the more immediately useful functions of a dictionary is to indicate how words are pronounced. When you learn a new word in your reading, you may want to use it in conversation—and you will want to pronounce it correctly.

Like other dictionaries, the *American Heritage College Dictionary* provides a pronunciation key on every page or two-page spread. This will help you understand what the symbols mean in the pronunciation guide for each word. If you look closely at the small print, you will see how each of the symbols listed next to the word should be pronounced. You can figure this out by looking first for the ′ mark, which indicates the syllable that is stressed or accented. Next take each vowel sound. Look at how it is configured with any marks and find the corresponding item in the pronunciation key.

ă	pat	oi	b**oy**
ā	p**ay**	ou	**ou**t
âr	c**are**	o͝o	t**oo**k
ä	f**a**ther	o͞o	b**oo**t
ĕ	p**e**t	ŭ	c**u**t
ē	b**e**	ûr	**ur**ge
ĭ	p**i**t	th	**th**in
ī	p**ie**	*th*	**th**is
îr	p**ier**	hw	**wh**ich
ŏ	p**o**t	zh	vi**s**ion
ō	t**oe**	ə	**a**bout, it**e**m
ô	p**aw**		

Stress marks:
′ (primary); ′ (secondary), as in
dictionary (dĭk′shə-nĕr′ē)

This chart contains two kinds of information. First, each sound is indicated by a short word that shows how it should be pronounced. The vowel combination *oi*, for example, sounds like the *oy* in *boy*. Second, the example of the word *dictionary* is given at the base of the chart to indicate primary and secondary accents. These heavier and lighter accent marks indicate which syllables you should stress when saying the word and which syllable receives the strongest stress or accent.

If you come across the word *epitome,* for example, you might wonder how to pronounce it. Does its ending rhyme with *Rome*? Is it accented on the first, second, or third syllable? Are the vowels long or short? Does the *e* sound like the *e* in *me* or the *e* in *get,* or some other way? Does the *i* sound like the *i* in *line* or the *i* in *lit*? And what of the *e* at the end of the word? Is it pronounced or not?

Here is how the word is shown to be sounded in the *Random House Webster's College Dictionary:*

e•pit•o•me (ĭ-pĭt′ə-mē)

Notice the little swirled line above the first letter of the pronunciation guide. It indicates that the first *e* in *epitome* sounds more like an *i*—a short *i* sound like the one in the word *it.* This is also the sound of the *i* in *pit* as well. Notice too that the accent falls on the *i*—the syllable *pit* is stressed when saying *epitome.* Look next to the end of the word, at the *e.* That sound is long, the *e* sound of *me.* Finally, look at the symbol designating the *o* sound in the word. This is a schwa, which looks like an upside down and backward letter *e.* The schwa is pronounced "uh"— the sound of *a* in *about.* It is never accented.

What you have been doing in breaking down the word *epitome* to understand how to pronounce it is similar to what you did earlier in breaking words down into their roots, prefixes, and suffixes to understand their meanings. In both types of learning you have been making careful observations about language. You also made connections between words that use similar roots, prefixes, and suffixes. In addition, you are connecting what you know about the sound values of short and long vowels to what you see provided in the dictionary pronunciation chart.

Exercise A-1

Look up the following words. Then in a small group, practice pronouncing the words for each other, until you can agree on the correct pronunciation. Use the dictionary pronunciation charts for guidance.

1. *hypothermia*

2. *mesomorph*

3. *metallurgy*

4. *obloquy*

5. *hematoma*   8. *hyperkinesis*

6. *loggia*   9. *marjoram*

7. *atomism*   10. *monetarism*

. . . .

■ Part of Speech

Your dictionary will also indicate the part of speech for each word. There are eight parts of speech: noun, pronoun, verb, adjective, adverb, preposition, conjunction, and interjection. The accompanying chart defines and illustrates each.

THE PARTS OF SPEECH

Part of Speech	Function	Example
verb	indicates action or state of being	*talk, think, care, seem, run*
noun	names a person, place, thing, concept, or quality	*George Washington, Shirley Jones, house, sister, dime, history, despair*
pronoun	takes the place of a noun	*I, you, he, she, it, us, her, they, ours, anyone, myself, himself*
adjective	describes (modifies or qualifies) a noun or pronoun	*handsome, tired, old, clever, desperate, clumsy*
adverb	describes a verb, adjective, or another adverb	*often, courteously, noisily, nevertheless, really*
preposition	indicates the relationship between a noun or pronoun and another word in a sentence	*to, from, with, behind, by, above, beyond, through*
conjunction	links or joins words, phrases, and clauses	*and, but, or, nor, for, so, yet*
interjection	expresses surprise or emotion	*Hey, Oh, Wow, Ah*

For words that can function as more than a single part of speech—such as *book*, which can be a noun *(I bought a book)* or a verb *(I need to book a room)*—dictionaries give separate meanings for each part of speech.

Dictionaries abbreviate the parts of speech. *Adjective,* for example, is usually abbreviated *adj.* to distinguish it from *adverb,* which is abbreviated *adv.* Nouns are abbreviated *n.,* and verbs are designated by *v.* If you are not sure what an abbreviation stands for, consult the glossary in the front or back of the dictionary, where all symbols are explained. If you're not sure what part of speech a word is, consult your dictionary.

Exercise A-2

Use your dictionary to identify the part of speech of each of the following words. Then use each word in a sentence. If a word functions as more than a single part of speech, write a sentence for each part of speech. The first one is done for you.

Example:

rose   PART(S) OF SPEECH: *noun; adjective; verb (past tense of "rise")*

SENTENCE(S):   *A single red rose adorned her dress. The dress*

was a deep rose color. I rose early this morning.

1.   *click*   PART(S) OF SPEECH: _____

SENTENCE(S): _____

_____

_____

2.   *engage*   PART(S) OF SPEECH: _____

SENTENCE(S): _____

_____

_____

3.   *charisma*   PART(S) OF SPEECH: _____

SENTENCE(S): _____

_____

_____

4. *justice*   PART(S) OF SPEECH: _____

    SENTENCE(S): _____

    _____

    _____

5. *flutter*   PART(S) OF SPEECH: _____

    SENTENCE(S): _____

    _____

    _____

. . . .

■ Meanings

This section is entitled *meanings,* with an *s,* because many words have more than one meaning. Sometimes the meanings are very different. Sometimes the meanings can be so different as to be opposite. *Cleave,* for example, means both "to split or divide," as with a cleaver, and "to adhere closely, to cling," as in a man should cleave to his wife.

Usually a word with multiple meanings will not contain opposite meanings, but rather a range of related meanings. The word *drum,* for example, means a musical percussion instrument, the act of playing on such an instrument, the sound of such an instrument, or the sound produced by striking a hollow tree or similar object—and so on. But there are also additional related meanings with the words *eardrum* and *drumfish.*

Chum offers a greater range of meanings, including these three very different ones: (1) a close companion or friend; (2) cut or ground bait dumped into the water to attract fish; and (3) a kind of salmon. The meanings for *chum* may be listed separately as *chum 1, chum 2,* and *chum 3.* Or the different meanings may simply be numbered in the same entry.

Here is how the *American Heritage College Dictionary* lists meanings for *chum:*

chum¹ (chŭm) *n.* An intimate friend or companion. —*intr.v.* **chummed, chum•ming, chums. 1.a.** To be an intimate friend. **b.** To display good-natured friendliness. **2.** To share the same room, as in a dormitory. [Perh. short for *chamber fellow,* roommate.]

continued

chum² (chŭm) *n.* Bait usu. consisting of oily fish ground up and scattered on the water. —*v.* **chummed, chum•ming, chums.** —*intr.* To fish with chum. —*tr.* To lure (fish) with chum. [?]
chum³ (chŭm) *n.* A chum salmon.

Exercise A-3

Look up the following words in your dictionary to determine their meanings. List the number of meanings provided for each. Make sure you check to see if the meanings are listed separately (as for *chum*) or all in a single entry, as is the usual pattern. Then write a sentence for each word using at least one of its meanings. The first one is done for you.

Example:

European   NUMBER OF MEANINGS: __2__

SENTENCE(S): *We went on a European holiday. My cousin, a European,*

is visiting for a week.

_____

1. *drake*   NUMBER OF MEANINGS: _____

SENTENCE(S): _____

_____

_____

2. *sovereign*   NUMBER OF MEANINGS: _____

SENTENCE(S): _____

_____

_____

3. *avalanche*   NUMBER OF MEANINGS: _____

SENTENCE(S): _____

_____

_____

4. *strike*   NUMBER OF MEANINGS: _____

SENTENCE(S): _____

_____

_____

5. *rook*   NUMBER OF MEANINGS: _____

SENTENCE(S): _____

_____

_____

6. *spike*   NUMBER OF MEANINGS: _____

SENTENCE(S): _____

_____

_____

7. *cardinal*   NUMBER OF MEANINGS: _____

SENTENCE(S): _____

_____

_____

8. *stream*   NUMBER OF MEANINGS: _____

SENTENCE(S): _____

_____

_____

9. *respite*   NUMBER OF MEANINGS: _____

SENTENCE(S): _____

_____

_____

10. *cuckoo*   NUMBER OF MEANINGS: _____

SENTENCE(S): _____

_____

_____

■ Origin

Your college dictionary also provides information about the origin, or etymology, of words. The word *dictator* derives from a Latin verb— *dicere,* meaning "to speak or tell." Your dictionary lists that derivation with the abbreviation *L.* for *Latin.* Other languages from which English words may be derived are also abbreviated, such as *OFr.* for *Old French* and *Gk.* for *Greek.*

Since English is a language with a rich history of derivation, you will find many words coming from other languages. From Italian, for example, English has taken *macaroni* and *volcano;* from French, *royal;* from Dutch, *easel, landscape,* and *cruise.* English has borrowed the words *alcohol* from Arabic, *coffee* from Turkish, *bazaar* from Persian, and *wampum* from Algonquian, to cite a few examples. A substantial portion of English words, however, derive from Anglo-Saxon, or Old English, and its later development into Middle English.

English actually was not the first language spoken in England. Celtic was apparently the native language there. But with the arrival of Germanic tribes—Angles, Saxons, and Jutes—who conquered the Celts, the earliest form of English emerged. This oldest form of English is designated *AS* for *Anglo-Saxon* and *OE* for *Old English.* Old English was written and spoken from about A.D. 400 to 1100, when Middle English emerged. During the period of Old English the language was enriched by words from Latin and Greek because those were the languages of scholarship in the Western world. During the Middle English period, English borrowed heavily from French, because the French conquered England in 1066, when William of Normandy won a major battle against the English. Middle English developed into the beginning of what we know as Modern English around 1500, half a century before the birth of Shakespeare in 1564.

With continued development of technology and increasing cultural exchange, English has borrowed a large number of words from many of the world's languages. At the same time, English has become one of the most important languages in the world, spoken not only in Great Britain and North America but also by people in Jamaica, South Africa, Australia, and New Zealand. English is also an officially recognized language in Kenya, Pakistan, Uganda, Liberia, India, and the Philippines.

When a word's dictionary definition includes information about the origin, or etymology, of a word, it will usually appear at the bottom of the definition. Look back at the definition of *marmoset* on page 498 for an example. The etymological information appears in brackets:

[ME *marmusette,* a small monkey < OFr. *marmouset,* grotesque figurine, alteration of *marmotte,* marmot. See MARMOT.]

This coded note lists the history of the word as it evolved over time. The codes differ slightly from dictionary to dictionary but are usually similar. To understand what you see in the etymological note, look for your dictionary's key to understanding the abbreviations and symbols—almost always in the first few pages of the book. In the case of *marmoset,* the abbreviation *ME* means *Middle English.* The Middle English version of the word, *marmusette,* changed into our modern word. The < that follows indicates that the Middle English version of marmoset came from the *OFr.,* or Old French, version, which didn't mean exactly the same thing as our current version. You can see here that it meant "grotesque figurine." Finally, the note indicates that more information can be found in the definition of *marmot.*

Exercise A-4

. . . .

Identify the origin of each of the following words. The first one is done for you.

Example:

    brazen ORIGIN: *Old English* _____

1. *isometric* ORIGIN: _____

2. *theory* ORIGIN: _____

3. *intention* ORIGIN: _____

4. *voodoo* ORIGIN: _____

5. *plaza* ORIGIN: _____

6. *horse* ORIGIN: _____

7. *sky* ORIGIN: _____

8. *samba*   ORIGIN: _____

9. *asteroid*   ORIGIN: _____

10. *sauna*   ORIGIN: _____

Exercise A-5
· ·

Read the sample dictionary entries and answer the questions that follow.

1. **con•tem•plate** (kŏn′təm-plāt′) *v.* **-plat•ed, -plat•ing, -plates.** —*tr.*
   1. To look at attentively and thoughtfully. See Syns at **see**¹. **2.** To consider carefully and at length; meditate on or ponder. **3.** To have in mind as an intention or possibility. —*intr.* To ponder; meditate. [Lat. *contemplārī, contemplāt-* : *com-*, com- + *templum,* space for observing auguries; see **tem-**.] — **con′tem•pla′tor** *n.*

   a. How many meanings are listed for the word? _____

   b. What language does *contemplate* derive from? _____

   c. What part of speech is it? _____

   d. Which syllable is accented in pronouncing it? _____

2. **ep•i•thet** (ĕp′ə-thĕt′) *n.* **1.a.** A term used to characterize a person or thing, such as *rosy-fingered* in *rosy-fingered dawn.* **b.** A term used as a descriptive substitute for a person's name or title, such as *The Great Emancipator* for Abraham Lincoln. **2.** An abusive or contemptuous word or phrase. **3.** *Biol.* A word in the scientific name of an animal or a plant following the genus name and denoting a species, variety, or other division of the genus, as *sativa* in *Lactuca sativa.* [Lat. *epitheton* < Gk., neut. of *epithetos,* added, attributed < *epitithenai,* to add to : *epi-,* epi- + *tithenai,* to place; see **dhē-**.] — **ep′i• thet′ic, ep′i•thet′i•cal** *adj.*

   a. In your own words, what is the general meaning of *epithet*?

   _____

   _____

   b. What is its specialized biological meaning?

   _____

   _____

   c. How many parts of speech can it function as? _____

   d. Which syllable is accented in pronunciation? _____

3. **kib•butz** (kĭ-bōōts′, -bōōts′) *n., pl.* **kib•but•zim** (kĭb′ōōt-sēm′, -ōōt-). A collective farm or settlement in modern Israel. [Heb. *qibbûs,* gathering < *qibbēs,* to gather.]

   a. What part of speech is the word? _____

   b. How many regular meanings does it have? _____

   c. What is its origin? _____

   d. What other form(s) of the word are listed? _____

4. **con•tend** (ken-tĕnd′) *v.* **-tend•ed, -tend•ing, contends.** —*intr.* **1.** To strive in opposition or against difficulties; struggle. **2.** To compete, as in a race; vie. **3.** To strive in controversy or debate; dispute. —*tr.* To maintain or assert. [ME *contenden* < Lat. *contendere* : *com-,* com- + *tendere,* to stretch, strive; see **ten-*.**] —**con•tend′er** *n.*

   a. From what Latin word does *contend* derive? _____

   b. What part of speech is it? _____

   c. What is its noun form? _____

   d. What is one of its synonyms? _____

   _____

5. **bun•ga•low** (bŭng′gə-lō′) *n.* **1.** A small house or cottage usu. having a single story and sometimes an attic story ? A thatched or tiled one-story house in India surrounded by a wide verandah. [Hindi *baṅglā,* Bengali (house) < *Bengali,* of Bengal.]

   a. What is the word's meaning? _____

   b. What is the word's origin? _____

Acknowledgments (continued)

Kenneth Blanchard, Charles Schewe, Robert Nelson, and Alexander Hiam, adaptations and excerpts from *Exploring the World of Business.* Copyright © 1996 by Worth Publishers. Used with permission of Worth Publishers.

Jim Bobryk, "Navigating My Eerie Landscape Alone" from "My Turn" column, *Newsweek,* March 8, 1999. All rights reserved. Reprinted by permission.

William Booth, "The Social Lives of Dolphins," copyright © 1996 by William Booth. Reprinted by permission of the author.

Susan Brink, adaptation from "Your Brain on Alcohol," *U.S. News & World Report,* May 7, 2001. Copyright © 2001 U.S. News & World Report, L.P. Reprinted with permission.

Michael Cole and Sheila R. Cole, "Schooling and Development in Middle Childhood" from *The Development of Children* by Michael Cole and Sheila R. Cole. Copyright © 2001 by Worth Publishers. Used with permission.

Consortium for Mathematics and Its Applications (COMAP), "The Mathematical Bernoullis" and other adaptations and excerpts from *For All Practical Purposes: Mathematical Literacy in Today's World* by COMAP. Copyright © 1988 by W. H. Freeman and Company. Used with permission.

Bill Cosby, "How to Read Faster" from *The Power of the Printed Word Program,* published by International Paper Company. Copyright © 1979 by Bill Cosby. Reprinted by permission of the author and the William Morris Agency.

Timothy W. Costello and Joseph T. Costello, "Personality Disorders" from *Abnormal Psychology,* 2nd ed., by Timothy W. Costello and Joseph T. Costello. Copyright © 1992 by Allyn & Bacon. Reprinted by permission.

Helena Curtis and Sue M. Barnes, excerpts and adaptations from *Invitation to Biology.* Copyright © 1994 by Worth Publishers. Used with permission.

Mac Daniel, "Mercury Levels in Fish Rising," *Boston Globe,* July 24, 2001. Copyright © 2001 by the Boston Globe. Reprinted by permission of the *Boston Globe* via The Copyright Clearance Center.

Amy Dickinson, "When Mommy or Daddy Dates," *Time,* July 16, 2001. Copyright © 2001 Time, Inc. Reprinted by permission.

Annie Dillard, exerpt from *An American Childhood* by Annie Dillard. Copyright © 1987 by Annie Dillard. Reprinted by permission of HarperCollins Publishers, Inc.

Rebecca J. Donatelle and Lorraine G. Davis, "Stress and the College Student" excerpted from *Access to Health,* 5th ed., by Rebecca J. Donatelle and Lorraine G. Davis. Copyright © 1998 by Allyn & Bacon. Reprinted by permission of Pearson Education, Inc.

David V. Edwards and Allessandra Lippucci, excerpt from *Practicing American Politics.* Copyright © 1998 by Worth Publishers. Used with permission.

D. Stanley Eitzen, excerpt from *Sport in Contemporary Society.* Copyright © 2001 by Worth Publishers. Used with permission.

Karen Epstein, "I'm a Barbie Girl," *Tufts Daily,* November 21, 1997. Reprinted by permission of the author.

Lanny B. Fields, Russell J. Barber, and Cheryl A. Riggs, excerpt from *The Global Past.* Copyright © 1998 by Bedford/St. Martin's. Reprinted with permission.

Robert H. Frank, "The Downside of Hearing Whoopi at the Mall," *New York Times,* August 7, 2001. Reprinted by permission of the author.

David Gergen, excerpt from "Keeping the Flame Alive," *U.S. News & World Report,* August 16, 1999. Copyright © 1999 U.S. News & World Report, L.P. Reprinted with permission.

Abbie Gibbs, "Witnessing Execution," *Daily O'Collegian,* Oklahoma State University, February 24, 1998. Reprinted by permission of Jack Lancaster, faculty advisor to the *Daily O'Collegian.*

Ellen Goodman, "The Suspected Shopper," *Boston Globe,* 1981. Copyright © 1981, The Boston Globe Newspaper Co./Washington Post Writers Group. Reprinted by permission.

Dana Hawkins, "Lawsuits Spur Rise in Employee Monitoring," *U.S. News & World Report,* August 15, 2001. Copyright © 2001 U.S. News & World Report, L.P. Reprinted with permission.

James A. Henretta, David Brody, and Lynn Dumenil, various excerpts and adaptations from *America: A Concise History.* Copyright © 2002 by Bedford/St. Martin's. Reprinted with permission.

James A. Henretta, David Brody, Susan Ware, and Marilynn S. Johnson, various excerpts from *America's History,* 4th ed. Copyright © 2000 by Bedford/St. Martin's. Reprinted with permission.

Don H. Hockenbury and Sandra E. Hockenbury, "Contemporary Trends in Psychology" and other adaptations and excerpts from *Discovering Psychology* by Don H. Hockenbury and Sandra E. Hockenbury. Copyright © 2001 by Worth Publishers. Used with permission.

Eva Hoffman, "Lost in Translation." "Paradise" from *Lost in Translation* by Eva Hoffman. Copyright © 1989 by Eva Hoffman. Used by permission of Dutton, a division of Penguin Putnam Inc.

William J. Kaufmann III and Roger A. Freedman, excerpts and adaptations from *Universe.* Copyright © 1999 by Freeman Publishers. Used with permission.

Rebecca Thomas Kirkendall, "Who's a Hillbilly?," *Newsweek,* November 27, 1995. All rights reserved. Reprinted by permission.

Ben Krull, "The Lost Art of Nicknaming," *New York Times,* May 10, 2001. Copyright © 2001 by The New York Times Co. Reprinted by permission.

Robert Kunzig, "Erectus Afloat," *Discover,* January 1999. Copyright © 1999 by Robert Kunzig. Reprinted by permission of the author.

Ellen J. Langer, "Automatic Behavior" from *Mindfulness* by Ellen J. Langer. Copyright © 1989 by Perseus Books. Reprinted by permission of Perseus Books.

Warren E. Leary, "Lift, Drag, Spin, and Torque: Sending . . . ," *New York Times,* June 20, 1995. Copyright © 1995 by The New York Times Co. Reprinted by permission.

Connie Leslie, "You Can't High-Jump If the Bar Is Set Too Low," *Newsweek,* November 6, 1995. All rights reserved. Reprinted by permission.

Sylvia S. Mader, adaptation from *Inquiry into Life* by Sylvia S. Mader. Copyright © 1994 by The McGraw-Hill Companies. Reprinted by permission of The McGraw-Hill Companies.

Bruce Maxwell, "Your Life and the Internet" adapted from *How to Find Information on the Internet* by Bruce Maxwell. Copyright © 1998 by Congressional Quarterly Inc.

Douglas McCollam, "The Bull Shark," *Slate,* July 17, 2001. Copyright © 2001 by *Slate* magazine. Distributed by United Feature Syndicate, Inc.

Susannah Meadows, "The Water of the Moment," *Newsweek,* July 30, 2001. All rights reserved. Reprinted by permission.

Miki Meek, "You Can't Hide Those Lying Eyes in Tampa," *U.S. News & World Report,* August 6, 2001. Copyright © 2001 U.S. News & World Report, L.P. Reprinted with permission.

Michael Meyer, excerpts from *The Bedford Introduction to Literature,* 6th ed. Copyright © 2002 by Bedford/St. Martin's. Reprinted with permission.

David G. Myers, "When Beliefs Collide with Psychological Science" and other excerpts and adaptations from *Psychology* by David G. Myers. Copyright © 2001 by Worth Publishers. Used with permission.

Jeffrey S. Nevid, Spencer A. Rathus, and Hannah R. Rubinstein, "Health in the New Millennium," "The Healthy Personality," "Benefits of Bone-Strengthening Exercise," and other excerpts and adaptations from *Health in the New Millennium* by Jeffrey S. Nevid, Spencer A. Rathus, and Hannah R. Rubinstein. Copyright © 1998 by Worth Publishers. Used with permission.

William G. Nickels and Marian Burk Wood, "Branding Reinforces Marketing Relationships" from *Marketing: Relationships, Quality, Value* by William G. Nickels and Marian Burk Wood. Copyright © 1998 by Worth Publishers. Used with permission.

Dan O'Hair, Gustav W. Friedrich, John M. Wiemann, and Mary Wiemann, "Developing and Maintaining Relationships," Chapter 7 of *Competent Communication* by Dan O'Hair, Gustav W. Friedrich, John M. Wiemann, and Mary Wiemann. Copyright © 1997 by Bedford/St. Martin's. Reprinted with permission.

Charles Panati, "Bad Luck Superstitions about Umbrellas" adapted from page 16 of *Panati's Extraordinary Origins of Everyday Things* by Charles Panati. Copyright © 1987 by Charles Panati. Reprinted by permission of HarperCollins Publishers, Inc.

Alexandra Powe-Allred and Michelle Powe, "Sports Choices" from *The Quiet Storm: A Celebration of Women in Sport* by Alexandra Powe-Allred and Michelle Powe. Copyright © 1997 by Alexandra Powe-Allred and Michelle Powe. Reprinted by permission of The McGraw Hill Companies.

Frank Press and Raymond Siever, excerpt from *Understanding Earth* by Frank Press and Raymond Siever. Copyright © 2001 by W. H. Freeman and Company. Used with permission.

William K. Purves, Gordon H. Orians, H. Craig Heller, and David Sadava, adaptation from *Life: The Science of Biology,* 5th ed. Reprinted by permission of Sinauer Associates, Inc.

Steve Rhodes and Kendall Hamilton, "Will Athletic Records Ever Stop Tumbling?," *Newsweek,* October 6, 1997. All rights reserved. Reprinted by permission.

James L. Roark, Michael P. Johnson, Patricia Cline Cohen, Sarah Stage, Alan Lawson, and Susan M. Hartmann, excerpt from *The American Promise,* 2nd ed. Copyright © 2002 by Bedford/St. Martin's. Reprinted with permission.

Ian Robertson, "Sport in American Society" from *Sociology* by Ian Robertson. Copyright © 1987 by Worth Publishers. Used with permission.

A. M. Rosenthal, "The Way She Died," *New York Times,* March 15, 1994. Copyright © 1994 by The New York Times Co. Reprinted by permission.

Mark Trahant, "Every Symbol Tells a Story," *MSNBC.com,* April 19, 2000. Reprinted with permission from MSNBC Interactive News L.L.C.

Timothy Tregarthen and Libby Rittenberg, excerpts from *Economics* by Timothy Tregarthen and Libby Rittenberg. Copyright © 2000 by Worth Publishers. Used with permission.

———, excerpts from *Macroeconomics* by Timothy Tregarthen and Libby Rittenberg. Copyright © 2000 by Worth Publishers. Used with permission.

Michael Utley, "My Personal Bolt of Lightning," *New York Times,* August 27, 2001. Copyright © 2001 by The New York Times Co. Reprinted by permission.

Stephen G. Wayne, G. Calvin Mackenzie, David M. O'Brien, and Richard L. Cole, various excerpts from *The Politics of American Government.* Copyright © 1999 by Bedford/St. Martin's. Reprinted with permission.

Betty Yorburg, various excerpts from *Family Relationships* by Betty Yorburg. Copyright © 1993 by Worth Publishers. Used with permission.

Cathy Young, "Trigger Guards Are Not Answer, but Moral Fiber Is," *Detroit News,* March 8, 2000. Reprinted by permission of the *Detroit News.*

Illustrations

Page 226: "Perceptual Sets" illustration, from *Psychology* by David G. Myers. Originally from *Mind Sights* by Roger N. Shepard. Copyright © 1981 by Roger N. Shepard. Reprinted by permission of W. H. Freeman and Company.

Page 288: Illustration from *The Global Past* by Lanny B. Fields, Russell J. Barber, and Cheryl A. Riggs. Copyright © 1998 by Bedford/St. Martin's. Reprinted with permission.

Page 374: Photograph of Joe Louis standing among a crowd of kids, © Bettmann/Corbis. Used with permission.

Page 375: Dennis Brack photograph, reprinted by permission of Black Star.

Pages 379, 381: Illustrations from *Exploring Psychology* by David G. Myers. Copyright © 2001 by Worth Publishers. Used with permission.

Page 380: Illustration from *Understanding Earth* by Frank Press and Raymond Siever. Copyright © 2001 by W. H. Freeman and Company. Used with permission.

Page 383: "How a Corporation Is Run" illustration, from *Exploring the World of Business* by Kenneth Blanchard, Charles Schewe, Robert Nelson, and Alexander Hiam. Copyright © 1996 by Worth Publishers. Used with permission.

Page 392: "Unemployment Rate in the Civilian Labor Force" table, from *1997 Information Please Almanac.* Copyright © 1997 by Inso Corporation. Reproduced by permission of Houghton Mifflin Company. All rights reserved.

Pages 399, 405: Nenad Jakesevic maps, copyright © 1999 by Nenad Jekesevic. Reprinted by permission of the illustrator.

Pages 401, 406: John Gurche photograph, copyright © 1999 by John Gurche. Reprinted by permission of the photographer.

Page 409: Illustration reprinted from *Inquiry into Life* by Sylvia S. Mader. Copyright © 1994 by The McGraw Hill Companies. Reprinted by permission of The McGraw Hill Companies.

Page 430: Richard Hutching photograph, reprinted by permission of Photo Researchers, Inc. Copyright © 1998 by Richard Hutching. Courtesy of Photo Researchers, Inc.

Page 442: Cathy Guisewite, cartoon featured in *Why Do the Right Words Always Come Out of the Wrong Mouth?* by Cathy Guisewite. Copyright © 1988 by Universal Press Syndicate. All rights reserved. Reprinted with permission of Andrews and McMeel, a Universal Press Syndicate Company.

Page 443: Nadine Markova photograph, reprinted by permission of Corbis/The Stock Market.

Page 449: Esbin-Anderson photograph, reprinted by permission of The Image Works.

Page 455: Michael Heron photograph, reprinted by permission of Woodfin Camp & Associates.